Contemporary Black Urban Music

The Revolution of Hip-Hop

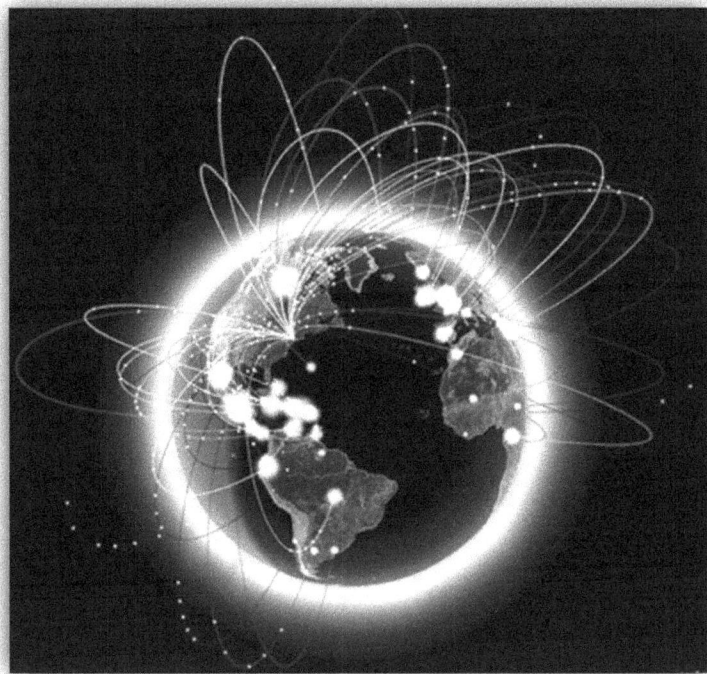

A Historical Survey

Contemporary Black Urban Music

The Revolution of Hip-Hop

By Ron Westray

FHB | FIRST HILL BOOKS

FIRST HILL BOOKS
An imprint of Wimbledon Publishing Company
www.anthempress.com

This edition first published in UK and USA 2023
by FIRST HILL BOOKS
75–76 Blackfriars Road, London SE1 8HA, UK
or PO Box 9779, London SW19 7ZG, UK
and
244 Madison Ave #116, New York, NY 10016, USA

British Library Cataloguing-in-Publication Data
A catalogue record for this book is available from the British Library.

Library of Congress Control Number: 2022934908
A catalog record for this book has been requested.

ISBN-13: 978-1-83998-5-270 (Hbk)
ISBN-10: 1-83998-5-275 (Hbk)

Cover image: Ron Westray

This title is also available as an e-book.

CONTENTS

PREFACE

I teach a course titled *Contemporary Black Urban Music*. Hip-Hop represents my generation, and I was excited to be asked to conduct this course upon starting my appointment at York University. Upon entering academe, my most difficult tasks were those of "harvesting" my mind for all of the data that is necessary and for building the curricula to support that information. Bolstering the development of an effective didactic process, teaching at the university level inspires my research; and it is inspiring to witness the progressive effect of "new information" upon the students' abilities—and the impact of teaching upon my own development. While the stimulus for my research bares a direct relationship to the weight of *history*, and the influence of like-minded contemporaries, the process of dispersing information also serves as an *impetus* for the *expansion* of the known. Overall, academe has amplified my goals and increased my effectiveness.

ACKNOWLEDGMENTS

I would like to thank David Lidov for the *fresh* insights in Chapters 1 & 2. I thank Dr. Ryan Bruce (a former Graduate Assistant for CBUM) for his vivid contribution to the Afro-modernism and jazz rap chapters; and thank you Adams Amaning (a former student of CBUM) for your timely commentary and astutely savvy suggestions. Furthermore, I thank the entire team at Anthem Press (and Deanta Global) for their tireless efforts. Finally, to all of my friends and family for their support, before, during, and after the completion of this textbook, thank you!

Chapter 1

LEARNING OBJECTIVES: INTRODUCTION

The whole earth had a common language and a common vocabulary

—Genesis 11:1–9

Reuniting the world through the common language of lived experience, and amid the syntax of personal-existence, Hip-Hop has emerged as a 'Babylonian' solution

—Ron Westray

Brief statement of the purpose:

This course will examine Contemporary Black Urban Music (CBUM) and its historical development by tracing the evolution of soul and funk music into rap and Hip-Hop.
A wide range of topics will be presented to the student in preparation for written essays, philosophical-flexibility, assessment, and the examination of CBUM/Hip-Hop as a *global force* factor.

Specific learning objectives for the student:

– Specific objectives of the book include the discussion of the historical evolution of CBUM/Hip-Hop, and the development (and retention) of an informed perspective regarding legendary figures, bands, and genres in CBUM. The examination of the historical, social, and economic implications of CBUM that lead to the globalization of Hip-Hop, an understanding of how CBUM is perceived and measured in society, and the student's ability to describe a range of effects fostered by the evolution of CBUM, all factor highly in this book.

"All great … music, like all great drama, is as *contemporary* as the vitality of the performance."

—Stanley Crouch

MEDIA:

❖ Duke Ellington, "Thanks for the Beautiful Land on The Delta," *The New Orleans Suite*, 1970. https://g.co/kgs/MzAQ4j

• ZOOM OUT: Tray Deuce, "Get IT," *Doin' IT, Live*, 2018. https://traydeuce1.bandcamp.com/track/get-it.

Welcome to CBUM. Duke Ellington was born in 1899. In the 1930s he was *a* 'King of Swing'; and by 1970 he was still conducting his jazz orchestra (after 50 years). *Thanks for the Beautiful Land on* <u>*The*</u> *Delta* is a musical metaphor of the relationship between jazz and Hip-Hop. From a rhythmic standpoint, this is [proto] Hip-Hop. You see, by 1970, James Brown had already broken the 'code', and Ellington is [musically] co-signing that fact. You could put any Emcee on this. That's Hip-Hop, baby! Put your hands in the air like this!

I "came up" in "The Trap" during the *rap-age*. Consequently, in structuring this course, I have harnessed my own experiences. More qualitative than comprehensive, this course is an 'authentic' survey of how CBUM came to be, and what it represents contemporarily—a historical overview of the events that shaped industry and fan-perception (and behavior) over time. Veritably Hip-Hop 101, this textbook is primarily designed for the *uninitiated*. Forming the backbone of this publication, via my original lectures, are text and media from a variety of public and online sources.

Ultimately, it is impossible to tell all the stories; and the chronology is not strict; but we will *explore* how Black American Music (BAM) came to be. However, we must cover some historical ground before we get to "Sugar Hill."

As this course is focused on Contemporary BLACK Urban Music, the focus is on Black artists. In art, as in life, to achieve a realistic viewpoint, we must allow for some overlap, sway (and exclusion). In the process, we will talk about other styles and eras. For instance, Bebop has a lot to do with Hip-Hop; and the societal elements that formed the respective genres are similar. The image of the bebopper still pervades the imagination of artists to this day. In fact, I think most "cats" [still] want to be regarded as "jazz-musicians" (the proto-Hip-Hop). Join me on this unique and colorful journey into CBUM.

Get a good seat!

The music is evolving at this moment. We must deal with the past, but we do include a very recent past. The past is the soil for what is emerging today. What matters is whether, or not, you know these eras—these artists.

By nature of the content, the student/reader may be exposed to the following: Provocative lyrics and innuendo, race, relations, consequences, and repercussions. But Hip-Hop is not a political movement, and I am not making a political statement; nor do I have a personal agenda for the material discussed. I encourage you to view this course material from a perspective of neutral social analysis. I am writing subjectively, from a range of experiences: as an African American from the good hood, as a consumer, as a virtuoso instrumentalist, and as a modern composer.

It's all good for the first months or so; but around midterm, everyone goes berserk; and students begin to scapegoat the Professors for their own shortcomings (e.g., lack of preparation, on your part, does not constitute an emergency on my part). But if you communicate effectively, I will try to assist. Unfortunately, rather than just do what you need to do in the course, some of you would prefer to create a Human Resource *issue* with me. For instance, last year, a student complained to my Department Chair that my email *response* was not long enough. Really? See, that student was stressed!

Chapter 2

CHARACTERISTICS OF MUSIC AND
MUSICAL TERMINOLOGY

Let's start with some terminology that musicians use, terms for the elements and characteristics of music that empower us to describe it. That way, when you hear the talk and their vocabulary, you can attach the intended ideas to them.

Terminology is a bridge that lets us pinpoint relationships between our musical experience and other aspects of our culture. We do it in writing and in conversation, even with what seems like a casual conversation. We said Hip-Hop is not a political movement. That's true, but it is an artistic movement, a cultural movement, that plays a HUGE role on political, sociological, and economic associations—huge like the *Romanticism* of the nineteenth century, or the *Enlightenment* of the seventeenth and eighteenth centuries. We are in the middle of learning to integrate the culture of Hip-Hop into our thinking and our worldview. And YOU, be you a student, teacher, researcher, or serious listener are participating in that vital work whenever you have a thoughtful conversation about the music. That is a good reason to dip your toes into a bit of terminology and the concepts the terminology represents and to know something of its limitations. Let us emphasize this limitation; because the biggest and hardest job of intelligence is to recognize and acknowledge ignorance.

Some readers will find much of this familiar and easy. Others may find it new and overwhelming. To the first, the old hands, we say, read it through; you may find some fresh angles. To the novices we say, don't sweat. Go through it the first time to start building a general understanding and then, think of it as a reference. Come back to it when and if it seems useful. Even though we do not use all this info in the rest of the book, you may find you are using it and that you start listening to our musician friends' chit-chat with new ears. We aim for comfort, not mastery. Musical terminology is not a walled garden protecting state secrets. Remember, infants learn words by using them, faking it till they make it. Not a bad strategy.

Apart from a very brief excursion—we will alert you— we are not "doing" science when we turn to musical terminology. Many of our terms are vague and general and do not permit strict formal definition. Of course, that is equally the case for plenty of our most important non-music terms: "justice," "freedom," "art," "balance," "beauty" and "success," not to mention the word "music" itself. No logical definitions. For music, the main exception to vagueness would be terms for the symbols used to write music on paper (like "half note," "sharp" and "time signature"). Those do indeed have strict definitions, but we don't need them in this course. Many terms we rely on may risk ambiguity. You are likely to already know many of the words we discuss but may not know that the vagueness or ambiguity is not your fault—an important point to recognize to avoid confusion or the illusion that five more hours of study would set things straight in the world of music theory.

For example, "Melody." Look in a dictionary. Let us know if you can find a clear definition. For practical purposes, let us just say a melody is something a person could sing. When there is more in the music than the melody alone (i.e., there is an "accompaniment"), the melody is the foreground, standing out above the rest of the music and is the part you're most likely to hum. "Rhythm": something a person could clap or dance. Find a textbook that is 100 years old or even 75 years old. You may read that song and dance are the foundation of music. But does that apply to rap? Due to the Hip-Hop revolution, we have invented a new term, "Flow." Flow does not reduce to melody and rhythm; it is not only related to both, but it also depends on speech.

Rap synthesizes music and speech to create flow. There are precedents a plenty for blending music and speech: In classical opera, "recitativo." In the English stage musical, the fast "patter song." In American vernacular music, the "talking blues." In South Indian music "solkatu." In many traditional rituals, "chants" that are very close to speech. Yet, none of those are music's main dishes. They are appetizers and side dishes. In rap, however, the synthesis of speech and music takes the center ring, and it establishes new values, incorporating persuasion, expression, wit, intelligence and more that we honor as "good flow." Flow is a very important term and musical concept but perhaps not ready for the dictionary.

Now, indulge us for a few paragraphs; even if you have no taste for science, we need this brief bit as our foundation to introduce the terms "pitch," "octave," and "scale" and "vibration." In casual talk we say, "sending you good vibrations," apparently a spiritual emanation. In music, we have a physical interpretation. Musical vibration entails some physical material (wood, air, and skin) moving back and forth very rapidly. Skin can be vocal cords or your eardrum or a drumhead. With a violin, vibrations in a "metal or gut string" make vibrations in the "wooden body." The vibrating wood makes the "air" vibrate. The air vibration makes your "eardrum" vibrate. The eardrum activates nerves. And then—the mysterious part that science has not cracked—your brain interprets the vibrations as sound. We DO NOT KNOW HOW THE BRAIN DOES THIS. The events preceding and transmitting the vibrations are mechanical and well-understood. The violin string goes back and forth, mainly sideways. The movements of the wooden sound box of the violin are extremely complex and we won't try to detail them, but they are physical motions too small and fast for our eyes but discernible with measuring devices. The air vibrations are of another sort; they alternate compression and expansion. The main point: these are all physical, material vibrations and not spiritual radiations. And they happen at a measurable speed.

Vibrations make all sounds, not only musical sounds. The slowest vibrations that the human ear interprets as sound, (very low/deep sound) move back and forth about 20 times in one second; the fastest (very high sound) about 20,000 times per second (40,000 for dogs). For random sounds, in general, the vibration speed, the "frequency" changes all the time. In music, the most characteristic sounds, or "tones," maintain a steady speed, but briefly, for a short-tone—and a prolonged speed for a long-tone. The tone we call "middle C" makes 256 vibrations per second (vps). The standard for tuning the orchestra, A 440, makes 440 (vps). That value, which is the "frequency," determines the "pitch" of the tone. People capable of knowing which note is which when they hear it (recognizing notes by ear) are said to have "perfect pitch" or "absolute pitch." Most musicians agree that perfect pitch doesn't make a big difference, but it certainly attracts some interesting research. It may turn out that this ability is quite common but usually unconscious.

If two different tones sound at the same time or one right after the other, we can refer to the pair of them as an "interval." "Interval" has two technical meanings in music. Interval means (a) a pair of tones and (b) the size of the distance between them. That is, the size of the frequency difference. We come back to (b) in a moment. First, (a) a pair of tones: if the vibration speed of one is exactly twice that of the other, they seem to blend into one. That is why high voices and low voices can sing the same song as if they were one voice.

The C above middle C), vibrating twice as fast, makes 512 vibrations per second. Music uses eight different "C's" from very low to very high. The interval of two tones with the same letter name (High C/Low C; High F/Low F; etc.) is called an "octave."

MEDIA:

❖ "What is an Octave?," Music Theory, Video Lesson.
   https://youtu.be/fV-p9n7upMc

A human voice or a violin can slide from a low C (or D, whatever) to the next higher C (or D, whatever) and slide back. A piano (or flute) cannot. Instead of sliding, the octave is conventionally divided by intermediate notes.

You can see on a keyboard that the standard modern division gives us 12 tones for each octave. The interval from one tone to the next is a "halftone." Played one after another, they form the "chromatic scale." However, it is much more common to set some notes aside and make music with scales of just seven tones ("major" and "minor" scales and modes) or six or five tones (pentatonic scales and hexatonic scales, both common in folk music).

Scales have a main note, a boss note, called the "tonic." The letter name of the tonic note is the "key" or the "tonality" of a piece. So, we say, "this song is in the key of D-minor" or maybe "this phrase [a short section] has the tonality of F-major." We can move the whole song up or down: "This song was originally composed in A major, but we are going to sing it a little lower in G-major." Scales provide a vocabulary from which we select and combine tones to make melodies and harmonies (paragraph below). This parallels language, where we select and combine words from our vocabulary to make sentences and some styles of painting, too, where the painter selects and combines colors to make visual forms from a vocabulary provided by their palette.

Scales provide a vocabulary from which we select and combine tones to make melodies and harmonies (paragraph below). This parallels language, where we select and combine words from our vocabulary to make sentences and some styles of painting, too, where the painter selects and combines colors to make visual forms from a vocabulary provided by their palette.

For most instruments, including wind instruments, string instruments, *voice* and electronic instruments, the division of the octave into 12 pitches is a necessary framework but not an absolute prison. We practice techniques to inflect or "bend" the pitches for ornamental and expressive purposes.

Bends make a very human, voice-like color, that are absolutely essential in jazz and many other styles.

"Harmony" is another huge concept that defies definition. It includes "chords," combinations of tones that can sound simultaneously and patterns of successive chords. When we combine just two tones, we'd probably call the pair an interval rather than a chord; yet when just two voices are singing somewhat independent melodies, we still say they "harmonize."

Chords are frequently classified as Consonant (pleasant, clear, and stable) or Dissonant (tense and complex). Although "harmony" commonly refers to tone combinations that seem to make sense (not to be defined!), we might also refer to chaotic combinations as dissonant or discordant "harmony." When music presents an unstable or discordant chord that is connected to a following chord which sounds stable and coherent, that is called "harmonic resolution" or "dissonance and resolution."

The terms "major" and "minor" that we mentioned as scale types are also chord types. They are associated in various cultures with emotional values, a complex and subtle aspect.

In all this terminology for melody and harmony there exists highly subjective judgments. There are theories aplenty to explain harmony; but it is a short path from textbook rules to "research." That interesting path is there for you to explore if your future lies that way. Meanwhile, don't ask us for tidy answers! Go with the flow—as even the experts must.

Notes must have length as well as a pitch. We have short notes and long notes. This brings us to "rhythm."

We have spelled out some elements of melody and harmony; but until we attach rhythm, we do not arrive at music. Music is a time art; and rhythm is a time *pattern*. Rhythm is arguably the most important element of music, the easiest to identify with and feel in our bodies. We generally associate rhythm with drums. But it is not only established by the drums—it is also established by pauses [silence]. You need to know that it is also the space (in between) that makes the rhythm— pauses that relate to the translation of the rhythm. In music notation, the silences are called "rests."

MEDIA:

❖ "Rests in Music," Music Theory, Video Lesson.
   https://youtu.be/ejxFVaH_A-Y

We make rhythm by joining notes (and silences) of long and short duration. Rhythm is also established by a regular pulse in the music called the Beat. If they are equal in duration, beats (pulses) can occur at any speed (the tempo). This is measured in beats per minute (BPM). The rhythm is supported by the pulse in the music—the beat. You thought rhythm and beat were the same things; they are not. We measure the beat by its tempo–the speed of the beat: 60 BPM (ballad/slow song); 120 BPM (pop hit); 240 BPM (Bebop!).

Additionally, the word "feel," has recently become an important term in music, perhaps not quite a "technical" term, but widely used, readily understood. We will come back to it.

Up top of this section, we said rhythm is what someone could clap or dance.

We skipped two major issues. First, we skipped the term "meter." Clapping and dancing are not fully interchangeable. Dancing has much more to do with "meter," a regular pattern of "beats," the ongoing steady stream of pulsation that frames the rhythm and which may be fully spelled out in the sound or just partly spelled out and partly left for implication and intuition. That last may sound like an appeal to intellect, but your feet get it before you have a chance to think. Little conscious intellect is involved. Most urban black music exploits a regular meter. Some music does not, but we needn't go there. In teaching and in practicing, meter is often marked by counting, the "One Two Three, One Two Three" of a waltz or the "One Two, One Two" of a rag. The numbers mark "beats" in one sense of that term, and they continue at a constant speed called the "tempo" of a musical composition.

We sometimes indicate tempo in terms of beats per minute (BPM).

We indicated tone frequency by vibrations per second, a way faster range. [Your human brain will not interpret a fast beat as a low tone. It will not interpret a low tone as a rhythmic beat or pulse. A whale brain might have a different opinion.]

A "measure" is a group of beats. Beats have functions and hierarchy. The beat that starts a measure is a "downbeat"; the beat that ends it is an "upbeat." The "backbeat" divides the time of a beat in half.

A "loop" is a continuously repeating unit. There are four versions: (1) beats emphasized, (2) downbeats emphasized more, (3) upbeats emphasized more and (4) backbeats emphasized more.

Using a reliable Digital Audio Workstation (DAW) we can change the "mix."

The *mix* controls the loudness (aka "volume" or "velocity") of separate elements of music; we can also determine how much to the left or right [channels] each element sounds—the "pan," or "panning."

Here is the second item we skipped over: In talking about clapping hands and dancing feet, we skipped the term "syncopation." To fully understand *syncopation*, you *must* use your hips. Syncopation refers to accents that do not line up with the beat hierarchy. If it is a matter of one syncopated note, we might ignore the hips, but if a sustained rhythmic pattern is syncopated, you may need loose, swinging hips to keep the pattern going in your body. Muscular impulses in legs-feet and arms-hand alternate, swinging the hips. Here you have ongoing energy tension of the beats versus the backbeats—and we love it.

An entirely alternative (though related) meaning of "Beat" does not appear in classical music theory. It originates in the production of Black Urban styles. This "Beat" is the repeating pattern or loop of sounds that sets the rhythmic framework and much of the style for a song or a rap. Drums, cymbals, and bass are typically dominant components of a beat, but the format is open. Making beats is an art form. A song often has a beat created by a disc jockey (DJ) independently of the rap or melody subsequently created by a master of ceremonies (MC) or vocalist.

There are even specialists who make and sell beats to vocalists, and the two creative artists don't necessarily work together more than that.

Affiliated with syncopation but not the same, we take note of "Swing." Whereas syncopation displaces accents, *swing* is generated by the ongoing unequal division of beats. Instead of

    Ta . . Ta . . Ta . . Ta . .
we might have
    Ta . . . Ta . . Ta . . . Ta . .
And maybe syncopated accents on the shorter Ta's.

But we shouldn't rely on spelling it out. Listen to examples and realize that the persistence and style of Swing is always a major part of the aesthetics of African-derived African derived music. (Though not all African music is itself characterized by swing.)

The summed totality of rhythmic nuance (swing, syncopation and other) repeated and maintained in the meter of a musical performance is its "feel." This originally causal term (from jazz and pop) is now a locus of study and research. It is not pinned down, but it refers to a phenomenon of undeniable importance and perhaps universal breadth. It can involve nuances of syncopation and swing and weight that we cannot count out nor analyze but that we do feel as a strong character identity of a musical style.

Some Very General Terms

Timbre: [pronounced "tamber"] In addition to pitch and length—which we can pin down pretty precisely—a note also has a color or "timbre." The difference between a trumpet and a violin playing the same note is timbre. This general quality is not immune to scientific analysis but is not necessarily fully resolved by analysis.

We are incredibly sensitive to timbre and can often recognize a friend's voice in less than a second just by hearing its color quality, and its timbre.

Texture: Obviously a metaphorical term (music is like a cloth . . .). Everything that goes into the soup to make the general, coloristic quality of a composition can be considered texture, including the mix of timbres but also the clarity or density of sound, its steadiness or volatility, and so on.

Texture in music refers to the nature or characteristic(s) of the sound as a totality. Identifying texture involves considering all the instruments sounding at one time. Each instrument contributes its own unique timbre. The totality is like fabric... dense, coarse, and smooth... Texture is based on instrumentation. It is not a precise, formal concept. But, as an exception to that cop-out, there are some standardized special usages for categories of sound structure. Thus, we speak of a "melody plus accompaniment texture" an "orchestral" texture and so on—an indefinite list of terms not worth enumerating if you aren't making a word-puzzle out of them.

Form: Form has both a cut-and-dried specific technical meaning in music (easy) and a general meaning that it shares with other media (more difficult). And those two can blend. The easy, technical idea, applies best to music that divides into repeating and contrasting sections and refers to the pattern made by sections, often represented by letters.

For example, a piece of music might readily divide into four sections with the first and third the same (or quite similar), and the second and fourth also similar to each other. We might symbolize that as ABAB or ABA'B'. Thus, we have "binary form," and we have "ternary form" the latter in three parts form, A-B-A or A-B-C. Other terms for form include "bridge" (in classical music, a transitional passage. In vernacular music, a middle section), "head," the main tune, and "hook," a brief passage that represents the character of a song and infects your memory like a friendly virus.

The other, general meaning of "form" is judgmental. A piece of music without formulaic divisions and repetitions may still strike us as having "good form."

Painters would say that a picture has good/bad "composition" meaning pretty much the same thing that we would judge as good/bad form—the overall shape.

Ornament: Not a specialized word. Basically, it means the same thing in music as it does in architecture or costume design or elsewhere. You can decorate one note with others; the decorating notes are ornaments. However, ornamentation is a special concept in music in the sense that music traditions around the world have cultivated very individual and very elaborate practices of ornamentation and have names for ornaments. We mentioned one, "bends." If you study vocal or instrumental performance formally, ornamentation will likely be your graduate course.

The standard Western tuning system, called equal temperament (meaning that the distance from note-to-note [scale] is equal) differentiates Western music from the music of Eastern cultures. Eastern/Asian scales may, sometimes, contain as little as five notes; whereas the typical Western scale (ordered sets of notes or "pitches"), most commonly the major/minor scales and the chromatic scale contains 7 notes and 12 notes, respectively. These scales are the most identifiable part of the sound of Western music; it is also differentiated by instrumentation (texture)—Ron Westray

Western 'Classical' music has become intensely committed to notation—a source of certain rigidities (possibly). However, notation is also the radix of enormous creativity and new stylistic directions (e.g., strict fugue or orchestral architecture.)

Conversely, the term "Western music" interiorizes a whole United States, and the history that it might want to dump; but what is the alternative? Originally the attempt was to designate the tradition of "educated" music born in and cultivated in Western Europe and specifically in Spain, Italy, Austria, Germany, England, Belgium, and the Netherlands. Complications: The original idea was associated with the upper classes. Among regular folks, song and dance traditions persisted that did not necessarily fit the aesthetic of the courts and churches. The Church of Rome had regulated its own sacred music to discourage Eastern styles that were too personal, wild, and expressive.

But those styles made a roaring comeback via professional street violinists, many entering (Vienna) from the east, who were listened to, attentively, by Beethoven—among others.

[That is "Gypsy music". "Gypsy," the term preferred by many of the Roma ethnicity, is a corruption of "Gypcien," short for Egyptian and certainly not "western" The Western idea of minor scales as sad or tragic owes much to Gypsy violinists].

Like what is now Canada, the USA and Mexico, the Western nations had colonies—where Europeans mixed (musically) with many cultures. Starting before 1600, voyaging guitarists from Spain were picking up rhythmic styles in Mexico that slaves from Africa were playing there, and they took these home for more distribution. Large orchestras dominated by strings are iconic for Western music; yet today you can hear them throughout Asia, playing expert compositions fitting into Asian aesthetics. Nobody asks permission. Is Hip-Hop Western music? Certainly, some of its chord patterns are.

The fact is that Western Europe did develop a fabulous, magnificent musical tradition or family of traditions, whatever term we choose to designate it. Feel free to own it. You don't need permission—D. Lidov.

Musical Terminology: Overview

Melody: Melodies are derived from scales (or ordered sets of pitches), most commonly the major or minor scales, in simple terms, it is the perceptible tune of a piece of music. It stands out above the rest of the music. For example, take a tune with lyrics, like "Twinkle, Twinkle, Little Star." The words you sing contain the melody. It stands out above the rest of the music and is the part you're most likely to hum.
Harmony: Harmony in music refers to when [at least] two notes sound simultaneously. It can be classified as Consonant (pleasant) or Dissonant (tense/complex). The harmony in music plays a foundational role to the melody, thus giving the melody deeper meaning. And so, harmony can be pleasant or tense. Chords occur in music when [at least] three notes sound simultaneously. "Chords and Harmony can be classified as Major or Minor—aesthetically happy and sad, respectively. **Rhythm**: Rhythms are the specific patterns of short and long durations given to the melody and harmony.

Rhythm is also established by percussion and silence. Rhythm accounts for much of the "style/feel" of a piece of music. Rhythms are also established by the **Beat**: A regular pulse in the music. These pulses, or "beats," can occur at any speed, or tempo. This speed is measured in BPM (Beats Per Minute). Texture: Texture in music refers to the nature or characteristic (s) of the sound. Identifying texture involves considering all the instruments sounding at one time. Each instrument has its own unique timbre, just as each ensemble has its own timbre. **Form**: Form is the organization of all the individual sections of a piece of music—sections of music that repeat—and sections of music that are contrasting.

Chapter 3

EVOLUTION OF EARLY AFRICAN AMERICAN MUSIC

Though West African and Afro Caribbean connections predominate, cross-ancestry with Native American and European cultures is also part of the development of African American music.

—Ron Westray

Cultures get transformed not deliberately or programmatically but by the unpredictable effects of social, political, and technological change, and by random acts of cross-pollination…

—Excerpt From "The Free World," by Louis Menand

When we think about African American music, we are not just dealing with one thing—we are also dealing with Native American and Euro influences. It takes this cultural-coalescence to produce a Bootsy Collins—a James Brown. … it is not just a black thing. That *mixture* gives us the opportunity to express the music that we have harnessed for hundreds of years—now.

In 1817, legislation was passed which permitted enslaved African Americans to meet and practice their ancestral traditions, such as drumming and the dancing of the "Bamboula," "Congo," and "Flat-Footed-Shuffle"—all of which played an important role in the development of Black American Music (BAM)—most notably, jazz.

Congo Square ("Place des Nègres," "Place Publique," later "Circus Square" or informally "Place Congo" at the "back of town" originated as a social and cultural meeting ground for the city's enslaved African American population. Presently, the 'square' is an open space within the Louis Armstrong Park– which is in the Tremé neighborhood of New Orleans, Louisiana (just across Rampart Street north of the French Quarter). The Tremé neighborhood is famous for its history of African American music.

MEDIA:
❖ Congo Square.
   https://youtu.be/yUSyJKElXos

The "BackBeat"

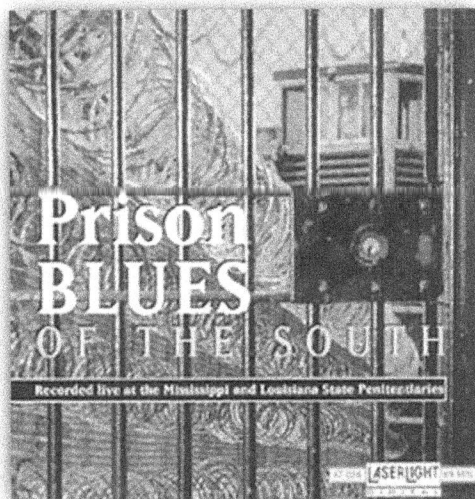

The BackBeat forms the framework that, controls and informs [nearly] all forms of popular and commercial-music; it can be identified by the accentuation of beats *two* and *four* of a four-beat cycle.

The "Back Beat" is at the core of all the music you respond to right now; it is the element of this music that makes "that" song, that song. Without it, music would be boring; for the BackBeat informs the framework within-which CBUM is built.

Western Music makes heavy use of a four-beat cycle that repeats with every measure. What are some of the sources of the BackBeat? From a Western standpoint, we can trace the implication of the BackBeat (the black beat) back to the 'spirituals' sung by Negro Slaves, forward, through the blues, to Work Songs and Prison Chain Gangs of North America, on up to its appropriation by commercial music, including rap and Hip-Hop. Metaphorically, it could be said that the term comes from the "backs" of those minority laborers and convicts; it is a veritable consequence of the nature of the industrialized prison complex in (and of) North America.

Sources of the BackBeat: Summary

❖ Work Songs
❖ Chants and 'Spirituals'
❖ Prison Blues
❖ The Chain Gang

MEDIA:

❖ "Early in the Morning," *Prison Blues of the South*, recorded by Alan Lomax, 1947–48.
   https://youtu.be/lw6GFCupesI
❖ Tray Deuce, "The Chain Gang," *Out the Box*, 2016.
   https://traydeuce1.bandcamp.com/track/the-chain-gang-orig-version

Vocal Blues

The music of the 1920s had qualities that closely resemble contemporary Hip-Hop. Artists like Robert Johnson were the first freestylers (an artist telling their story 'off the cuff'). Arguably, the three-stanza blues form is a prototype of 'freestyling' in Hip-Hop. Similarly, Bessie Smith—the "Queen of the Blues" (e.g., the Beyoncé of the 1920s), and the idea of telling a real-life story, represents another Hip-Hop prototype.

Check out Brazilian culture and music. These trends that are popping up are an extension of things that were already there. In other words, *twerking* did not just come about. *Human nature has not changed in thousands of years; society has changed.*

Key Artists:

❖ Robert Johnson
❖ Son House
❖ Ma Rainey
❖ Bessie Smith (The Queen of the Blues)

The archetype of the "Hellhound" refers to the hounds that police would use to track down escaped slaves and convicts of the time.

"Hellhounds" identifying slave DNA through their nostrils is something you worried about—back then.

Lyrics:

"I got to keep movin', I got to keep movin'
Blues fallin' down like hail, blues fallin' down like hail
Hmm-mmm, blues fallin' down like hail, blues fallin' down like hail
And the days keeps on worryin' me
Tha' hellhound on my trail, hellhound on my trail, Hellhound on my trail

You gotta think back … It doesn't get any more popular for music in 1920.

Robert Leroy Johnson

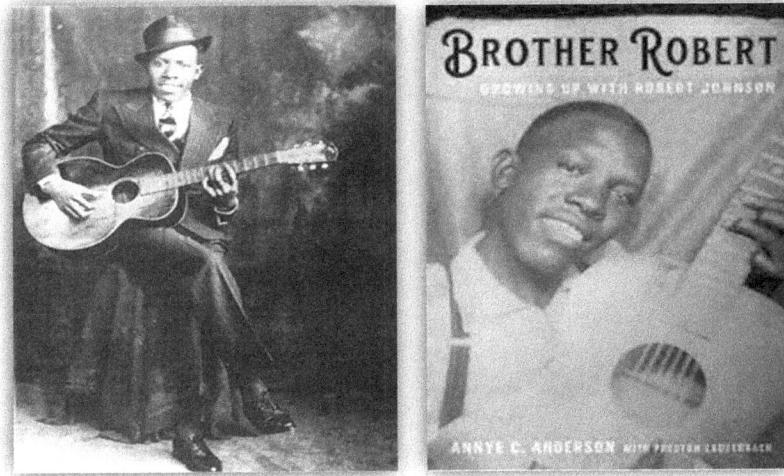

Robert Leroy Johnson was an American blues musician and songwriter. His landmark recordings in 1936 and 1937 display a combination of singing, guitar skills and songwriting talent that has influenced later generations of musicians. He is now recognized as a master of the Delta Blues style of guitar playing.

MEDIA:

❖ Robert Johnson, "Hellhound on My Trail," 1937.
  https://youtu.be/OHAIgpih86E

Edward James "Son" House Jr.

Son House was an American Delta Blues singer and guitarist, noted for his highly emotional style of singing and slide guitar playing. After years of hostility to secular music, as a preacher and for a few years also working as a church pastor, he turned to blues performance at the age of 25.

MEDIA:

❖ Son House, "Death Letter Blues," 1965.
  https://youtu.be/NdgrQoZHnNY

Bessie Smith

Bessie Smith (April 15, 1894–September 26, 1937) was an American singer widely renowned during the Blues Era. She was the most popular female blues singer of the 1920s and 1930s. She is often regarded as one of the greatest singers of her era and was a major influence on her contemporaries (including jazz singers like Billie Holiday). Her recording career on Columbia Records began in 1923; but her performing career was cut short by a car crash that killed her at the age of 43.

MEDIA:

❖ Bessie Smith, "St. Louis Blues," 1929.
   https://youtu.be/5Bo3f_9hLkQ?t=25

Ma Rainey

Gertrude "Ma" Rainey was an American blues singer and influential early blues recording artist. Dubbed the "Mother of the Blues," she bridged earlier vaudeville and the authentic expression of southern blues (influencing a generation of blues singers).

MEDIA:

❖ Ma Rainey, "Ma Rainey's Black Bottom," 1927.
  https://youtu.be/cph7qZoE5d8

Mahalia Jackson

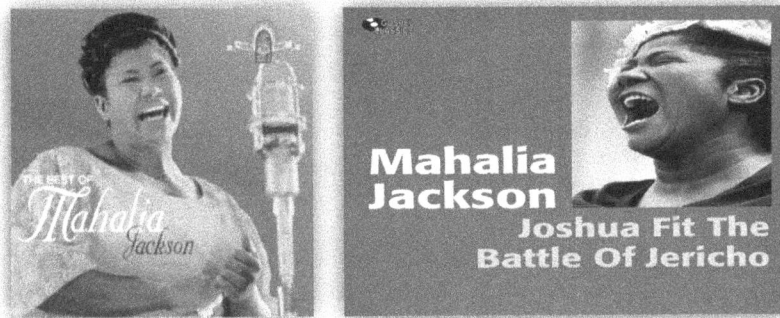

Mahalia Jackson is widely considered one of the most influential vocalists of the 20th century. With a career spanning 40 years, Jackson was integral to the development and spread of gospel blues in black churches throughout the U.S. She is a symbol of American gospel music—another one of those *proponents* of Hip-Hop—*the way it is.*

MEDIA:

❖ Mahalia Jackson, "Joshua Fit the Battle of Jericho," 1956.
  https://youtu.be/BHFGRI5lyDg?t=26

Joshua fit the battle of Jericho, Jericho, Jericho.
Joshua fit the battle of Jericho, and, the walls came tumbling down....

Ragtime (RT)

RT presents itself as a transition between Blues and Jazz around the late 1800s and two of the most significant names within that genre are Scott Joplin and James P. Johnson. RT is the music you would associate with a Saloon in the Wild West. Looking at the music of Joplin, we see a combination of Western Classical Music and "Hood Swag." Similarly, the music of J. P. Johnson would be a significant influence on the development of Duke Ellington.

Key Artists:

❖ Scott Joplin
❖ James P. Johnson

Scott Joplin

Scott Joplin was an African American composer and pianist. Joplin is also known as the "King of Ragtime" because of the fame achieved for his ragtime compositions (music that was born out of the African American community).

MEDIA:

❖ Scott Joplin, "The Entertainer," 1902.
  https://youtu.be/p3UjFFi434o

James Price Johnson

J. P. Johnson was an American pianist and composer. A pioneer of stride piano, he was one of the most important pianists in the early era of recording; and like Jelly Roll Morton, he is one of the key figures in the evolution of ragtime to jazz.

MEDIA:

❖ James P. Johnson, "Carolina Shout," 1944.
  https://youtu.be/nRKTpobVidw

Early Jazz

Transitioning out of the RT era of the late 1800s (the formation of the western frontier), brings us to the Early Jazz era from approximately 1900 to 1920. The "Father of Jazz" is most certainly Louis Armstrong, who combined African American rhythmic values with Western Classical Music traditions to forge a new genre of music. In his youth Armstrong was taught and mentored by Joe "King" Oliver (another important contributor to the development of this music). Another important name in Early Jazz is "Jelly Roll" Morton and in addition to his musical contributions, he also serves as a prototype for the Black Identity that would later be forged by the Beboppers a few decades later. In 1900, a time before integration and civil rights with wall-to-wall racism, and at a time before Blacks in America could even vote, Morton named himself "Jelly Roll," as an early example of the swagger that would become part of the African American identity, even in the face of the adversity of the time.

Key Artists:

❖ Jelly Roll Morton
❖ King Oliver
❖ Louis Armstrong (Father of Jazz)

Joseph Nathan "King" Oliver

King Oliver was an American jazz cornet player and bandleader. He was particularly recognized for his playing style and his pioneering use of mutes in jazz.

MEDIA:

❖ King Oliver's Creole Jazz Band: "Dippermouth Blues," 1923.
   https://youtu.be/BEF9QeHxrYw

Ferdinand Joseph LaMothe

Jelly Roll Morton was an American RT and jazz pianist, bandleader, and composer. Proving that a genre rooted in improvisation could retain its essential characteristics when notated, Morton is widely recognized as jazz's first orchestrator.

MEDIA:

❖ Jelly Roll Morton, "Black Bottom Stomp," 1926.
  https://youtu.be/bVUyvwtHTnw

Louis Daniel Armstrong, nicknamed "Satchmo," "Satch," and "Pops,"

Louis Armstrong was an American trumpeter and vocalist from New Orleans, Louisiana. With a career that spanning five decades and several eras He is widely considered to be the single most influential figure in the history of jazz.

MEDIA:

❖ Louis Armstrong and His Hot Five, "West End Blues," 1928.
  https://youtu.be/4WPCBieSESI

Swing Era

Key Artists:

❖ Duke Ellington
❖ Count Basie

By far the most significant contributor to the development of Hip-Hop has been Jazz; and this really starts to take shape in the 1930s with the Swing Era. The artists that represent this period are Count Basie, and most importantly, Duke Ellington. He was born in 1899 and was the King of Swing during the 1930s. Flash forward to 1970. Ellington (who was in his early 1970s and still conducting his big band) has been on the road for 50 years. He was commissioned to write a suite of music which culminated in *The New Orleans Suite*. In listening to the track "Thanks for the Beautiful Land on Delta" we can see how Ellington could hear what was coming—revealing the direct connection between Jazz and Hip-Hop. Without Duke Ellington, we may never have witnessed the emergence of black 'urban' music.

Edward Kennedy "Duke" Ellington

Duke Ellington was an American composer, pianist, and bandleader born in Washington, D.C., Based in New York City, Duke gained a national profile through his orchestra's appearances at the Cotton Club in Harlem.

MEDIA:

❖ Duke Ellington, "Tourist Point of View," *The Far East Suite*, 1966.
  https://youtu.be/_xqR6E26Tz4

William James "Count" Basie

Count Basie was an American jazz pianist, organist, bandleader, and composer. In 1935, he formed the Count Basie Orchestra. The following year he took the band to Chicago for a string of performances, and the band's first commercial recording. The rest (as they say) is history!

MEDIA:

❖ Count Basie, "Lester Leaps In," *Count Basie at Newport*, 1957.
  https://youtu.be/VKO_FUKbaDw

Chapter 4

BEBOP: AFRO MODERNISM VIA THE AFRICAN DIASPORA

Migration, integration, social and economic progress, and urbanization

Terminology: African Diaspora

African diaspora: descendants of African peoples relocated to other parts of the world; in many cases, this relates to the dispersion of peoples to the Caribbean and Americas during the Atlantic slave trade. African diaspora importance: African cultures were brought to the New World. Over time, cultural customs are adapted to different social, political and economic surroundings. Artistic expression is transformed within new contexts, for example, forms of music that are influenced by African American identity, social customs, religion, and dance. E.g., slave work songs, blues; and later: jazz; Rhythm & Blues; Hip-Hop.

- Hip-Hop Example: "The musical components of hip hop are a hybrid form nurtured by the social relations of the South Bronx, wherein Jamaican sound system culture was transplanted in the 1970s and put down new roots."
- Afrocentric vs. Eurocentric: binary opposites of viewpoints on musical activity (or the musical activity itself). Ethnically essential concepts.
- Eurocentrism: ideology based on the preeminence of European culture.
- Afrocentrism: ideology in response to Eurocentrism that asserts the African (and Pan-African) culture to be central to African American history, culture, and identity.
- Alternate theories (music): Eurological vs. Afrological
- Some musical practices overlap; aspects are assimilated by both European and
- African procedures or customs follow different streams that are historically emergent rather than ethnically *essential*..

The Shape of Afro-modernism:

Afro-modernism: "is connected to the new urbanity of African American communities, the heady momentum of socio-political progress during the first half of the twentieth century, and the changing sense of what constituted African American culture (and even American culture generally speaking) at the post [World War II] moment. The term helps us understand race music appearing at that time as historically specific social discourses. This social energy circulating then shaped the formal procedures of race music and helped give it meaning and coherence for its audiences." (Guthrie Ramsey Jr., Race Music: Black Cultures from Bebop to Hip-Hop, 2003 p. 28)

Strategies of Afro-modernism:

Music, fashion, speech, dance, and other activities are related to signaling membership in a particular subculture through the symbolic uses of these styles. This sense of identity helped shape the Civil Rights and Black Power Movements of the 1950s–1970s.

Summary of Afro-modernism: It is *cultural* (not just musical).

Connected to:

- The urban environment of African American communities
- The sociopolitical progress of the early 1900s

- A changing sense of African American culture beginning around 1945
- Music that reflects this social energy (giving it meaning and coherence for it's audience).

Identities in Jazz: Bebop of the 1940s and 1950s.

The Greatest Photo in Bebop History:

Charles Mingus (bs), Roy Haynes (dr), Thelonious Monk (p) and Charlie Parker.

Bebop was the voice of the disenfranchised urban African American youth.

> *"Bop's mocking defiance made a virtue of isolation," where the "social position of this modernism—distanced from both the black middle class and the white consensus—gave aesthetic self-assertion political force and value."—Eric Lott*

The Dress of Bebop:

- Zoot suits were in defiance of War rationing efforts, a symbol of anti-patriotism.
- Expensive dress: a symbol of financial success, dignity, and self-respect.
- The idea of "being fly" starts with the bebop musicians.
- Hyper-materialism as overcompensation in relation to Eurocentrism.

John Birks "Dizzy" Gillespie

Dizzy Gillespie, from South Carolina, is a genius of the trumpet. He had ego in a time when you could get lynched for having self-pride. There is a story that is told wherein Dizzy Gillespie was seated, getting a shoeshine; in racist anger, a white man (who was supposed to be next), grabbed Dizzy and pulled him out of the seat by his necktie. Dizzy [sarcastically] apologized for existing—moments before knocking him out cold, with one punch, and casually walking off—readjusting his necktie.

This is the era wherein *identity* is replacing *insecurity*. The way is opened!

[Photo: Thelonious Monk, Howard McGhee, Roy Eldridge and Teddy Hill posed outside Minton's Playhouse in New York circa 1940].

Speech/Argot: Some examples typically used by Lester Young (Talking Jive).

- "I feel a draft." (I detect racism in our midst.)
- "How's your feelings?" (How are you?)
- "Can madam burn?" (Can you/he/she cook?)
- "Startled doe, two o'clock." (There's an attractive doe-eyed woman off to the right.)
- "How does the bread smell?" (How much does this job pay?)

Bebop and Dance

The central esthetic of bebop was that it asserted itself as musical art or art music rather than entertainment for dancing (musicians playing for a dance hall).

Jazz, Drugs and Alcohol

Narcotics and alcohol proliferated jazz culture during the 1940s. Marijuana and alcohol were prevalent, although many abused amphetamines. Heroin became the drug of choice among young musicians; many believed it would make them play better, following the virtuosity of Charlie Parker.

Parker, as well as others, would die of overdoses or drug-related abuse in the 1940s and 1950s.

Masculinity and Bebop

With bebop, the masculinist tendencies of jazz became enshrined within a gendered aesthetic of "hipness" that marked "the emergence of the figure of the modern black jazzman as a defiant, alternative, and often exotic symbol of male masculinity."

Note: A common term for this identity is the "hipster."

The "Pimp" Aesthetic

This version of Afro-modernism sets the stage for social and cultural norms in some African American communities. Hip-Hop later capitalized on these themes of cultural performance, albeit in a different expression.

Bebop and Misogyny

Miles Davis was known as a womanizer.

Charlie Parker is well-known for his many mistresses and sexual excesses.

In his autobiography, *Myself When I Am Real*, Charles Mingus writes about his former life as a pimp. By asserting a male-oriented Afro-modernism—concurrent to inscribed notions of gender roles. This is evidenced by the general exclusion of women from the history and development of bebop (with exceptions).

Changes in Jazz Identity

The late 1950s: Narcotics are a known problem in jazz culture during the 1950s.

- Some die from drug use (e.g., Charlie Parker's 1955 overdose) prompting many to kick their habits.
- The 1960s: a new generation of jazz musicians generally refrained from drug use.
- The late 1950s-1960s: "Cool Jazz" (as opposed to bebop) gains more prominence, and with it, a different identity (e.g., more white listeners and college students).
- The 1970s: Jazz institutionalized as art music.
- The 1980s-present: neoclassicism—jazz is a concert hall music. Appealing to, and in some cases, promoted to the upper class.

From left, Tommy Potter, Charlie Parker, Dizzy Gillespie and John Coltrane at Birdland, the New York nightclub named after Parker, in 1951.

MEDIA:

❖ Charlie Parker, "Ko-Ko," 1945.
   https://youtu.be/okrNwE6GI70

Jazz and Hip Hop:

In 1991 (the year of his death), and in response to the popularity of Gangsta rap, Miles Davis produced his only Jazz/Hip-Hop fusion album, *doo-bop*, released posthumously in 1992.

Miles Davis

Miles Dewey Davis III was an American trumpeter, bandleader, and composer. He is among the most influential and acclaimed figures in the history of jazz and popular music.

MEDIA:

❖ Miles Davis, Doo-Bop (Produced by Easy Mo Bee for Def Jam Records), *Doo-Bop*, 1992.
   https://youtu.be/HT2TTFv0-4U

Moving on, this example has more to do with the inherent Rhythmic (Groove) connection between jazz and Hip-Hop (to come)—a portent of the future.

Milt Jackson and Sonny Stitt

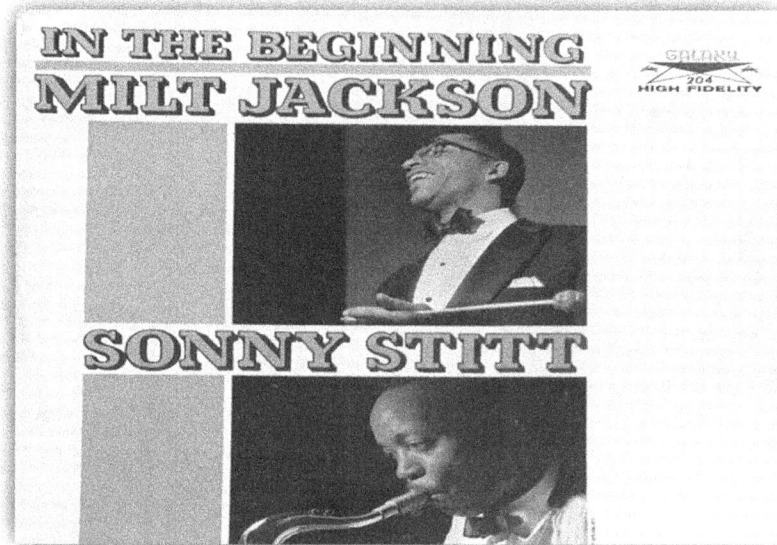

MEDIA:

❖ Milt Jackson and Sonny Stitt, "Baggy's Blues," *In the Beginning*, 1948.
   https://acerecords.co.uk/the-roots-of-modern-jazz-1948-sensation-sessions

Bebop Vocalists: Hip-Hop Prototypes
King Pleasure

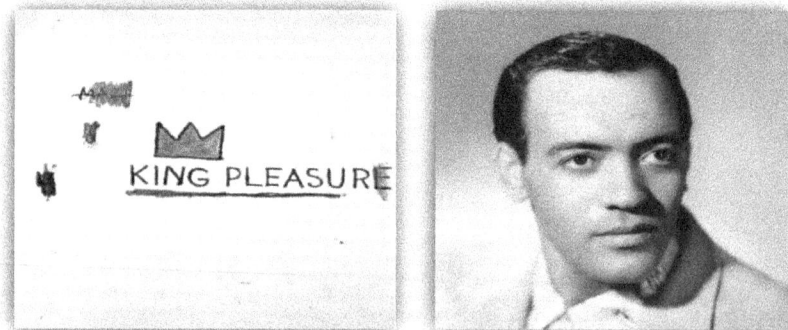

Clarence Beeks, known as King Pleasure, was an American jazz vocalist and an early master of *vocalese*, where a singer sings words to a well-known instrumental solo (e.g., James Moody, Charlie Parker, etc.).

Above: Jean Michel Basquiat, Graffiti Art.

MEDIA:

❖ King Pleasure, "Parker's Mood," 1953–54.
  https://youtu.be/U2N8bVpRneQ
❖ King Pleasure, "Moody's Mood for Love," 1972.
  https://youtu.be/0BAeHpSu24Y

Eddie Jefferson & Coleman Hawkins

Eddie Jefferson was an American jazz vocalist and lyricist. He is credited as an innovator of vocalese, a musical style in which lyrics are set to an instrumental composition or solo. Jefferson credits Leo Watson as his main influence.

Coleman Randolph Hawkins, nicknamed "Hawk" and sometimes "Bean," was an American jazz musician—one of the first prominent tenor saxophonists.

MEDIA:

❖ Coleman Hawkins' most famous performances—1939 recording of "Body and Soul".
  A proto-Hip-Hop style/feel known as the 'Foxtrot'. Dig the funk.
  https://youtu.be/62Qx-ExiAWs
❖ Eddie Jefferson, "Body and Soul," *The Jazz Singer*, 1968.
  https://youtu.be/ly8esocvae4

• ZOOM OUT: Ron Westray, "Soul," *Gemini*, 2018.
  https://traydeuce1.bandcamp.com/track/soul

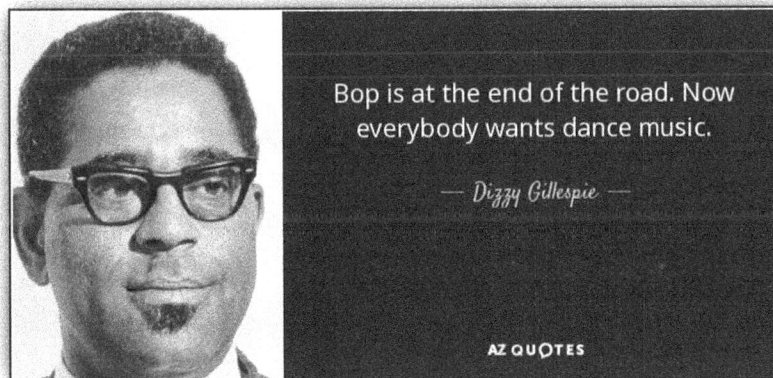

Bop is at the end of the road. Now everybody wants dance music.

— Dizzy Gillespie —

AZ QUOTES

Ultimately, Bebop was no longer danceable (e.g., too fast, too complex); the popular audience wanted Rhythm and Blues.

Chapter 5

RHYTHM AND BLUES: THE PROTO-ROCK AND ROLL

When we consider jazz's relationship to Rhythm and Blues, we can see that Jazz is fundamentally responsible for Rock & Roll, too.

Moving on from Swing in the 1930s and Bebop in the 1940s, during the 1950s we see the rise of a new genre that would be labelled as "Rhythm and Blues." In a sense this genre was a response to Bebop, which was becoming too complex and intellectual to be popular music. In short, the rise of both Bebop and Rhythm and Blues marked the end of Jazz as the popular dance music of the day. **Transitioning** from Swing as *the* popular/dance/music, Rhythm and Blues provided a solution to complex jazz. Still a lot like jazz at the core rhythmic levels, it did not do away with everything associated with Jazz; rather, it took the "bells and whistles" from Jazz and used them to create a new format—utilizing the core rhythmic values of Swing and Jazz, but exploiting an "Overt Back Beat," while also making heavy use of the 12-bar-blues-form (the word "bar" is a more casual word for the term "measure"). In Western Music, the vertical lines on the music staff represent one bar. In a very general sense, Western Music is largely based on 4/4 ("four–four") time, with 4 beats to a bar; thus, if there are 4 beats to a bar and 12 bars to a form, there are 48 beats in each 12-bar blues form. Within this structure the **BackBeat** gets placed on beats 2 and 4 of every bar (and not on 1 and 3). The 12-bar blues form is such a core part of American and African American music that, to this day, even contemporary artists such as Twista of Chicago use the 12-bar blues form in their music. Another key element to this new music form was the **"Riff,"** which is essentially a repeated musical figure that comes out of jazz. In its simplest form it could be the horn section repeating a "Charleston" rhythm. Also borrowed from Jazz was the **Shuffle/Triplet** Rhythm: The Shuffle is based on the Triplet, which is the subdivision of each beat in a bar into three equal beats. Of course, "what is old is new again," and many rappers today are "stuck" on this "new" rap rhythm. To arrive at the Shuffle rhythm, simply take the first and last parts of each triplet and leave out the middle beat.

Rhythm and Blues Characteristics:

❖ 12-bar blues.
❖ Riff-oriented.
❖ Solution to bebop/complex jazz.
❖ Transition out of swing as popular music.
❖ Overt backbeat.
❖ Shuffle/Triplet.
  • 1 Measure
  • 4 Beats per bar
  • 3 Triplets per beat
  • Shuffle is on the first and third triplets of each beat.

• ZOOM OUT: Example of the 'Triplet' Rhythm in Rapping.

❖ Twista, "Talk to Me," *Category F5*, 2009.
  https://youtu.be/uzUnshYkARo

• ZOOM OUT: Example of the Blues Progression in Hip-Hop.

❖ Twista, "Like a 24 (feat. T.I. and Liffy Strokes)," *Kamikaze*, 2004.
  https://youtu.be/NKN0R3Y87mQ

Key Artists:

Chuck Berry

Charles Edward Anderson Berry was an American singer, songwriter and guitarist who pioneered Rock and Roll.

MEDIA:

❖ Chuck Berry, "Johnny B. Goode," *Live, 1958.*
  https://youtu.be/6ROwVrF0Ceg

Little Richard

Richard Wayne Penniman, known professionally as Little Richard, was an American musician, singer and songwriter. He was an influential figure in popular music and culture for seven decades. From Elvis Presley to James Brown to Jimi Hendrix to Michael Jackson to Prince Rogers Nelson and Ru Paul—they all owe a huge debt of gratitude to Sir 'Little' Richard!

MEDIA:

❖ Little Richard, "Lucille," 1957.
   https://youtu.be/u0Ujb6lJ_mM

Chapter 6

MEMPHIS SOUL-CHICAGO SOUL

Memphis Soul is a shimmering, sultry style of soul music produced in the 1960s and the 1970s at Stax Records and Hi Records in Memphis, Tennessee. It featured *melancholic and melodic horns, organ, bass and drums,* as heard in recordings by Hi's Al Green and Stax's Booker T. & the M.G.'s. The latter group also played in the harder-edged *Southern Soul* style. The Hi Records house band (Hi Rhythm Section) and producer Willie Mitchell developed a surging style heard in the label's 1970s hit recordings. Amid recordings which had their own unique sound, many Stax recordings fit into the aforementioned [soul] style.

MEDIA:

❖ Al Green, "Tired of Being Alone," on PBS' *Soul!* 1973.
   https://youtu.be/422vdlO8eJQ?t=47

Curtis Mayfield & The Impressions helped to develop the sound that later earned him a reputation as the Godfather of Chicago Soul. As a member of The Impressions, Mayfield infused a *call-and-response style of group singing* that came from gospel and influenced many other groups of the era. Chicago Soul is also known as "Northern Soul." In 1968, Mayfield founded the record label Curtom Records with Impressions Manager Eddie Thomas; he left The Impressions in 1970 to embark on a solo career.

The track "Keep on Pushing" took on deeper significance when it was adopted as an anthem of the Civil Rights Movement during the 1960s; and while we have talked about music being played in 4/4 time, "Keep on Pushing" is an example of a composition in 3/4 time, meaning that there are three beats to each measure. "I Loved and I Lost," along with "Move On Up" show us how past genres such as Chicago Soul have gone on to influence and inform Hip-Hop: "I Loved and I Lost" was sampled by Common on his 2011 track "Lovin' I Lost," as well as Tray Deuce for his 2016 instrumental track "Lost," While Kanye West sampled "Move On Up" for his 2005 track "Touch The Sky." The track "Pusher Man" represents one Mayfield's most significant efforts as a solo artist, the soundtrack to the 1972 Blaxploitation film *Super Fly.*

MEDIA:

❖ Curtis Mayfield & The Impressions, "Keep on Pushing," *Keep on Pushing,* 1964.
   https://youtu.be/HU-mEsCk3D8
❖ Curtis Mayfield & The Impressions, "I Loved & I Lost," *We're a Winner,* 1968.
   https://youtu.be/lIpgjRQdgkg
❖ Common, "Lovin' I Lost," *The Dreamer/The Believer,* 2011.
   https://youtu.be/z6Undk2Vwks
❖ Tray Deuce, "Lost," *Out the Box,* 2016.
   https://traydeuce1.bandcamp.com/track/lost
❖ Curtis Mayfield, "Move on Up," *Curtis,* 1970.
   https://youtu.be/6Z66wVo7uNw
❖ Kanye West, "Touch the Sky," *Late Registration,* 2005.
   https://youtu.be/B95OUKk7alM

❖ Curtis Mayfield, "Pusher Man," on *Soul Train*, 1973.
  https://youtu.be/YFMUERIJRPM
❖ Super Fly (trailer), 1972.
  https://youtu.be/VYZUWzv_FaY

Though his music had more of a traditional blues influence to it, another important artist associated with Chicago Soul/ Northern Soul was **Little Milton Campbell.** In Campbell's music we hear yet another association with Hip Hop, when Campbell's "Packed Up and Took My Mind" was sampled by Ghostface Killah on his track, "Walk Around." Here, Ghostface Killah also flips the self-deprecating metaphor of Campbell's song to that of having to shoot someone in the grocery store aisle:

MEDIA:

❖ Little Milton Campbell, "Packed Up and Took My Mind," *Tin Pan Alley*, 1975.
  https://www.youtube.com/watch?v=hjQtXaRAIZw
❖ Little Milton Campbell, "If You Talk in Your Sleep," on *Soul Train*, 1975.
  https://youtu.be/NivDiCuCUfk

• ZOOM OUT: Ghostface Killah, "Walk Around," *The Big Doe Rehab*, 2007.
  https://youtu.be/4V8iFguVTYU

It was him, the corner store, and a buttered roll
The shit dropped when I gave him two stomach holes—G.K.

Chapter 7

MOTOWN

Motown Record Corporation was formed in Detroit, Michigan in 1960 by Berry Gordy Jr. The name is a reference to Detroit's nickname of "Motor City" (automotive manufacturing that the city had become famous for). Motown was an immensely influential record label with an equally important roster of artists and staff. Some of Motown's "key artists" include William Smokey Robinson, Marvin Gaye, and Michael Jackson.

MEDIA:

❖ Michael Jackson, "One Day in Your Life," on *Soul Train*, 1975.
  https://youtu.be/5OY99WubWBo
❖ Marvin Gaye, "Distant Lover," on *Soul Train*, 1973.
  https://youtu.be/BNUDlqSnxZk

• ZOOM OUT: Kanye West, "Spaceship," *The College Drop Out*, 2004.
  https://youtu.be/mn77gzjBl1U

Another important Motown group was The Isley Brothers lead by Ronald Isley (also known as Mr. Biggs [as named by R. Kelly]). The Isley's 1983 track "Between the Sheets" was sampled by DJ Magic Mike for his 1990 track "For the Easy Listeners," which served as a precursor to Notorious B.I.G. for his 1994 track "Big Poppa," which also sampled "Between the Sheets."

MEDIA:

❖ The Isley Brothers, "It's Your Thing," *The Isleys Live*, 1973.
  https://youtu.be/Tqc_EhmL8-E
❖ The Isley Brothers, "Living for The Love of You," *The Heat Is On*, 1975.
  https://youtu.be/WMdBs7uTLHw

• ZOOM OUT: Ron Westray, "Lyfe," *Beats and Time, 2017.*
  https://traydeuce1.bandcamp.com/track/lyfe

❖ The Isley Brothers, "Between the Sheets," *Between the Sheets*, 1983.
  https://youtu.be/TNDb8qKZEX8
❖ DJ Magic Mike, "For the Easy Listeners," *Bass Is the Name of the Game*, 1990.
  https://youtu.be/veKvQzm7JUE
❖ Notorious B.I.G., "Big Poppa," *Ready to Die*, 1994.
  https://youtu.be/phaJXp_zMYM?t=6
❖ The Isley Brothers, "Pop That Thang," on *Soul Train*, 1972.
  https://youtu.be/tC4BBybp5-U

Don Cornelius and *Soul Train*

Donald Cortez Cornelius was an American television show host and producer widely known as the creator of the nationally syndicated dance and music show *Soul Train*, which he hosted from 1971 until 1993. Cornelius sold the show to MadVision Entertainment in 2008. One of the major cultural institutions of the time was the television program *Soul Train*, created and hosted by Don Cornelius in the early 1970s. Cornelius was from Chicago and first started his program in that city, the birthplace of "Chicago Soul," until production was moved to Hollywood after the show gained national syndication shortly after its creation. Airing weekly for several decades, this show presented all manner of Soul, Rhythm and Blues, Gospel, Funk and, eventually, Hip-Hop artists across the country. *Soul Train* was the first Black-owned program to achieve this level of success; the show gained a following among White audiences as well. A few other notable *Soul Train* artists include Johnnie Taylor, The Staple Singers, Gladys Knight and the Pips, Thelma Houston (Auntie of Whitney Houston) and the O'Jays, whose leader Eddie Levert was the father of Gerald Levert.

MEDIA:

❖ Johnnie Taylor, "Disco Lady," on *Soul Train*, 1975.
https://youtu.be/-3JkEoQ0Cz8

• ZOOM OUT: Ron Westray, "Boogah," *Beats and Time*, 2017.
https://traydeuce1.bandcamp.com/track/boogah

❖ The Staple Singers, "If You're Ready (Come Go with Me), on *Soul Train*, 1974.
https://youtu.be/gxPIvTDeEho
❖ The Staple Singers, "Let's Do It Again," *Let's Do It, Again*, 1975.
https://g.co/kgs/XakruH

• ZOOM OUT: Ron Westray, "Slyme," *Beats and Time*, 2017.
https://traydeuce1.bandcamp.com/track/slyme

❖ Gladys Knight and the Pips, "Best Thing That Ever Happened to Me," on *Soul Train*, 1974.
https://youtu.be/Z7-1g-a7WtM
❖ Thelma Houston, "I Want to Go Back There Again," on *Soul Train*, 1972.
https://youtu.be/Pz2_ygbiJrY
❖ The O'Jays, "Give the People What They Want," on *Soul Train*, 1975.
https://youtu.be/Vir6swQpfbY

It is important to note that the two terms "R&B" and "Rhythm and Blues" are not [necessarily] interchangeable.
R&B, as a genre, occurs after Rhythm and Blues, and developed out of Rhythm and Blues. Rhythm and Blues and jazz both express the swing rhythm—a "circular" rhythm aesthetic..

Aretha Franklin

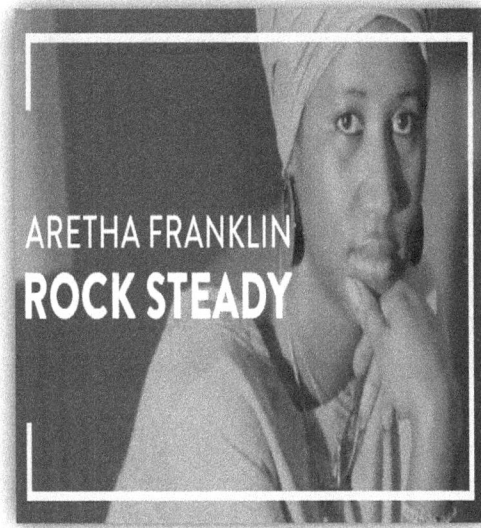

One final "key artist" from this era was Aretha Franklin, who is often referred to as "The Queen of Soul." While Franklin is often incorrectly associated with the Motown label, she was in fact signed to Arista Records (after leaving Atlantic records). Musically, Franklin spans the genres of Rhythm & Blues and Soul to Funk, and was among several artists, including The Isley Brothers and Curtis Mayfield who transitioned from Soul to Funk. Ultimately, she recorded for Arista Records; but Aretha is an indelible part of Rhythm & Blues, Soul and Funk—representing all three genres—as do The Isley Brothers and a host of other artists who influenced the transition from soul to funk.

MEDIA:

❖ Aretha Franklin, "Rock Steady," *Young, Gifted and Black*, 1971.
   https://youtu.be/EXJx2NnnxA0

• ZOOM OUT: Tray Deuce, "Deez Nutz," *Beats and Time*, 2019.
   https://traydeuce1.bandcamp.com/track/deez-nutz

❖ Aretha Franklin, "Sparkle," on *Soul Train*, 1976.
   https://youtu.be/sLfavmdPEbg

Fish Sandwich Music: "Butterfat"

Betty Wright

Bessie Regina Norris, better known by her stage name Betty Wright, was an American soul and R&B singer, songwriter and background vocalist. Beginning her professional career in the late 1960s as a teenager, Wright rose to fame in the 1970s with hits such as "Clean Up Woman" and "Tonight Is the Night."

MEDIA:

❖ Betty Wright, "Clean Up Woman," *I Love the Way You Love*, 1972.
   https://g.co/kgs/LlmXWH
❖ Betty Wright, "Tonight is the Night," *Danger, High Voltage*, 1974.
   https://g.co/kgs/Yb3UgG

• ZOOM OUT: Kendrick Lamar, "Holy Key (feat. Betty Wright and Big Sean, prod. By DJ KHALED)," *Major Key*, 2016.
   https://g.co/kgs/nkzZfd.

Bishop BULLWINKLE

Bernard Thomas, better known as Bishop Bullwinkle, was an American singer/comedian best known for appearing in the viral YouTube video "Hell to the Naw Naw."

• ZOOM OUT: Bishop Bullwinkle, "Hell To Da Naw Naw Naw," 2017.
   https://g.co/kgs/s6fxGP

Chapter 8

TRANSITION TO FUNK

Funk is an amalgamation (mixture/combination) of soul music, jazz, and R&B. Funk (and Soul) expresses what's known as the "Funky Four Corners"—a "square" rhythmic-aesthetic: a *linear* sound.

These 'shape' associations can help to explain why the genres of Funk, Soul and Hip-Hop can be rhythmically differentiated from Jazz and Rhythm and Blues (Circular).

(Bobby Byrd)
What you gon' PLAY now?
(James Brown)
Bobby … I don't know; but whuss-n-evuh I PLAY,
It's got to be funky!
(B.B.)
Yeeeah!

James Brown

"The Godfather of Soul"

James Brown started out in Rhythm and Blues. "*I Feel Good*," for instance, is early James Brown. Additionally, songs like "*Papa's Got A Brand New Bag*" are still *swinging*. His evolution into Funk was a result of all these musical experiences. By the 1960s he was in his prime; and his music started to take on a highly syncopated (the accenting of the weak beat, the 'off-beat', the 'upbeat') rhythmic feel–this along with catchy vocals and extensive vamps and riffs from the ensemble.

> *Brown's frenzied vocals, frequently punctuated with screams and grunts, channelled the "ecstatic ambiance of the black church" in a secular context.*

Brown's innovations (e.g., first MC/Rapper?) pushed the funk music style further to the forefront with releases such as "Cold Sweat" (1967), "Mother Popcorn" (1969) and "Get It Up (I Feel Like a Being A) Sex Machine" (1970). Discarding even the 12-bar blues featured in his early music, Brown's later music was overlaid with "catchy, anthemic vocals" based on "extensive vamps"—in which he also used his voice as "a percussive instrument with frequent rhythmic grunts and with rhythm section patterns… [resembling] West African polyrhythms"—a tradition evident in African American work songs and chants. As characterized by tracks such "I Feel Good" and "Papa's Got a Brand-New Bag," by the mid-1960s, James Brown had developed his signature groove called, "The One," which emphasized the first beat of every measure, as exemplified by tracks such as "Make It Funky," "Good Foot," "The Payback," and "Lickin' Stick." His musical innovations pushed the funk music style further to the forefront with hit tracks such as "Cold Sweat" (1967), "Mother Popcorn" (1969) and "Get Up (I Feel Like Being A) Sex Machine" (1970).

Brown's backing band The J.B.'s would occasionally issue albums and singles on their own, though James Brown would still produce the music and sometimes would even play the organ or synthesizer on these tracks. One such recording was Bobby Byrd's "I Know You Got Soul," which was later sampled by Eric B. & Rakim.

MEDIA:

❖ James Brown, "I Got You (I Feel Good)," 1964.
  https://youtu.be/BlwOK9yGUYM
❖ James Brown, "Papa's Got a Brand-New Bag," 1965.
  https://youtu.be/QE5D2hJhacU
❖ James Brown, "Licking Stick-Licking Stick," *Say It Live and Loud: Live in Dallas*, 1968.
  https://youtu.be/f-597SOXFgs
❖ James Brown, "Funky Drummer Pt.1&2," *In the Jungle Groove, 1970.*
  https://youtu.be/QXw6YZltKJk
❖ James Brown, "Make It Funky," 1971.
  https://youtu.be/RJHjkS0eFHM
❖ James Brown, "Super Bad," 1971.
  https://youtu.be/XV9a3tUPqTo
❖ James Brown, "Make It Funky," 1972.
  https://youtu.be/E2D2oUNTbjU
❖ James Brown, "Good Foot," 1972.
  https://youtu.be/KzlxUHUKlrA
❖ James Brown, "The Payback," *The Payback*, 1973.
  https://youtu.be/istJXUJJP0g
❖ James Brown, "Super Bad," on *Soul Train*, 1974.
  https://youtu.be/Jk8D7L7EPcg
❖ James Brown, "Cold Sweat," *Live*, 1968.
  https://youtu.be/tvltTXEg5kI

ZOOM OUT:

• Bobby Byrd, "I Know You Got Soul," 1971.
  https://youtu.be/ny-g9dYVP74
• Ron Westray, "Take Me Thur," *Beats and Time*, 2017.
  https://traydeuce1.bandcamp.com/track/take-me-thur
• Hank Ballard, "From the Love Side," on *Soul Train*, 1974.
  https://youtu.be/zKKcArCApx0
• Lynn Collins, "Mama Feel Good," *Black Ceasar*, 1973.
  https://youtu.be/mXcdpPDHzlM

"It was James Brown's restaurant—but Fred's kitchen!"—Ron Westray

Fred Wesley

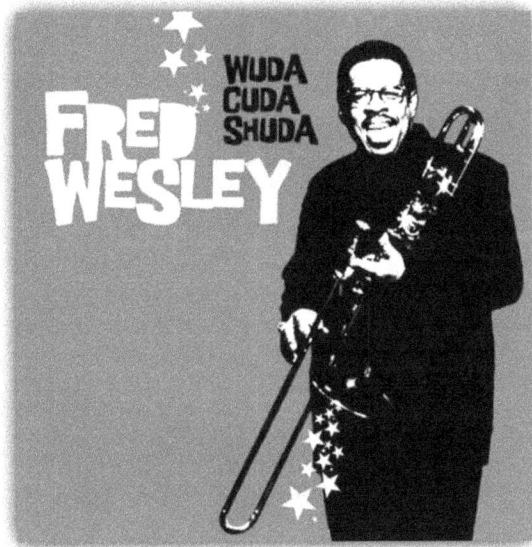

Fred Wesley is an American trombonist, composer and soloist who architected the sound, and composed *many* of the hits, for James Brown in the 1960s and 1970s—and was an integral part of the success of Parliament-Funkadelic.

FUN FACT: What Ever Happened to MDLT?

The Jackson Five produced a girl group in 1974. They were a family of four sisters from Ohio called Maxine, Diane, Laverne and Tina (MDLT) Willis. They had one release on Joe Jackson's Ivory Tower International Records label called "What's Your Game."
It's rumored that they were blackballed from the industry because one of the girls tried to seduce Michael...lol.

George Clinton

"The Picasso of Funk"

George Edward Clinton is an American musician, singer, songwriter, bandleader and record producer. His Parliament-Funkadelic collective developed an influential and eclectic form of funk music during the 1970s that drew on science fiction, outlandish fashion, psychedelia and surreal humor.

Parliament-Funkadelic is an American music collective of rotating musicians headed by George Clinton, primarily consisting of the funk bands Parliament and Funkadelic, both active since the 1960s.

In the 1970s and early 1980s, a new group of musicians further developed the "funk rock" approach innovated by George Clinton, with his main bands *Parliament* and, later, *Funkadelic*. Together, they produced a new kind of funk sound heavily influenced by jazz and psychedelic rock. The two groups had members in common and often are referred to collectively as "Parliament-Funkadelic." The breakout popularity of Parliament-Funkadelic gave rise to the term "P-Funk," which referred to the music by George Clinton's bands and defined a new sub-genre.

Bernie Worrell: MVP

George Bernard Worrell, Jr., a founding member of P-Funk. was an American keyboardist and record producer best known for his work on synth (and as the ex-officio musical director of the band). In 1997, he was inducted into the Rock and Roll Hall of Fame alongside fifteen other members of Parliament-Funkadelic. Worrell was described as "the kind of sideman who was as influential as many bandleaders."

MEDIA:

❖ Parliament, "Chocolate City," *Chocolate City*, 1975.
  https://youtu.be/DZaVA3NS7zE
❖ Parliament, "Mothership Connection (Star Child)" *Mothership Connection*, 1975.
  https://youtu.be/4aGnuLXCruc
❖ Funkadelic, "One Nation Under a Groove," *One Nation Under A Groove*, 1978.
  https://youtu.be/3WOZwwRH6XU
❖ George Clinton, "Atomic Dog," *Computer Games*, 1982.
  https://youtu.be/YAaVpVUgGfE

Bootsy

William Earl "Bootsy" Collins is an American funk bassist, singer, and songwriter. Rising to prominence with James Brown in the late 1960s, and with Parliament-Funkadelic in the 1970s, Collins driving bass guitar and humorous vocals established him as one of the leading names in funk. Collins is a member of the Rock and Roll Hall of Fame, inducted with 15 other members of Parliament-Funkadelic. Associated acts include Parliament-Funkadelic, Bootsy's Rubber Band, James Brown, Axiom Funk, Praxis, Material, Fatboy Slim, Snoop Dogg, Deee-Lite and Buckethead.

MEDIA:

❖ Bootsy's Basic Funk Formula: "The One".
  https://youtu.be/IHE6hZU72A4

❖ Bootsy Collins, "I'd Rather Be With You," *Stretchin' Out In Bootsy's Rubber Band*, 1976. https://youtu.be/0tgYr03o3dE

❖ Bootsy Collins, "Munchies for Your Love," *Ahh… the Name Is Bootsy, Baby!*, 1977. https://youtu.be/kVYwZ1hgNiU

• ZOOM OUT: Snoop's Parliament Connection-Sonic Examples of Stylistic Influence

MEDIA:

❖ Nite L.O.C.s (feat. Kokane, Snoop Dogg, Goldie Loc, Quaze, *Welcome to Tha. House Vol.1, 2002*. https://youtu.be/unmhvHW8SC8

❖ Snoop Dogg, *Welcome to Tha. House Vol. 1* (feat. Latoiya Williams), 2002. https://youtu.be/XafX31rKxrk

• *ZOOM OUT II*:

First released as a single in 1980, and made famous for its extensive use of the **"Izzle"** (infix form of slang), "Double Dutch Bus" was a hit [funk] single composed by Frankie Smith.

❖ Frankie Smith, "Double Dutch Bus," *Double Dutch Bus*, 1981. https://youtu.be/fK9hK82r-AM

Chapter 9

FUNK JAZZ

In the early 1970s, when funk was becoming more mainstream, artists like Parliament Funkadelic, Earth Wind and Fire, Sly and the Family Stone as well as *The Ohio* Players, among others, were successful in getting radio play; but according to *Billboard Magazine*, only Sly & the Family Stone had singles which made it to #1. In 1970, "Thank You (Falettinme Be Mice Elf Agin)" hit # 1 as did "Family Affair" in 1971, affording Sly and Funk crossover success and greater recognition, unlike some of their equally talented but moderately popular peers, before the onslaught of Disco, around the middle of the 1970s, remaining hugely popular through the early 1980s. Disco music owed a great deal to funk. Many early disco songs and performers came directly from funk-oriented backgrounds. Some disco music hits, for example "I'm Your Boogie Man" by KC & The Sunshine Band and "Le Freak" by Chic, included riffs or rhythms very similar to funk music.

MEDIA:

❖ Commodores, "Brick House," *Commodores*, 1977.
   https://youtu.be/rrBx6mAWYPU

• ZOOM OUT: Ron Westray, "Get Brycks," *Beats and Time*, 2017.
   https://traydeuce1.bandcamp.com/track/get-brycks

❖ Earth, Wind & Fire, "Shining Star," *That's The Way of the World*, 1975.
   https://youtu.be/Zu9a29UR2dU
❖ Ohio Players, "Skin-Tight," *Skin-Tight*, 1974.
   https://youtu.be/oBG3qpYj5DU
❖ Heatwave, "Always and Forever," *Too Hot to Handle*, 1976.
   https://youtu.be/9tXVK7fh -kI
❖ Heatwave, "Boogie Nights," *Too Hot to Handle*, 1976.
   https://youtu.be/2XEmFuEbpzM

• ZOOM OUT: Ron Westray, "Weave," *Beats and Time*, 2017.
   https://traydeuce1.bandcamp.com/track/weave

❖ Side Effect, "Keep That Same Old Feeling," *What You Need*, 1976.
   https://youtu.be/IhXt_J-6Ick
❖ KC & The Sunshine Band, "I'm Your Boogie Man," *Part 3*, 1976.
   https://g.co/kgs/CmHafq
❖ Average White Band, "Pick Up the Pieces," AWB, 1974.
   https://g.co/kgs/eDyNc2
❖ Average White Band, "A Love of Your Own," *Soul Searching*, 1976.
   https://g.co/kgs/iUoNTA

MEDIA:

❖ The Ohio Players, "Who'd She Coo?" on *Soul Train*, 1976.
   https://youtu.be/fmFc7RwIvAg
❖ War, "All Day Music," on *Soul Train*, 1972.
   https://youtu.be/GxiqgFLSK3U
❖ Sly & The Family Stone, "Thank You (Falettinme Be Mice Elf Agin)," on *Soul Train*, 1974.
   https://youtu.be/wj5VODa-eTY

Grover Washington, Jr.

Grover Washington, Jr. was an American jazz-funk and soul-jazz saxophonist. Along with Wes Montgomery and George Benson, he is considered by many to be one of the founders of the smooth jazz genre. Grover authored much of his own material.

MEDIA:

❖ Grover Washington, Jr. "Mister Magic," *Mister Magic*, 1975.
   https://youtu.be/UbsbqkgzxWM

• ZOOM OUT: John Coltrane, "Mr. Day," *Coltrane Plays the Blues*, 1960.
   https://youtu.be/Q5V-gQBfJc4

Chapter 10

HYPER FUNK

In the 1980s, largely as a reaction against what was seen as the overrated popularity of disco, many of the core elements that formed the foundation of the P-Funk formula began to be usurped by electronic machines and synthesizers. Disco music owed a great deal to funk. Many early disco songs and performers came directly from funk-oriented backgrounds. Some disco music hits, for example "I'm Your Boogie Man" by KC & The Sunshine Band and "Le Freak" by Chic, included riffs or rhythms very similar to funk music. Horn sections of saxophones and trumpets were replaced by synths and keyboards. The classic keyboards of funk, like the Hammond B3 organ and the Fender Rhodes piano began to be replaced by the new digital synthesizers such as the Yamaha DX7. Electronic drum machines began to replace the drummers of the past; and the slap and pop style of bass playing were often replaced by the synth keyboard bass lines. As well, the lyrics of funk songs began to change from suggestive double-entendres to more graphic and sexually explicit content. Bands that began during the P-Funk era incorporated some of the uninhibited sexuality of Prince and state-of-the-art technological developments to continue to craft funk hits. Cameo, Zapp, The Gap Band, The Bar Kays and The Dazz Band all found their biggest hits in the 1980s; but by the latter half of the 1980s, funk had lost its commercial impact.

Prince

The other artist who embodies Hyper Funk and who without question represents the epitome of 1980s production values is Prince.

Using a stripped-down instrumentation, and combining eroticism, technology, and musical complexity (as well as an outrageous image and stage show), **Prince** went on to have as much of an impact on the sound of funk as James Brown—ultimately creating a 'musical world' that was as ambitious and imaginative as George Clinton and P-Funk. Prince was integrally involved with the group Morris Day and 'The Time' (who were originally conceived as an opening act for him). Exploiting the "Minneapolis Sound," a hybrid mixture of funk, R&B, rock, pop, new-wave, tight musicianship and sexual themes, **The Time** went on to define their *own* sound..

MEDIA:

❖ Prince, "I Wanna Be Your Lover," *Prince*, 1978.
https://youtu.be/Rp8WL621uGM

CHIC

Chic, also known as Nile Rodgers & Chic, is an American band that was organized in 1972 by guitarist Nile Rodgers and bassist Bernard Edwards.

MEDIA:

❖ Chic, "Le Freak," *C'est Chic* 1978.
https://g.co/kgs/oU4q6m

Rick James

Rick James was the first funk musician to assume the funk mantle dominated by P-Funk in the 1970s. His 1981 album *Street Songs* with the singles "Give It To Me Baby" and "Super Freak" resulted in James becoming a star, and paved the way for the future direction of explicitness in funk. A subtle connection between Funk and Hip-Hop can be observed in two of James' tracks: Before "Bustin' Out'" (with the funk), the intro of the track "You and I" (1978) parodies and mocks the Disco *style* (foreshadowing an anti-disco, Hip-Hop *mentality*). Meanwhile, the song "Loosey's Rap" (1988) prominently features the rapper Roxanne Shanté.

MEDIA:

❖ Rick James, "You and I," *Come Get It*, 1978.
  https://youtu.be/dWZkxYamLUs
❖ Rick James, "Loosey's Rap," *Wonderful*, 1988.
  https://youtu.be/qNOrMPhTevU
❖ Rick James, "Super Freak," *Street Songs*, 1981.
  https://youtu.be/QYHxGBH6o4M

Con Funk Shun

Con Funk Shun is an American R&B and funk band whose popularity began in the mid-1970s and ran through the 1980s. They were influenced by funk legend James Brown and Sly and the Family Stone.

MEDIA:

❖ Confunkshun, "Love's Train," *To the Max*, 1982.
  https://g.co/kgs/PC5U12

Cameo

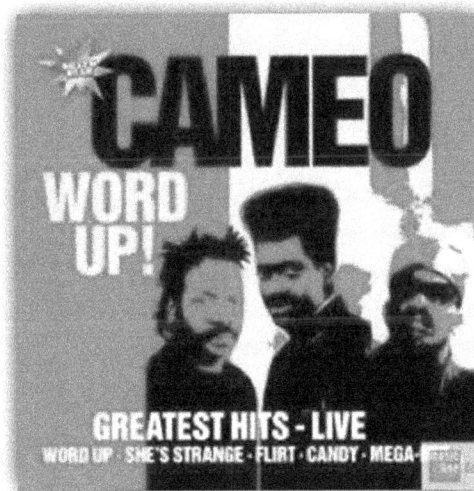

Cameo is an American funk band that formed in 1974. Cameo was initially a 14-member group known as the New York City Players; this name was later changed to Cameo. Along with "Candy," "She's Strange" and "Alligator Woman," Cameo had the hit single "Word Up" (giving rise to the phrase "word up," which later became "word"), Among other qualities of these tracks, we can hear how the sonic quality of the back beat is evolving as part of the transition from live drummers to the use of drum machines. On "Candy," the sax solo by renowned jazz saxophonist Michael Brecker is notable in that it reflects the sound of true-jazz-harmony (something that was not prevalent in earlier Funk solos—with their dependence on the blues and pentatonic scale). Cameo topped the R&B charts for more than a decade, has sold more than 18 million albums and is widely considered to be one of the most popular funk bands of it's era.

Larry Blackmon: MVP

Born in New York, NY, Larry Ernest Blackmon was an American vocalist and musician who gained acclaim as the lead singer, founder and frontman of the 1980s Hyper-Funk band, Cameo.

MEDIA:

❖ Cameo, "Alligator Woman," *Alligator Women*, 1982.
 https://youtu.be/3hMttCO2yIo
❖ Cameo, "She's Strange," *She's Strange*, 1984.
 https://youtu.be/jUgsmsvSYow
❖ Cameo, "Word Up!" *Word Up!* 1986.
 https://youtu.be/MZjAantupsA
❖ Cameo, "Candy," *Word Up!* 1986.
 https://youtu.be/sn8KYD1Vco0

Chapter 11

DUB

Characteristics and Key Artists

The final historical element leading up to the formation of Hip-Hop can be found in the Dub music that came out of Jamaica. While the Dub genre grew out of Reggae in the 1960s and is commonly considered a sub-genre, it has developed and extended beyond the scope of Reggae. The verb Dub is defined as making a copy of one recording to another. The process of using previously recorded material, modifying the material, and subsequently recording it to a new master mix, in effect transferring or "dubbing" the material, was utilized by Jamaican producers when making dubs. Dub is a genre of music which grew out of Reggae music in the 1960s, and is commonly considered a sub-genre, though it has developed to extend beyond the scope of Reggae. Music in this genre consists predominantly of instrumental remixes of existing recordings and is achieved by significantly manipulating and reshaping the recordings, usually by removing the vocals from an existing music piece, emphasizing the drum and bass parts. Other techniques include dynamically adding the drum and bass parts. Other techniques include dynamically adding extensive echo, reverb, panoramic delay, and occasional dubbing of vocal or instrumental snippets from the original version or other works. Dub was pioneered by Osbourne "King Tubby" Ruddock, Lee "Scratch" Perry, Erol Thompson and others in the late 1960s. Similar experiments with recordings at the mixing desk outside of the dancehall environment were also done by producers Clive Chin and Herman Chin Loy. These producers, especially Ruddock and Perry, looked upon the mixing desk as an instrument, manipulating tracks to come up with something new and different. Dub has influenced many genres of music, including rock (most significantly the sub-genre of post-punk and other kinds of punk), pop, Hip-Hop, disco, and later house techno, ambient and trip hop. Dub has also become a reference for the genres of jungle, drum "n" bass and dubstep. *That's Dub's contribution: technical information from the Jamaican dub artists, rather than direct musical influence.*

Key Artists:

- Osbourne "King Tubby" Ruddock
- Lee "Scratch" Perry
- Errol Thompson

MEDIA:

❖ King Tubby & Santic Allstars, "Shooter Dub," 1976.
  https://youtu.be/9quKFiOC89U
❖ The Revolutionaries, "Nuclear Bomb," *Reaction in Dub*, 1977.
  https://youtu.be/PJVD2IXnDjo

Chapter 12

ORIGINS OF EAST COAST HIP-HOP

Pigmeat Markham

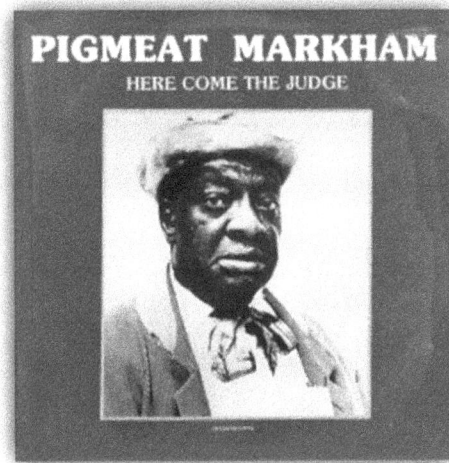

Dewey "Pigmeat" Markham was an American entertainer. Though best known as a comedian, Markham was also a singer, dancer and actor. His nickname came from a stage routine, in which he declared himself to be "Sweet Poppa Pigmeat." He was sometimes credited in films as Pigmeat "Alamo" Markham. While DJ Kool Herc pioneered Deejaying, DJ Hollywood holds the distinction of creating rapping as we know it today. DJ Hollywood was in turn influenced by the comedian "Pigmeat" Markham, whose 1968 single "Here Comes the Judge" is widely considered a precursor to rapping. Young Kurtis Blow, at home in Grandma's attic, also heard that record.

MEDIA:

❖ Pigmeat Markham, "Here Come' the Judge," 1968.
  https://g.co/kgs/jnRQMF

Gilbert Scott-Heron

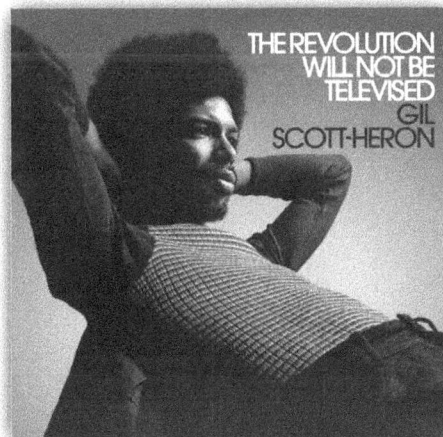

Gilbert Scott-Heron, from Chicago, IL, USA, was an American soul and jazz poet, musician, and author, known primarily for his work as a spoken-word performer in the 1970s and 1980s. His poem "The Revolution Will Not Be Televised," delivered over a jazz-soul beat, had a major influence on the development of urban music and Hip-Hop.

MEDIA:

❖ Gil Scott-Heron, "The Revolution Will Not Be Televised," *Pieces of a Man*, 1971.
https://youtu.be/vwSRqaZGsPw

There will be no slow motion or still life of Roy Wilkins
Strolling through Watts in a red, black, and green liberation jumpsuit
That he has been saving for just the proper occasion-G.S.H.

❖ Excerpt from the movie, *Uptown Saturday Night*, 1974.
https://youtu.be/jmpt502R_ZM?t=2520

Chapter 13

THE ARRIVAL OF HIP-HOP

The Griots of West Africa (a group of traveling singers and poets) whose vocal style is like that of rappers, also resembles the Jamaican tradition of "toasting" (boasting, impromptu poetry and sayings over music) and dates back hundreds of years. Like jazz, the roots of Hip-Hop are found in African American music.

When the historic aftershocks of urban renewal, gentrification, and capital flight settled, a new social and economic order had emerged in America. In the wake of massive shifts, the gap between America's cities, populated by black and brown bodies, and the suburbs, whiter and more affluent, grew wider and more severe. But, during the volatile surge of social and economic change, an exuberant youth culture started to take shape. What began in basements, on street corners, in public parks, and throughout the still of the night, would furnish young people with a fertile environment for crafting new identities, explosive art forms, and whole industries.

Cultural Origins

Hip-Hop is a cultural movement that developed in New York City in the 1970s, primarily among the Black Americans and Latino Americans. As with earlier forms of African American music that fused African and European or African and Native influences, here we see the fusing of African and Latino influences. Of course, the distinctly African influence on the development of this music is still prevalent.

Cultural precedents for rapping and Hip-Hop can be found in the Griots of West Africa (a group of traveling singers and poets) whose vocal style, dating back hundreds of years, is like that of rappers (and resembles the Jamaican tradition of "toasting" — boasting, impromptu poetry and sayings over music). The Griots and Toasting are the prototypes of rap *in* Hip-Hop.

It was DJ Afrika Bambaataa that outlined the five pillars of Hip-Hop culture: MCing, DJing, breaking, graffiti, writing and knowledge. Other elements include beatboxing, Hip-Hop fashion, and slang.

Hip-Hop culture extends far beyond the purview of music and lyrics; and there are numerous key cultural and technical elements, associated with this culture, that have branched off, and taken a on a life of their own.

Essential Elements:
- Rapping (MC/Emceeing)
- DJing (Including Sampling/Beat Making)
- Breaking (B-boyin'/B-girlin')
- Graffiti (Graf)
- Beat Boxing

Other Cultural Foundations:

- ❖ Rhyming
- ❖ Storytelling
- ❖ Poetry
- ❖ Comedy
- • Redd Foxx
- • Richard Pryor
- • Eddie Murphy
- • Robin Harris
- • Bernie Mac
- • Dave Chappelle
- • Chris Rock
- • Pigmeat Markham

There is no Hip-Hop without comedy; and it might be said that you can't be a Hip-Hop artist without being somewhat of a comedian. It is at the core of the Hip-Hop music you like. But to be a comedian you must be smart (they aren't funny because they are dumb) Comedy demands a high level of intellect. The greatest comedians are, all, geniuses of social observation. – R.W.

Rudy Ray Moore: *The Godfather of Rap*

Rudolph Frank Moore, known as Rudy Ray Moore, was an American comedian, singer, actor, and film producer. Using personas that he had developed during his early comedy recordings, he created the character Dolemite (the character from the 1975 film Dolemite)—and its sequels: The Human Tornado and The Dolemite Explosion.

Rapping/MCing:

During the 1970s, Rapping (which can be defined as "the rhythmic spoken delivery of rhymes and wordplay delivered either over a beat or without accompaniment) developed into the commercial form we know today during DJ Kool Herc's street parties in the Bronx. Again, we can trace the roots rapping to the Jamaican tradition of "toasting" (and even further back several hundred years to the Griots of West Africa). It is also important to remember that rap developed inside, and outside, of Hip-Hop culture. 1970s rapping evolved into MC-ing (a further refinement of rapping that is more metaphorically and more rhythmically advanced than rap, and is often performed over complex, multi-layered beats). The term "MC" is derived from "Master of Ceremonies." As well, the content evolved: Though "novelty rap" songs were still a regular occurrence in the 1980s, "The Message" (1982) by Grandmaster Flash and the Furious Five is cited as the birth of "serious" Hip-Hop; and the work of future Emcees did much to help Hip-Hop be taken seriously—as a mature art form, rather than a novelty.

Early DJs, Crews and Rappers:

The creation of Hip-Hop can be traced directly to the street parties hosted by DJ Kool Herc (born Clive Campbell) hosted in the Bronx borough of New York City and is considered the "Father of Hip-Hop." Campbell was born in Jamaica and during his youth was exposed to the Jamaican tradition of Boasting, as well as Dub artists in dance halls, prior to his family moving to New York City. Eventually Campbell began hosting parties where he would function as the DJ. One of the earliest innovations Campbell, along with several other DJs pioneered was "The Break," which is the isolation of one section of a musical composition, to serve for an Emcee, or for B-Boys/B-Girls to dance to. Campbell never recorded any albums (and subsequently never profited from his artistry). However, Kool Herc had an immediate influence on several artists in the Bronx (as well as in other NYC boroughs that would help define this new genre of Hip-Hop).

"DJ Hollywood is the reason the industry wanted to record rap," the reason Kurtis Blow got a record deal. He laid the groundwork but isn't widely recognized.

When the music industry heard DJ Hollywood, they realized that this new genre of music had presented itself as a viable industry; while DJ Hollywood effectively laid the groundwork, it was Kurtis Blow (born Kurtis Walker) who holds the distinction of being the first commercially successful rapper (as well as the first to sign with a major record label)— thanks, in part, to the contribution of DJ Hollywood.

MEDIA:

❖ DJ Hollywood and Starski, Live at the Armory, 1979.
   https://youtu.be/EqLL9Tw2i6c

Rap can be seen as a revolt against Disco (as listeners began to grow tired of the previous genre). However, there exists a certain irony in the fact that the most important commercial rap song of all time (Rapper's Delight) was based on a sample of the disco hit, "Good Times" by the band 'Chic'.

Fun Fact: Like a singer, *every Rapper (or MC) has a distinct pitch or frequency that distinguishes the "sound" of their voice. The artist will normally adjust or adapt their voice to the frequency, sound, or pitch of the beat. This evolution of Singer/Rappers can best be observed in performers today such as Snoop Dogg, Kanye West, Jay-Z, Little Wayne, Drake, J. Cole, Wiz Khalifa and a host of younger artists who utilize pitch. Andre Romelle was a Singer in the WCWC before he was the husky voiced Dr. Dre from NWA we know today. At close inspection, the rapper Notorious B.I.G. has a vocal range like that of the singer Teddy Pendergrass.*

THE SUGAR HILL GANG: RAPPER'S DELIGHT: EARLY RAPPERS

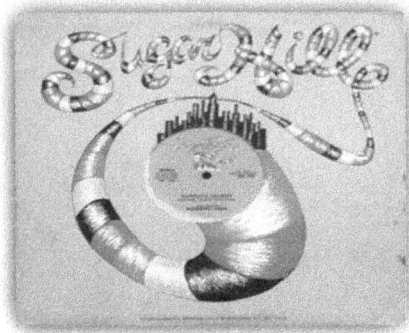

Performed over the breakdown section of a disco hit, which involved proto-sampling techniques via editing the studio tape or by having a DJ cut them into the track, Rapper's Delight is generally considered to be the song that first popularized Hip-Hop in the United States and around the world. The track is notable in that it uses the breakdown section of Chic's "Good Times." A group of live musicians known as "Positive Force" plays the opening vamp that we know so well. While contemporary ears would assume that the beat was in fact sampled electronically, the "opening vamp" had to be performed, live, by the band (similar to what we see in current production techniques). However, it was not long before the technology allowing rappers and DJs to create samples directly from recordings resulted in live musicians swiftly disappearing from Hip-Hop.

MEDIA:

- ❖ Chic, "Good Times," *Risque*, 1979.
  https://youtu.be/Er9xGRolrT4
- ❖ The Sugarhill Gang, "Rapper's Delight," 1979.
  https://youtu.be/ZjRi-S7J70Y
- ❖ Sugarhill Gang's "8th Wonder," 1981.
  http://www.youtube.com/watch?v=_rwpBYQn3S8

Busy Bee Starski

Hitting the New York City music scene in 1977, when rap music and Hip-Hop culture was still in its infancy stages in New York City, David Parker, also known as Busy Bee Starski, a.k.a. Chief Rocker Busy Bee, who worked with many of Hip-Hop's founding fathers, including Melle Mel and Afrika Bambaataa, is an old-school Hip-Hop musician and MC. Known for his comedic rhymes, Busy Bee originally gained a large following through MC rap battles in Staten Island, Brooklyn, and New Jersey. In 1981, in one of the earliest documented rap battles, he was famously 'roasted' by Kool Moe Dee at *Harlem World* in Manhattan, NY, In the early 1980s, Afrika Bambaataa asked Busy to join his Zulu Nation where the young MC would DJ for Bambaataa's Zulu Nation parties. Busy Bee continues to rhyme today, most recently appearing on KRS-One and Marley Marl's collaborative 2007 album, Hip-Hop Lives.

Kurtis Blow

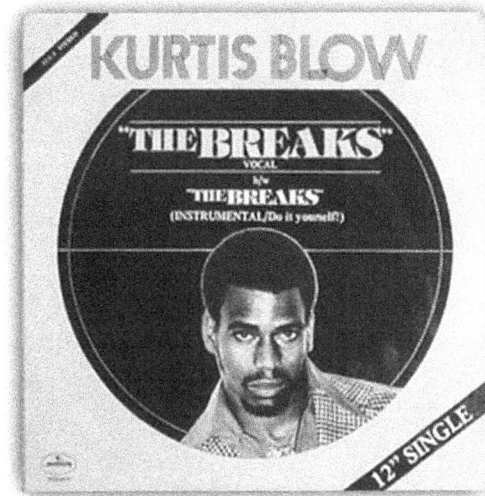

Emanating from Harlem, NY, USA, Kurtis Walker aka Kurtis Blow holds the distinction of being the first commercially successful rappers, as well as the first to sign with a major record label, thanks in part to the contribution of DJ Hollywood. Among many "firsts" Kurtis Blow's hit single "The Breaks" from his 1980 self-titled debut album holds the distinction of being the first rap song to be certified gold by the R.I.A.A.

MEDIA:

❖ Kurtis Blow, "The Breaks," *Kurtis Blow*, 1980.
   https://g.co/kgs/MrrdTy

RUN DMC

RUN DMC emerged from the Hollis neighborhood in Queens, NYC. The group consisted of members Joseph "Run" Simmons (brother of Hip-Hop mogul Russel Simmons), Daryl "D.M.C." McDaniels and Jason "Jam-Master Jay" Mizell.

The group released their self-titled debut album in 1984, following the release of their first single "Sucker M.C.'s (Krush-Groove 1)" the previous year. The members of the group are notable for establishing "The Look," defined as "the stripped-down look," that mirrors their approach to music, which stripped out all other instrumentation leaving only the drums. The group is notable for their collaboration with (white) producer Rick Ruban, who in turn orchestrated a collaboration with vocalist Steven Tyler and guitarist Joe Perry of the Rock band Aerosmith, resulting in a Hip-Hop version of Aerosmith's 1979 track "Walk This Way" on Run-D.M.C.'s third album *Raising Hell*. This collaboration, the very first Rock and Rap crossover proved immensely successful—and had a profound effect on the careers of Run–D.M.C. and Aerosmith and helped bring to and gain acceptance from many audiences who had previously ignored Hip-Hop or had dismissed it as a novelty. In total, the group released seven studio albums, and was instrumental in implementing Rock samples into their music. Run–D.M.C. was named Greatest Hip-Hop Group of All Time by MTV.com; the Greatest Hip Hop Artist of All Time by VH1 and were the second Hip-Hop group (after Grandmaster Flash and The Furious Five) to be inducted into the Rock and Roll Hall of Fame in 2009.

MEDIA:

❖ Run–D.M.C., "Sucker M.C.'s (Krush-Groove 1)," *Run-D.M.C.*, 1984.
   https://youtu.be/iOKMWSR2Aio
❖ Run-D.M.C., "Walk This Way," *Raising Hell*, 1986.
   https://youtu.be/4B_UYYPb-Gk

Kool Moe Dee

Mohandas Dewese, a.k.a. Kool Moe Dee, is an American MC from New York City, NY, USA. He was one of the first rappers to earn a Grammy Award and the first to perform at the Grammys. In the late 1970s, Kool Moe Dee met Special K, DJ Easy Lee and LA Sunshine to form the influential Hip-Hop group The Treacherous Three on Enjoy Records. It was with The Treacherous Three in 1981 that Kool Moe Dee performed his freestyle on-stage roast of party rapper Busy Bee Starski, a performance frequently cited as a pivotal moment in the development of the battle rap. Kool Moe Dee attended Norman Thomas High School on 33rd and Park Avenue in New York City and was known as a quiet, eccentric young man, always holding a pen and a pad ready to write rhymes. In 1981, The Treacherous Three moved to Sugar Hill Records along with Grandmaster Flash and the Furious Five. The Treacherous Three became well known for their singles "Feel the Heart Beat" and "Whip It." They were featured in the 1984 breakdance cult-movie, Beat Street, performing the song "Xmas Rap" with Doug E. Fresh.

Fresh Gordon

Fresh Gordon's first vinyl appearance was on "Brooklyn Style" by The Choice MCs on Rocky Records early in 1985.

Heavy D and the Boyz

Dwight Arrington Myers, better known as Heavy D, was a Jamaican-born American rapper, record producer, singer, and actor.

Early Hip-Hop Terminology (Slang)

- **Beats:** Many MCs call the music they perform to, beats. Their producers "make beats."
- **Freestyle:** To vocally improvise or make up rhymes in lyrical fashion across a range of subject matter, or in a "DIS-ing" fashion, in battle.
- **Flow:** Flow describes a lyricist's cadence. It is in the interaction of words with musical arrangements, with beats or the way the lyricist creates the rhythm with words, the intermingling of words with rhythmic patterns.
- **MC:** Traditionally, MC has stood for master of ceremonies. This is the same in the realm of the Hip-Hop culture.
- **Rapping:** Rhyming is synonymous with the word rapping.
- **Old School:** Reminiscent of past processes, virtues, or actions.

- **Underground:** Underground refers to music that is not mainstream/ radio.
- **Whack:** This word is used to describe work of poor quality, someone that is a nuisance, or that it reflects a poor decision.
- **Beef:** As disagreement or conflict.
- **Bite:** Plagiarism. To steal styles, concepts, or lyrics from someone else (highly subjective).
- **Da Bomb (The Bomb):** Describing something of high quality.
- **Crew:** Organized group of writers, Rappers and MCs.
- **Def:** Derived from the word definite.
- **Dope:** Excellent and of the highest order.
- **Diss:** To discount, reduce or reject.
- **Down:** Willing to participate.
- **DT:** Plain-clothes police officer or detective.
- **5-O:** Slang for police (Derived from the television series Hawaii 5-O).

The DJ

Of equal importance to the Rapper or MC in Hip-Hop is that of the Disk Jockey (DJ). The DJ employs a variety of techniques throughout a performance such as looping, sampling, and remixing of another artist's music (sometimes without the original artist's consent). This process can be viewed as a by-product of Jamaican Dub tradition (with a direct connection to Hip-Hop's Jamaican born **DJ Kool Herc**, who is credited with *creating* Hip-Hop music; and it is a hallmark of the Hip-Hop style. Overtime, production has evolved *around* the DJ; and presently the DJ is involved in the sampling, the beat-making, the production (and more)—they are essential to the creation of *the music*.

Essential DJ Techniques

❖ Mixing/cutting
❖ Scratching
❖ Spinning
❖ Sampling
❖ Song Choice/Criteria

DJ Kool Herc

Clive Campbell also known as Kool DJ Herc, a Jamaican-born DJ who is credited with originating Hip-Hop music. The Break: One of the key responsibilities for the DJ essentially from the very beginning of Hip Hop was the creation of "breaks," in other words, the isolation of one section of a musical composition, which served as a vamp for an MC, or for B-boys/B-girls to dance to. Because the percussive breaks on the source records were generally short, DJ Kool Herc and other DJs began extending them using an audio mixer and two copies of a record: using this setup, the DJ would play the break on one record, while simultaneously searching for and cuing the same break on the other record, using the mixer to alternate between the two records at the right time, allowing the DJ to play a break for as long as is needed. As such, mixers, amplifiers, speakers and various other pieces of electronic music equipment from an essential part of a DJ's arsenal. The breakdown is at the core of the evolution of B-Boy/B-Girl culture. Given the technological nature of being a DJ, it wasn't long before it grew into a field of its own, with the DJ's turntable evolving into a new instrument played by "Turntablists." Because of the high-level technical skills developed by these Turntablists, it was only natural that many of them became producers.

Grandmaster Flash and the Furious Five

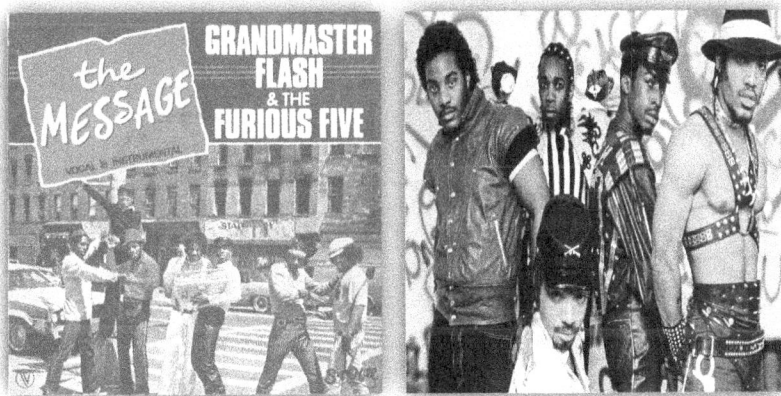

In a genre of music that owed as much to technical developments as it did to artistry, the technical aspect of Rap and Hip-Hop developed at a furious pace. Grandmaster Flash (born Joseph Sadler) and the Furious Five from South Bronx, NYC (a distinct region in The Bronx) is considered one of the pioneers of DJ techniques such as cutting and mixing. By being among the first rap groups to discuss life in the Hood (as in the song "The Message"), Grandmaster Flash and the Furious Five had a profound influence on the artistic development of Hip-Hop.

Joseph Saddler, professionally known as **Grandmaster Flash**, is an American Hip-Hop musician and DJ, and one of the pioneers of Hip-Hop DJing, cutting and mixing. "The Message" (1982) by Grandmaster Flash and the Furious Five (verse by Melle Mel) is oftentimes cited as the birth of "serious" Hip-Hop. Grandmaster Flash and the Furious Five were inducted into the Rock and Roll Hall of Fame in 2007, becoming the first Hip-Hop/rap artists to be so honored.

The Furious Five:

- Keef Cowboy (deceased)
- Melle Mel
- The Kidd Creole
- Scorpio
- Rahiem

MEDIA:

❖ Grandmaster Flash and the Furious Five, "The Message," *The Message*, 1982.
https://youtu.be/gYMkEMCHtJ4

• ZOOM OUT: Ice Cube, "Check Yo' Self," *The Predator*, 1992.
https://youtu.be/5aAbOgdbTbM

❖ Grandmaster Flash and the Furious Five, "It's Nasty," *The Message*, 1982.
https://youtu.be/Hcn5oHh4RX8

Tom Tom Club & Mariah Carey

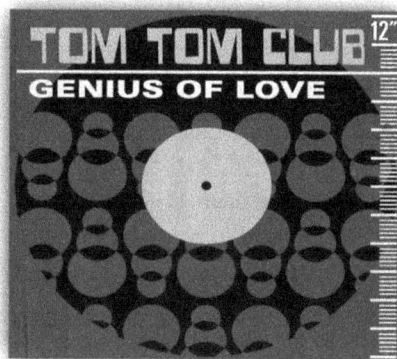

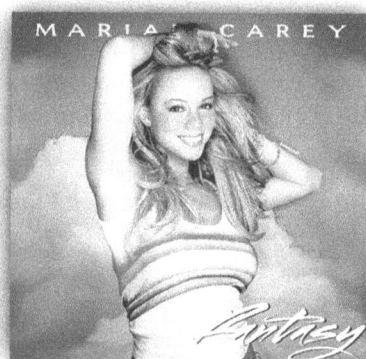

Tom Tom Club is an American new wave band founded in 1981 by husband-and-wife team Chris Frantz and Tina Weymouth and as a side project from Talking Heads. Tom Tom Club enjoyed early success in the dance club culture of the early 1980s with the hits "Genius of Love."

Mariah Carey *is an American singer, songwriter, actress, and record producer; she is noted for her five-octave-range and her skills as a songwriter. Carey rose to fame in the 1990s.*

MEDIA:

❖ Tom Tom Club, "Genius of Love," *Tom Tom Club*, 1981.
https://youtu.be/aCWCF19nUhA

"Genius of Love" is sampled by Mariah Carey in "Fantasy."
❖ Mariah Carey—"Fantasy" (Remix) feat. O.D.B, 1995.
https://youtu.be/-tCTm5M3Cp8

Breaking (B-boyin'/B-girlin'): The Dance Equivalent to Hip-Hop

Breaking, an early form of Hip-Hop dance, is a dynamic style of dance which developed as part of the East Coast hip hop culture. Breaking began to take form in the South Bronx alongside the other elements of Hip-Hop. The "B" in B-boy stands for break, as in break boy (or girl). The term "B-boy" originated from the dancers at DJ Kool Herc's parties, who saved their best dance moves for the break section of the song. B-boying is one of the major elements of Hip-Hop culture. The DJs of Hip-Hop created that breakdown, where everything drops out except for the beat. Every time the DJ broke the music down, dancers would run up to the stage, to "dance" on the "break." That's how they earned their name. The DJ and the breakdown are two core elements of "breaking" culture.

Breakin' came from the East; but Poppin' came from the West—Mr. Animation, The Air Force Crew

Notable East Coast Dance Crews:

❖ The Rock Steady Crew
❖ The New York City Breakers

West Coast Dance Styles

-Dance styles that evolved independently during the late 1960s in the West Coast are also a part of Hip-Hop culture.

Locking (The first professional street dance on the west coast)

- Ticking
- Struttin'
- Popping
- The Boogaloo
- Hittin'

MEDIA:

❖ "The Freshest Kids: The History of the B-Boy," 2002.
   https://youtu.be/RxoWyGFSGuk

Fred Berry a.k.a. "Re-Run"

- ZOOM OUT: "Re-Run," from the television show "*What's Happening*," was a professional pop-locker. https://youtu.be/RxoWyGFSGuk?t=2192.

Flashdance was the first movie to feature B-boyin' and B-girlin' (breakdancing). It was also the first time the West Coast 'locker' saw East Coast 'breakin'. A coalescing of styles ensued shortly thereafter.

MEDIA:

❖ "Flashdance," 1983 (Trailer). https://youtu.be/YdXqyECQzck

Krumping and Beyond: The Dance Equivalents to Hip-Hop

Krumping is a style of street dance popularized in the United States, described as Afro-diasporic dance, characterized by free, expressive, exaggerated, and highly energetic movement. Krumping was created by two dancers: Ceasare "Tight Eyez" Willis, and Jo'Artis "Big Mijo" Ratti in South Central, Los Angeles, during the early 2000s. Clowning is the less aggressive predecessor to krumping and was created in 1992 by Thomas "Tommy the Clown" Johnson in Compton, California.

Graffiti: The visual equivalent of Hip-Hop

In America, around the late 1960s, graffiti was used as a form of expression by political activists (as well as by gangs and crews). Graffiti can be described as urban, mural artwork usually created with spray paint, and on existing surfaces such as trains and buildings.

For some, it is a means of exemplifying craftsmanship, while for others reflects rivalry among disparate graffiti artists. The relationship between graffiti and Hip-Hop culture arises from early graffiti artists practicing *other* aspects of Hip-Hop that were still evolving. Graffiti is recognized as a visual expression of rap music, just as *breaking* is viewed as a physical expression.

Early Terminology:

- Graf—Short for Graffiti.
- Bombing—Graffiti in which the entire train car is covered with "Graf."
- Fade: Graduation/gradation of colors.
- Families: Rows of graffiti of the same name/crew.
- Floaters: "Graf" done on subway car panels at window level.
- Freights: The railroad cars/trains.
- Flats: Painted steel subway cars with flat surfaces.

MEDIA:

- ❖ *Wild Style*, 1982.
  https://youtu.be/mKUGA0ezG8A
- ❖ *Beat Street*: The "Roxy" Battle, 1984.
  https://youtu.be/zNsMEP0i8aM
- ❖ *Krush Groove*: RUN-DMC Scene, 1985.
  https://youtu.be/65HHssDkSHA

TAKI 183

TAKI 183 is one of the most influential graffiti writers. His "tag" was short for Demetaki, a Greek alternative for his birth-name Demetrius, and the number 183 came from his address on 183rd Street in Washington Heights. He worked as a foot messenger in New York City and would write his "tag" around New York.

- ZOOM OUT: *Just to Get a Rep* (Graffiti Documentary), 2004.
  https://youtu.be/GT0WbXfPXM0

Jean-Michael Basquiat

Jean-Michel Basquiat was an American artist who rose to success during the 1980s as part of the Neo-expressionism (including Graffiti) movement in NYC.

Beatboxing

The term "beatboxing" refers to the human imitation of instruments and is derived from the mimicry of the first generation of drum machines, then known as beatboxes, as well as the Latin instrument, the Cuica [pronounced "Kweyka"]. Popularized by Doug E. Fresh, beatboxing represents the vocal percussion language of Hip-Hop culture and is primarily concerned with the art of creating beats, rhythms and melodies using the human mouth. The art form enjoyed a strong presence in the 1980s with artists like Darren "Buffy, the Human Beat Box" Robinson of the Fat Boys and Biz Markie. Beatboxing declined in popularity along with break dancing in the late 1980s, and almost slipped even deeper than the underground. Beatboxing has resurged since the late 1990s, marked by the release of "Make the Music 2000" by Rahzel of The Roots (who is known for even singing while beatboxing).

MEDIA:

❖ The Fat Boys, "Human Beat Box," *Fat Boys*, 1984.
   https://youtu.be/6c7b-Kfg0fU
❖ Biz Markie, "Just A Friend," *The Biz Never Sleeps*, 1989.
   https://youtu.be/9aofoBrFNdg?t=34
❖ Biz Markie and Will Smith Beatbox in *Men In Black II*, 2002.
   https://youtu.be/lr7pyggTmmY?t=78

Chapter 14

EARLY SNEAKER CULTURE

We're going to take a diversion and watch a video about sneakers and look at the relationship of tennis shoes to Hip-Hop—and Hip-Hop to tennis shoes.

Basketball is credited with being responsible for sneaker culture. While the element of style in sneaker culture is credited to Hip-Hop, it was *comfort* that initially determined the selection of sneakers by B-Boys and B-Girls. Supporting fashions included your shirt, shoes, pants, and cap (Kangol, Nylon T-shirt, Levi /Lee Jeans, Adidas and Fat Shoelaces).

B-Boys and B-Girls dominated the sneaker look of the 1980s; and the mindset of cleaning your sneakers (as opposed to purchasing new ones) came from the conditions of economic necessity (poverty). Back then, your shoelaces matched your outfit; and without the proper laces, your sneakers meant nothing.

In the 1980s, to stretch your shoelaces, an electric-iron was used; while the concept of lace-less sneakers comes from prison culture. Around this time, Jerald Deas (a community member who feared the burgeoning movement of Hip-Hop) came up with the term "Felon Sneakers." Ultimately, the fashions of the 1980s revolved around the individual. Flagship endorsements, such as the Adidas brand, became synonymous with the rap group RUN–D.M.C. Sporting the classic all leather looks, known in the city as the Stick-Up-Kid, Run–D.M.C.'s initial contract with Adidas was for one million dollars. Russell Simmons (Run's brother) came up with the slogan "My Adidas!" In 1984, Michael Jordan, specifically, introduced the Nike Air Ship (followed by the Air Jordan "1" in 1985). Fresh Gordon had "My Filas." Heavy D had the Nike endorsement, Busy Bee had Converse, The Beastie Boys had Suede Adidas and LL Cool J had the Troop endorsement.

MEDIA:

❖ *Just for Kicks*, Sneaker Documentary, 2005.
   https://vimeo.com/3684841

Chapter 15

ELECTRO-FUNK

The sub-genre of Electro-Funk was one that emerged early in the history of Hip-Hop and is associated with artists such as Afrika Bambaataa and groups such as, The Jonzun Crew and Newcleus. Also known as Electro, some of the characteristics of this genre include a minimalist machine-driven style of funk making heavy use of synthesizers and drum machines such as the Roland TR-808, as well as themes rooted in science fiction.

TR-808 Drum Machine

As drummers and live musicians began to be replaced by drum machines, one of the most prolific of these was the TR-808 made by Roland. As an indication of how esteemed this machine was in the eyes of the Hip-Hop community, The TR-808 is responsible for changing the sound of Hip-Hop and generated most of the sound-templates we are familiar with.

• ZOOM OUT: Kanye West titled his fourth album "808s & Heartbreak".

Afrika Bambaataa:

Lance Taylor, a.k.a. Afrika Bambaataa, is an American DJ from South Bronx, New York City, who was instrumental in the early development of Hip-Hop and Electro-Funk. Inspired by DJ Kool Herc, he began hosting Hip-Hop parties in 1982, and is one of the three originators of breakbeat DJing—earning him the titles of "Grandfather," "Godfather" and "Father" of Electro-Funk. Heavily influenced by the group *Kraftwerk*, he *created* "electro-funk," a minimalist machine-driven style of funk, with his single, "Planet Rock." Also known simply as *electro*, this style of funk was driven by synthesizers and the electronic rhythm of the TR-808 drum machine. Later, through his co-opting of the street gang, the Black Spades, into the music and culture-oriented Universal Zulu Nation, he is responsible for spreading Hip-Hop culture throughout the world. Bambaataa helped to ratify "electronica" as an industry-certified trend, and designated "turntablism" as its own sub-genre in the late 1990s.

Kraftwerk

Kraftwerk is a German band formed in Düsseldorf in 1969 by Ralf Hütter and Florian Schneider. Widely considered innovators and pioneers of electronic music, Kraftwerk were among the first successful acts to popularize the genre.

MEDIA:

- ❖ Kraftwerk, "Numbers," *Computer World, 1981.*
  https://youtu.be/4YPiCeLwh5o
- ❖ Afrika Bambaataa & Soulsonic Force, "Planet Rock," *Planet Rock: The Album*, 1982.
  https://youtu.be/9J3lwZjHenA
- ❖ Talib Kweli, "We Got The Beat," *The Beautiful Struggle*, 2004.
  https://youtu.be/svnunOifOLk

The Jonnzun Crew

The Jonzun Crew was a Boston, Massachusetts Electro-Funk group formed by three Florida-born brothers, Michael Johnson, Soni Johnson and Larry Johnson (aka Maurice Starr), in the 1980s. They were an "electro" and early funk/Hip-Hop group that was active in the 1980s. The group's most famous track is named *Pack Jam*. Musically, the group was inspired by the sci-fi themes that were present in the music of Parliament-Funkadelic, reinforced by many space-themed-songs and album titles. The group's sound was unique for the time—as the synthesizer parts were played by a musician rather than being sequenced; while live drummers were used for the main drum track, most of their songs used the drum machine added to the mix.

MEDIA:

❖ Jonzun Crew, "Pack Jam (Look out for the OVC)," *Lost In Space*, 1982.
    https://youtu.be/oXPng1dQag

NEWCLEUS:

Members:

- Ben "Cozmo D" Cenac
- Yvette "Lady E" Cook
- Monique Angevin (Cenac's cousin)
- Bob "Chilly B" Crafton

Formed by Ben "Cozmo D" Cenac, Yvette "Lady E" Cook, Monique Angevin (Cenac's cousin), and Bob "Chilly B" Crafton, **Newcleus** was another Electro-Funk group that helped bring the genre to a wider audience. Formed in Brooklyn, New York City in the late 1970s, out of a group of DJs who would throw block parties throughout the borough, their 1983 demo track "Jam-On Revenge" entered the Top 40 on the Billboard R&B chart in 1983 and was followed by the track "Jam on It" the following year—reaching the Top Ten, and peaking at number 56 in the Hot 100.

MEDIA:

❖ Newcleus, "Jam on It," *Jam on Revenge*, 1984.
   https://youtu.be/Q1Qdcl4ja1Y

Chapter 16

EARLIER STYLES VERSUS LATER STYLES

YOUR SPACE HAS BEEN INVADED

- *Break beats versus No break beats*
- *Drum machines versus Sampled drum line*
- *Tape loops versus Sampler*

Mixtapes Then

In Hip-Hop's earliest days, the music only existed in live form, and the music was spread via tapes of parties and shows. Hip-Hop mixtapes first appeared in the mid-1970s in New York City, featuring artists such as Kool Herc and Afrika Bambaataa. As more tapes became available, they began to be collected and traded by fans. In the mid-1980s, DJs, such as Brucie B, began recording their live music and selling their own mixtapes, which was soon followed by other DJs such as Kid Capri and Doo Wop. Ron G moved the mixtape forward in the early 1990s by blending R&B acapella with Hip-Hop beats (known as "blends"). Blend tapes became increasingly popular by the mid-1990s, and fans increasingly looked for exclusive tracks and freestyles on the tapes. In the Hip-Hop scene, mixtape is often displayed as a single-term mixtape. Throughout the 1980s, mixtapes were a highly visible element of youth culture. However, the increased availability of CD burners and MP3 players and the gradual disappearance of cassette players in cars and households have led to a decline in the popularity of the compact audio cassette as a medium for homemade mixes. The high point of traditional mixtape culture was arguably the publication of Nick Hornby's novel High Fidelity in 1995. Since then, mixtapes have largely been replaced by mix CDs and shared MP3 playlists, which are more durable, can hold more songs and require minutes (rather than hours) to prepare.

Chapter 17

TURNTABLISM: THE EARLY YEARS

The word *turntablist* was originated by Luis "DJ Disk" Quintanilla.

In order to describe the difference between a DJ who simply plays and mixes records and one who performs by physically manipulating the records, stylus, turntables, turntable speed controls and mixer to produce new sounds, (and coinciding with the resurgence of Hip-Hop DJing during the '90s) DJ Babu popularized the term in 1995.

MEDIA:

❖ Scratch, (A Turntablism Documentary), 2002.
   https://youtu.be/A8aMMpoSUSQ

Overview:

Jamaican Dubbing tradition from the 1970s is the prototype to turntablism and DJing. A turntablist's basic setup is two turntables, a mixer, monitoring-headphones, an amplifier, and speakers. A combination of mixing, cutting, scratching, and sampling occurring simultaneously is called "beat juggling." The art of searching for albums, beats, to "harvest" for samples, is called "digging" or "crate digging." DJ "Shadow" was well known for being a good crate-digger. Started in 1987, the Disco Mix Club ("DMC") is one of the largest organized DJ battles. You only have six minutes to perform your routine at the DMC ("Six minutes Dougie Fresh, you're on!"). The crew that's known for "sounding like a band," credited with "orchestrating" their compositions are the Invisibl Skratch Piklz, formed in 1989. The three core members of the Invisibl Skratch Piklz are DJ Qubert, Mix Master Mike, and DJ Apollo, aka "the subliminal kid" (Paul D. Miller). Meanwhile, DJ Spooky pioneered a style of scratching called "illbient"—a cross between the words *ill* (excellent or dope) and *ambient*. First DJ to blend records together: Francis Grasso. Technical term for blending records: slip-cueing; synchronizing the switch bay between records. Grand Wizard Theodore came up with a new technique for scratching: the baby-scratch.

Other (early) Scratching techniques:

• The Flare
• The Transformer
• The Crab

Grand Mixer DXT was on the Herbie Hancock Video Rockit, from the 1984 Grammy awards.

Herbie Hancock

Herbert Jeffrey Hancock is an American jazz pianist, keyboardist, bandleader, and composer.

Hancock started his career with trumpeter Donald Byrd's group and architected the sounds of the 1960s Miles Davis bands.

Other notable artists for the technological advances of this time were Thomas Morgan Robertson, known by the stage name *Thomas Dolby*—an English musician, producer, composer, entrepreneur, and teacher—and Hans Hugo Harold Faltermeier, known professionally as Harold Faltermeyer: a German musician, composer and record producer. Faltermeyer is best known for composing the "Axel F" theme for the feature film Beverly Hills Cop, an influential synth-pop hit in the 1980s.

MEDIA:

❖ Thomas Dolby, "She Blinded me with Science," *The Golden Age of Wireless*, 1982.
   https://youtu.be/wdSUnV2fJGk
❖ Herbie Hancock, "Rockit," *Future Shock*, 1983.
   https://youtu.be/Ecw8vaKMiC4
❖ Harold Faltermeyer - "Axel F," *Beverly Hills Cop* (Soundtrack), 1984.
   https://youtu.be/Qx2gvHjNhQ0

Return of the DJ, Vol. 1 is a 1995 compilation, and the first all DJ (turntablist) album ever released.
The album features artists and crews such as DJ Babu, The Beat Junkies, Invisibl Skratch Piklz, The Cut Chemist, and DJ Z-Trip.

❖ *Return of the DJ, Vol. 1, 1997.*
   https://youtu.be/ucRc7BPohJQ

Chapter 18

BATTLE ROYALE: DISSING ON RECORD

The Juice Crew

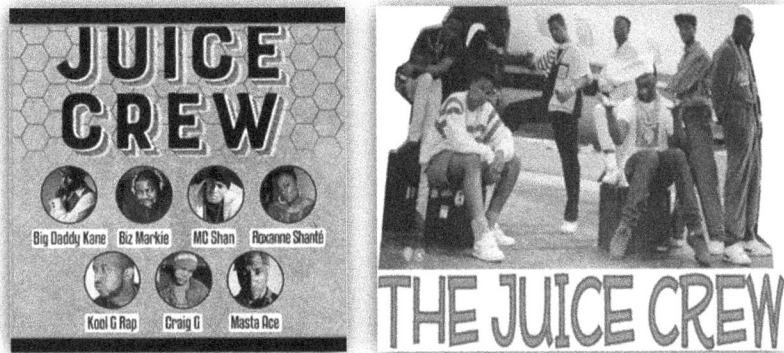

The Juice Crew was a Hip-Hop collective of largely Queensbridge, New York, USA-based artists in the mid-to-late 1980s. Founded by producer Marley Marl and radio DJ Mr. Magic and housed by Tyrone William's Cold Chillin' Records. Tragedy the Intelligent Hoodlum and Marley Marl began the Juice Crew's long tradition of answer records with their first release—1983's "Sucker DJs (I Will Survive). Ultimately, the Juice Crew introduced *New School* artists MC Shan, Big Daddy Kane, Masta Ace, Biz Markie, Roxanne Shanté, Craig G, and Kool G Rap. The crew produced many "answer" ('diss') records and "beefs," primarily with rival radio jock Kool DJ Red Alert and the South Bronx's Boogie Down Productions."

Roxanne Shanté

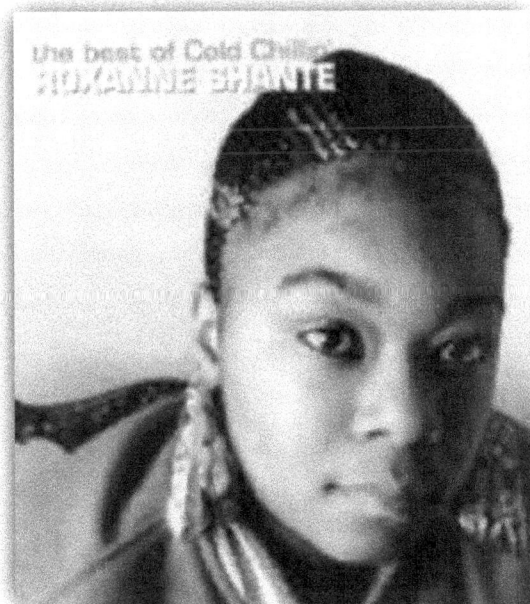

Lolita Shanté Gooden, better known by her stage name Roxanne Shanté, is an American rapper and The First Commercial Female Rapper. Born and raised in the Queensbridge Projects of Queens, New York City, Gooden first gained attention through the *Roxanne Wars*.

MEDIA:

❖ Roxanne Shanté, "Roxanne's Revenge," 1984.
   https://youtu.be/0eckRNcHCKA

The Roxanne Wars

In 1984, the group UTFO from Brooklyn, New York City, released a track titled "Roxanne, Roxanne," describing a fictitious encounter with a woman named Roxanne who would not respond to their advances, which quickly turned into a hit single. That same year a young rapper named Lolita Shanté Gooden happened to run into Tyrone Williams, DJ Mr. Magic, and Marley Marl of the Juice Crew outside their home in the Queensbridge housing project in Queens, NYC, and overheard them complaining about how UTFO had failed to show up for an engagement they had previously committed to. During this conversation, Gooden came up with the idea of writing a rebuttal to "Roxanne, Roxanne," called "Roxanne's Revenge" and in the process adopted the name Roxanne Shanté. The song was originally the B-side of the lesser-known single "Hangin' Out." The original release of "Roxanne's Revenge" proved to be an immediate hit, quickly selling 250,000 copies in the New York City area alone, however "Roxanne's Revenge" used the original beat from "Roxanne, Roxanne" and was also filled with profane language. Soon after its release lawsuits were filed; and in 1985 the track was reissued with a new beat and the obscene lyrics removed. The success and challenge of "Roxanne's Revenge" prompted UTFO to record another track in response, which too became a hit record. On the heels of the success of the original three tracks, it was not long before many other artists began rapping about this mythical woman Roxanne, and as a result, between 30 and 100 additional "answer records" were released during this time, entrenching in Hip-Hop culture, the power and appeal of disses and beefs.

UTFO

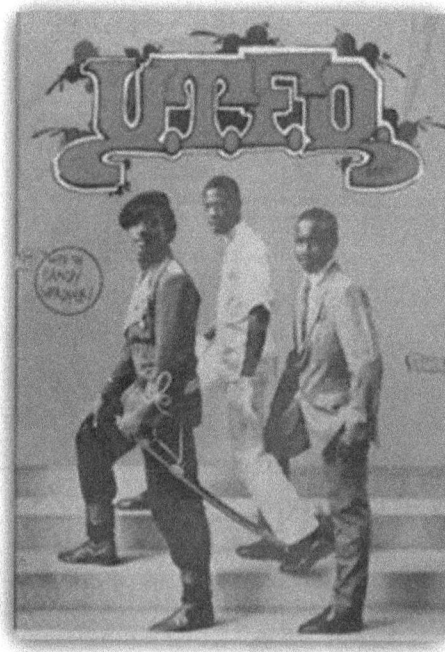

UTFO (which stands for Untouchable Force Organization) is an old school Hip-Hop group from Brooklyn, New York, USA that was popular in the 1980s. The group consists of the Kangol Kid (Shiller Shaun Fequiere), the Educated Rapper (Jeffrey Campbell) (also known as EMD), Doctor Ice (Fred Reeves) and Mix Master Ice (Maurice Bailey). The group's best-known single is "Roxanne, Roxanne," a widely acclaimed Hip-Hop classic, which created a sensation on the Hip-Hop scene soon after it was released and inspired numerous answer records, most notably by Marley Marl.

MEDIA:

❖ UTFO, "Roxanne, Roxanne," 1984.
   https://youtu.be/sgaedPLT43k
❖ Roxanne Shanté, The Roxanne Wars.
   https://youtu.be/3jVxBPHUpH8?t=157

MC SHAN

Emanating from Queensbridge Houses, NYNY, USA, Shawn Moltke better known by his stage name MC Shan, is an American Hip-Hop and R&B recording artist. He is best known for his song "The Bridge" produced by Marley Marl, and for collaborating on "Informer," the international number-one hit single.

The Bridge Wars

On the heels of the Roxanne Wars, members of Queensbridge's Juice Crew soon found themselves embroiled in the Bridge Wars with South Bronx's Boogie Down Productions member KRS-One. The real source of animosity between KRS-One, and Juice Crew founders Mr. Magic and Marley Marl can be traced back to when Mr. Magic and Marley Marl rejected KRS-One from the Juice Crew, though initially KRS-One claimed his attacks were a response to Juice Crew member MC Shan's 1986 track "The Bridge," which discussed the origins of the Juice Crew in the Queensbridge housing projects. That same year KRS-One released his own track titled "South Bronx" in which he claimed that Shan was in fact asserting that Hip-Hop had grown out of Queensbridge, disparaged Shan, and reasserted the genre's well-established origins in South Bronx and the street parties of DJ Kool Herc. To further fuel the flames of this conflict, KRS-One, in a demonstration of his "Blastmaster" persona, chose a rap battle in Cedar Park to unveil "South Bronx" live following a performance of "The Bridge" by MC Shan, which for the first time, saw one MC attacking another directly, instead of for the purpose of exciting the audience, with KRS-One being viewed as prevailing in that battle. In the second round of the Bridge Wars, MC Shan released the track "Kill That Noise" on his 1987 debut record *Down by the Law*, which was soon followed by "The Bridge Is Over," by KRS-One on Boogie Down Productions' 1987 album *Criminally Minded*, which concluded the feud with KRS-One emerging victorious. The results of this war had lasting effects on the careers of both KRS-One and MC Shan, with victor KRS-One going on to achieve consider success and loser MC Shan largely fading from the scene. Years later KRS-One and Marley-Marl would reconcile their differences and collaborate on the 2007 album *Hip Hop Lives*, and KRS-One has subsequently explained that his true motivations for attacking MC Shan, Marley Marl and Juice Crew were in fact necessitated by his then-status as a struggling artist, his initial rejection by Marley Marl and Mr. Magic, as well the understanding, in the wake of the Roxanne Wars, that attacking other artists could provide a much-needed boost to his career, which it did. Despite all of this, years later MC Shan would remake "The Bridge" as "The Bridge 2000" in which he denied that the Bridge War "was over" with the lyrics:

The Bridge was never over
We left our mark
This jam is dedicated to you and your boys
I brought my Queensbridge thugs to kill that noise-MC Shan

While the Bridge Wars had a lasting effect on the careers of KRS-One and MC Shan, it also shaped the future direction of Hip-Hop. KRS-One's live attack on MC Shan at the Cedar Park rap battle is credited with innovating the "aggressive side" of freestyle battling, while the Bridge War in general helped cement the roll of beefs, disses, attacks and answers, as a necessary 'tool' for emerging rap-artists to establish their careers.

Summary:

- KRS-One: Credited with establishing the aggressive battles, battling MC Shan in Cedar Park.
- Juice Crew came out with a single called "The Bridge" (meaning, "don't cross this bridge that separates the two boroughs").
- KRS-One (BDP) responded with "South Bronx" which obliterated "The Bridge."
- The Juice Crew put out "Kill That Noise" in response.
- BDP shut it down with "The Bridge is Over."
- So, "The Bridge" (JC), "South Bronx" (BDP), "Kill That Noise" (JC) and "Bridge Is Over" (BDP).
- To this day, BDP is regarded as the 'dopest' crew.

MEDIA:

- ❖ MC Shan, "The Bridge," 1986.
  https://youtu.be/dS4RpBR0Zn0
- ❖ Boogie Down Productions, "South Bronx," *Criminal Minded*, 1987.
  https://youtu.be/vsrOy32nJdI
- ❖ MC Shan, "Kill That Noise," *Down by The Law*, 1987.
  https://youtu.be/KkpLn-6O6cc
- ❖ Boogie Down Productions, "The Bridge Is Over," *Criminal Minded*, 1987.
  https://youtu.be/r0Sy4twXSn0
- ❖ *MC Shan KRS-One battle*, Beef I Documentary.
  https://youtu.be/Kr22KYAMbcI?t=1126

Big Daddy Kane

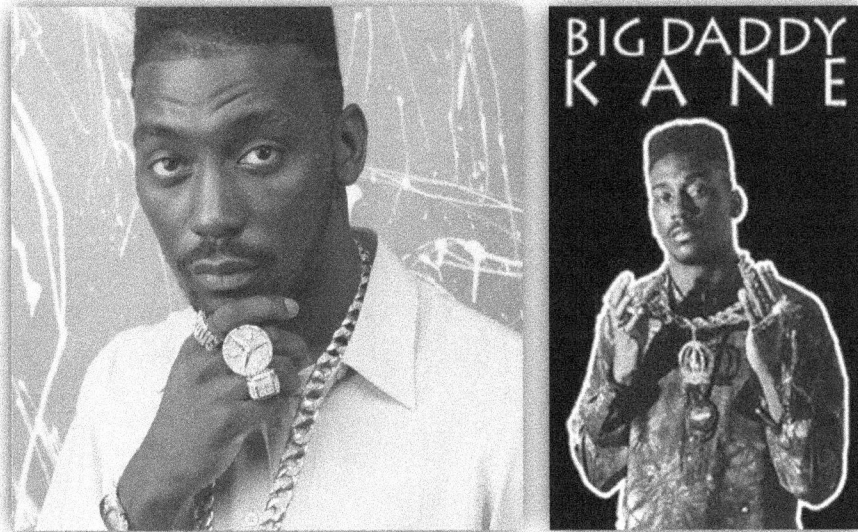

Emanating from Bedford-Stuyvesant, Brooklyn, New York City, NY, US, Antonio Hardy, better known by his stage name Big Daddy Kane, is an American rapper who started his career in 1986 as a member of the rap group the Juice Crew. He is considered to be one of the most influential and skilled Emcees in Hip-Hop.

Tragedy Khadafi

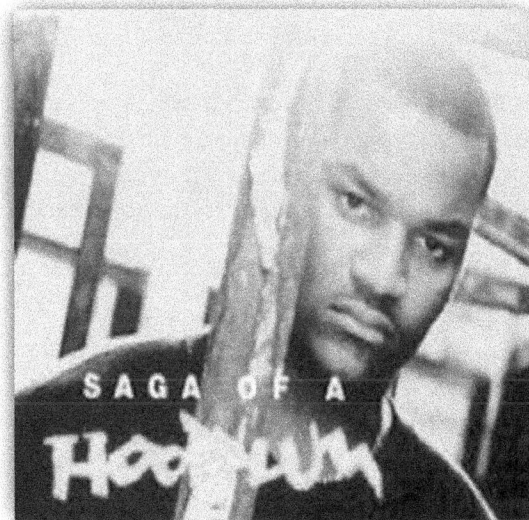

Percy Chapman IV, (born August 13, 1971, in Queens, NY, USA) known by his stage name Tragedy Khadafi, and formerly known as Intelligent Hoodlum, is an American rapper and producer from the Queensbridge housing projects in Queens, New York, who helped spawn other Hip-Hop artists such as Nas, Cormega, Mobb Deep, Capone-N-Noreaga and many others both through production and influence. His name is a reference to former Libyan head of state Muammar Gaddafi. He was one-half of the group the Iron Sheiks, along with Imam T.H.U.G., which produced the underground classic "True Confessions." Tragedy Khadifi, was the first single released by the Juice Crew.

KRS-One

Lawrence "Kris" Parker, better known by his stage names KRS-One and "The Teacha", is an American rapper, lyricist and occasional producer from New York. He rose to prominence as part of the Hip-Hop group Boogie Down Productions, which he formed with DJ Scott La Rock in the mid-1980s.

(KRS-One), Scott La Rock

- Debut Album, Criminal Minded in 1987.
- First-time rappers brandished guns and ammunition on a record cover.
- Credited as setting the template for the burgeoning genres of hardcore and gangsta rap.
- La Rock was killed in a shooting later that year.

Boogie Down Productions released their debut album Criminal Minded in 1987. The album, whose cover pictured BDP draped in ammunition and brandishing guns, is often credited with setting the template for the burgeoning genres of hardcore and gangsta rap. Scott La Rock was killed in a shooting later that year.

KRS-One: The Blastmaster

KRS-One is credited with innovating the "aggressive side" of freestyle battling via MC Shan Battles in Cedar Park. The song that's associated with this battle is "South Bronx" and "The Bridge." KRS-One began his recording career as one-half of the hip hop group Boogie Down Productions or BDP alongside DJ Scott La Rock. After being rejected by radio DJs Mr. Magic and Marley Marl, KRS-One would go on to diss the two and those associated with them, sparking what would later be known as The Bridge Wars.

KRS-One: The Teacha

"**K**nowledge **R**eigns **S**upreme **O**ver **N**early **E**veryone"

"KRS-One" was originally Parker's graffiti tag, short for "Kris Number One." He began using it as his stage name and later devised an acronym for the name "Knowledge Reigns Supreme Over Nearly Everyone. During this time KRS-One also gained acclaim as one of the first MCs to incorporate Jamaican style into Hip-Hop. Using the Zungazung melody, originally made famous by Yellowman in Jamaican dance halls earlier in the decade. While KRS-One used Zunguzung styles in a more powerful and controversial manner, especially in his song titled "Remix for P is Free," he can still be credited as one of the more influential figures to bridge the gap between Jamaican music and American Hip-Hop. As Parker adopted this "humanist," less violent approach, he turned away from his "Blastmaster" persona and toward that of "The Teacha."

"Kristyle" is an original and un-released documentary featuring KRS-One backstage @ the*Wu* Tang Clan's 36 *Chambers* recording studio, NYC, circa 2003.

Medical Cures for the Chromatic Commands is the soundtrack from this unreleased documentary.

ZOOM OUT: Ron Westray, Medical Cures for the Chromatic Commands of the Inner City, 2008.
https://youtu.be/gX841ITDw6E

[Hip-Hop is] **H**is (or Her) **I**nfinite **P**ower **H**elping **O**ppressed **P**eople;

Hip-Hop is a Reflection of the Reality of the Inner City—KRS-One

YOUR SPACE HAS BEEN INVADED

AKAI-S900 Sampler

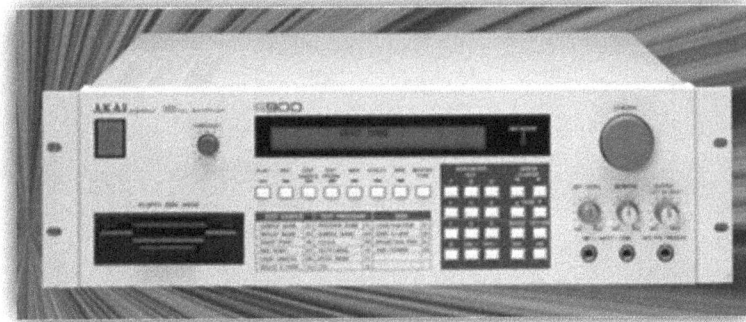

    With the emergence of a new generation of samplers, DJs were, at last, free of tape loops. The AKAI-S900 sampler, that emerged in the late 1980s, allowed the DJ to loop record breaks into breakbeats (a task that was previously done manually. During its 'Golden Age' this machine became such an important part of Hip-Hop that, veritably, all the music was being created using this machine; and just like the Roland TR-808, the AKAI-S900 brought about a drastic change in the overall "sound" of the music while presenting a new way of making music (a technical innovation as well as a process innovation) In short, this is one of those technological improvements that changed everything.

Breakdown of Song to Sample

With the advent of sampling, which is a process in which a pre-existing piece of recording was manipulated in various ways, it wasn't long before a set of procedures were adopted for the manipulation of such content. One technique involved the diminishing or augmentation of the original sample, which primarily involved changing the pitch of the existing recording to fit into a new key signature. Next, the tempo of the source recording could be changed by either increasing or decreasing tempo, an example of this is J Dilla's "Take Notice," which samples the synth part from Peter Baumann's 1976 track "Phase By Phase," which increases the tempo of the original sample. Lastly, new beats, instrumentation, solos, or vocals could also be added to the mix. Outside of the technical realm, the artist could find clever ways of metaphorical manipulation through the substitution or alteration of an original philosophical theme, such as in the case of Ghostface Killah's 2007 track "Walk Around," which sampled Little Milton's "Packed Up and Took My Mind" and flipped the metaphor.

Summary:

- Diminishing/augmentation of original sample.
- Tempo increase/decrease (BPM).
- Addition of beats/instruments/solos/vocals.
- Substitution and/or alteration of original philosophical theme.

We are ready to transition to the Golden Age via "The [Hip-Hop] British Invasion." The break-beat goes away; and the drum machine is rendered, nearly, obsolete by the sampler. Sampling takes externally recorded sounds and digitally manipulates them—a digital-recorder versus the drum machine which can be programmed. Concurrently, a certain **consequential polytonality** was introduced: the musical use (or occurrence) of multiple-musical-tonalities (keys) during digital-production.

Chapter 19

THE BRITISH INVASION: PROTO-NEO-SOUL

Loose Ends

Formed in London in 1980, **Loose Ends** was a successful British R&B band that produced many *urban-contemporary* hits. The group was initially composed of vocalist and guitarist Carl McIntosh, vocalist Jane Eugene, and keyboard player, writer, and founder Steve Nichol. The prevalence of the Roland TR-808 in production was a hallmark of the band's sound.

MEDIA:

❖ Loose Ends, "Slow Down," *Zagora*, 1986.
https://youtu.be/qdKdnCSeJwQ

THE BRITISH INVASION: cont.
Soul II Soul

Soul II Soul is a British group that was created in London in 1988. They are best known for their 1989 UK chart-topper and US Top 5 hit, "Back to Life (However Do You Want Me)."

LAURYN HILL

Lauryn Noelle Hill is an American singer-songwriter, rapper, record producer and actress from South Orange, NJ, USA.

Early in her career, she established her reputation as a member of the Fugees. In 1998, she launched her solo career with the release of the commercially successful and critically acclaimed album, The Miseducation of Lauryn Hill. The recording earned Hill five Grammy Awards, including the coveted Album of the Year and Best New Artist. In more recent years, she has recorded songs for soundtracks and mixtapes, as well as performing live at several music festivals.

THE FUGEES

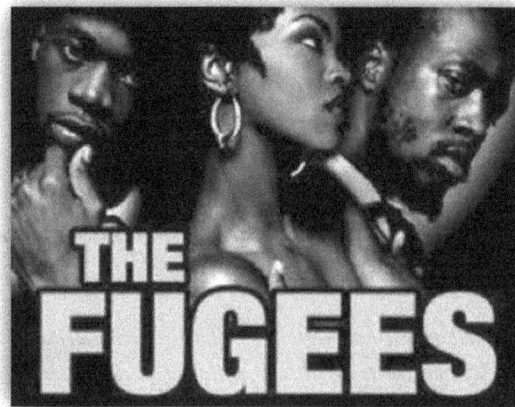

The Fugees were a Haitian American Hip-Hop group who rose to fame in the mid-1990s. Their repertoire included elements of Hip-Hop, soul, and Caribbean music, particularly reggae. Deriving their name from the term refugee, Jean and Pras are Haitian—while Hill is American. The group recorded two albums—one of which, The Score (1996), was a multi-platinum and Grammy-winning success—before disbanding in 1997.

THE ROOTS

Composed of [original] members Black Thought, ?uestlove, Mark Kelley, Kamal Gray, Captain Kirk Douglas, F. Knuckles, Damon "Tuba Gooding, Jr." Bryson and James Poyser, The Roots is an American Hip-Hop/neo-soul band from Philadelphia, Pennsylvania, USA (originally called The Square Roots). They are known for a jazzy, eclectic approach to Hip-Hop which includes live instrumentals. The Roots released an independently produced debut album, Organix, in 1993. In 1995, with the label DGC Records, the band released Do You Want More? Their next album, Illadelph Halflife, was released in 1996. With Illadelph Halflife the band again gained members in Scratch and Dice Raw. The band's next album, Things Fall Apart, was a breakthrough album in that it was their first album to break the top 10 of the Billboard 200 In addition to becoming the house band on Late Night with Jimmy Fallon, The Roots have generated a great deal of critical acclaim and have influenced numerous rap and R&B groups. Associated Acts are Soulquarians, Jill Scott, John Legend, and Dave Chappelle.

Chapter 20

THE GOLDEN AGE OF HIP-HOP

Overview:

Entering the *Golden Age* of Hip-Hop, there were certain stylistic issues that emerged, distinguishing older styles from newer trends. One of first changes in this regard was the method of creating beats; whereas we have seen the drummer replaced by the drum machine, such as the Roland TR-808, the drum machine was now replaced by the sampler, typically the AKAI-S900. The technique of sampling involves capturing a pre-existing sound and manipulating that sound in various ways to create a beat, versus programming a drum machine. As part of the adoption of the sampler, another part of that transition involved phasing out the use of tape loops.

Artists began to cease including break beats in their music (which had previously been a hallmark of Hip-Hop). By the mid to late 1980s, Hip-Hop had spread from its birthplace in the South Bronx, and new artists were emerging from places other than the Bronx and Queens. Here we begin to see Hip-Hop artists from Philadelphia, Newark, Long Island and even Oakland, California on the West Coast. This new cohort would build on the foundations laid by their peers earlier in the decade and attain previously unheard-of commercial success as well as critical acceptance, in the form of both R.I.A.A. gold and platinum certifications, and awards such as the first Best Rap Performance Grammy introduced at the end of the decade.

Meanwhile, Long Island's Public Enemy made a name for themselves; and on the West Coast, out of Oakland California came Digital Underground (most notable for launching the career of Tupac Shakur). Female Hip-Hop artists were also establishing themselves as well during this time. The Queens based trio Salt-N-Pepa have established themselves as the most commercially successful female rap group through the sales of over 15 million records and singles, with six of their albums being certified gold or platinum by the R.I.A.A. Also emerging during this time was Newark-based Queen Latifah, who has had a prolific career that has branched out from Hip-Hop and into film and television.

Eric B. & Rakim

Eric B. & Rakim are an American Hip-Hop duo formed on Long Island, New York, in 1986, composed of members Eric Barrier aka Eric B. and William Michael Griffin Jr. a.k.a MC Rakim.

During rap's golden age in the late 1980s, Eric B. & Rakim were almost universally recognized as the premier DJ/MC team in Hip-Hop. The Long Island duo proved to be quite influential on the course of Hip-Hop with their debut album *Paid in Full* which had a lasting effect on both DJ-ing and MC-ing). Following Rakim's response to Eric B.'s search for a rapper to complement his disc jockey work, the duo recorded the album at Hip-Hop producer Marley Marl's home studio and Power Play Studios (NYC) in 1985, following Rakim's response to Eric B.'s search for a rapper to complement his disc jockey work in 1985. When "Paid in Full" was released in 1987, Eric B. and Rakim left a mushroom cloud over the Hip-Hop community. The album was captivating, profound, innovative, and instantly influential. With an emphasis on James Brown, Eric B. had an ear for picking out loops and samples that were drenched with soul. Rakim's use of *internal rhymes* in Hip-Hop set a higher standard of lyricism in the genre—forming the template for future rappers. His "slow flow," "mesmeric" lyrics and his "methodical" approach to rapping provided a stark contrast to the typically energetic, irreverent MCs such as Run, D.M.C., Chuck D. and KRS-One. The *"Seven Minutes of Madness"* remix of "Paid in Full" is also considered a milestone in Hip-Hop. *Paid In Full* would peak at Number 58 on the Billboard 200 chart, attain gold certification by the R.I.A.A. in 1995, and be ranked number 227 on *Rolling Stone Magazine's* list of the 500 greatest albums of all time. The album peaked at number 58 on the Billboard 200 chart and produced five singles, "Eric B. Is President," "I Ain't No Joke," "I Know You Got Soul," "Move the Crowd," and "Paid in Full." Ultimately, Paid in Full is credited as a benchmark album of golden age Hip-Hop. The Recording Industry Association of America (RIAA) certified it platinum in 1995.

MEDIA:

❖ Eric B. & Rakim, "Paid in Full (Seven Minutes of Madness—The Coldcut Remix)," *Paid in Full*, 1987. https://youtu.be/yUHBwErQmw4

• ZOOM OUT (Sample): Soul II Soul, "Back to Life," *Club Classics* vol. 1, 1989. https://youtu.be/oUOKf-UzHVo

LL Cool J

James Todd Smith, better known as LL Cool J, is an American rapper and actor from Queens, New York, USA. "LL Cool J" stands for "Ladies Love Cool James." With the breakthrough success of his single "I Need a Beat" and the Radio LP, LL Cool J became an early hip hop act to achieve mainstream success along with Kurtis Blow and Run-DMC. He is also known for romantic ballads such as "I Need Love," "Around the Way Girl" and *"Hey Lover" as well as pioneering Hip-Hop such as "I Can't Live Without My Radio," "I'm Bad," "The Boomin' System" and "Mama Said Knock You Out." He has also appeared in several films, and the network television series "CSI."

MEDIA:

❖ LL Cool J, "I Can't Live Without My Radio," *Radio*, 1985: Live.
   https://youtu.be/GdkamS5axHQ

Queen Latifah

Dana Elaine Owens aka Queen Latifah is an American singer, rapper, and actress from Origin: Newark, New Jersey, USA. Associated Acts are Jungle Brothers, A Tribe Called Quest and De La Soul.

MEDIA:

❖ Queen Latifah, "U.N.I.T.Y," *Black-Reign*, 1993.
   https://youtu.be/f8cHxydDb7o

TOMMY BOY RECORDS

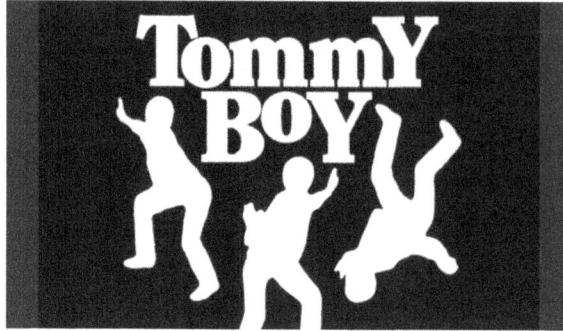

Tommy Boy Entertainment
Founded: 1981 by Tom Silverman
Location: New York, NY, USA

After borrowing $5,000 from his parents, the label was an outgrowth of Tom Silverman's Disco News bi-weekly publication (later titled Dance Music Report), which spanned 14 years, beginning in September 1978. In 1985, Warner Bros. Records bought 50 percent of the label, eventually buying all of it in 1990.

DEF JAM RECORDS

Def Jam Recordings is an American multinational record label owned by the Universal Music Group. It is based in Manhattan, New York City, specializing predominantly on Hip-Hop, contemporary R&B, soul and pop. The label has a London-based, UK arm known as 0207 Def Jam and is currently operated through EMI Records.

Slick Rick

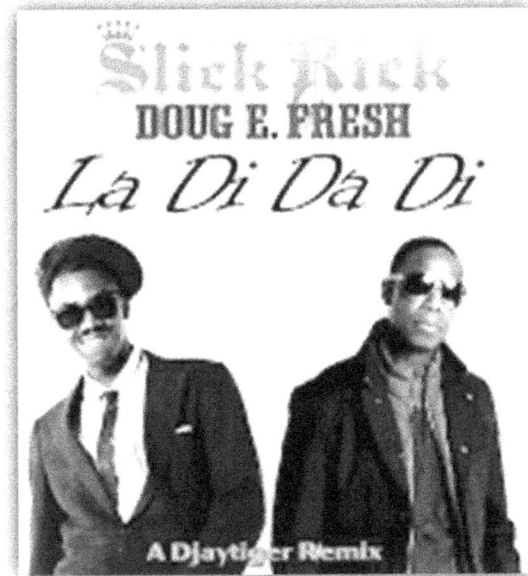

Richard Martin Lloyd Walters, better known as Slick Rick, is an English American rapper and record producer. He rose to prominence with Doug E. Fresh & the Get Fresh Crew in the mid-1980s. Their songs "The Show" and "La Di Da Di" are considered early Hip-Hop classics.

MEDIA:

❖ Doug E. Fresh & the Get Fresh Crew, La Di Da Di (feat. Slick Rick), 1995.
   https://youtu.be/waY_ng-is-E

DJ Jazzy Jeff and The Fresh Prince

The Philadelphia duo DJ Jazzy Jeff (Jeffrey Townes) and The Fresh Prince (Will Smith) helped bring Hip-Hop to an even wider audience. While known for his "clean" approach to Emceeing. Will Smith's profanity-free lyrics helped Hip-Hop increase in both popularity and critical recognition as the duo's single "Parents Just Don't Understand," received the very first Grammy Award for Best Hip-Hop Performance, while their album *He's the DJ, I'm the Rapper* was certified multi-platinum by the R.I.A.A. Two years later the duo would win a second Grammy award for the track "Summertime" which also reached #4 in the Billboard Hot 100 charts. As a further service to Hip Hop, Will Smith starred in the television show *The Fresh Prince of Bel-Air*, which gave Rap and Hip-Hop an even greater exposure, while occasionally featuring his partner DJ Jazzy Jeff in several episodes as well as up-and-coming Hip-Hop stars such as Queen Latifah and LL Cool J—other artists whose careers would branch out into film and television.

MEDIA:

❖ DJ Jazzy Jeff and The Fresh Prince, "Parents Just Don't Understand," *He's The DJ, I'm the Rapper,* 1988 (First Rap Grammy).
    https://youtu.be/LYHJ3c78yNc

❖ DJ Jazzy Jeff and The Fresh Prince, "Summertime," *Homebase,* 1991.
    https://youtu.be/Kr0tTbTbmVA

• ZOOM OUT (Sample Source): Kool & The Gang, "Summer Madness," *Light Of The World,* 1974.
    https://www.youtube.com/watch?v=2SFt7JHwJeg

Salt-n-Pepa

Salt-N-Pepa is a Grammy Award-winning American Hip-Hop trio from Queens, New York, that came onto the music scene in 1985. The group, consisting of Cheryl James ("Salt," now Cheryl Wray), Sandra Denton ("Pepa"), and Deidra "Dee Dee" Roper (Spinderella) were signed to Next Plateau Records and released their single "Push It" in 1987, which hit number one in three countries and became a top 10 or top 20 hit in various countries. The group has sold over 15 million albums and singles worldwide. Salt-N-Pepa is the best-selling female rap duo/group, [citation needed] and six of their single releases have been certified either platinum or gold in America by the RIAA. Associated Acts are Roxanne Shante, MC Lyte, Run DMC, Fat Boys, and Kid 'n Play.

MEDIA:

❖ Salt-N-Pepa, "Push It," *Hot, Cool & Vicious,* 1988.
    https://youtu.be/vCadcBR95oU

Public Enemy

Public Enemy, also known as PE, is an American Hip-Hop group consisting of Chuck D (Carlton Douglas Ridenhour), Flavor Flav (William Jonathan Drayton, Jr.), Professor Griff and his S1W group, Sister Souljah and DJ Lord, who replaced Terminator X in 1999. Formed on Long Island, New York in 1982, they are known for their politically charged lyrics and criticism of the American media, with an active interest in the frustrations and concerns of the African American community.

MEDIA:

❖ Public Enemy, "Fight the Power," *Fear of a Black Planet*, 1989.
https://youtu.be/jRJKjiCtVco

EPMD:

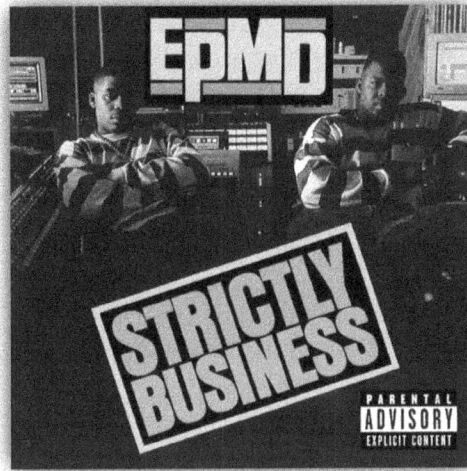

EPMD is an American Hip-Hop duo from Long Island, New York. The group name is an acronym for "Erick and Parrish Making Dollars," referring to its members: Erick Sermon and Parrish Smith.

MEDIA:

❖ EPMD, "You Gots to Chill," *Strictly Business*, 1988.
https://youtu.be/APMJNyaDC78
❖ EPMD, "Strictly Business," *Strictly Business*, 1988.
https://youtu.be/z26QCzYZH4w

Kwamé

Kwamé Holland, also known as K-1 Million, K1 Mil, is an American rapper and record producer from Queens, New York. Originally starting out as a rapper in the late 1980s, Holland later sought greater success with behind the scenes work as a producer. Associated acts include Jade Ewen and Beyond Belief.

JAZZ RAP

"Jazz elements were in early rap, but not in a sustained way until the late 1980's"

Another Hip-Hop sub-genre that emerged during this time was Jazz Rap, the evolution of which was motivated by the necessity to establish the cultural legitimacy of Hip-Hop by making it part of a lineage connecting African diasporic music to Hip-Hop via Jazz. The genre was also a reaction to the negative stereotypes perpetuated in the violent and misogynistic lyrics of Gangsta Rap and its connection to "the street," and accomplished this through politically oriented and socially progressive lyrics—and by tapping into the perception of Jazz in the 1980s as "well-mannered" art music. While Rap in its earliest incorporated jazz elements, before groups such as Eric B. and Rakim and Digital Underground set the template for Hip-Hop through the heavy use of Funk samples, Jazz Rap groups such as Stetsasonic and Gang Starr began to consistently ground their songs in jazz samples.

Overview:

- Alternative to stereotypes perpetuated by Gangsta Rap.
- Alternative to the authenticity of "the street"
- Jazz is used to provide lineage of African diasporic music into Hip-Hop.
- The art-music and "well-mannered" identity of jazz (1980s) is a strategy for *cultural legitimacy*.
- Characterized by politically oriented and socially progressive lyrics.

Stetsasonic

Stetsasonic is an American Hip-Hop band formed in 1981, in Brooklyn, New York. Around 1988, KISS-FM radio personality James Mtume challenged the artistic legitimacy of the burgeoning Hip-Hop movement. In response, Stetsasonic released the track "Talkin' All That Jazz," with the goal of establishing the legitimacy of Hip-Hop by connecting it to jazz. The liner notes from the album, *In Full Gear*, make this view clear—explaining how rap is "the most progressive music since jazz."—"progressive" being used here to describe the advancements made by African American musicians, in general (and to corroborate the fact that rap was a "progressive" *new* development for African American cultural progress)—this, in contradiction to the critical notions that deny Hip-Hop the status of art. Stetsasonic was also one of the first Hip-Hop acts to perform with a full band, and use live instrumentation on their recordings—paving the way for the future of Hip-Hop.

MEDIA:

❖ Stetsasonic, "Talkin' all that Jazz," *In Full Gear*, 1988.
  https://youtu.be/2kdQ4soLcac

GANG Starr

Gang Starr was an American Hip-Hop duo, consisting of Texas record producer DJ Premier and Massachusetts rapper Guru. Gang Starr was at its height from 1989 to 2003 and are considered one of the best MC-and-producer duos in Hip-Hop history. They are recognized for being one of the pioneers of jazz rap. Their first single, released in 1989, was "Words I Manifest." Providing an alternative to Gangsta Rap and misogynistic lyrics, they purport "knowledge, wisdom and understanding." There is also frequent use of jazz samples in many of their tracks. "Jazz Music" from 1989 gained the attention of film director Spike Lee who asked Gang Starr to create a theme, "Jazz Thing" for his *Mo Better Blues* movie in 1990. To this end, the group composed the track "Jazz Thing" which was essentially a chronology of jazz from its origins in the chain gangs, to the present day. The ensuing production (single and video), features the lineage of prominent jazz musicians, alternative to stereotypes perpetuated by Gangsta Rap (and it's "authenticity of the street") Essentially, the "art-music" and "well-mannered" identity of jazz, is used to provide lineage of African diasporic music into Hip-Hop.

MEDIA:

❖ Gang Starr, "Jazz Thing," soundtrack to the film *Mo Better Blues*, 1990.
  https://youtu.be/3kg0mh3lu9Q

"Jazz Thing" Analysis

  Now listen see, the real mystery is how music history
  Created Paul Whiteman or any other white man
  That pretended he originated...

And contended that he innovated—a jazz thing.

  ...The music called Jazz
  Its roots are in the sounds of the African
  Or should I say the mother, bringin' us back again
  From the drummin' on the Congo.

Lyrics: Discussion of Africa "or should I say the mother"

Gang Starr brings attention to the appropriation of African American music by white musicians.

While the lyrics to "Jazz Thing" are largely a chronology of Jazz from the days of the Chain Gang to the present, it does touch on several societal issues as well.

At first glance the lyrics are referring to several of Coltrane's compositions including "A Love Supreme," "Wise One," "Impressions," "Afro Blue," "The Promise" and "Giant Steps," however Dr. Jesse Stuart suggests the line, "The promise that was not kept" hints at the oppressive social conditions that surrounded Coltrane's music, as well as those surrounding Jazz, Hip-Hop and African American experience more generally.

Another important issue the song brings attention to is the cultural appropriation of African American culture, as well as the co-opting of the innovations of African American musicians by White musicians, and in particular, Paul Whiteman, the self-proclaimed "King of Jazz" during the 1930s swing era, and the creation of a parallel historical narrative that ignores the African American origins of jazz.

One verse deals specifically with John Coltrane:

John Coltrane, a man supreme, he was the cream.
He was the "Wise One."
The impression of "Afro Blue,"
and of "The Promise" that was not kept,
he was a Giant Step.

MEDIA:

❖ John Coltrane, "Acknowledgment," *A Love Supreme*, 1965.
https://youtu.be/5Pi5ZJZ07ME

Chapter 21

MIAMI BASS: 2 LIVE CREW/EAST COAST DIRTY RAP

2 Live Crew

2 Live Crew is an American hip hop group from Miami, Florida, which had its greatest commercial success from the late 1980s to the early 1990s. The group's most well-known line up was composed of Luke Campbell, Fresh Kid Ice, Mr. Mix, and Brother Marquis.

J Prince

Rap-A-Lot is a Hip-Hop record label founded by James Smith aka James Prince aka J Prince in 1987. He is the CEO of the Houston-based record label Rap-A-Lot. Rap-A-Lot was first distributed by A&M Records with the release of Raheem's 1988 debut The Vigilante. The label was distributed through the 1990s by EMI's Priority Records, Noo Trybe Records and Virgin Records. He is best known as the person who had originally introduced Canadian rapper Drake to Lil Wayne and helped him get signed to Young Money Entertainment in 2009.

Beastie Boys

Beastie Boys is an American rap group from New York City, formed in 1981. The group was composed of Michael "Mike D" Diamond, Adam "MCA" Yauch and Adam "Ad-Rock" Horovitz.

MEDIA:

❖ Beastie Boys, "Paul Revere," *License to Ill*, 1986.
   https://youtu.be/P_PQ52SCDQE

DJ MAGIC MIKE

DJ Magic Mike (born Michael Hampton, May 9, 1966) is a "Miami-Bass" record producer, rapper, and the first plat-inum selling recording artist from Orlando, Florida. Magic Mike made his debut in 1986. He landed a solo deal with Cheetah Records, releasing his first batch of solo singles in 1988. Those led to a full-length album in 1989 entitled "DJ Magic Mike and The Royal Posse," which featured many guest crews and rappers all based on his production and turntable antics. His following album Bass is the Name of the Game in 1990 saw the Miami Bass genre reach a zenith both creatively and commercially.

Chapter 22

THE NEW DIVAS

MC LYTE

Born: October 11, 1970, Brooklyn, New York, Lana Michele Moorerbetter known by her stage name MC Lyte, is an American rapper, DJ, actress and entrepreneur. Considered one of the pioneers of female rap, Lyte first gained fame in the late 1980s, becoming the first solo female rapper to release a full album with 1988's critically acclaimed Lyte as a Rock. Other associated acts are Audio Two, and Xscape.

Sisters with Voices

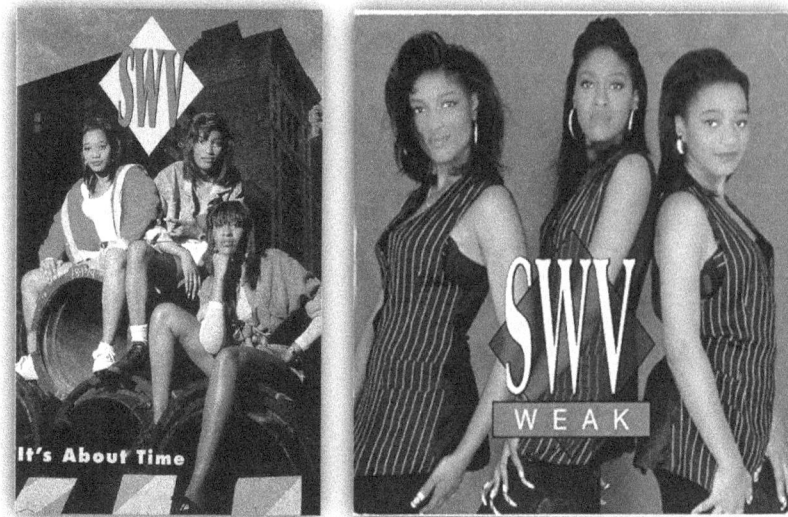

Composed of members Leanne "Lelee" Lyons, Cheryl "Coko" Clemons, and Tamara "Taj" Johnson-George, SWV (Sisters with Voices), is an American female R&B trio from New York City, NY. Formed in 1990 as a gospel group, SWV became one of the most successful R&B groups of the decade. They had a series of hits, including "Weak," "Right Here/ Human Nature," "I'm So Into You," and "You're the One." The group disbanded in 1998, to pursue solo projects, and reunited in 2005.

MISSY ELLIOT

Melissa Arnette "Missy" Elliott (born July 1, 1971), known as Missy Elliot, is an American rapper, singer-songwriter, record producer, dancer, and actress. A five-time Grammy Award winner, Elliott, with record sales of over seven million in the United States, is the only female rapper to have five albums certified platinum by the RIAA, including one double platinum for her 2002 album Under Construction. Elliott is known for a series of hits and diverse music videos, including "The Rain (Supa Dupa Fly)," "Hot Boyz," "Get Ur Freak On," "One Minute Man," "Work It," "Pass That Dutch" and "Lose Control." In addition, she has worked extensively as a songwriter and producer for other artists, both alone and with her fellow producer and childhood friend Timbaland, with whom she received her first production credit on R&B singer Ginuwine's 1996's album Ginuwine...the Bachelor. Associated acts include Timbaland, Magoo, Aaliyah, Aaliyah, Ginuwine, Jodeci and Ludacris.

Mary J. Blige

Mary Jane Blige (/'blaɪʒ/; born January 11, 1971) in The Bronx, NY, US. is an American singer–songwriter, record producer and actress. She is a recipient of nine Grammy Awards and four American Music Awards and has recorded eight multi-platinum albums. She is the only artist with Grammy Award wins in Pop, Rap, Gospel and R&B. Blige started her musical career in 1992, releasing her debut album, What's the 411? on MCA Records and Uptown. With her tenth album, My Life II... The Journey Continues (Act 1) (2011), she had 10 consecutive albums debut in the top 10 on the Billboard 200. Blige's work has defined the course of R&B/Hip-Hop music. My Life is considered among the greatest albums ever recorded according to Rolling Stone, Time, and Vibe. For her part in combining Hip-Hop and soul in the early 1990s and its subsequent commercial success, Blige received the World Music Awards "Legends Award." In 2007, the American Society of Composers, Authors and Publishers awarded her its "Voice of Music" Award. ASCAP stated that her music has been the voice of inspiration to women worldwide in both struggle and triumph." That same year, Time included her in its "Time 100" list, a collection of the year's 100 most influential individuals around the world.

Lil Kim

By way of Brooklyn, New York, US, Kimberly Denise Jones, a.k.a., Lil Kim was heavily influenced by other female MC'S like MC Lyte and Lady of Rage. Impressed, Notorious B.I.G. invited her to the stage in 1995 via the group Junior M.A.F.I.A, which was also formed and mentored by Notorious B.I.G. Her album Hard Core (1996) was certified double platinum and spawned three consecutive #1 rap hits that included: "No Time" "Not Tonight (Ladies Night remix)" and "Crush on You." Lil Kim was the only female rapper, besides Missy Elliott, to have at least three platinum albums in early Y2K.

FOXY BROWN

Inga DeCarlo Fung Marchand (born September 6, 1978), better known as Foxy Brown, is an American rapper known for her solo work as well as numerous collaborations. Her father, Keith Stahler held a career at ERAC Records. Her albums include Ill Na Na in 1996, followed by Chyna Doll in 1999, and Broken Silence in 2001.

After 2002, she continued recording but did not release any albums; canceling the release of her Ill Na Na 2 album, she left the Def Jam label in 2003. She returned to the label in January 2005 after Jay-Z signed her for the Black Roses album. A fourth studio album, which originally was a mixtape, was released in May 2008. Associated acts include Jay-Z, Nas, Fox-5, Gravy, The Firm, and Rick Ross.

SUGA-T

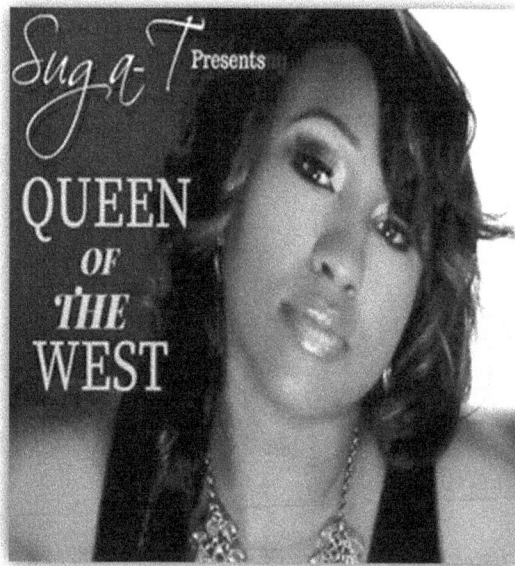

Tenina Stevens, better known by her stage name SUGA-T, is an American rapper and actress from Vallejo, California. She is a founding member of The Click, a rap group that includes her brothers E-40 and D-Shot, along with her cousin B-Legit.

Ladybug Mecca

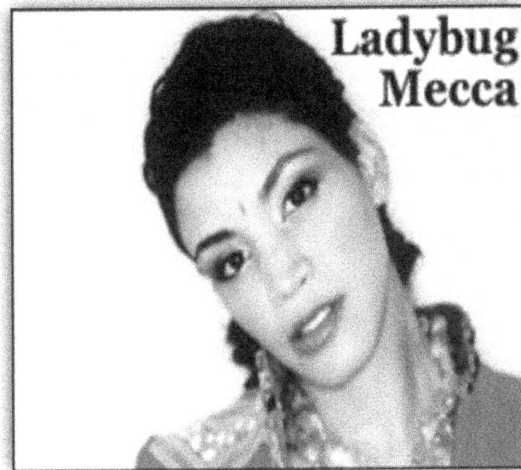

Khalilah-Azraa Vieira (born Mary Ann Vieira), better known by her stage name Ladybug Mecca or simply Ladybug, is an American rapper from Silver Spring, Maryland. She is best known for being a member of the group Digable Planets during the early 1990s. She is a pioneer of female equality in Hip-Hop, expressing non-sexualized lyrics, setting the template for the pro-feminist movement in Hip-Hop.

ZOOM OUT:

- Ladybug Mecca was discussing pro-life versus abortion issues before it was cool.

MEDIA:

- ❖ Digable Planets, "Le femme fetal," *Reachin' (A new Refutation Of Time and Space)*, 1993. https://youtu.be/3DfMksmOIME

Trina

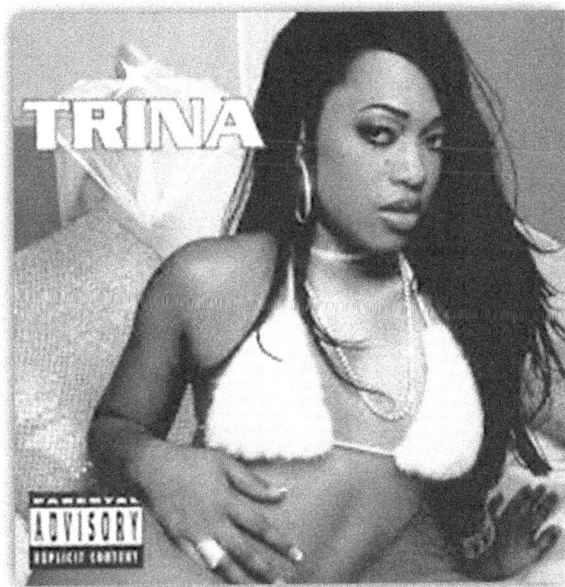

Katrina Laverne Taylor (born December 3, 1978), better known by her stage name Trina, is an American rapper, songwriter and model from Miami, Florida. Trina first gained notoriety in 1998 with her appearance on Trick Daddy's second studio album www.thug.com to the single "Nann Nigga." Since then, she has released five moderately successful studio albums and has been named The Most Consistent Female Rapper of All-Time by XXL Magazine. Da Baddest Bitch was certified Gold in November 2000 by the RIAA. It stayed on the Billboard 200 chart for 29 weeks and on the Hip-Hop/R&B album chart for 49 consecutive weeks.

MEDIA:

❖ Trina, "Killin U Hoes," *Still da Baddest*, 2008.
  https://youtu.be/Pb7v8EjQ6Yk

RIHANNA

Robyn Rihanna Fenty, born February 20, 1988, in Saint Michael (and raised in Bridgetown) Barbados, is a singer, actress, and businesswoman., Rihanna auditioned for American record producer Evan Rogers who invited her to the United States to record a demo tape. After signing with Def Jam in 2005, she soon gained recognition with the release of her first two studio albums, both of which peaked within the top ten of the USA Billboard 200 chart.

Harnessing the chart-topping single "Umbrella," Rihanna's third album, Good Girl Gone Bad (2007), established her status as a sex symbol in the music industry and earned Rihanna her first Grammy Award, catapulting her to global stardom. Rihanna is one of the best-selling and wealthiest female artists alive, with sales of over 250 million records worldwide and estimated net worth of $1.4 billion (circa 2022).

Aside from music, Rihanna is known for her involvement in humanitarian causes, entrepreneurial ventures, and the fashion industry. She is the founder of a nonprofit organization, a cosmetics brand (Fenty Beauty), and fashion house Fenty under Moët Hennessy Louis Vuitton (LVMH) Rihanna has also ventured into acting, appearing in many major roles. She was appointed as an ambassador of education, tourism, and investment by the Government of Barbados in 2018 and was declared a National Hero on the first day of the country's parliamentary republic in 2021, entitling her to the status of "The Right Excellent" for life.

Chapter 23

WHAT'S BEEF?—NOT MEAT

It's when you make enemies

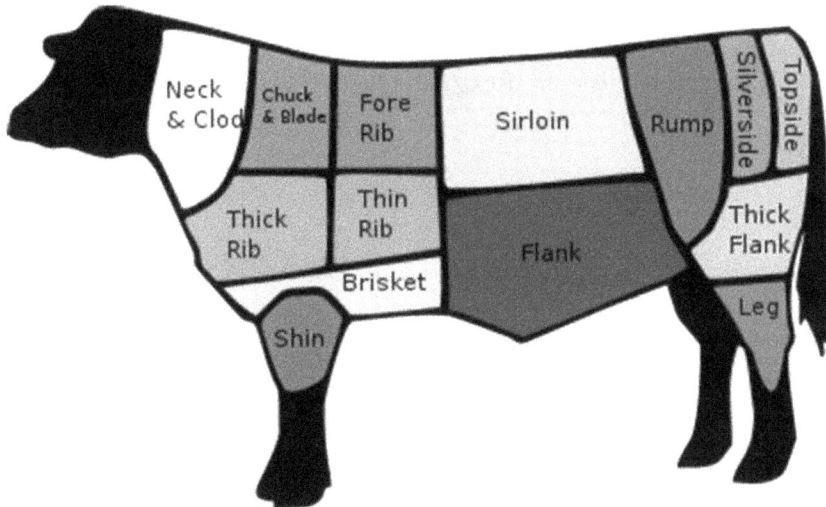

Neck & Clod Chuck & Blade Fore Rib Sirloin Rump Silverside Topside

Thick Rib Thin Rib Flank Thick Flank

Brisket Leg

Shin

As we saw with the Roxanne and Bridge wars of the 1980s, Hip-Hop artists discovered that "diss," "answer" and "battle" records and tracks could help a young artist make a name for themselves; consequently, feuding or "beefs" became an integral part of Hip-Hop culture. However, somewhere along the way "beef" took on a sinister life of its own to the point that artists were now resolving disputes in physical combat, rather than on the stage or on the radio. Before "beef" began taking on a literal dimension, we can find its direct origins in the Hip Hop that immediately preceded it, within which we can find the routine use of contextual "false" misogyny, the use of fiction, and the extensive use of metaphors, which were used as modules for socio-political observation or the telling of fictional stories. It is important to note that the violence in Hip-Hop did not originate in, nor is it exclusive to, that culture. The fact is that violence is pervasive across American culture as a whole—harnessing many cultural foundations (where the bloody battles of Cowboys versus Indians, Mobsters versus Hustlers, Drug Dealers and Gangs are regular fare in all forms film and media). What changed was the nature of the criminal element, as criminals in the vein of "Scarface" began to be supplanted by criminals of the "Superfly" variety; over time, rappers simply usurped the violence that already existed in American culture.

Steeped in so much violence, it was only a matter of time before virtual reality, once the home of metaphors, evolved into reality; as the continuous exposure to violent material and subject matter can adversely twist one's take on reality, influencing aggression in today's world. Another part of this was a shift in perceptions and interpretations of other's actions versus [their] intentions—the world of real and false beefs. As everyone became hyper-sensitized to perceived threats, compounded by desensitization to this formerly metaphorical violence, the final step in the creation of this violence is, of course, *enactment*.

Foundations of Violence, Key Aspects:

- Contextual "false" misogyny
- Extensive use of metaphors
- Metaphors used as modules for socio-political observation or fiction

Societal Influences:

- Crack Cocaine "Germ Warfare" on the community
- Reaganomics (inflation, etc.)
- Disenfranchised Urban America—late 1980s early 1990s
- Community rage expressed through music

Cultural Foundations:

- Rappers appropriated the violence that already existed in American culture (they did not originate it)
- Cowboys versus Indians, Mobsters, Hustlers, Dealers, Gangs and "Scarface" versus. "Superfly")
- Virtual Reality versus Real Conflict (Virtual-reality could, in reality, influence aggression)

Other Ideas:

- Perceptions and interpretations versus intentions (Real/False Beefs)
- Desensitization:
    a) Enactment

MEDIA:

❖ Hydrogen vs. Boost (Original).
    https://youtu.be/O1W_u5GPDys
❖ Hydrogen vs. Boost (Translated).
    https://youtu.be/pdxIDrs2Uc4

West Coast Gangsta Rap to East Coast Mafioso Style

"The New York EGO worked against the imitation (flattery) and admiration from other regions."

First East Coast / West Coast "Beefs" on Wax: The Seeds of Rap Animosity

MEDIA:

❖ (East) Tim Dog, "Fuck Compton," *Penicillin on Wax*, 1981.
    https://youtu.be/AwzeM2J3Emk
❖ (West) Tweety Bird Loc, "Fuck The South Bronx, Nigga This Is Compton" (Single), 1982.
    https://youtu.be/-J6cTLyPiRw

- ZOOM OUT (Sample Source): The Dramatics, "Get Up and Get Down," *Whatcha See Is Whatcha Get*, 1971.
    https://youtu.be/hZfMpbcI1NQ

Evolution of a Gangsta Sample: Evolution of a Gangsta Sample: "P.S.K. What Does It Mean?" (also written as "P.S.K. (What Does It Mean?)") is a song released in 1985 by Philadelphia rapper Schoolly D on his independent label Schoolly D Records. P.S.K. is the abbreviation for Park Side Killas (a street gang with which Schoolly D was affiliated). The highly influential song is considered the first gangsta rap and hardcore rap song and features incidents of graphic sex, gunplay, drug references—this along with one of the first uses of the word "nigga" in a rap song (notwithstanding "Family Rap" in 1979 and "New York New York in 1983).

MEDIA:

❖ Schoolly D, "P.S.K. What Does It Mean?," *Schoolly D*, 1985.
    https://youtu.be/fQc4A-XBzBY
❖ Ice T., "6 in The Mornin'," *Rhyme Pays*, 1987.
    https://youtu.be/izuMglGGnMc
❖ Eazy E, "Boyz N The Hood," *N.W.A. and the Posse*, 1987.
    https://youtu.be/64mx7TiCbuY

Chapter 24

EAST COAST MAFIOSO RAP

Mafioso rap is a hardcore Hip-Hop sub-genre founded by Kool G Rap in the late 1980s. It is the pseudo-Mafia extension of East Coast hardcore rap and is considered the counterpart of West Coast G-Funk rap. Mafioso rap is characterized by lavish, self-indulgent and luxurious subject matter, with many references to famous mobsters, organized crime, materialism, drugs, and expensive champagne. Though the genre died down for several years, it re-emerged in 1995 when Wu-Tang Clan member Raekwon released his critically acclaimed solo album, Only Built 4 Cuban Linx .... 1995 also saw the release of Doe or Die by Nas' protégé AZ. These two albums brought the genre to mainstream recognition, and inspired other East Coast artists, such as Nas, Notorious B.I.G. and Jay-Z, to adopt the same themes as well with their albums It Was Written, Life After Death and Reasonable Doubt. Though Mafioso rap declined in the mainstream by the late 1990s, it has seen somewhat of a revival in more recent years with Ghostface Killah's Fishscale, Jay-Z's American Gangster, Rick Ross's Deeper than Rap, and Raekwon's Only Built 4 Cuban Linx II. Similarly, in recent years, many rappers, such as T.I., Fabolous, Jadakiss, Jim Jones and Cassidy have maintained popularity with lyrics about self-centered urban criminal lifestyles or "hustling."

KOOL G RAP

Nathaniel Thomas Wilson (born July 20, 1968), better known by his stage names Kool G Rap (or simply G Rap), Kool G Rap and Giancana (Meaning of the abbreviation "G"), is an American rapper, from the Corona neighborhood of Queens, New York City. He began his career in the mid-1980s as one half of the group **Kool G Rap & DJ Polo** and as a member of the Juice Crew. He is a pioneer of mafioso rap/street/hardcore content and multisyllabic rhyming. On his album The Giancana Story, he stated that the "G" in his name stands for "Giancana" (after the mobster Sam Giancana) but on other occasions he's stated that it stands for "Genius." Associated Acts include Eminem, Nas, Jay Z, Big Pun, RZA and Ghost Face Killah.

MEDIA:

❖ Kool G Rap, "Two to the Head" (feat. Ice Cube, Bushwick Bill and Scarface), *Live and Let Die*, 1992. https://youtu.be/hDxa0ze_AfI

• ZOOM OUT (Sample Source): George Clinton, "Mommy, What's a Funkadelic?," *Funkadelic*, 1970. https://youtu.be/c-53pFRA9IQ

Bad Boy Records

Bad Boy Records (originally Bad Boy Entertainment) is a record label founded in 1993 by producer/rapper/entrepreneur Sean "Diddy" Combs. Today it operates as a subsidiary of Warner Music Group and is distributed by Atlantic Records. After his climb from a non-paying internship to becoming an A&R executive at Uptown Records, Diddy was abruptly terminated in 1993 by then CEO John Galante and Andre Harrell—reportedly due to his own difficulty to work with David E. Thigpen/Nassau. Together with school friend Mark Pitts—who had interned with Combs at Uptown—the pair founded Bad Boy Records in 1993. The label's first release was "Flava in Ya Ear" by Craig Mack, followed quickly by Mack's debut album, "Project: Funk Da World" in 1994. On the heels of these releases came "Juicy" and "Ready to Die," the lead single and debut album from The Notorious B.I.G. aka "Biggie Smalls," released the same year. While Mack's album went gold, "Ready to Die" achieved multi-platinum success. Dominating the charts into 1995, B.I.G. became Bad Boy's premier star. Also in 1995, the label continued its success with platinum releases by Total and Faith Evans. Bad Boy, meanwhile, staffed a bevy of in-house writer/producers, including Chucky Thompson, Easy Mo Bee, Nashiem Myrick and D Dot—all of whom were instrumental in producing many of Bad Boy's most noted releases during this time.

Craig Mack

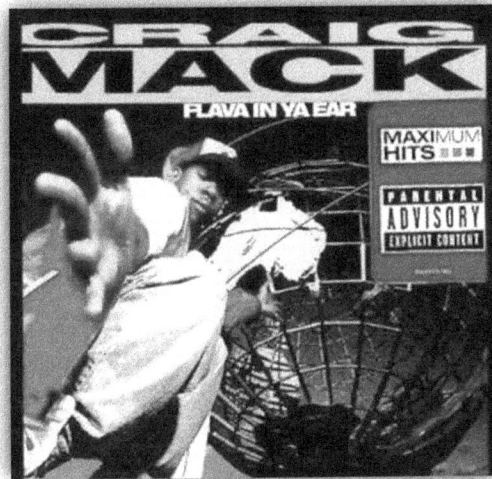

Born on May 10, 1970, in The Bronx, NYC, Craig Jamieson Mack (a.k.a. Craig Mack) was an American rapper and record producer. He helped build the foundation for Bad Boy Records, one of hip hop's most influential labels. He died on March 12, 2018, in Walterboro, South Carolina, USA.

MEDIA:

❖ Craig Mack, "Flava In Ya Ear," *Funk da World*, 1994.
  https://youtu.be/-iP-_zycd-M

THE NOTORIOUS B.I.G.

"Rappers are not different from human beings"—Notorious B.I.G.

Originally known as MC QWEST, Christopher George Latore Wallace, aka, NOTORIOUS B.I.G. was from Brooklyn. NY, USA. His emceeing style involved a loose, easy, flow, with dark semi-autobiographical lyrics and genius-storytelling-abilities. He also displayed "a talent for piling multiple rhymes on top of one another in quick succession, and for making multi-syllabic rhymes sound smooth. Wallace's lyrics and themes included mafioso tales, his drug dealing past, materialistic bragging, as well as humor and romance.

MEDIA:

❖ Notorious B.I.G., "Juicy" *Ready To Die*, 1994.
https://youtu.be/_JZom_gVfuw

• ZOOM OUT (Sample Source): Juicy is based on the 1980's song, *Juicy Fruit*, by the group Mtume.
https://youtu.be/MucY5wRYByU

❖ The Notorious B.IG., Party and Bullshit, *Who's the Man?* 1993.
https://youtu.be/rEaPDNgUPLE

• ZOOM OUT (Sample Source): The Last Poets, When The Revolution Comes, 1970.
https://youtu.be/8M5W_3T2Ye4

Jadakiss

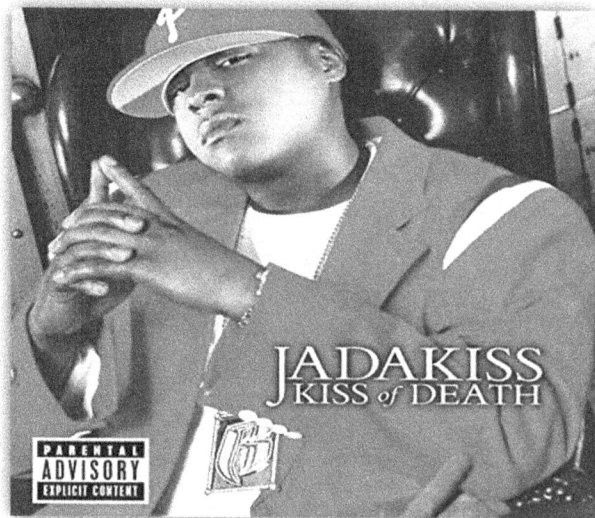

Jason Terrance Phillips, better known by his stage name Jadakiss, is an American rapper from Yonkers, New York. He began his career in the 1990s as a member of the rap trio The Lox, managed by Ruff Ryders and signed with Bad Boy Records. After leaving the label in 1999, they signed a joint venture deal with Interscope Records and Ruff Ryders. Jadakiss' debut solo album, *Kiss Tha Game Goodbye*, was released in 2001. He has also released an album with fellow MC Fabolous. Jada signed with Roc-A Fella and Def Jam in 2007, co-releasing his 2009 album, *The Last Kiss*, with Ruff Ryders. Jada has released five studio albums, most recently *Ignatius* in 2020.

MEDIA:

❖ Jadakiss, "Kiss of Death" (feat. Styles P.), *Kiss of Death*, 2004.
https://youtu.be/mcxjRe4-cbc

MOBB DEEP

Mobb Deep was an American Hip-Hop duo from New York City. The duo consisted of rappers Prodigy and Havoc. They are among the principal progenitors of hardcore East Coast Hip-Hop in the mid-1990s. Mobb Deep became one of the most successful rap duos of all time, having sold over three million records. Associated acts include Big Noyd, Nas. Raekwon, and Tragedy Khadafi.

MEDIA:

❖ Mobb Deep, "Survival of the Fittest," *The Infamous*, 1995. https://youtu.be/Dz5VzLz67WA
❖ Mobb Deep, "The Start of Your Ending," *The Infamous*, 1995. https://youtu.be/005GRsukWMc

WU-TANG CLAN

Wu-Tang Clan is an American Hip-Hop group formed in Staten Island, New York City, in 1992. Its original members include RZA, GZA, Ol' Dirty Bastard, Method Man, Raekwon, Ghostface Killah, Inspectah Deck, U-God, and Masta Killa. Close affiliate Cappadonna later became an official member. Loud Records, LLC. is a record label founded by

Steve Rifkind and Rich Isaacson in 1991. The label released material by acts such as Wu-Tang Clan, Big Pun, Mobb Deep and Krayzie Bone. Other associated acts include The Killa Beez, DJ Stretch Armstrong and DJ Doo Wop.

MEDIA:

❖ Wu-Tang Clan, "Protect Ya Neck," *Enter the Wu-Tang*, 1993.
   https://youtu.be/OFhXivuXq00?t=6
❖ Wu-Tang Clan "Triumph" (feat. Cappadonna), *Wu-Tang Forever*, 1997.
   https://youtu.be/7AFEWPAir8s
❖ Wu-Tang Clan "Unpredictable," *8 Diagrams*, 2007.
   https://youtu.be/80E_TW76IOA

• ZOOM OUT: The Evolution of the "WU"

The Cold Crush Brothers

The Cold Crush Brothers are an American Hip-Hop group that formed in 1978 in the Bronx, New York City. They were especially known for their memorable routines which included harmonies, melodies and stage-stomping performances, setting the pace for groups such as, The Force MD's.

The Force MD's

Formerly the Force MC's, are an American R&B vocal group that was formed in 1981 in the Stapleton section of Staten Island, New York (aka "Shaolin"). Although the group is perhaps best known for two tunes that are widely considered 1980s quiet storm classics, "Tender Love" and "Love is a House," they are also the "inspiration" for groups such as The Wu Tang Clan.

Ol' Dirty Bastard (ODB)

Russell Tyrone Jones, better known by his stage name Ol' Dirty Bastard, was an American rapper. He was one of the founding members of the Wu-Tang Clan, a rap group primarily from Staten Island, New York City, which rose to mainstream prominence with its 1993 debut album Enter the Wu-Tang.

Ghostface Killah

Born on Staten Island, New York, USA, Dennis Coles, also known as Ghostface Killah, is an American rapper, and a prominent member of the Wu-Tang Clan. Ghostface Killah debuted his solo-career with Ironman in 1996, which was well received by music critics. He has continued his success over the following years with critically acclaimed albums such as Supreme Clientele (2000) and Fishscale (2006). His stage name was taken from one of the characters in the 1979 kung fu film Mystery of Chessboxing. Ghostface Killah is critically acclaimed for his loud, fast-paced flow and his emotional stream-of-consciousness narratives containing cryptic slang and non-sequiturs. He is widely considered to be one of rap's finest storytellers. Associated acts include Theodore Unit, MF DOOM, and Rakim.

Master P

Percy Robert Miller Sr, better known by his stage name Master P, is a 54-year-old American rapper, record executive, actor, and entrepreneur. He was born and raised in New Orleans, Louisiana. Master P gained fame in the mid 1990s from the success of his Hip-Hop group, TRU, as well as his fifth solo rap album *Ice Cream Man*. In 1997, after the success of his platinum single "Make 'Em Say Uhh!," his popularity expanded. He is the founder of the record label No Limit Records. As of 2022, Master P's net worth is approximately $200 million USD.

MEDIA:

❖ Master P, "Make 'Em Say Ugh," *Pooti Tang*, 1997.
   https://youtu.be/h1fBYUWxaKQ

DMX

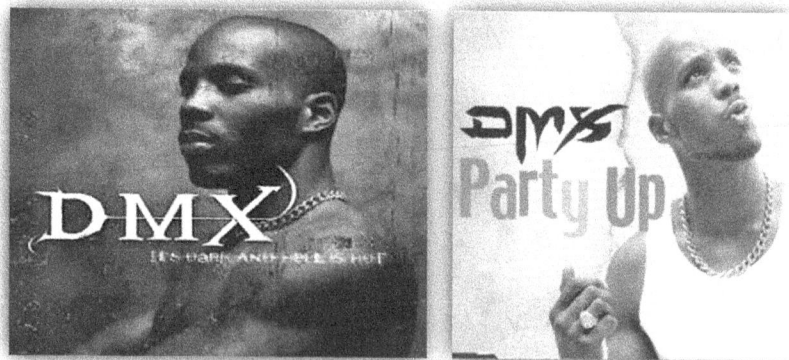

Born on December 18, 1970, Mount Vernon, NY, USA, Earl Simmons, known by his stage name DMX, was an American rapper and actor. He began rapping in the early 1990s and released his debut album "It's Dark and Hell Is Hot" in 1998, to both critical acclaim and commercial success, selling 251,000 copies within its first week of release. DMX died on April 9, 2021, at White Plains Hospital, White Plains, New York, USA.

MEDIA:

❖ DMX, "Slippin'," *Flesh of My Flesh, Blood of My Blood*, 1998.
https://youtu.be/9Ww-TQUeA3E

❖ DMX, "Party Up" (Up in Here), *And Then There Was X*, 2000.
https://youtu.be/thIVtEOtlWM

Pusha T

Born on May 13, 1977, in Bronx, NY, USA, Terrence LeVarr Thornton, better known by his stage name Pusha T, is an American rapper and record executive. He rose to prominence as one-half of the Hip-Hop duo Clipse, which was mainly active from 1994 to 2010, alongside his older brother No Malice.

MEDIA:

❖ Pusha T, "The Games We Play," *Daytona*, 2018.
https://g.co/kgs/ZNVS5D

• ZOOM OUT: Ron Westray, "Games," *Gemini*, 2018.
https://traydeuce1.bandcamp.com/track/games

Chapter 25

ORIGINS OF WEST COAST HIP-HOP

THE WATTS PROPHETS

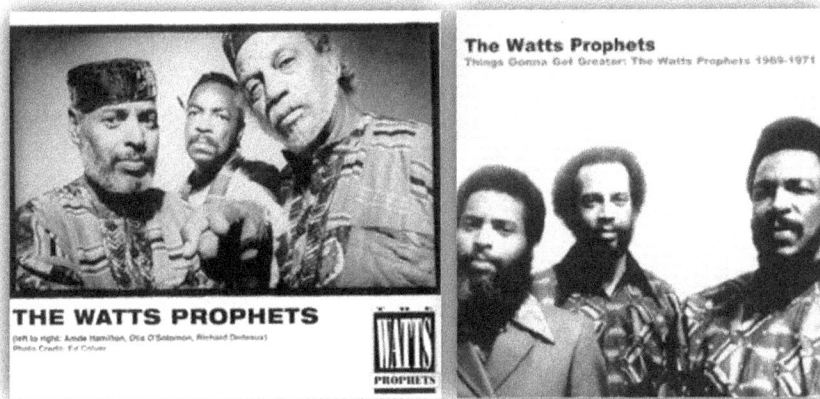

Formed in 1967, and consisting of the members Anthony Hamilton Richard Dedeaux, and Otis O'Solomon, The Watts Prophets are a group of musicians and poets from Watts, Los Angeles, California, USA. Like their contemporaries, The Last Poets, the group combined elements of jazz music and spoken word performance, making the trio one that is often seen as a forerunner of contemporary Hip-Hop music.

MC HAMMER

Stanley Kirk Burrell, also known as (M.C. Hammer, Hammer, Hammer time and King Hammer) is an American rapper, entrepreneur, record producer and actor from Oakland, California. He had his greatest commercial success and popularity from the late 1980s until the mid-1990s. Remembered for a rapid rise to fame before losing most of his fortune, Hammer is also known for his hit records, including "U Can't Touch This," flamboyant dance movements and trademark Hammer pants. Hammer's superstar-status made him a household name and pop icon. He has sold more than 50 million records worldwide.

MEDIA:

❖ MC Hammer, "U Can't Touch This," *Please Hammer Don't Hurt 'Em*, 1990. https://youtu.be/otCpCn0l4Wo?t=14

• ZOOM OUT (Sample Source): Rick James, "Super Freak," *Street Songs*, 1981. https://youtu.be/wnKc4zi0MLA

Chapter 26

WEST COAST 'GANGSTA' AND THE MIDWEST

Gangsta-rap Aka West Coast Hip-Hop Aka G-Funk is a subgenre of Hip-Hop that was pioneered in the mid-1980s by rappers such as Schoolly D and Ice-T and was later popularized by groups like N.W.A. in the early 1990s. The genre evolved from hardcore Hip-Hop and purports to reflect urban crime and the violent lifestyles of inner-city youths. The lyrics in Gangsta-rap vary from accurate reflections to highly fictionalized accounts.

Rap (Industry) versus Hip-Hop (Culture):

West Coast Gansta emphasized skills in the street as much as, if not more than, skills on the mic; ultimately, the need to "Keep it real" blurred the line between business and the streets.

Gangster Rap, Sociological Identifiers:

- **Ethnocentrism**: A pattern of increased hostility toward outgroups accompanied by increased loyalty to one's ingroup.
- **Frustration–aggression hypothesis**: The theory that frustration causes aggression.
- **Actor–observer effect**: The tendency for people to attribute their own behavior to external causes but that of others to internal factors.
- **Aggressive script**: A guide for behavior and problem solving that is developed and stored in a person's memory, and is often characterized by aggression.
- **Anti-conformity**: Opposition to social influence on all occasions, often caused by psychological reaction.

CMW

Straight out of Compton, California, USA, **Compton's Most Wanted**, consisting of leaders MC Eiht and Tha Chill, are pioneers of the West-Coast-Gangsta-Rap-Hip-Hop scene. They can be viewed as a prototype for the group NWA.

- ZOOM OUT (Bi-Coastal Sample Usage): The Notorious B.I.G's "Warning" uses the same sample as "Hood Took Me Under"; both versions sampled Isaac Hayes' "Walk On Bye," (Later used by Jay-Z, and Ludacris.)

MEDIA:

- ❖ Compton's Most Wanted, "Hood Took Me Under," *Music to Driveby*, 1991.
  https://youtu.be/RI2rCOFN43E
- ZOOM OUT: The Notorious B.I.G., "Warning," *Ready To Die*, 1994.
  https://youtu.be/TbSm6HsX_ek

Ruthless Records

Ruthless Records was an American record label founded by Eric "Eazy-E" Wright and Jerry Heller in Compton, California in 1986, where all the Ruthless trademarks have been owned by Comptown Records, Inc. since 1997.

N.W.A.: Niggaz Wit Attitudes

Widely considered as one of the seminal groups of the Gangsta Rap sub-genre, N.W.A. (short for Niggaz Wit Attitudes or Niggaz with Attitude) was a Hip-Hop group from Compton, California. From 1986 to 1991, the group endured controversy due to the explicit nature of their lyrics)and was subsequently banned from many mainstream US radio stations)—and even prevented from touring. Ultimately, the group sold tens of millions of 'units' in the US, alone. The original lineup consisted of Arabian Prince, DJ Yella, Dr. Dre, Eazy-E, Ice Cube and MC Ren. Their debut album Straight Outta Compton marked the beginning of the new Gangsta Rap era (as the production and social commentary in their lyrics were revolutionary within the genre). Associated acts came to include the groups Above the Law, C.I.A., Fila Fresh Crew J. J. Fad, Snoop Dogg and The D.O.C.

EAZY E

Eric Lynn Wright (September 7, 1963–March 26, 1995), better known by his stage name Eazy-E, was an American rapper who performed solo and in the Hip-Hop group N.W.A. Wright was born to Richard and Kathie Wright in Compton, California. After dropping out of high school in the tenth grade, he supported himself primarily by selling drugs before investing in Ruthless Records and becoming a rapper. When Ruthless artists Dr. Dre and Ice Cube wrote "Boyz-n-the-Hood," Dre, Cube and Eazy formed N.W.A.

After DJ Yella, MC Ren, and Arabian Prince joined the group, N.W.A released N.W.A. and the Posse. In 1988, they released their most controversial album, Straight Outta Compton. The group released two more albums and then disbanded after Eazy released Dr. Dre from his contract. Eazy's main influences included 1970s funk groups, contemporary rappers, and comedians. When reviewing Eazy's albums, many critics noted his unique overall style, with Steve Huey of the All Music Guide saying this:

"While his technical skills as a rapper were never the greatest, his distinctive delivery (invariably described as a high-pitched whine), over-the-top lyrics, and undeniable charisma made him a star." On February 24, 1995, Eazy was admitted into Cedars Sinai Medical Center in Los Angeles with what he believed to be asthma but was instead diagnosed with AIDS. Ultimately dying from complications due to the AIDS virus, rumor had it that Eazy was "emotionally-scarred" by the disses from his former homies.

Eazy Duz It: Royalties?

NWA versus Eazy E Beef: Summary

- Jerry Heller- Ex Rock Manager teamed with Eazy E. Eazy 'sold out' and didn't want to split the royalties with the band.
- A 75,000 check was presented to the members of NWA to sign a limited, and biased, contract.
- The botched deal was the beginning of the end for the group.

ZOOM OUT: Above the Law

Above the Law was an American Hip-Hop group from Pomona, California, founded in 1989 by Cold 187um, KMG the Illustrator, Go Mack, and DJ Total K-Oss. *Black Mafia Life was the third album by gangsta rap group Above the Law, released on February 2, 1993; being released after their popular debut Livin' Like Hustlers, Black Mafia Life was a surprising success.*

ICE CUBE

Known professionally as Ice Cube, O'Shea Jackson Sr. is an American rapper. While his political rap solo albums AmeriKKKa's Most Wanted (1990), Death Certificate (1991), and The Predator (1992) were critically and commercially successful, his contribution to the N.W. A 1988 album, Straight Outta Compton, heavily influenced Gangsta Rap's widespread popularity. He has also had and acting film and acting career since the early 1990s. 'Cube' was inducted into the Rock and Roll Hall of Fame as a member of N.W.A in 2016.

MEDIA: Ice Cube versus NWA BEEF (Sequence)

❖ Ice Cube's, "Amerikkka's Most Wanted," *Amerikkka's Most Wanted*, 1990.
  (Goes Gold in just 2 weeks He did not diss NWA on the album; yet they retaliated)
  https://youtu.be/8zK6eHWqjtw
❖ NWA attacks w/"100 Miles and Runnin'," *100 Miles and Runnin (EP)*, 1990.
  https://youtu.be/GiDti_Xnnmo
❖ Ice Cube releases "Jackin' for Beats," *Kill at Will (EP)*, 1990.
  https://youtu.be/k3Vn12rvPfM
❖ NWA retaliates with bigger diss "Real Niggaz," *100 Miles and Runnin (EP)*, 1990.
  https://youtu.be/6-ihjmlTTeA
❖ Ice Cube retaliates with "No Vaseline," *Death Certificate*, 1991.
  https://youtu.be/csm6jilQwcw?t=64

Dr. Dre

Andre Romelle Young, known professionally as Dr. Dre. is an American rapper and record producer. Prior to becoming a founding member of the Gangsta-Rap group NWA, 'Dre' was a singer in the group World Class Wreckin Crew Dr. Dre is the co-founder of Beats Electronics, which was acquired in 2014 for $3.4 billion by technology giant Apple Inc.

Dr. Dre versus Eazy E Beef:

- Dr. Dre finds fault w/NWA, Eazy and the group manager Jerry Heller;
- Dr. Dre started Death Row Records with Marion "Suge" Knight in 1991, upon Dr. Dre's departure from N.W.A.
- Physically threatens Eazy E and Jerry Heller for his release from the binding agreement.
- Dr. Dre is finally released from his contract with Ruthless Records.
- *Eazy Refers to Dr. Dre's World Class Wrecking Crew days, claiming that, "Dr. Dre didn't start hollering, "Compton!" until he joined NWA."*
- Death Row (with Snoop Dogg) versus Eazy E.

MEDIA:

❖ Dr. Dre, "Fuck with Dre Day (And Everybody's Celebratin')," *The Chronic*, 1992.
  https://youtu.be/NbQz5kgKHhA
❖ Eazy E, "Real Muthaphuckkin' G's," *It's on (Dr. Dre) 187 um Killa*, 1993.
  https://youtu.be/fJuapp9SORA

Excerpt from, Eazy E, "Real Muthaphuckkin' G's," 1993: Dresta verse (partial).

"Knowin ya ain't seen no parts of the streets, G.
Think ya tryna bang around the time of the peace treaty."

Death Row Records

Death Row Records is a record label founded in 1991 by Marion "Suge" Knight Jr. and Andre Young (Dr. Dre). Though most of the artists departed from the label after its demise (following the murder of Tupac Shakur in 1996), it was home to many popular West Coast Hip-Hop artists.

MEDIA:

❖ Dr. Dre, "THE UP IN SMOKE TOUR," 2000.
   https://youtu.be/PFSI9nwqPSc
❖ Video from 28:20-44:25.
   https://youtu.be/Kr22KYAMbcI?t=1700
❖ Video from 42:05.
   https://youtu.be/Kr22KYAMbcI?t=2525

-West Coast Succeeds East in Record Sales

- Feuds escalated from battling (as Emcees) to who's crew would prevail in physical combat.
- At the 1995 Soul Train Music Awards, Suge Knight Disses Sean 'Puffy' Combs. Death Row Records (West Coast) and Bad Boy Records (East Coast) clash – ending any possible East-West unity.

Ganster Rap violence aspects: (Hip-Hop conveys positive or negative energy, i.e., the blues)

- Lyrical Content Changed
- More Threatening (i.e., mafia threats)
- Artists come from a rugged point of view
- Streets enter the business
- 50 percent thugs (your crew)
- 50 percent business (including the artist)
- Thugs want stripes to prove their loyalty to the artist.
- Many times, the artist is accused of deeds of the crew or crew member (furthering the complexity of the picture).
- Emotional arousal makes artists take things personally.
- Crews can influence the artist to "react."

The Mid 1990s: Overview

The Media propagandizes Gangsta-Rap; and the West Coast grows weary of being stereotyped.

Notable Peacemakers in Hip-Hop:

- ZULU Nation
- Jim Brown (Ex-NFL; Actor; Activist)
- Russell Simmons

To resolve disputes, peacefully, Farrakan calls for intervention.

Prominent East versus West: Overview

Vibe magazine gets the heat for instigating the WC/EC feud.
Tupac was around the wrong crowd—starts fight with Orlando Anderson—a well known Los Angeles gang member.
Several hours later, Tupac is shot dead in his car (BMW 500 series) just off the Las Vegas strip.
    a. Soldiers (Crew/Thugs) failed at their job, while looting the resources.

Sept 13, 1996 Tupac is killed
March 9, 1997, B.I.G. is killed

- Allure of financial reward influences artist to do anything for the money.
- Most important figures have been killed grievously.

MEDIA:

- ❖ Suge Knight Disses Sean 'Puffy' Combs, 1996.
  https://youtu.be/mv2OMXngkEs?t=29
- ❖ Beef 1, West Coast vs East Coast.
  https://youtu.be/Kr22KYAMbcI?t=2955
- ❖ BIG and TUPAC SPLIT: Tupac Shakur, "Hit 'em Up," 1996
  https://youtu.be/4lqC3w3UUkU

- • ZOOM OUT: TUPAC and B.I.G., *Before the Feud*

- ❖ *Tupac*, "*Runnin*' From Tha' *Police*," (feat. **Notorious B.I.G.**), *Hit Machine 18*, 1995.
  https://youtu.be/H1VKbF3GvjI
- ❖ Biggie and Tupac (2002), Documentary.
  https://youtu.be/UvdXXis291I

Summary:

- We've pushed through the early years of gangster rap. The old generation grew into it, but the new guys came into the business like that.
- 1996 the apex of the east coast-west coast rivalry. Tu-Pac put out a video following the Soul Train Awards called Signaling the 'beginning of the end' of the east coast-west coast feuding. Tupac's Hit '*Em Up* from 1996, a very insulting video (veritably) guaranteed the deaths of Tu-Pac Shakur and The Notorious B.I.G.

TUPAC

Born Lesane Parish Crooks, Tupac is one of the best-selling music artists in the world, with 75 million albums sold to date. 2Pac was born in the East Harlem section of Manhattan in New York City. He was renamed Túpac Amaru II, after the Peruvian revolutionary who led an indigenous uprising against Spain and was subsequently executed. His mother, Afeni Shakur, was an active member of the Black Panther Party in New York in the late 1960s and early 1970s; Shakur was born just one month after her acquittal on more than 150 charges of "Conspiracy against the United States government and New York landmarks" in the New York Panther 21 court case.

He was later shot five times and robbed in the lobby of a recording studio in New York City. Following the event, Shakur grew suspicious that other figures in the rap industry had prior knowledge of the incident and did not warn him; the controversy helped spark the East Coast–West Coast Hip-Hop rivalry. On the night of September 7, 1996, Shakur was shot four times in a drive-by shooting in the Las Vegas metropolitan area in Nevada. He died six days later of respiratory failure and cardiac arrest at the University Medical Center.

MEDIA:

❖ Tupac, "Keep Ya Head Up," *Strictly 4 My N.I.G.G.A.Z*, 1993.
   https://youtu.be/XW--IGAfeas
• ZOOM OUT (Sample Source): Zapp, "Be Alright," *ZAPP*, 1980.
   https://youtu.be/UvZAt7VnJls
• ZOOM OUT: *Look for Me in the Whirlwind: From the Panther 21 to 21st-Century Revolutions*, contains rare poetry and prose from Afeni Shakur (Tupac's Mother).

E-40

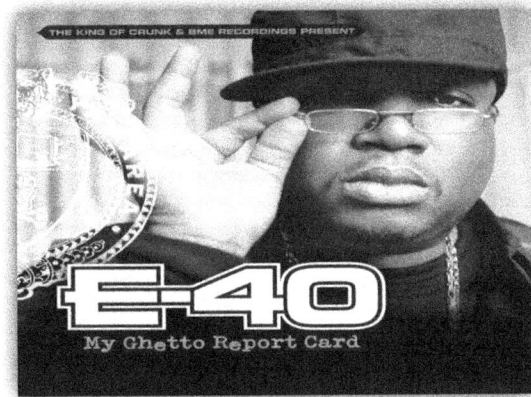

Earl Tywone Stevens Sr., better known by his stage name E-40, is an American rapper. He is a founding member of the rap group the Click, and the founder of Sick Wid It Records.

COMMON

Lonnie Rashid Lynn, Jr. (born March 13, 1972), better known by his stage name Common (previously Common Sense) is an American Hip-Hop artist and actor. He debuted in 1992 with the album, Can I Borrow a Dollar? and maintained a significant underground following into the late 1990s, after which he gained notable mainstream success through his work with the Soulquarians. His first major-label album, Like Water for Chocolate, received widespread critical acclaim and tremendous commercial success His first Grammy award was in 2003 for Best R&B Song for "Love of My Life (An Ode to Hip-Hop)" with Erykah Badu. Its popularity was matched by May 2005's Be, which was nominated in the 2006 Grammy Awards for Best Rap Album. Common was awarded his second Grammy for Best Rap Performance by a Duo or Group, for "Southside" (featuring Kanye West), from his July 2007 album Finding Forever. His best-of album, Thisisme Then: The Best of Common, was released on November 27, 2007.
Common versus Westside Connection (Ice Cube)

- In 1994 he wrote "I used to love her," talking about Hip-Hop as a metaphor: "She" comes out to the West Coast and ends up with a pimp.
- West Coast rappers didn't like that he implied that the "Gangsta" style ruined Hip-Hop.
- WestSide Connection with Ice Cube picked up and responded saying "why are you dissing the West Coast," came out with a Diss Video called "The WestSide Slaughterhouse," a diss directed at Common.
- Transcending his normally conscious style, Common fires back with the single, "Tha Bitch in Yoo."

Two Ways in which the media propagandizes information: **Instigation and Publicity**

MEDIA:

❖ Common Vs. WestSide Connection.
 https://youtu.be/9H8DbHyaapA

NELLY

Cornell Iral Haynes Jr., better known by his stage name Nelly, is an American rapper, singer, and entrepreneur. He embarked on his music career with the Midwest Hip-Hop group St. Lunatics in 1993. Nelly signed to Universal Records in 1999.

MEDIA:

❖ Nelly, "Hot In Herre," *Nellyville*, 2002.
 https://g.co/kgs/dhC6Nz
❖ Krs-One versus Nelly.
 https://youtu.be/3jVxBPHUpH8?t=2960

Bone Thugs-N-Harmony

Bone Thugs-N- Harmony (aka B.O.N.E. Enterprises) is an American Hip-Hop group from Cleveland, OH, USA, consisting of rappers Bizzy Bone, Wish Bone, Layzie Bone, Krayzie Bone and Flesh-n-Bone. The group was signed to Ruthless Records in late 1993, when they debuted with their EP Creepin on ah Come Up. The EP included their break-out hit single "Thuggish Ruggish Bone." Associated Acts are Eazy E, Mariah Carey, Twista, and Snoop Dogg.

MEDIA:

❖ Bone Thugs and Harmony, "Tha Crossroads," *E. 1999 Eternal*, 1995.
   https://youtu.be/WRGzLl1DTqo

• ZOOM OUT (Sample Source):

• The Isley Brothers, "Make Me Say It Again Girl," *The Heat Is On*, 1975.
   https://youtu.be/SHH_EMeRjGA

The Dayton Family

The Dayton Family is an American Hip-Hop group from Flint, Michigan, composed of Ira "Bootleg" Dorsey, Raheen "Shoestring" Peterson and Matt "Backstabba" Hinkle. The group's name is derived from the infamous 'Dayton Street'—one of *Flint's* most crime-ridden streets..

Priority Records

Priority Records is an American record label, owned and operated by EMI, which has made a name for itself dealing primarily in Hip-Hop, pop and world music. Priority has also provided distribution for other labels such as Rap-A-Lot Records, Ruthless Records, Death Row Records, Wu-Tang Records, Rawkus Records, No Limit Records, Roc-A-Fella Records, Scarface Records, Black Market Records, Rhythm Safari and Tass Radio Records.

Snoop Dogg

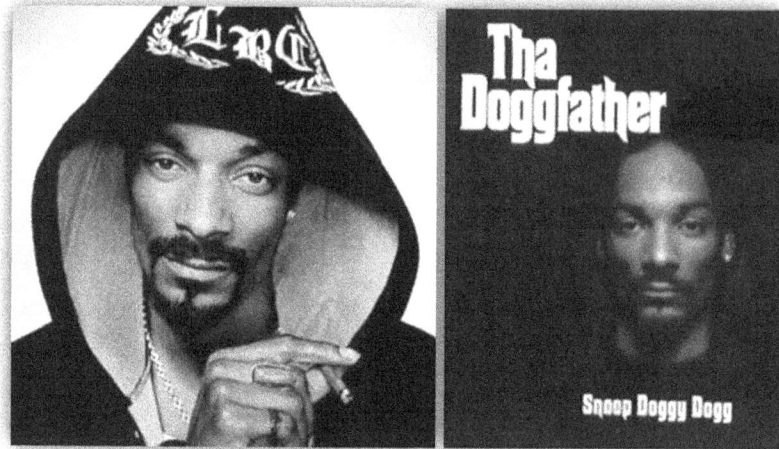

Calvin Cordozar Broadus, Jr. (born October 20, 1971), better known by his stage name Snoop Dogg, is an American rapper, singer, record producer and actor. Snoop is best known as a rapper in the West Coast Hip-Hop scene (and for being one of Dr. Dre's most notable protégés). In 1994, Snoop released a soundtrack on Death Row Records for the short film Murder Was the Case, starring himself. His second album,Tha Doggfather, also debuted at No.1, with the single, "Snoop's Upside Ya Head" being certified double platinum in 1997. Tha Doggfather was his last release for Death Row before he signed with No Limit Records (releasing his next three albums). Snoop Dogg signed with Priority/Capitol/ EMI Records in 2002—signing with Geffen Records in 2004. In recent decades (in addition to maintaining a legendary status as a rapper) Snoop Dogg has starred in motion pictures and hosted several television shows. Associated acts include groups such as Tha Dogg Pound, Dr. Dre, Nate Dogg, 2Pac, Ice Cube, 50 Cent, Eminem and Wiz Khalifa.

MEDIA:

❖ Snoop Dogg, "Gin and Juice," *Doggystyle*, 1993.
　https://g.co/kgs/2tfAkU
❖ Snoop Dogg, "Blueberry," *Tha Doggfather*, 1996.
　https://youtu.be/q-LKGzFWE84

DJ QUIK

David Martin Blake was born on January 18, 1970 in Compton, California is better known by his stage name DJ Quik. He is an MC and record producer, and was chiefly inspired by funk and soul artists, such as Roger Troutman and George Clinton. David's love for music began at 2 years old. By the age of 12, he was already playing instruments. By age 21, David was a platinum-selling artist.

MEDIA:

❖ DJ Quik, "Tonite," *Quik is the Name,* 1991.
   https://youtu.be/WWSLM2lFjvg

ICE T

Tracy Lauren Marrow, better known by his stage name Ice-T, is an American rapper, songwriter, actor, and producer born in Newark, New Jersey, USA. He grew up in Crenshaw, Los Angeles, California, and began his career as an underground rapper in the 1980s. Releasing his debut album, *Rhyme Pays, he*, was signed to Sire Records in 1987. Before his major role debut, starring as police detective Scotty Appleton in the film *New Jack City* (1991), Ice-T played small parts in several films during the 1980s. Since 2000, he has portrayed NYPD Detective/Sergeant Odafin Tutuola on the NBC police drama *Law and Order: Special Victims Unit.*

MEDIA:

❖ Ice T, "Ain't New Ta This," *Home Invasion*, 1993.
  https://youtu.be/el19D6zhoRk
❖ Ice T, "Mixed Up," *Home Invasion*, 1993.
  https://youtu.be/nZqpFbnJi0s

SUGA FREE

Dejuan Rice (born January 17, 1970), better known by his stage name Suga Free, is an American rapper from Pomona, California. Suga Free was born in Oakland and raised in Compton, later becoming based in Pomona, California.

He began his professional rapping career working with DJ Quik, with Quik serving as the producer on his debut album, Street Gospel, released in 1997, which reached number 27 on the Billboard R&B albums chart. He made guest appearances on Xzibit's Restless and Snoop Dogg's Tha Last Meal in 2000, and released a second album in 2004, The New Testament, which peaked at number 23 on the R&B albums chart and number 72 on the Billboard 200. Just Add Water followed in 2006, described by Allmusic: "Just Add Water may not be the complete handbook to being a pimp, but it certainly is a kind of missive on the life of Suga Free." The album was described as "charismatic and funny, with a rapid- fire-yet-conversational style".

Digital Underground:

Digital Underground was an American Hip-Hop group from Oakland, California. Gregory "Shock G" Jacobs (also known as Humpty Hump) formed the group in 1987 with Jimi "Chopmaster J" and Kenneth "Kenny-K" Waters. Heavily influenced by the various funk bands of the 1970s, Digital Underground became a defining sound of West Coast rap (and is notable for launching the career of Tupac Shakur and [singer] Mystic).

MEDIA:

❖ Digital Underground, "Kiss You Back," *Sons of the P*, 1991.
  https://youtu.be/OIXQk0Uej-Y

WEST COAST DIRTY RAP
TOO $HORT

Todd Anthony Shaw, born April, 1966, is better known by his stage name: Too Short (stylized as Too $hort). With lyrics often based on pimping, promiscuity, drug culture and street survival, he is an American rapper and record producer who became famous in the West Coast Hip-Hop scene of the late 1980s. Associated acts include artists such as Ant Banks, Lil' Jon, E-40, Travis Porter, George Clinton, Wiz Khalifa, and Cee-Lo Green.

MEDIA:

❖ Notorious B.I.G. "The World is Filled" (feat. Too $hort and Puff Daddy), *Life After Death*, 1997.
  https://youtu.be/9X7izkqRLxs
❖ Ant Banks, "4 tha Hustlas (feat. Too $hort, 2Pac and M.C. Breed)," *Big Thangs*, 1997.
  https://youtu.be/KcxMztIAmUI
❖ Too $hort "Six Figga Niggas" (feat. Jay-Z), 2006.
  https://youtu.be/HhEUpys6wGo

BEEF: PART II

A generation of MC's that don't know the line between the streets and the business: "Raised on BEEF"

50 Cent

Curtis James Jackson III, known professionally as 50 Cent, is an American rapper, actor, and businessman. Known for his impact in the Hip-Hop industry, he has been described as a "master of the nuanced art of lyrical brevity." He made his name by battling and dissing dozens of artists who took his disses seriously. Fortuitously, he even dissed Jay-Z, who responded with the hook, "I'm about dollars; who the fuck is 50 Cent?"—validating 50 Cent as a rapper to be contended with.

50 Cent versus Murder Inc: Summary

a. 50's biggest challenge
b. Ja Rule (main nemesis)
c. The 'Beef' was based on 50's association with a person who robbed Ja Rule.
d. Each crew accuses the other of not being Hustlas/Ganstas, or not having street cred.
e. Black Child (BC) of Murder Inc. stabs 50 Cent in a brawl at the studio, The Hit Factory, NYC.
f. 50 pressed charges; and Black Child is arrested.

- BC emasculates 50 Cent publicly about the order of protection
- 50 Cent denied it; but it was later proven to be true as per court records

MEDIA:

❖ 50 Cent vs. Ja Rule Beef.
   https://youtu.be/DxNrXdcQHNs

Other Notable Beefs

- Cypress Hill vs. Westside Connection
- Foxy Brown vs. Lil Kim
- Canibus vs. LLCool Jay
- Jermaine Dupree vs. Dr. Dre
- Jay Z vs. Mobb Deep
- DMX vs. Ja Rule
- Benzino vs. Eminem

Jay Z versus Nas: Summary

MEDIA:

❖ In the first round of disses in 2001 Jay-Z came out with the track "Takeover" (dissing Nas).
   https://youtu.be/Aht7DVRRNiQ
❖ In the second round of disses in 2002, Nas fired back with H to the OMO
   (Jay-Z Freestyle Diss) used Eric B and Rakim's "Paid in Full" beat.
   http://www.youtube.com/watch?v=9gYPipNBcLs
❖ Jay-Z responded with "Supa Ugly" (dissing Nas).
   https://youtu.be/6geZaShQZiQ
❖ Nas responded with "Ether" (dissed Jay-Z).
   https://youtu.be/zfyQ8muKLdc

   - *Beef between Jay-Z and NAS elevated the entire game.*
   - *Because they lived thru BIG and TUPAC, they are savvier—with a more worldly mentality regarding the effect of their actions upon others; and beefs are resolved on recordings.*

The Game

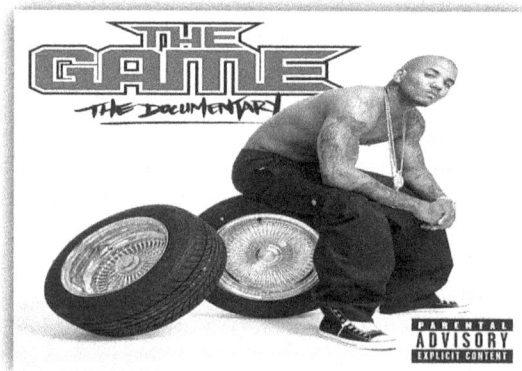

Jayceon Terrell Taylor, better known by his stage name The Game (aka 'Game'), is an American rapper. Born in Compton, California, he initially released a series of mixtapes under the wing of fellow West Coast rapper JT the Bigga Figga. After releasing his debut independent album Untold Story in 2004, he was discovered and signed to Dr. Dre's *Aftermath Records* label.

Chapter 27

BEATS AND RHYMES AND BEYOND

Jada Kiss argues that most violent lyrics are for entertainment and should not be taken literally, much like action movies are accepted as fantasy.

Dr. Beverly Guy-Shefthall states, "Generally speaking, Black people do not believe that misogyny, sexism and violence against women are urgent issues."

Media educator—Sut Jhally—suggests that, "Hip-Hop culture is not separate from the rest of American culture ... the objectified female bodies are everywhere."

Chuck D. argues that instead of challenging the notion that black male violence is natural, the industries that produce popular culture exploit the stories and images of black death—for profit.

Professor Jelani Cobb argues that "music videos have taken a view of women of color that is not radically different from the views of 19th century white slave owners."

"The notion of violent masculinity is at the heart of American identity"—Michael Eric Dyson.

"We have trusted the media and the corporations to define what Hip-Hop is.... We have never let the media define us, so why are we doing that now?"—Brooklyn-bred Hip-Hop artist, Talib Kweli.

"We're playing a role from the time we're seven and we're walk-ing down the street and someone calls us a sissy, sucker, church boy, and we start playing that [tough]role."—Rev. Conrad Tillard.

Associated Definitions:

- **Fantasy:** the faculty or activity of imagining things that are impossible or improbable.
- **False misogyny:** Contextual or Lexicon based misogyny.
- **Homoerotic:** sexual desire centered on a person of the same sex.
- **Homophobia:** an extreme and irrational aversion to homosexuality and homosexual people.

Summary:

• American culture, at its very historical core, is hyper-violent and hyper-masculine.
• Violence is so much a part of American culture that we have become desensitized to it. It is found not only in rap music, but across the culture in movies, sports, video games and the real-world politics of militarism and war.
• Rap also grew out of a long tradition of male boasting in African American culture, a tradition of boys and men fighting for respect by projecting and proclaiming their own power and ability while simultaneously denigrating other men.
• This societal neglect is itself a form of violence in America—a systematic, structural form of violence historically directed at poor people.
• Hip-Hop and rap were born out of poverty, created in what Kevin Powell calls urban "war zones," cityscapes torn apart by neglectful and abusive government policies.
• This vision of violent masculinity is not found only in rap music. In fact, it is a longstanding and central part of American culture and American identity.
• The ability to use words skillfully and aggressively is central to being masculine in the Hip-Hop world, as is the ability to survive the violence that is so much a part of young, poor, and working-class men's lives.
• Michael Eric Dyson points to the early years of America, the expansion of the frontier, and the way guns were equated with manhood and the ability to protect and care for one's family. Guns in American culture are in fact a standard symbol of masculinity.

Chapter 28

NEO-SOUL

Overview:

Every genre we've talked about (Rhythm and Blues, Soul, Funk, Jazz, Hip-Hop, and so on) has fed into the development of Neo-Soul. The sound of Neo-Soul is part of the progression of Hip-Hop—and we will witness a return to live instrumentation. It is a mix of values between electronic music and live musicians; and that's what makes it such a unique and important genre in the evolution of CBUM.

Let's discuss some of the artists who do it best: Erykah Badu, D'Angelo, Maxwell, and Angie Stone.

Erykah Badu

Erica Abi Wright (born February 26, 1971), is better known by her stage name Erykah Badu (pronounced /ˈɛrɪkə bɑːˈduː/), is an American singer–songwriter, record producer and actress. Her work includes elements from R&B, Hip-Hop and jazz. She is best known for her role in the rise of the neo-soul sub-genre, and for her eccentric, cerebral musical stylings and sense of fashion. She is known as the "First Lady of Neo-Soul" or the "Queen of Neo-Soul." Early in her career, Badu was recognizable for wearing very large and colorful headwraps. For her musical sensibilities, she has often been compared to jazz great Billie Holiday. She was a core member of Soulquarians.

Jill Scott

Jill Scott (born April 4, 1972) is an American soul and R&B singer–songwriter, poet, and actress. In 2007, Scott made her cinematic debut in the films Hounddog (as Big Mama Thornton) and in Tyler Perry's feature film, Why Did I Get Married? That year, her third studio album, The Real Thing: Words and Sounds Vol. 3, was released on September 25, 2007. She has won numerous Grammy Awards.

D'Angelo

Michael Eugene Archer (born February 11, 1974), better known by his stage name D'Angelo, is an American R&B and neo-soul singer-songwriter, multi-instrumentalist and record producer. He is known for his production and songwriting talents as much as for his vocal abilities, and often draws comparisons to his influences, Marvin Gaye, and Prince. D'Angelo was one of the most influential artists during the rise of the neo-soul movement. Associated acts include groups such as Soulquarians, Questlove, Raphael Saadiq, The RH Factor, Common, and De La Soul.

Maxwell

Gerald Maxwell Rivera, known as Maxwell. from Brooklyn, New York, USA is an American R&B, funk and neo-soul musician. He played an important role in the development of the soul sub-genre, Neo-Soul. Maxwell's debut album, "*Urban Hang Suite*," was released in 1996. Heavily inspired by the sound of classic soul music, Maxwell's Urban Hang Suite did not catch on with audiences until the release of the second single, "Ascension (Don't Ever Wonder)," which became a hit. Maxwell's "Urban Hang Suite" would go on to sell over 2,000,000 copies, earning 2X platinum status and was nominated for a Grammy Award.

Angie Stone

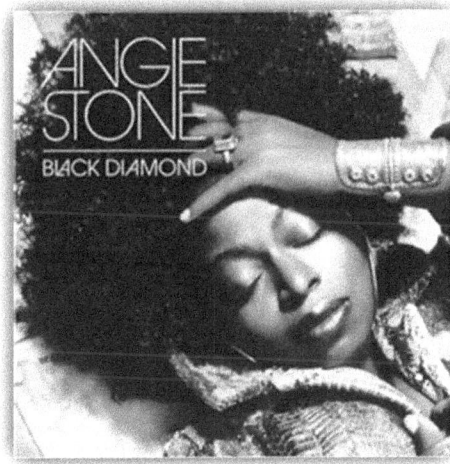

Angie Stone, was born in Columbia, South Carolina, USA. She is an American R&B and soul singer–songwriter, and record producer. Angie Stone has been nominated for three Grammy Awards; but has been more successful on the R&B charts, with numerous Top 10 albums, and has sold millions of albums in US and internationally. Associated acts include groups such as The Sequence, Vertical Hold, Mantronix, Devox, Joss Stone and Anthony Hamilton.

Fun Facts:

Before she was Angie Stone, she was Angela Laverne Brown in a band named *Sequence.*

Around the time that the Sugar Hill Gang came out with "Rapper's Delight," the label (Sugar Hill Records) picked up Sequence's hit single, "Funk You Up" (1980)—the first all-female rap group on the record label.

Soulquarians

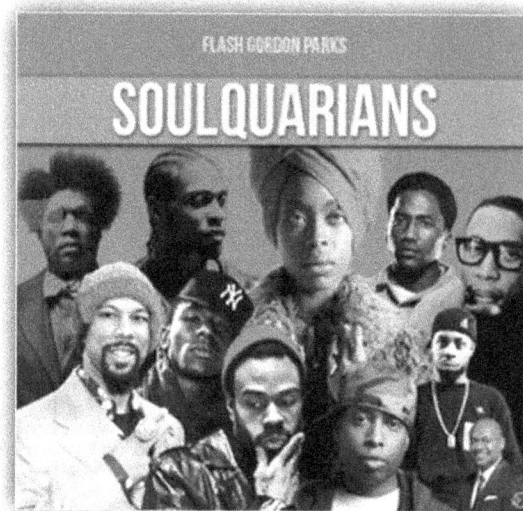

Soulquarians is a neo soul and Hip-Hop-informed musical collective with members Erykah Badu (Dallas),D'Angelo (Richmond),James Poyser (Philadelphia), Mos Def (New York City),Q-Tip (New York City), Talib Kweli (New York City) Pino Palladino (Cardiff) and J Dilla (Detroit) (deceased). The collective formed during the late 1990s, continuing into the early 2000s, and produced several well-received albums. Before its formation, members Common, Talib Kweli, Mos Def and Q-Tip were members of the Native Tongues Posse.

Producer and drummer Ahmir "Questlove" Thompson of Hip-Hop band The Roots acted as the "musical power-house" behind several of the collective's projects during the late 1990s and early 2000s, including The Roots' Things Fall Apart (1999), D'Angelo's Voodoo (2000), Erykah Badu's Mama's Gun (2000), and Common's Like Water for Chocolate (2000). Associated acts Blackalicious, Dave Chappelle, Cee-Lo, Cody ChesnuTT, Musiq Soulchild, Vinia Mojica, OutKast, Karriem Riggins, The Roots, Raphael Saadiq, Jill Scott, Slum Village, The Soultronics, A Tribe Called Quest and Zap Mama.

Chapter 29

UNDERGROUND HIP-HOP

Underground Hip-Hop is an umbrella term for Hip-Hop music outside the general commercial canon. It is typically associated with independent artists, signed to independent labels or no label at all. Underground Hip-Hop is often characterized by socially conscious, positive, or anti-commercial lyrics. However, there is no unifying or universal theme—Allmusic suggests that it "has no sonic signifiers." "The Underground" also refers to the community of musicians, fans and others that support non-commercial, or independent music. Some underground Hip-Hop is also sometimes known as alternative Hip-Hop. It is important to note that many artists who are considered "underground" today, were not always so—possibly having previously broken the Billboard charts.

J Dilla

James Dewitt Yancey better known by the stage names J Dilla and Jay Dee, and Dilla Dawg was an American Grammy Nominated record producer who emerged from the mid-1990s underground Hip-Hop scene in Detroit, Michigan. According to his obituary at NPR.org, he "was one of the music industry's most influential Hip-Hop artists, working for big-name acts like De La Soul, Busta Rhymes and Common." Other associated acts include Phat Kat, The Ummah, Slum Village, Guilty Simpson, A Tribe Called Quest, Kanye West, Soulquarians, Royce Da 5'9, Frank-n-Dank, The Roots, Proof, Pete Rock, Busta Rhymes, Mos Def, Erykah Badu, Jaylib, Talib Kweli, Raekwon, Madlib, The Pharcyde, and Janet Jackson.

Percee P

Percee P (born John Percy Simon) is a Hip-Hop artist from the Patterson Projects in The Bronx, New York City, United States. Though his debut commercial album *Perseverance* was not released until September 18, 2007 (produced by Madlib), Percee P has been writing and performing since 1979. He was known within the 'underground' community of artists and fans for selling his mixtapes in front of the *Fat Beats* store in New York City (a practice he continues today by selling his Stones Throw albums and his other mixtapes at his shows).

Chapter 30

CONSCIOUS COMMERCIAL

Madlib

Madlib (Mind Altering Demented Lessons in Beats) (born Otis Jackson Jr. on October 24, 1973 in Oxnard, California, United States) is a Grammy nominated California-based DJ, multi-instrumentalist, rapper, and music producer. Known under a plethora of pseudonyms, he is one of the most prolific and critically acclaimed Hip-Hop producers of the 2000s. Having influenced a generation of producers and musicians, Madlib has described himself as, "DJ first, Producer, second, and Emcee, last."

Jaylib–Champion Sound

Champion Sound is a studio album by the duo Jaylib (Hip-Hop musicians J Dilla and Madlib). Half of the songs are produced by Madlib and feature J Dilla on vocals, and the other half are produced by J Dilla and feature Madlib on vocals. This album was the first of the Madlib duo collaboration albums made during the 2000s on the Stones Throw record label. The album was released in October of 2003.

Madvillain

Madvillain is a Hip-Hop group consisting of MF DOOM (MC/producer) and Madlib (MC/producer). Their debut album Madvillainy was met with wide critical acclaim for its unique approach—short songs, obscure lyrics, few choruses and a sound which was generally unfriendly to commercial radio.

MF DOOM

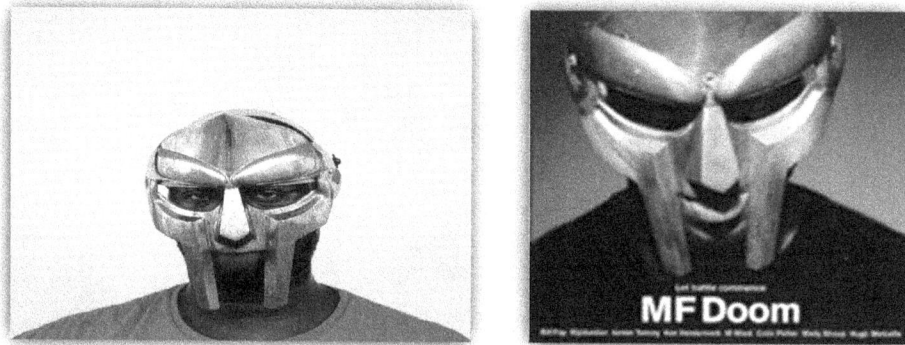

Daniel Dumile, best known by his stage name MF Doom or simply Doom (seen here wearing his symbolic Kifwebe [Songye] mask), was a British American rapper and record producer from Long Island, New York, United States. Noted for his intricate wordplay, signature metal mask, and "supervillain" stage persona, Noted for his intricate wordplay, signature metal mask, and "supervillain" stage persona, Dumile became a major figure of underground and alternative Hip-Hop. Associated acts include Ghostface Killah, Wu-Tang Clan, Madvillain (with Madlib), Danger Mouse and Cee-Lo Green.

MEDIA:

❖ J Dilla, "Take Notice," *Ruff Draft*, 2003.
https://youtu.be/UjWtTmLY4OU

• ZOOM OUT (Sample Source): Peter Bauman, Romance '76, *Phase By Phase*
https://youtu.be/pnWLzU_RuRE

❖ Jaylib, "The Exclusive," *Champion Sound*, 2003.
https://youtu.be/ammzSxTPzpo

❖ Jaylib, "No Games," (Feat. Percee P), *Champion Sound*, 2003.
https://youtu.be/DRaVKKykOwM

❖ Madvillain, *Madvillainy* (Full Album) 2004.
https://youtu.be/WffJfQPp7kE

❖ Percee P, "Last of The Greats" (Feat. Prince Po), *Perserverance*, 2007.
https://youtu.be/98vcQsWpuaE

Talib Kweli

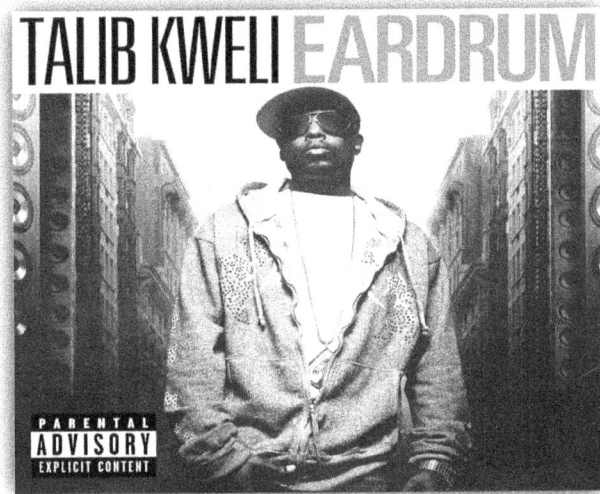

Talib Kweli Greene (/tæˈlɪb kwɑːˈliː/) is an American rapper. He earned recognition early on through his collaboration with fellow Brooklyn rapper Mos Def in 1997, when they formed the group Black Star. Kweli's musical career continued with solo success including collaborations with producers and rappers Kanye West, Just Blaze, and Pharrell Williams. His most recent album is titled Gotham, released in 2020. In 2011, Kweli founded his own record label, Javotti Media.

Mos Def

Dante Terrell Smith-Bey, from Bedford-Stuyvesant, Brooklyn, New York City, also known as Yasiin Bey, but more commonly as Mos Def, is an American rapper, singer, songwriter, and actor. He began his professional music career in 1994, alongside his siblings in the short-lived rap group Urban Thermo Dynamics—after which they appeared on albums by Da Bush Babees and De La Soul. Associated acts include Soulquarians, Black Star, Talib Kweli, Native Tongues Posse, Kanye West, The Roots, Common and K'naan.

Black Star

Black Star is a heralded Hip-Hop collaboration between Yasiin Bey (also known as Mos Def) and Talib Kweli.

NAS

Nasir bin Olu Dara Jones, from Queens, New York, better known by his stage name Nas, is an American rapper. The son of jazz musician Olu Dara, Nas is regarded as one of the greatest rappers of all time. Having adopted the moniker of "Nasty Nas," his musical career began in 1989 recording demos for the rapper Large Professor. Associated acts include Sean Combs, The Firm, The Game, Group Therapy, Jay-Z, Kool G Rap, Mobb Deep, Damian Marley and Raekwon.

MEDIA:

❖ Nas, "It Ain't Hard To Tell," *Illmatic*, 1994.
  https://youtu.be/3hOZaTGnHU4
❖ Mos Def, "Black on Both Sides," *Mathematics*, 1999.
  https://youtu.be/PwK1WkmOeZE
❖ Madlib, "Distant Land," *Shades of Blue*, 2003.
  https://youtu.be/EQcuwVLx01o
❖ MF Doom, "Camphor," *Special Herbs Volumes 7&8*, 2004.
  https://youtu.be/XIaAewzL3aM
❖ Madvillain, "Curls," *Madvilliany*, 2004.
  https://youtu.be/tv2q9vQ7GOI
❖ Talib Qweli, "We Got The Beat," *Beautiful Struggle*, 2004.
  https://youtu.be/5Fsg3lXuNHc
❖ Nas, "Street's Disciple," *Street's Disciple*, 2004.
  https://youtu.be/TmM4oGRzLVU

Chapter 31

SOUTHERN EXPOSURE: "STREET FAME"

Scarface

After releasing the 12" single "Scarface," he would go on to sign with Rap-A-Lot Records and join the group Geto Boys, replacing a member and releasing the group's second album Grip It! On That Other Level (1989), a highly successful album that garnered the group a large fanbase, despite their violent lyrics keeping them from radio and MTV. He took his stage name from the 1983 film Scarface. In addition to his career as a rapper, Scarface has also been the coordinator and president of Def Jam South since 2000, where he has fostered the career of popular rapper Ludacris, whom he originally signed to the label.

MEDIA:

❖ Scarface, "The Diary," *Scarface*, 1994.
  https://youtu.be/yzbq9CGdqjY
❖ Scarface and the Geto Boys, "Mind Playing Tricks on Me," *We Cant Be Stopped*, 1991.
  https://youtu.be/IJtHdkyo0hc

ZOOM OUT:

• Ron Westray, "Gemini," *Gemini*, 2018.
  https://traydeuce1.bandcamp.com/track/gemini

UGK

UGK (short for Underground Kingz) was an American hip hop duo from Port Arthur, Texas, formed in 1987, by Chad "Pimp C" Butler and Bernard "Bun B" Freeman. They released their first major-label album Too Hard to Swallow, in 1992, followed by several other albums charting on the Billboard 200 and Top R&B/Hip-Hop Albums charts, including the self-titled Underground Kingz album, which debuted at number one on the Billboard 200, in August 2007. Associated acts include DJ Screw, Paul Wall, Three 6 Mafia, 8Ball & MJG, Slim Thug, Outkast and Jay-Z.

MEDIA:

❖ UGK, "Pocket Full of Stones," *Too Hard To Swallow, 1993.*
   https://youtu.be/MnP1XmxyqxA

Ludacris

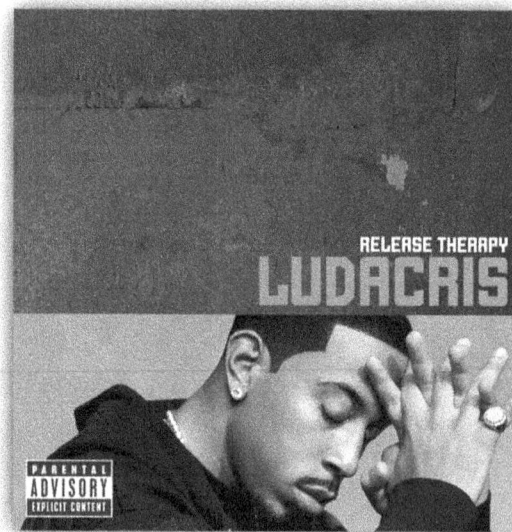

Christopher Brian "Chris" Bridges (born September 11, 1977) better known by his stage name Ludacris, is an American Hip-Hop recording artist and actor from Atlanta, Georgia. Along with fellow Atlanta-based rappers Big Boi and Andre 3000 of Outkast, Ludacris was one of the first and most influential "Dirty South" rappers to achieve mainstream success during the early 2000s.

MEDIA:

❖ Ludacris, "Undisputed," *Theater Of The Mind*, 2008.
  https://youtu.be/1ewTjHCND-w

LITTLE BROTHER

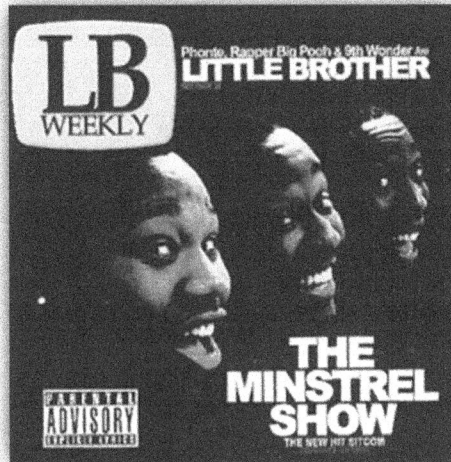

Little Brother is an American alternative Hip-Hop group from Durham, North Carolina, composed of artists Phonte (Phonte Coleman), Big Pooh (Thomas Jones) and DJ 9th Wonder (Pat Douthit). The group produced four acclaimed studio albums and six mixtapes during their nine-years existence. The official debut for Little Brother came in August 2001 with their first recording, "Speed." In 2003, the group released their first full length studio album, *The Listening*, to critical acclaim. National recognition for the group, and particularly DJ 9th Wonder, came when rapper Jay-Z tapped in for the song "Threat."

MEDIA:

❖ Little Brother, "Lovin' It," *The Minstrel Show*, 2005.
  https://youtu.be/q-qg2Q_zxFQ

TIMBALAND

Emanating from Norfolk, Virginia, Timothy Zachery Mosley a.k.a DJ Timmy a.k.a. T/Timbo, Timbaland began his producing career strictly for R&B acts. In the early- to mid-1990s he produced a few songs for R&B acts such as Jodeci and Sista. His trademark sound was very much rooted in Hip-Hop with its fast-paced nature and clear drum breaks. Timbaland's clean, electronic and non-sample-based productions were something very new to Hip-Hop audiences. Amid numerous Grammy Awards and Nominations, he was named Producer of the Year in 2007, and Songwriter of the Year in 2008.

Goodie Mob

Goodie Mob is an American Hip-Hop group based in Atlanta, Georgia. It was formed in 1991 by Big Gipp, Khujo, CeeLo Green and T-Mo. In 1995, Goodie Mob released their debut album, Soul Food, which was critically acclaimed and certified Gold.

MEDIA:

❖ Goodie Mob, "Cell Therapy," *Soul Food*, 1995.
  https://youtu.be/6Uh5-Pz_pe0

OutKast

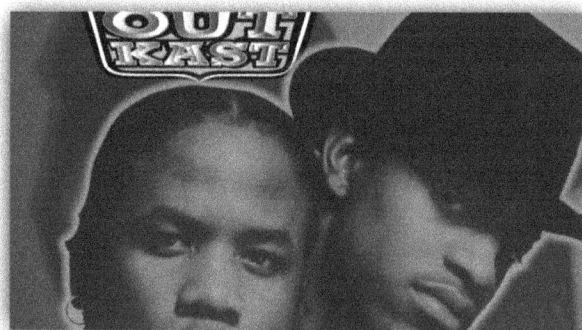

OutKast is an American Hip-Hop duo formed in 1991, in East Point, Atlanta, Georgia. Composed of Atlanta-based rappers André "André 3000" Benjamin (Formerly known as Dré) and Antwan "Big Boi" Patton, the duo achieved both critical acclaim and commercial success in the 1990s and early 2000s–popularizing Southern Hip-Hop, creating distinctive alter-egos, and experimenting with diverse genres such as funk, psychedelia, techno and gospel.

MEDIA:

❖ Outkast, "Southernplayalisticadillacmuzik," *Southernplayalisticadillacmuzik*, 1994.
  https://youtu.be/RIaDSpLpbg4

T. I.

Clifford Joseph Harris, Jr., formely known as T.I. Kawan, is an American rapper and actor. The record executive "KP" Prather discovered and signed him while he was still a teenager. Upon signing with Arista Records' subsidiary, LaFace Records, in 2001, he shortened his name to T.I. His second album *Trap Muzik*, which was released through Grand Hustle Records, debuted at number four and sold over 100,000 copies in the first week.

MEDIA:

❖ T.I. versus Lil' Flip.
   https://youtu.be/9C75vvApo-o?t=2502

Rick Ross

William Leonard Roberts II (born January 28, 1976), known professionally as Rick Ross, is an American rapper. In 2005, alongside fellow Florida rappers Gunplay and Torch, Ross was a lead member of the group *Triple C's*. He signed a multi-million-dollar deal with Jay Z on Def Jam Recordings in 2006. Later that year, debuting at the top spot on the U.S. Billboard album chart, Ross released his debut album *Port of Miami*. He released his second studio album, *Trilla*, in 2008 (again debuting atop the *Billboard* 200). Ross founded the record label Maybach Music Group in 2009, and has released ten studio albums, including, *God Forgives*, I Don't, which includes artists such as rappers Future, Wale, and singer Jazmine Sullivan, Other prominent industry acts that have also been signed to Rick Ross through the Maybach Music label, include, among others, Meek Mill, and French Montana.

MEDIA:

❖ Rick Ross, "Rich Off Cocaine," *Deeper Than Rap*, 2009.
    https://youtu.be/BGYmm_CQ3r4

Lil Boosie

Torence Ivy Hatch (born November 14, 1982), better known by his stage name Boosie BadAzz or simply Boosie (formerly Lil Boosie), is an American rapper. Hatch began rapping in the 1990s as a member of the Hip-Hop collective Concentration Camp with rapper C-Loc. He made his debut on C-Loc's fifth album, It's A Gamble, and eventually pursued a solo career in 2000 with the release of his debut album Youngest of da Camp. After leaving the label the following year, he signed with Pimp C's Trill Entertainment to release his second studio album, For My Thugz (2002). One of the most prominent figures of Southern Hip-Hop, Hatch has gone on to release seven solo studio albums, as well as six collaborative albums and scores of mixtapes.

MEDIA:

❖ Lil Boosie "I'm That Nigga Now" (feat. Quick), *BooPac*, 2011.
    https://youtu.be/agNhRBM-PSQ

Webbie

Originally from Baton Rouge, Louisiana, USA, Webster Gradney, a.k.a. Webbie was signed to the independent Trill Entertainment label from 2003 to 2005. In 2005 he came into the Hip-Hop scene with "Gimme That" featuring Bun B. His songs "Bad Bitch" and "Swerve" were featured on Gangsta Musik, his 2003 group album with Lil Boosie, and in the 2005 movie Hustle & Flow. Webbie's second album, Savage Life 2, was released in the fall 2008 with the hit single "Independent" featuring Lil Boosie and Lil Phat. Trill began a deal to sign Webbie to the Warner Bros. Records subsidiary label Atlantic Records. He was signed there, and his major-label debut Savage Life was released in 2005, debuting at number 8 on the Billboard 200 chart.

Juicy J

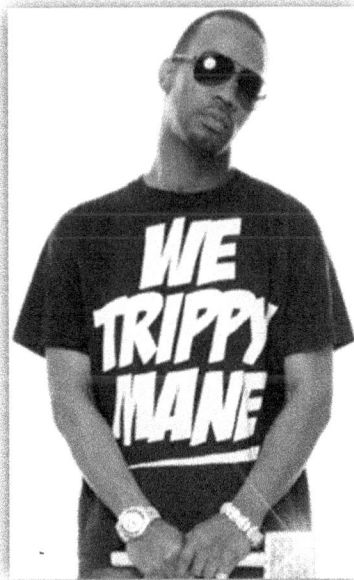

Originally from Memphis, Tennessee, Jordan Houston, otherwise known as Juicy J, is most notable for his crunk style of rapping, highlighted by his patented "heavy-breathing" and "stomping" background sound effects. Juicy J's production style is characterized by fast-rolling high hats, sharp snares and deep cinematic bass. He also incorporates samples from classic soul artists such as Willie Hutch, David Ruffin and Isaac Hayes. Co-founder and a member of the duo Three 6 Mafia (aka Triple Six Mafia). He won an Academy Award for Best Original Song for "It's Hard out Here for a Pimp." Juicy J is a member of Wiz Khalifa's "Taylor Gang."

MEDIA:

❖ Juicy J, "Flood Out the Club (ft. Casey Veggies)," *Blue Dream and Lean,* 2011.
   https://g.co/kgs/FUPHBt

Gucci Mane

Emanating from Birmingham, Alabama, rapper, Radric Davis, better known as Gucci Mane, released his independent debut album called Trap House, which featured the successful single "*Icy*" with Young Jeezy. Hard to *Kill* followed in 2006, which included the hit single "*Freaky Gurl.*" Throughout his career, Gucci Mane has released 14 studio albums and over 71 mixtapes. In 2007, he founded his own label, 1017 Records. The official remix of Freaky Gurl featuring Ludacris and Lil Kim was included on his commercial debut album *Back to the Trap House*. Gucci Mane appeared on OJ da Juiceman's "*Make Tha Trap Say Aye*" and began working on various mixtapes. Gucci Mane signed to Warner Bros. Records in May 2009. Following a string of critically and commercially successful mixtape releases, Gucci Mane released his fourth studio album *The State vs. Radric Davis*, his first gold-certified album. On May 26, 2016, Gucci Mane was released from prison. The next day, he released the first single under his new deal with Atlantic Records, "*1st Day Out tha Feds,*" re-emerging with several critically acclaimed projects, including Everybody Looking (2016) along with a collaboration with Rae Sremmurd, titled "*Black Beatles,*" Gucci Mane's first number-one single on the US Billboard 100 chart.

Young Scooter

Kenneth Edward Bailey, from Walterboro, South Carolina, is better known by his stage name Young Scooter. He is affiliated with *Freebandz, 1017 Brick Squad Records*, and is CEO of his own label, Black Migo Gang.

- **ZOOM OUT:**
  Young Scooter, "77 Birds" (feat. Gucci Mane), *Married to The Streets*, 2012.
  https://youtu.be/UsRO44QhOn8

Young Jeezy

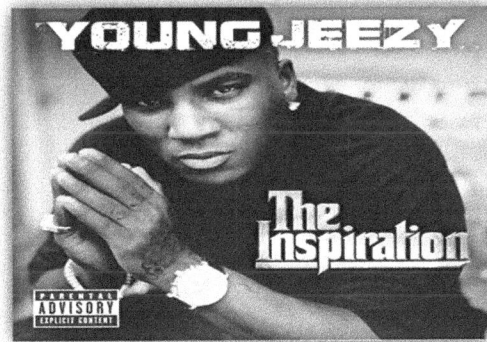

Jay Wayne Jenkins, known by his stage name Jeezy (or Young Jeezy), is an American rapper from Columbia, South Carolina, USA. Jeezy began his music career in 2001 as Lil J with the release of Thuggin' Under the Influence (T.U.I) and was signed to Def Jam Records in 2004. His label debut, *Let's Get It: Thug Motivation 101* was released the following year. Jeezy is credited, along with fellow Atlanta-based rappers T.I. and Gucci Mane for pioneering and popularizing trap music for a mainstream audience. Jeezy released his tenth studio album, *The Recession 2* in 2020.

2 CHAINZ

Tauheed K. Epps, known professionally as 2 Chainz, is an American rapper. Born and raised in College Park, Georgia, he initially gained recognition as one-half of the Southern Hip-Hop duo Playaz Circle, alongside his long-time friend and fellow rapper Earl "Dolla Boy" Conyers. Epps signed a solo deal with Def Jam Recordings in 2012, releasing his debut studio album, *Based on a True Story* later that year to huge commercial success. The album produced three hit singles: all of which charted in the top 50 of the Billboard Hot 100 and were certified Gold (along with the album being certified Gold). His second studio album was released on September 11, 2013, producing the lead single *Feds Watching*. In 2017 2 Chainz began working with on a show called *Most Expensivest* on the Viceland TV network. The show aired for three seasons.

Chapter 32

ALTERNATIVE HIP-HOP

Digable Planets

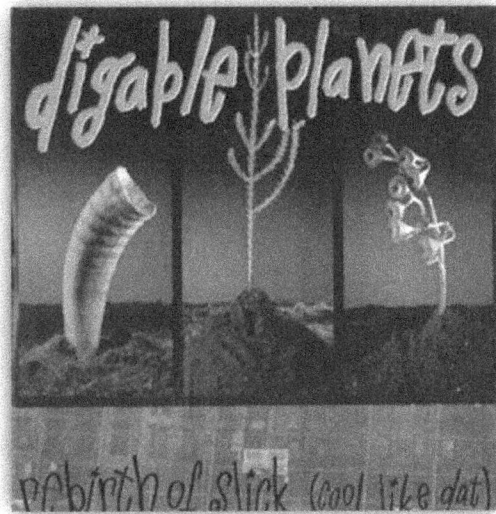

Composed of Ishmael "Butterfly" Butler (from Seattle), Craig "Doodlebug" Irving (from Philadelphia) and Mary Ann "Ladybug Mecca" Vieira (from Washington, D.C.), Digable Planets is a Grammy Award-winning American [alternative] Hip-Hop group based in New York City. Silkworm (King Britt) later embarked on a solo career. With a Grammy award for Best Rap Performance for the track "Rebirth of Slick (Cool Like Dat)" in 1994, and collaborations such as "Verses from the Abstract.," with jazz bassist Ron Carter, Digable Planets helped bring the genre commercial and critical success.

MEDIA:

❖ Digable Planets, "Rebirth of Slick (Cool Like Dat)," *Reachin (A New Refutation of Time and Space)*, 1992: https://youtu.be/kSa7cKUtt5M

De La Soul

De La Soul is an American Hip-Hop trio formed in 1987 on Long Island, New York. The band is best known for their eclectic sampling, quirky lyrics and contributions to the evolution of the jazz rap and alternative Hip-Hop subgenres. The members are Kelvin Mercer, David Jude Jolicoeur and Vincent Mason, known under a variety of nicknames. The three formed the group in high school and caught the attention of producer Prince Paul with a demo tape of the song "Plug Tunin'." With their playful wordplay, innovative sampling, and witty skits, the band's debut album, *3 Feet High and Rising*, is considered to be a Hip-Hop masterpiece.

MEDIA:

❖ De La Soul, "Me, Myself and I," *3 Feet High and Rising, 1989.*
   https://youtu.be/tD_crXNhzKs

• ZOOM OUT (Sample Source): Funkadelic, "(Not Just) Knee Deep," *Uncle Jam Wants You*, 1979.
   https://youtu.be/_20BvG3H6DY

A Tribe Called Quest

A Tribe Called Quest is an American Hip-Hop group, formed in 1985, and is composed of rapper/producer Q-Tip (Kamaal Ibn John Fareed, formerly Jonathan Davis), rapper Phife Dawg (Malik Taylor) and DJ/producer Ali Shaheed Muhammad. A fourth member, rapper Jarobi White, left the group after their first album but rejoined in 2006. Along with De La Soul, the group was a central part of the Native Tongues Posse and enjoyed the most commercial success out of all the groups to emerge from that collective. Preferring metaphor and socially conscious lyrics over the realism of Gangsta-Rap, Native Tongues originally consisted of Jungle Brothers, De La Soul, A Tribe Called Quest, and a latter affiliation with Digable Planets. While some songs are directed toward topics such as Spousal Abuse: *"Description of a Fool"* and Date Rape: *"The Infamous Date Rape,"* other tracks are influenced by jazz (including jazz samples), and other forms of popular music—*alternative identity framed in Afrocentricism.* Their innovative fusing of Hip-Hop and jazz has had a lasting impact on hip hop music, helping to expand the art of Hip-Hop production. Many of their songs, such as "Bonita Applebum," "Can I Kick It?" "I Left My Wallet in El Segundo," "Scenario," "Check the Rhime," "Jazz (We've Got)," "Award Tour" and "Electric Relaxation" are regarded as classics.

MEDIA:

❖ A Tribe Called Quest, "Youthful Expression," *People's Instinctive Travels and the Paths of Rhythm,* 1990.
   https://youtu.be/RBRaAQNTpoo

• ZOOM OUT (Sample Source): Marvin Gaye, "Make Me Wanna Holler,"*What's Going On,* 1971.
   https://youtu.be/WRLwTO_T52U?t=30

❖ A Tribe Called Quest, "Verses from the Abstract," *The Low End Theory,* 1991.
   https://youtu.be/p8iGF3M4IHc

Lupe Fiasco

Wasalu Muhammad Jaco (born February 16, 1982), better known by his stage name Lupe Fiasco (loo-pay), is an American rapper, record producer and entrepreneur. Fiasco is noted for his anti-establishment views. As an entrepreneur, Lupe is the CEO of 1st and 15th Entertainment. He rose to fame in 2006 following the success of his debut album, *Lupe Fiasco's Food & Liquor.* He also performs as the front man of rock band Japanese Cartoon under his real name. Raised in Chicago, Fiasco developed an interest in Hip-Hop after initially disliking the genre for its use of vulgarity. After adopting the name Lupe Fiasco and recording songs in his father's basement, 19-year-old Fiasco joined a group called Da Pak. The group disbanded shortly after its inception, and Fiasco soon met rapper Jay-Z who helped him sign a record deal with Atlantic Records. In 2006, Fiasco released his debut album *Lupe Fiasco's Food & Liquor* on the label, which received three Grammy nominations. He released his second album, Lupe Fiasco's The Cool, in December 2007. The lead single "Superstar" peaked at number 10 on the Billboard Hot 100. After a two-year delay. In addition to music, Lupe has pursued other business ventures, including fashion. In 2010 he recorded a benefit single for the victims of the Haiti Earthquake. Lupe's album *Lasers* was released in 2011. Associated acts include Child Rebel Soldier, Kanye West and Pharrell.

Chapter 33

THE NEO CANNABIS CREW

Wiz Khalifa

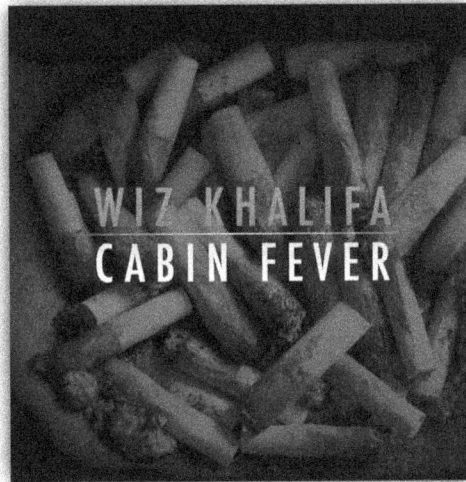

Cameron Jibril Thomaz (born September 8, 1987), better known by his stage name Wiz Khalifa, is an American rapper, singer, songwriter, and actor. He released his debut album, Show and Prove in 2006 and signed to Warner Bros. Records in 2007. Thomaz parted with Warner Bros. and released his second album, Deal or No Deal, in November 2009. He released the mixtape Kush and Orange Juice in 2010; he then signed with Atlanic Records. His debut single for Atlantic, "Black and Yellow," a veritable tribute to his hometown of Pittsburg, PA debuted at number 100 and eventually peaked at number 1 on the Billboard Hot 100. The song became the lead single for his third album Rolling Papers, which was released in 2011. The album's success was followed up by the singles, "Work Hard and Play Hard" and "Remember You" in 2012. Wiz released his fifth album Blacc Hollywood in August 2014, backed by the lead single "We Dem Boyz". In March 2015, he released "See You Again" for the soundtrack of Furious Seven. The song peaked at number one on the Billboard Hot 100 for 12 weeks. On April 20, 2020, Khalifa released a new EP, The Saga of Wiz Khalifa. The album included many collaborations. In 2021, Khalifa competed on the TV show The Masked Singer as "Chameleon". Khalifa is open about his use of marijuana, and he has claimed in many interviews that he spends $10,000 a month on cannabis, and also smokes daily. As of early 2014, Khalifa no longer pays for cannabis and is sponsored by The Cookie Company, a medical marijuana dispenser which sells his "Khalifa Kush" (KK) strain, which he partnered with RiverRock Cannabis to create.

MEDIA:

❖ Wiz Khalifa, "Middle of You (feat. Chevy Woods)," *Cabin Fever*, 2011 (*Planet Rock* Sample). https://g.co/kgs/Mp5TcW

SMOKE DZA

Sean Pompey, better known by his stage name Smoke DZA, is an American rapper and songwriter from Harlem, NY, USA. DZA decided on his moniker after being influenced by Chris Tucker's character Smokey from the movie *Friday*; and the acronym DZA stands for "Dream Zone Achieve". He was discovered by Cinematic Music Group in 2002 and went on to write for numerous rappers. He later partnered to become one half of the group Smoke & Numbers—until going solo in 2008.

MEDIA:

❖ Smoke DZA, "Profit" (feat. Trademark Da Skydiver), *The Hustler's Catalog*, 2011.
   https://youtu.be/z2UqJjpgBYw

Fabolous

John David Jackson, better known by his stage name Fabolous, is an American rapper and singer from New York, NY, USA. While still a senior in high school, he first gained recognition performing live on DJ Clue's radio show on Hot 97.

MEDIA:

❖ Fabolous, "Wolves in Sheep's Clothing" (Feat. Paul Cain), *The S.O.U.L Tape (Mixtape)*, 2011.
   https://youtu.be/YZ0QLz1BNus

Chapter 34

THE MAINSTREAM

Jay-Z

Shawn Corey Carter, better known by his stage name Jay-Z, is an American rapper from Brooklyn, New York, U.SA, He is a record producer, philanthropist, and entrepreneur. Having earned a net worth of over $450 million by 2010, Jay-Z is one of the most financially successful Hip-Hop artists and entrepreneurs in America. In addition to dozens of Grammy Awards for his musical work, and numerous additional nominations, he has sold hundreds of millions of albums world-wide. Jay-Z is consistently ranked as one of the greatest rappers of all-time. Associated acts include Memphis Bleek, FoxyBrown, Jaz-O, The Notorious B.I.G., Beyoncé, Rihanna, Kanye West, and Big L.

Roc-A-Fella Records, LLC. is an American Hip-Hop record label and music management company founded by record executives and entrepreneurs Damon "Dame" Dash, Kareem "Biggs" Burke and Shawn "Jay-Z" Carter in 1994.

• **ZOOM OUT:** Before there was Jay-Z…. there was….

Jaz-O

"Street phrases amaze scholars. We coin phrases for dollars."—Jaz-O

Jonathan Burks, better known by his stage name Jaz-O, is an American rapper and record producer active in the late 1980s through the 1990s, best known for being the mentor of Brooklyn rapper Jay-Z. Burks is nicknamed "the Originator," and had a song titled "The Originators" that featured a young Jay-Z in 1990.

Eminem

Eminem is an American rapper, record producer, songwriter, and actor. Eminem's popularity brought his group project, D12, to mainstream recognition. As well as being a member of D12, Eminem is also one half of the Detroit Hip-Hop duo Bad Meets Evil, with Royce da 5'9". Eminem is one of the best-selling artists in the world and is the best-selling artist of the 2000s. He has been listed and ranked as one of the greatest artists of all time by many magazines including Rolling Stone magazine. His popularity brought his group project, D12, to mainstream recognition. As well as being a member of D12, Eminem is also one-half of the Detroit hip hop duo Bad Meets Evil, with Royce da 5'9". Eminem quickly gained popularity in 1999 with his major-label debut album, The Slim Shady LP. That first album, The Marshall Mathers LP and his third major album and The Eminem Show, all won Grammy Awards. The Marshall Mathers LP is also considered one of Eminem's best and most successful albums. making Eminem the first artist to win Best Rap Album for three consecutive LPs. Eminem then went on a hiatus after touring in 2005. He released his first album since 2004's Encore, titled Relapse, on May 15, 2009. In 2010, Eminem released his seventh studio album Recovery, which was an international success.

Beanie Sigel

Dwight Equan Grant, better known by his stage name Beanie Sigel, is an American rapper from South Philadelphia, Pennsylvania. He first became known for his association with Jay-Z and Roc-A-Fella Records, releasing his debut studio album The Truth through Roc-A-Fella in February 2000 to critical and commercial success. Sigel's second studio album, *The Reason*, saw similar commercial success His third album, the B. Coming, was critically acclaimed, and peaked at number 3 on the Billboard 200. Sigel returned to Roc-A-Fella in 2007 and released his fourth studio album *The Solution* to positive reviews. After leaving Roc-A-Fella, Sigel's fifth and sixth studio albums were released independently. Sigel appeared in the 2011 film *Rhyme and Punishment, a documentary* about hip hop artists who have served time in county jail or state/federal prison. The film features an interview with Sigel in which he discusses his conviction and life while incarcerated. *This Time*, the sixth studio album by Sigel, was released in 2012; it was the first album released under the newly relaunched Ruffhouse Records.

Kendrick Lamar

Considered to be one of the most influential hip hop artists of his generation, Kendrick Lamar Duckworth (born June 17, 1987) is an American rapper and songwriter from Compton, California. He is known for his progressive musical style and socially conscious songwriting, Lamar began his career as a teenager performing under the stage name K.Dot. He quickly garnered local attention which led to him signing a recording contract with Top Dawg Entertainment (TDE) in 2005. After becoming a founding member of the Hip-Hop supergroup Black Hippy, Lamar started using his first and middle names professionally. In 2011, he released his debut studio album Section 80, which included his debut single "*HiiiiPower*". Kendrick acquired a record deal with Dr' Dre's Aftermath Entertainment in 2012 and released his second studio album *Good Kid, M.A.A.D. City*, a gangsta-rap influenced album that garnered widespread critical recognition and commercial success. A visit to South Africa inspired Lamar's third studio album *To Pimp a Butterfly* (2015). Having sold over 70 million records in the United States alone, all of Lamar's studio albums have been certified platinum (or higher) by (RIAA). He has received numerous accolades and awards throughout his career, including 14 Grammy Awards. In 2015, Lamar received the California State Senate's Generational Icon Award; and three of his studio albums were included on *Rolling Stone's* 2020 ranking of the 500 Greatest Albums of All Time.

A$AP ROCKY

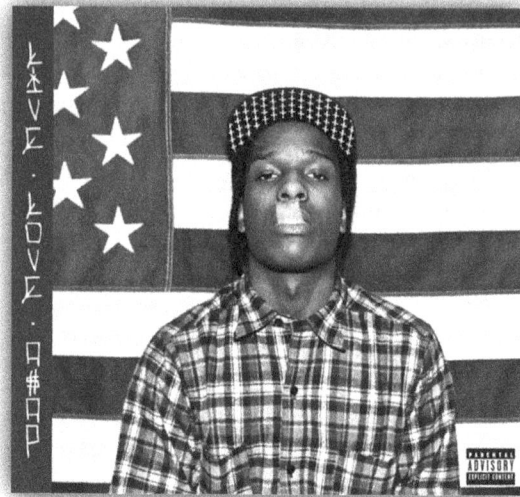

Rakim Athelaston Mayers, known professionally as A$AP Rocky, is an American rapper, singer and record producer. He is a member of the Hip-Hop collective A$AP Mob, from which he adopted his moniker. In August 2011, Rocky's single "Peso" was leaked online and within weeks received radio airplay.

Jay Electronica

Timothy Elpadaro Thedford (born September 19, 1976), better known by his stage name Jay Electronica, is an American Hip-Hop recording artist and record producer from (Magnolia Projects) New Orleans, Louisiana, USA. Jay Electronica first gained significant attention after the release of the musical composition Act I: Eternal Sunshine (the pledge), made available on a MySpace page in 2007. It is nine continuous minutes of music, without drums, built from Jon Brion's soundtrack to the film Eternal Sunshine of the Spotless Mind. In late 2009 he released two songs, both produced by Just Blaze, "Exhibit A (Transformations)" and "Exhibit C" the latter of which won a Sucker Free

Summit Award for Instant Classic. On November 12, 2010, it was announced Jay Electronica had become an official member of Jay-Z's Roc Nation record label. Associated acts include J Dilla, Erykah Badu, Just Blaze, Nas, Mos Def and Talib Kweli.

J. Cole

Jermaine Lamarr Cole (born January 28, 1985) is an American rapper and record producer. He was raised in Fayetteville, North Carolina, USA. Cole initially gained recognition as a rapper following the release of his debut mixtape, *The Come Up*, in early 2007. After signing to Jay Z's Roc Nation imprint, He went on to release two additional mixtapes, *The Warm Up* (2009) and *Friday Night Lights* (2010). Debuting at number one on the US *Billboard* 200, in 2011, Cole released his debut studio album, Cole Word: The Sideline Story. It. His next album, Born Sinner (2013), also topped the Billboard 200. Moving into more conscious themes, 2014 Forest Hills Drive (2014) topped the Billboard 200 and earned Cole a Best Rap Album nod at the 2015 Grammy Awards. His jazz influenced fourth album, 4 Your Eyez Only (2016), debuted at number one on the *Billboard* 200. KOD, Cole's fifth album (2018), became his fifth number-one album on the *Billboard* 200 and featured a then-record six simultaneous top twenty hits on the Billboard Top 100, tying him with the Beatles. Studio album number six, The Off Season, which earned him his sixth number-one album, was released on May 14, 2021.

MEDIA:

❖ J. Cole, "Villematic," *Friday Night's Light Mixtape*, 2010.
   https://g.co/kgs/kaawGM

Mac Miller

Malcolm James McCormick, better known by his stage name Mac Miller, was an American rapper and record producer. Miller began his music career in 2007, at the age of fifteen, and achieved mainstream success with his mixtapes K.I.D.S. and Best Day Ever. His debut studio album, Blue Slide Park, became the first independently distributed album to top the US Billboard 200 chart since 1995. Miller struggled with addiction and substance abuse, which was often mentioned in his lyrics. On September 7, 2018, he died from an accidental drug overdose at the age of 26.

Birdman

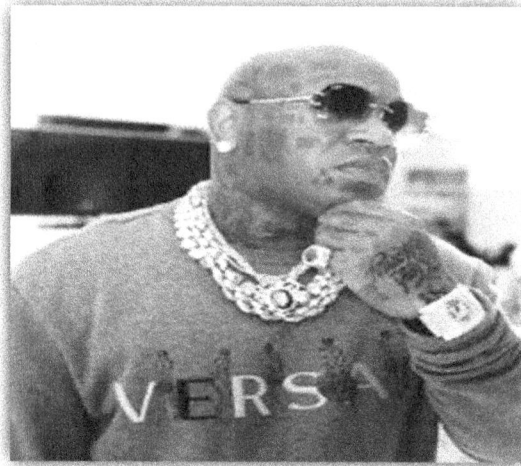

Bryan Christopher Williams, previously known as Baby, is better known by his stage name, Birdman. He is an American rapper, record executive, and co-founder of *Cash Money Records* (which he founded with his older brother Ronald "Slim" Williams in 1992). *Birdman* (2002) is the title of the debut solo album by Baby. Aside from his solo career, along with producer Mannie Fresh, Birdman is also a member of the Hip-Hop duo Big Tymers.

Juvenile

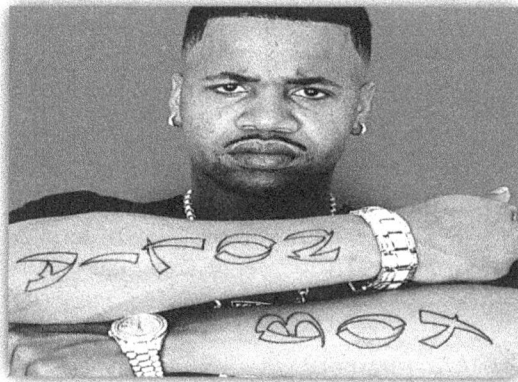

Terius Gray, better known by his stage name Juvenile, is an American rapper best known for his work with Birdman's Cash Money Records in the late 1990s and early 2000s (solo and as a member of the label's flagship group, Hot Boys).

Lil Wayne

Dwayne Michael Carter Jr. (born September 27, 1982), known professionally as Lil Wayne, is an American rapper, singer, songwriter, and record executive. His career began in 1995, at the age of 12, when he was signed by Birdman, joining Cash Money Records as the youngest member of the label, before ending his association with the company in 2018. His solo, breakthrough, debut album Tha Block Is Hot (1999) was followed by his fourth album Tha Carter (2004) and fifth album Tha Carter II (2005), as well as several mixtapes and collaborations throughout 2006 and 2007 reaching even higher popularity. He gained more prominence with his sixth album Tha Carter III (2008, winning the Grammy for Best Rap Album. In March 2010, Lil Wayne began serving an 8-month jail sentence in New York after being convicted of criminal possession of a weapon stemming from an incident in 2007. His eighth studio album was released during his incarceration; and his 2011 album Tha Carter IV was released following his release (selling near 1 million copies in the first week). Tha Carter V was released in 2018, Lill Wayne's thirteenth album was released in 2020. Regarded as one of the most influential hip hop artists of his generation by XXL, Lil Wayne has sold over 120 million records worldwide, including more than 20 million albums and 70 million digital tracks in the United States. He is often cited as one of the greatest rappers of all time.

DRAKE

Rapper and Singer, Aubrey Drake Graham (aw-BREE), was born in 1986 in Toronto, Ontario Canada. Is a Canadian. Drake has been credited for popularizing singing and R&B sensibility in Hip-Hop. He gained recognition by starring as Jimmy Brooks in the CTV teen drama series Degrassi: T.N.G., and subsequently pursued a career in music releasing his debut mixtape Room for Improvement in 2006. Drake's first three albums were all critical successes and propelled him to the forefront of Hip-Hop. Featuring the record-setting single "One Dance," his fourth album, Views (2016), stood atop the Billboard 200 for 13 weeks (making it the first album by a male artist to do so in over a decade). Drake released the double album, Scorpion, in 2018 which contained the three number-one singles: "God's Plan," "Nice for What," and "In My Feelings". Drake's widely anticipated sixth album, Certified Lover Boy (2021), achieved nine top 10 hits on the Hot 100. Among the world's best-selling artists, with over 170 million records sold, Drake ranked as the highest-certified digital singles artist in the United States by the RIAA. He has won four Grammys, six American Music Awards, an astonishing 34 Billboard Music Awards, two Brits, and three Juno Awards.

KANYE WEST

Born in Atlanta, and raised in Chicago, Kanye Omari West (KAHN-yay), also known as, Ye (YAY), is an American rapper, singer, songwriter, record producer, and fashion designer. He initially gained recognition as a producer for Roc-A-Fella-Records in the early 2000s, producing singles for several artists. He released his debut studio album, *The College Dropout* in 2004 to critical and commercial success. Later that year, he founded the record label GOOD music. With over 160 million records sold, he is one of the best-selling music artists of all time. West has won 22 Grammys and 75 nominations; and six of West's albums were included on Rolling Stone's 2020 *500 Greatest Albums of All Time*. Rolling Stones also named him one of the *100 Greatest Songwriters of All Time*. As a fashion designer, he has collaborated with Nike, among others, on clothing and footwear and he led the Yeezy collab with Adidas.

FUTURE

Better known by the stage name Future, Nayvadius DeMun Wilburn is an American rapper and singer from Atlanta, Georgia, USA. Known for his mumble-influenced vocal range and prolific output, Future is considered a pioneer of the use of melodies and vocal effects in the modern "trap" idiom. Future is considered a pioneer of the use of melodies and vocal effects in modern trap music. Based on his meteoric rise, Future has been called one of the most influential rappers alive.

Sean Kingston

Kisean Paul Anderson, better known by his stage name Sean Kingston, is an American-Jamaican singer and rapper. He is known for his hit songs "Beautiful Girls," "Fire Burning," "Take You There," and his collaboration with Justin Bieber, "Eenie Meenie."

Meek Mill

Robert Rihmeek Williams known professionally as Meek Mill, is an American rapper. Born and raised in Philadelphia, Pennsylvania. Meek embarked on his music career as a battle rapper and later formed a short-lived rap group, The Bloodhoundz. In 2008, T.I. signed Meek Mill to his first record deal. In 2011, after leaving Grand Hustle Records, Mill signed with Miami-based rapper Rick Ross' (MMG). Mill's debut album for MMG, Dreams and Nightmares, was released thereafter. The album, preceded by the lead single "Amen" (featuring Drake), peaked at number two on the *Billboard* 200. In July 2015, Meek Mill publicly criticized Drake, calling him out for not writing his own lyrics. In a series of tweets, the rapper claimed that Drake used a ghostwriter for a song on Mill's second album, *Dreams Worth More Than Money*. In addition, Meek was admittedly upset that Drake did not promote the album on Twitter. In November 2017, he was sentenced to two to four years in prison for violating parole, before being released while his trial continues after serving five months. In August 2019, a documentary series about his battle with the criminal justice system, Free Meek was released. Mill served as executive producer on the series alongside fellow rapper Jay-Z The two also became the co-founders of nonprofit organization Reform Alliance, which focuses on justice, parole, and probation reform. After Mill's release from prison in 2018, the feud was officially squashed; and Drake was featured on Mill's song "Going Bad," from his post-incarceration album *Championships*.

Chapter 35

GLOBALIZATION: THE REVOLUTION OF HIP-HOP

In his book *In Search of Africa*, Manthia Diawara explains that Hip-Hop is really a voice of people who are down and out in modern society. He argues that the "Worldwide spread of hip hop as a market revolution" is actually global "expression of poor people's desire for the good life," and that this struggle aligns with "the nationalist struggle for citizenship and belonging, but also reveals the need to go beyond such struggles and celebrate the redemption of the black individual through tradition. To suggest that rap is a black idiom, that prioritizes black culture and that articulates the problems of Black urban life does not deny the pleasure of participation of others. In fact, many Black music(s) before rap (e.g., the blues, jazz, and early rock "n" roll) have also become American popular music(s) precisely because of extensive white participation (Rose, 1994, p. 4).

… as Hip Hop emerges from the deindustrialization meltdown where social alienation, prophetic imagination, and yearning intersect. It is the tension between cultural fractures produced by post-industrial oppression and the binding ties of black cultural expressivity that sets the critical frame for the development of Hip-Hop (Rose, 1994, p. 21).

Global Innovations

Though created in the United States by African Americans, Hip-Hop culture and music is now global in scope. While Canada, France, Germany, the UK, Poland, Brazil, Japan, Africa, Australia and the Caribbean have long-established Hip-Hop followings, youth culture and opinion is meted out in both Israeli and Palestinian Hip-Hop. According to the U.S. Department of State, Hip-Hop is "now the center of a mega music and fashion industry around the world," that crosses social barriers and cuts across racial lines.

The Audacity of Hip-Hop—From Hip-Hop World by Dalton Higgins

It's a Hip-Hop world, and you're just living in it. For most music-addicted earthlings, Hip-Hop culture is the predominant global youth subculture of today. For the non-music-initiated, Hip-Hop has become the black, jewelry-laden elephant in a room filled with rock, country and classical music—an attention-grabber whose influence is impossible to miss on the daily news, in school playgrounds, during water cooler conversations or in a political debate. What is Hip-Hop, and why should you care about it?

LOCALIZATION

"Rather, globalization intensifies localization rather than leads to a flattening out of local cultures." (Basu, Lemelle, p.3).

"Allan Murray notes: while transnational media enterprises and the global culture industries have a powerful influence over what gets circulated into world markets, there are no guarantees as to how cultural commodities will be incorporated into localized practices and lived experiences of subjective pleasure and desire" (ibid. p.5).

Hip-Hop Politics? With Volume!

Hip-Hoppers and their responses to social and political issues, before rap's golden age

Clifton Watson, Department of History, North Carolina Central University

It is also important that the neighborhood-based social change efforts involving artists or the ways by which artists' politics are articulated through their music are not wholly dismissed as insignificant. When we become diligent to this end, we may discover ways to socialize a generation of youth that some have written off as apathetic about the importance of civic activism on a local, national, and even international scale.

Jazz, Rap Hip-Hop Politics: Deconstructing the Myth
by Yvonne Bynoe

In the 1980s and early 1990s, rap artists…. produced socially conscious songs… the emergence of a Hip-Hop inspired political movement…. During this period, it was rap artists who…connected with disenfranchised urban youth. The commercial success of "conscious" rap artists…helped to spawn the raptivist (a rap artist who dabbles in activism on the side).

All about The Beat?

Is the Hip-Hop Generation a political movement worth taking seriously?

Excerpt from John McWhorter *All about the Beat*

There is apparently something about Hip-Hop that distracts people into, in some part of their brains, seeing something in it that is… inspirational. It is so seductive that it can discourage reflection; and in the case of the idea of rap as politically significant, I think it is doing, precisely, that.

***

Chapter 36

LAMONT COLEMAN: 'BIG L'—IN MEMORIAM

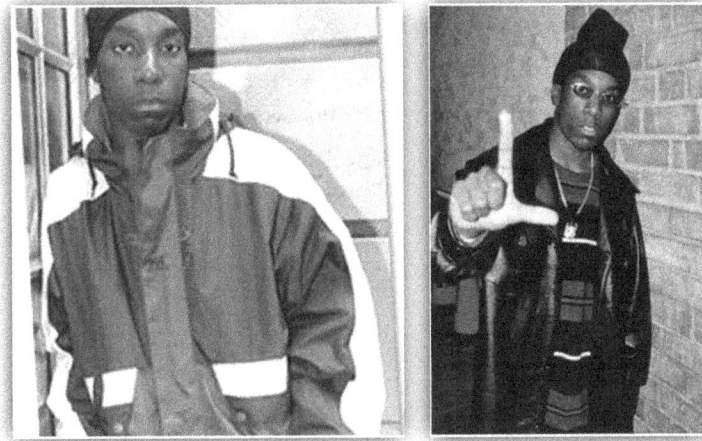

Lamont Coleman (May 30, 1974–February 15, 1999), also known by his stage name Big L, was an American rapper who made significant contributions to the New York City music scene in the 1990s as a member of the Hip-Hop collective D.I.T.C. He was shot and killed in February 1999 before releasing his second album. Lamont Coleman was born on May 30, 1974, in New York City and grew up in uptown Harlem which he references regularly in his lyrics (139th Street and Lenox Avenue). Big L began rhyming in 1990 and his first professional appearance came on the B-side of "Party Over Here" by Lord Finesse in 1992, the song was the remix to "Yes, You May." Around this time, L founded the Harlem-based rap group Children of the Corn with fellow aspiring MC's Killa Cam, Murda Mase and Killa Cam's cousin Bloodshed while Darrell "Digga" Branch provided production. Unfortunately, the group folded in 1996 when Bloodshed died in a car accident. In 1993, L was signed to Columbia Records and released his first single "Devil's Son." Big L's debut solo album, Lifestylez ov da Poor & Dangerous, was released in March 1995. The album featured guest appearances from several artists, notably Kid Capri, Lord Finesse, and then-unknown Cam'ron and Jay-Z. Two singles, "M.V.P." and "Put It On," were released from the album, both of which reached the top twenty-five of Billboard's Hot Rap Tracks. The album itself also reached the Billboard 200, but due to its poor commercial status Big L was dropped from Columbia Records. From 1997 to 1999, Big L worked on his second album The Big Picture through his own Flamboyant Entertainment label. He released the acclaimed single "Ebonics" in 1998 (it took Big L a year to write the song); that same year, he joined Bronx-based Hip-Hop collective Diggin' in the Crates Crew and appeared on their first single "Dignified Soldiers." The Big Picture was released posthumously in August 2000 and featured guest appearances by Fat Joe, Guru of Gang Starr, Kool G Rap and Big Daddy Kane among others. Jay-Z has said that Big L was set to sign with his Roc-A-Fella label but was murdered the week before. The Picture was Big L's last recorded album. It was put together by his manager and partner in Flamboyant Entertainment, Rich King. It contains songs that L had recorded and a cappella recordings that were never used, completed by producers and guest MCs that Big L respected or had worked with previously. The album was certified gold a month later.

Everybody in Hip-Hop hates Gerard Woodley, because he is the man that took Big L's life. Well, Cam'ron is from Harlem and things are deeper than you know. The word on the street is that Cam'ron attended the funeral of Woodley and there is Instagram proof. You all know, Cam and Big L used to rap together back in the day so one would assume that he'd hate Woodley. Not the case. On Instagram, he said, "Me and Kev at G-LOVE funeral Rip #139th St."

MEDIA:

❖ Big L, "Ebonics" (Criminal Slang), *The Big Picture*, 2000.
https://youtu.be/TMeFcVHNT1Q

APPENDIX: ASSESSMENT INDEX

Quiz 1 Question Bank

Quiz 1-1) Rhythm is established by (_____) as well as by (_____).

a) Percussion
b) The beat
c) Harmony
d) Melody
e) Rhythms
f) Tempo p
g) Texture
h) Silence

Quiz 1-2) Rhythm is established by Texture as well as by Silence.

a) False

Quiz 1-3) What do percussion and silence establish?

a) The beat
b) Harmony
c) Melody
d) Rhythm
e) Tempo
f) Texture

Quiz 1-4) (_____) often differentiates (_____) music from the music of other cultures

a) Equal Temperament Instrumentation
b) Meantone Temperament Instrumentation
c) Just Temperament Instrumentation
d) Eastern
e) Western
f) Southern
g) African
h) North American

Quiz 1-5) (_____) is the perceptible tune of a piece of music

a) Percussion
b) The beat
c) Harmony
d) Melody

e) Rhythm
f) Tempo
g) Texture

Quiz 1-6) Melody is the perceptible (_____) of a piece of music

a) Tune
b) Beat

Quiz 1-7) Two or more notes sounding simultaneously produces (_____)

a) Percussion
b) The beat
c) Harmony
d) The tune
e) Rhythm
f) The tempo
g) Texture

Quiz 1-8) (_____) sounding simultaneously produces harmony

a) Two or more notes
b) Silence
c) Rhythm
d) The beat
e) Consonance
f) Dissonance
g) Texture

Quiz 1-9) List the two 'Swing Era' musicians mentioned in the lecture.

a) Duke Ellington
b) Count Basie
c) Mahalia Jackson
d) King Oliver
e) Louis Armstrong
f) Jelly Roll Morton
g) Bessie Smith
h) Robert Johnson
i) Son House

Quiz 1-10) Specific [musical] patterns of long and short duration are called (_____).

a) Rhythms
b) Percussion
c) The beat
d) The harmony
e) The tune
f) The tempo
g) The texture

Quiz 1-11) (BPM) is an acronym for (_____) and refers to the (_____), or speed of a piece of music.

a) BPM
b) RPM
c) CPM
d) Beats Per Minute
e) Cycles Per Minute
f) Revolutions Per Minute
g) Tempo
h) Rhythm
i) Texture
j) The Beat

Quiz 1-12) Harmony can be described as (_____) (pleasing) or (_____) (clashing).

a) Consonant
b) Dissonant
c) Distasteful
d) Melodious
e) Harmonious
f) Musical

Quiz 1-13) Consonance refers to a (_____) sound.

a) Pleasing
b) Clashing
c) Ugly
d) Funky

Quiz 1-14) Dissonance refers to a (_____) sound.

a) Pleasing
b) Clashing
c) Ugly
d) Funky

Quiz 1-15) ABA form structure is also known as which of the following:

a) Binary form
b) Ternary form
c) Tertian form
d) Blues form

Quiz 1-16) Which of the following form structures represents Ternary Form?

a) ABA
b) AAB
c) AA'B
d) AABA
e) ABACA
f) AB

Quiz 1-17) ABA form is known as Tertian Form

a)   False

Quiz 1-18) AB form is known as Ternary Form

a)   False

Quiz 1-19) Which of the following form structures represents Binary Form?

a)   ABA
b)   AAB
c)   AA'B
d)   AABA
e)   ABACA
f)   AB

Quiz 1-20) The (Three Stanza Blues) is a prototype of (_____) in Hip-Hop.

a)   Three Stanza Blues
b)   Binary Form
c)   Tertian Form
d)   Freestyle
e)   Break Beat
f)   Slow Flow

Quiz 1-21) Name two prototypes to freestyle in Hip-Hop:

a)   Three stanza blues
b)   Blues vocals
c)   Beat Boxing
d)   Rapping
e)   Scratching
f)   Locking

Quiz 1-22) Son House was an "Early Jazz" legend mentioned in the lecture

a)   False

Quiz 1-23) Name two "Early Jazz" legends mentioned in the lecture:

a)   King Oliver
b)   Louis Armstrong
c)   Jelly Roll Morton
d)   Duke Ellington
e)   Count Basie
f)   Mahalia Jackson
g)   Bessie Smith
h)   Robert Johnson
i)   Son House

Quiz 1-24) King Oliver was an "Early Jazz" legend

a)   True

Quiz 1-25) King Oliver was a "Vocal Blues" legend

a)   False

Quiz 1-26) Jelly Roll Morton was a "Vocal Blues" legend

a)   False

Quiz 1-27) List two "Vocal Blues" legends mentioned in the lecture:

a)   King Oliver
b)   Louis Armstrong
c)   Jelly Roll Morton
d)   Duke Ellington
e)   Count Basie
f)   Mahalia Jackson
g)   Bessie Smith
h)   Robert Johnson
i)   James P. Johnson
j)   Son House
k)   Jelly Roll Morton

Quiz 1-28) Name the Gospel artist mentioned in the lecture:

a)   King Oliver
b)   Louis Armstrong
c)   Jelly Roll Morton
d)   Duke Ellington
e)   Count Basie
f)   Mahalia Jackson
g)   Bessie Smith
h)   Robert Johnson
i)   Son House
j)   Jelly Roll Morton

Quiz 1-29) Mahalia Jackson was the Gospel artist mentioned in the lecture.

a)   True

Quiz 1-30) Louis Armstrong was the Gospel artist mentioned in the lecture.

a)   False

Quiz 1-31) Melodies are derived from (_____) or ordered sets of pitches from low to high or high to low.

a) Scales
b) Rhythms
c) Beats
d) Textures
e) Harmonies

Quiz 1-32) The organization of all the individual sections of a piece of music is referred to as the form.

a) True

Quiz 1-33) (_____) and/or (_____) refers to the characteristics or nature of the sound.

a) Texture
b) Timbre
c) Consonance
d) Dissonance
e) Rhythm
f) Harmony

Quiz 1-34) Rhythm and/or Harmony refers to the characteristics or nature of the sound.

a) False

Quiz 1-35) Texture and/or timbre refers to the characteristics or nature of the sound.

a) True

Quiz 1-36) Name two "musical" sources (genres) for the "backbeat" in Urban Music:

a) Work Songs
b) Chain Gang
c) Plainchant
d) Western Art Music
e) Ragtime
f) Gospel

Quiz 1-37) Chords can be classified in two ways: (_____) (happy) or (_____) (sad)

a) Major or Minor
b) Major or Augmented
c) Diminished or Minor
d) Minor or Augmented

Quiz 1-38) The "backbeat" represents beats (_____) in a measure with 4 beats.

a) 1 and 2
b) 1 and 3
c) 1 and 4
d) 2 and 3
e) 2 and 4
f) 3 and 4

Quiz 1-39) The rhythmical accenting of beats two and four is referred to as the what?

a)   BackBeat
b)   Break Beat
c)   Down Beat
d)   Up Beat
e)   The Beat
f)   The One

Quiz 1-40) Harmony is established by a minimum of (_____) note(s).

a)   One
b)   Two
c)   Three
d)   Four
e)   Five

Quiz 1-41) Music born in Americas and Europe is referred to as Western music.

a)   True

Quiz 1-42) Music born in Africa and Asia is referred to as Western Music.

a)   False

Quiz 1-43) The Rhythm exists within the (_____), which exists within the (_____).

a)   Beat
b)   Form
c)   Texture
d)   Harmony
e)   Measure

Quiz 1-44) A minimum of three notes, sounding simultaneously, produces (_____).

a)   A chord
b)   Rhythm
c)   Texture
d)   Form
e)   Consonance
f)   Dissonance

Quiz 1-45) The Major scale has (7) notes in it.

a)   4
b)   5
c)   6
d)   7
e)   8
f)   11
g)   12

Quiz 1-46) The Chromatic scale has (_____) notes in it.

a) 4
b) 5
c) 6
d) 7
e) 8
f) 12
g) 13

Quiz 1-47) Though (West African) connections may predominate, (_____) within Native American and European cultures is also part of the development of African-American music.

a) West African
b) Caribbean
c) Mediterranean
d) Middle Eastern
e) East African
f) Cross Ancestry
g) Isolation
h) Assimilation

Quiz 1-48) The sound "Color" or characteristic of the sound can be described as which of the following?

a) Texture/Timbre
b) Mood
c) Style
d) Form
e) Harmony

Quiz 1-49) List the two artists from the Ragtime Era mentioned in the lecture:

a) James P .Johnson
b) Scott Joplin
c) Louis Armstrong
d) Mahalia Jackson
e) Duke Ellington
f) King Oliver
g) Count Basie

Quiz 1-50) The sound "Color" or characteristic of the sound can be described as Texture/Timbre?

a) True

Quiz 1-51) The sound "Color" or characteristic of the sound can be described as Form?

a) False

Quiz 1-52) James P. Johnson is an artist associated with the Ragtime era.

a) True

Quiz 1-53) James P. Johnson is an "Early Jazz" legend mentioned in the lecture.

a)   False

Quiz 1-54) Who performed "The Entertainer"?

a)   Jelly Roll Morton
b)   Scott Joplin
c)   Louis Armstrong
d)   King Oliver
e)   Robert Johnson
f)   James P. Johnson

Quiz 1-55) The Major Scale has 9 notes in it.

a)   False

Quiz 1-56) The Chromatic Scale has 11 notes in it.

a)   False

Quiz 1-57) The Chromatic Scale has 12 notes in it.

a)   True

Quiz 1-58) The Major Scale has 12 notes in it.

a)   False

Quiz 1-59) Which of the following scales has 7 notes in it?

a)   Major Scale
b)   Augmented Scale
c)   Chromatic Scale
d)   Whole Tone Scale
e)   Diminished Scale
f)   Pentatonic Scale

Quiz 1-60) Ragtime is one of the "musical" sources (genres) for the "backbeat" in Urban Music.

a)   False

Quiz 1-61) Work Songs are one of the "musical" sources (genres) for the "backbeat" in Urban Music.

a)   True

Quiz 1-62) Beats 1 and 3 represent the "backbeat" in a measure with 4 beats.

a)   False

Quiz 1-63) Duke Ellington represents which music genre?

a)   Swing
b)   Vocal Blues
c)   Ragtime
d)   Early Jazz
e)   Gospel

Quiz 1-64) King Oliver represents which music genre?

a)   Swing
b)   Vocal Blues
c)   Ragtime
d)   Early Jazz
e)   Gospel

Quiz 1-65) AB form is known as Binary Form

a)   True

Quiz 1-66) Louis Armstrong represents which music genre?

a)   Swing
b)   Vocal Blues
c)   Early Jazz
d)   Ragtime

Quiz 2 Question Bank

Quiz 2-1) Identify two characteristics of Rhythm and Blues:

a)   Twelve bar blues
b)   Riff oriented
c)   Tertian Form
d)   Led to development of Bebop/Complex jazz
e)   Transition into Swing as popular music
f)   Straight Eighths
g)   Break Beats

Quiz 2-2)

a)   Solution to Bebop/complex jazz
b)   Transition out of Swing as popular music
c)   Tertian Form
d)   Led to development of Bebop/Complex jazz
e)   Transition into Swing as popular music
f)   Straight Eighths
g)   Break Beats

Quiz 2-3)

a)   Shuffle/Triplet
b)   Overt backbeat

c) Tertian Form
d) Led to development of Bebop/Complex jazz
e) Transitioned into Swing as popular music
f) Break Beats
g) Straight Eighths

Quiz 2-4)

a) Chuck Berry
b) James Brown
c) Rick James
d) Marvin Gaye
e) Aretha Franklin

Quiz 2-5)

a) Little Richard
b) Fats Domino
c) Rick James
d) Marvin Gaye
e) Aretha Franklin

Quiz 2-6) Identify two Rhythm and Blues artists:

a) Isley Brothers
b) Little Richard
c) Rick James
d) Marvin Gaye
e) Aretha Franklin

Quiz 2-7) Identify two Motown Artists

a) William Smokey Robinson
b) Michael Jackson
c) Aretha Franklin
d) Little Richard
e) Chuck Berry
f) James Brown

Quiz 2-8) Identify two Motown Artists:

a) Marvin Gaye
b) Isley Brothers
c) Aretha Franklin
d) Little Richard
e) Chuck Berry
f) James Brown

Quiz 2-9) Identify two Motown Artists:

a) Marvin Gaye
b) Michael Jackson
c) Aretha Franklin

d) Little Richard
e) Chuck Berry
f) James Brown

Quiz 2-10) Identify two Motown Artists:

a) William Smokey Robinson
b) Marvin Gaye
c) Aretha Franklin
d) Little Richard
e) Chuck Berry
f) James Brown

Quiz 2-11) The Shuffle/Triplet is a characteristic of Rhythm and Blues.

a) True

Quiz 2-12) The Isley Brothers were Motown Artists.

a) True

Quiz 2-13) Chuck Berry was a Motown Artist.

a) False

Quiz 2-14) Marvin Gaye was a Motown Artist.

a) True

Quiz 2-15) Little Milton Campbell and Curtis Mayfield represent what subgenres?

a) Chicago Soul
b) Soul
c) R&B
d) Funk

Quiz 2-16) The Isley Brothers and Marvin Gaye represent the genre of Chicago Soul.

a) False

Quiz 2-17) Name the song played in the lecture by Curtis Mayfield and the Impressions:

a) "I Loved and I Lost"
b) "In Between The Sheets"
c) "For The Easy Listeners"

Quiz 2-18) Name the song played in the lecture by Curtis Mayfield and the Impressions:

a) "Move On Up"
b) "In Between the Sheets"
c) "For the Easy Listeners"

Quiz 2-19) Name the song played in the lecture by Curtis Mayfield and the Impressions:

a) "Keep on Pushing"
b) "In Between the Sheets"
c) "For the Easy Listeners"

Quiz 2-20) Memphis soul is a shimmering, sultry style of soul music produced in the 1960s and 1970s at (_____) and (_____) in Memphis, Tennessee, as heard on recordings by vocalist (_____).

a) Stax Records
b) Hi Records
c) Al Green
d) Motown Records
e) Capital Records
f) Ronald Isley
g) Marvin Gaye

Quiz 2-21) (_____) is a shimmering, sultry style of (_____) produced in the 1960s and 1970s at (_____) and (_____) in (_____), as heard on recordings by vocalist (_____)

a) Memphis Soul
b) Chicago Soul
c) Rhythm and Blues
d) Soul Music
e) Blues
f) Gospel
g) Chicago, Illinois
h) Memphis, Tennessee

Quiz 2-22) (_____) also known as (_____) is the lead singer for The Isley Brothers.

a) Ronald Isley
b) Curtis Mayfield
c) Chuck Berry
d) Jimmy Isley
e) Mr . Biggs
f) Mr. Biggy
g) Big Mister

Quiz 2-23) Chuck Berry was also known as Mr. Biggs.

a) False

Quiz 2-24) Marvin Gaye was also known as Mr. Biggs.

a) False

Quiz 2-25) What was the name of the Isley Brothers' track used for Notorious B.I.G.'s "Big Poppa"?

a) "Keep on Pushing"
b) "Move on up"
c) "I Loved and I Lost"

d)   "In Between the Sheets"
e)   "For the Easy Listeners"

Quiz 2-26) Which artist used the track "In Between the Sheets" by the Isley Brothers for the track "Big Poppa?"

a)   Notorious B.I.G.
b)   Sean "Puff Daddy" Combs
c)   Snoop Dogg
d)   Ghostface Killah

Quiz 2-27) Sean "Puff Daddy" Combs used the track "In Between the Sheets" on the track "Big Poppa."

a)   False

Quiz 2-28) Name the artist and the track mentioned in lecture that served as the precursor to Notorious B.I.G.'s "Big Poppa."

a)   DJ Magic Mike
b)   Ghostface Killah
c)   Sean "Puff Daddy" Combs
d)   "Keep on Pushing"
e)   "Move On Up"
f)   "I Loved and I Lost"
g)   "In Between The Sheets"
h)   "For The Easy Listeners"

Quiz 2-29) The track "For the Easy Listeners" by Notorious B.I.G. served as the precursor to DJ Magic Mike's "Big Poppa."

a)   False

Quiz 2-30) The track "For the Easy Listeners" by DJ Magic Mike served as the precursor to Notorious B.I.G.'s "Big Poppa."

a)   True

Quiz 2-31) Aretha Franklin was a Motown Artist.

a)   False

Quiz 2-32) Aretha Franklin was signed to Arista Records

a)   True

Quiz 2-33) Aretha Franklin was the "Queen of Soul"

a)   True

Quiz 2-34) Aretha Franklin was the "Queen of Gospel"

a)   False

Quiz 2-35) Aretha Franklin was signed to Stax Records

a)   False

Quiz 2-36) Name the Queen of Soul and the name of her record label.

a)   Aretha Franklin
b)   Bessie Smith
c)   Mahalia Jackson
d)   Erykah Badu
e)   Stax Records
f)   Motown Records
g)   Arista Records

Quiz 2-37) Funk is represented by a circular and continuous rhythmic cycle (circle) that is less defined.

a)   False

Quiz 2-38) Funk is represented by an angular rhythmic cycle with four distinct designations of the beat (square).

a)   True

Quiz 2-39) An angular rhythmic cycle with four distinct designations of the beat (square) is best represented by which genre of music?

a)   Funk
b)   Polka
c)   Jazz
d)   R&B

Quiz 2-40) A circular and continuous rhythmic cycle that is less defined (circle) is best represented by which genre of music?

a)   Jazz/R&B
b)   Funk
c)   Hip-Hop
d)   Blues
e)   Polka

Quiz 2-41) Jazz is represented by an angular rhythmic cycle with four distinct designations of the beat (square).

a)   False

Quiz 2-42) Jazz is represented by a circular and continuous rhythmic cycle (circle) that is less defined.

a)   True

Quiz 2-43) What is the name of Curtis Mayfield's record company?

a)   Stax Records
b)   Hi Records

c) Arista Records
d) Curtom Records
e) Motown Records

Quiz 2-44) Curtis Mayfield founded Stax Records.

a) False

Quiz 2-45) Curtis Mayfield founded Motown Records

a) False

Quiz 2-46) Curtis Mayfield founded Curtom Records

a) True

Quiz 2-47) Which subgenre is characterized by a call-and-response style of group singing?

a) Gospel
b) Memphis Soul
c) Chicago Soul
d) Soul

Quiz 2-48) Chicago Soul is also known as:

a) Northern Soul
b) Southern Soul
c) Memphis Soul
d) Eastern Soul

Quiz 2-49) Memphis soul is characterized by a call-and-response style of group singing.

a) False

Quiz 2-50) Northern Soul is also known as:

a) Chicago Soul
b) Western Soul
c) Memphis Soul
d) Eastern Soul

Quiz 2-51) Who is the "godfather" of Chicago Soul?

a) Curtis Mayfield
b) Marvin Gaye
c) James Brown
d) Don Cornelius

Quiz 2-52) What is the name of the Curtis Mayfield song and the associated 1970s blaxploitation film mentioned in the lecture?

a) "Pusherman"
b) Shaft

c)   Superfly
d)   "Keep on Pushing"
e)   "Move on up"
f)   "I Loved and I Lost"
g)   "In Between The Sheets"
h)   "For The Easy Listeners"
i)   Sweet Sweetback's Baadasssss Song
j)   Blacula
k)   Space Is the Place

Quiz 2-53) *Superfly* is a film in the blaxploitation genre.

a)   True

Quiz 2-54) Name the host of the show "Soul Train" during the 1970s.

a)   Don Cornelius
b)   Berry Gordy
c)   Marvin Gaye
d)   James Brown
e)   Curtis Mayfield

Quiz 2-55) What city was the show "Soul Train" first recorded in?

a)   Philadelphia, Pennsylvania
b)   Chicago, Illinois
c)   Memphis, Tennessee
d)   Harlem, New York City
e)   Detroit, Michigan

Quiz 2-56) Who founded Motown Records?

a)   Berry Gordy
b)   Marvin Gaye
c)   James Brown
d)   Don Cornelius

Quiz 2-57) What is the name of Berry Gordy's record company?

a)   Stax Records
b)   Hi Records'
c)   Arista Records
d)   Curtom Records
e)   Motown Records

Quiz 2-58) Motown Records was founded by James Brown.

a)   False

Quiz 2-59) Stax Records was founded by Berry Gordy

a)   False

Quiz 2-60) Motown Records was located in Philadelphia, Pennsylvania.

a)   False

Quiz 2-61) Motown Records was founded in Detroit, Michigan

a)   True

Quiz 2-62) Hi Records was founded in Detroit, Michigan

a)   False

Quiz 2-63) Philadelphia, Pennsylvania is also known as "Motor City"

a)   False

Quiz 2-64) What city is known as "Motor City" and why?

a)   Detroit, Michigan
b)   Philadelphia, Pennsylvania
c)   Memphis, Tennessee
d)   Chicago, Illinois
e)   Automotive Production
f)   Drag Races
g)   Reputation for funky music

Quiz 2-65) The (_____) genre is an amalgamation (mixture) of soul music, jazz, and R&B.

a)   Hip-Hop
b)   Funk
c)   Chicago Soul
d)   Memphis Soul
e)   Ragtime

Quiz 2-66) The Hip-Hop genre is an amalgamation (mixture) of soul music, jazz, and R&B.

a)   False

Quiz 2-67) The Funk genre is an amalgamation (mixture) of soul music, jazz and R&B.

a)   True

Quiz 3 Question Bank

Quiz 3-1) What is James Brown's signature groove, emphasizing the downbeat, referred to as?

Quiz 3-2) James Brown's signature groove, emphasizing the downbeat, is referred to as The Backbeat.

a)   False

Quiz 3-3) James Brown's signature groove, emphasizing the downbeat, is referred to as The One.

a)   True

Quiz 3-4) James Brown's signature groove, emphasizing the downbeat, is referred to as The Break Beat.

a) False

Quiz 3-5) Prince represents the epitome of 80s production.

a) False

Quiz 3-6) Prince represents the low point of 80's production.

a) False

Quiz 3-7) Scratch represents the epitome of 80s production.

a) False

Quiz 3-8) Identify the two Funk Jazz bands of the 1970s:

a) The Ohio Players
b) Earth Wind and Fire
c) The Chi-Lites
d) The Contours
e) Three Ounces of Love
f) The Dynamic Superiors
g) High Energy
h) The Lost Nation
i) Sunday Funnies

Quiz 3-9) Identify the two Funk Jazz bands of the 1970s:

a) Sly and Family Stone
b) Earth Wind and Fire
c) The Chi-Lites
d) The Contours
e) Three Ounces of Love
f) The Dynamic Superiors
g) High Energy
h) The Lost Nation
i) Sunday Funnies

Quiz 3-10) Identify the two Funk Jazz bands of the 1970s:

a) War
b) Sly and The Family Stone
c) The Chi-Lites
d) The Contours
e) Three Ounces of Love
f) The Dynamic Superiors
g) High Energy
h) The Lost Nation
i) Sunday Funnies

Quiz 3-11) Identify the two Funk Jazz bands of the 1970s:

a) The Commodores
b) Stylistics
c) The Chi-Lites
d) The Contours
e) Three Ounces of Love
f) The Dynamic Superiors
g) High Energy
h) The Lost Nation
i) Sunday Funnies

Quiz 3-12) Identify the two Funk Jazz bands of the 1970s:

a) The Commodores
b) Heatwave
c) The Chi-Lites
d) The Contours
e) Three Ounces of Love
f) The Dynamic Superiors
g) High Energy
h) The Lost Nation
i) Sunday Funnies

Quiz 3-13) Parliament Funkadelic was heavily influenced by (_____) and (_____).

a) Jazz
b) Psychedelicrock
c) Punk Rock
d) Rockabilly
e) Psychobilly
f) Reggae

Quiz 3-14) Parliament Funkadelic was heavily influenced by Reggae and Psychobilly.

a) False

Quiz 3-15) Parliament Funkadelic was heavily influenced by Jazz and Psychedelic Rock.

a) True

Quiz 3-16) Parliament Funkadelic was heavily influenced by Jazz and Punk Rock.

a) False

Quiz 3-17) Identify the genre that these statements apply to "Horn sections were replaced by synth keyboards" and "Electronic drum machines began to replace the 'funky drummers' of the past and the lyrics of funk songs became more graphic and sexually explicit."

a) Hyper Funk
b) P-Funk
c) R&B

d) Soul

e) Gospel

Quiz 3-18) Features of Hyper Funk include "horn sections replaced by synth keyboards"; Funky drummers replaced by electronic drum machines"; and "more graphic and sexually explicit lyrics."

a) True

Quiz 3-19) Features of Hyper Funk include "synth keyboards replaced by live horn sections" and "Electronic drum machines replaced by 'funky' drummers, and less graphic and sexually explicit lyrics."

a) False

Quiz 3-20) Features of P-Funk include "horn sections replaced by synth keyboards"; Funky drummers replaced by electronic drum machines"; and "more graphic and sexually explicit lyrics."

a) False

Quiz 3-21) Parliament-Funkadelic, also known as (_____), was founded by (_____).

a) P-Funk

b) Hyper Funk

c) Soul

d) Punk-Funk

e) George Clinton

f) Bill Clinton

g) Berry Gordy

Quiz 3-22) Parliament-Funkadelic, also known as Punk-Funk, was founded by Bill Clinton.

a) False

Quiz 3-23) Parliament-Funkadelic, also known as P-Funk, was founded by George Clinton.

a) True

Quiz 3-24) In the 1980s, largely as a reaction against what was seen as the overrated popularity of Disco many of the core elements began to be usurped by electronic machines and synthesizers.

a) Disco

b) P-Funk

c) Hyper Funk

d) Soul

e) R&B

f) Dub

Quiz 3-25) In the 1980s, largely as a reaction against what was seen as the overrated popularity of Hyper Funk many of the core elements began to be usurped by electronic machines and synthesizers.

a) False

Quiz 3-26) In the 1980s, largely as a reaction against what was seen as the overrated popularity of Disco many of the core elements began to be usurped by electronic machines and synthesizers.

a) True

Quiz 3-27) Which beat does James Brown's signature groove, "The One" emphasize?

a) The Downbeat
b) The Break Beat
c) The Two
d) The Up Beat
e) The Backbeat

Quiz 3-28) Identify the title and the year of the James Brown Hit mentioned in the previous lecture.

a) "Cold Sweat"
b) "Candy"
c) "She's Strange"
d) "Give it to Me Baby"
e) "Super Freak"
f) 1966
g) 1967
h) 1968
i) 1969
j) 1970

Quiz 3-29) Identify the title and the year of the James Brown Hit mentioned in the previous lecture.

a) "Mother Popcorn"
b) "Candy"
c) "She's Strange"
d) "Give it to Me Baby"
e) "Super Freak"
f) 1966
g) 1967
h) 1968
i) 1969
j) 1970

Quiz 3-30) Identify the title and the year of the James Brown Hit mentioned in the previous lecture.

a) "Get Up (I Feel Like Being A) Sex Machine"
b) "Candy"
c) "She's Strange"
d) "Give it to Me Baby"
e) "Super Freak"
f) 1966
g) 1967
h) 1968
i) 1969
j) 1970

Quiz 3-31) "She's Strange" is one of the James Brown hits mentioned in the previous lecture.

a)   False

Quiz 3-32) "Super Freak" is one of the James Brown hits mentioned in the previous lecture.

a)   False

Quiz 3-33) "Give it to Me Baby" is one of the James Brown hits mentioned in the previous lecture.

a)   False

Quiz 3-34) "Get Up (I Feel Like Being A) Sex Machine" is one of the James Brown hits mentioned in the previous lecture.

a)   True

Quiz 3-35) "Mother Popcorn" is one of the James Brown hits mentioned in the previous lecture.

a)   True

Quiz 3-36) "Cold Sweat" is one of the James Brown hits mentioned in the previous lecture.

a)   True

Quiz 3-37) Identify the title of one of the Cameo tracks played in the previous lecture

a)   "Mother Popcorn"
b)   "Get Up (I Feel Like Being A) Sex Machine"
c)   "Candy"
d)   "Cold Sweat"
e)   "Give it to Me Baby"
f)   "Super Freak"

Quiz 3-38) Identify the title of one of the Cameo tracks played in the previous lecture

a)   "Mother Popcorn"
b)   "Get Up (I Feel Like Being A) Sex Machine"
c)   "She's Strange"
d)   "Cold Sweat"
e)   "Give it to Me Baby"
f)   "Super Freak"

Quiz 3-39) "Cold Sweat" is one of the Cameo tracks played in the previous lecture.

a)   False

Quiz 3-40) "Get Up (I Feel Like Being A) Sex Machine" is one of the Cameo tracks played in the previous lecture.

a)   False

Quiz 3-41) "Candy" is one of the Cameo tracks played in the previous lecture.

a)   True

Quiz 3-42) "She's Strange" is one of the Cameo tracks played in the previous lecture.

a)   True

Quiz 3-43) Dub legend Osbourne Ruddock's nickname is "Scratch."

a)   False

Quiz 3-44) Dub legend Errol Thompson's nickname is "King Tubby."

a)   False

Quiz 3-45) Dub legend Lee Perry's nickname is "King Tubby."

a)   False

Quiz 3-46) Dub legend Osbourne Ruddock's nickname is "King Tubby."

a)   True

Quiz 3-47) Select two Dub legends mentioned in the lecture:

a)   Osbourne Ruddock
b)   Richard Riddick
c)   Errol Thompson
d)   Errol Garner
e)   James Brown
f)   Rick James

Quiz 3-48) Select two Dub legends mentioned in the lecture

a)   Osbourne Ruddock
b)   Richard B. Riddick
c)   Lee Perry
d)   Lee Marvin
e)   James Brown
f)   Rick James

Quiz 3-49) Lee "Scratch" Marvin and Richard "King Tubby" Riddick were two of the Dub Legends mentioned in the lecture.

a)   False

Quiz 3-50) Lee "Scratch" Marvin and Errol Garner were two of the Dub Legends mentioned in the lecture.

a)   False

Quiz 3-51) Osbourne "King Tubby" Ruddock and Lee "Scratch" Perry were two of the Dub Legends mentioned in the lecture.

a) True

Quiz 3-52) Errol Thompson and Lee "Scratch" Perry were two of the Dub Legends mentioned in the lecture.

a) True

Quiz 3-53) Osbourne "King Tubby" Ruddock and Errol Thompson were two of the Dub Legends mentioned in the lecture.

a) True

Quiz 3-54) Select two Dub legends mentioned in the lecture.

a) Errol Thompson
b) Errol Garner
c) Lee Perry
d) Lee Marvin
e) James Brown
f) Rick James

Quiz 3-55) Rick James and James Brown were two of the Dub legends mentioned in the lecture.

a) False

Quiz 3-56) Which two of these singles/songs resulted in Rick James becoming a star and paved the way for the future direction of explicitness in funk?

a) "Give it to Me Baby"
b) "SuperFreak"
c) "Mother Popcorn"
d) "Get Up (I Feel Like Being A) Sex Machine"
e) "Candy"
f) "Cold Sweat"

Quiz 3-57) The singles/songs "Get Up (I Feel Like Being A) Sex Machine" and "Cold Sweat" resulted in Rick James becoming a star and paved the way for the future direction of explicitness in funk.

a) False

Quiz 3-58) The singles/songs "Mother Popcorn" and "Candy" resulted in Rick James becoming a star and paved the way for the future direction of explicitness in funk.

a) False

Quiz 3-59) The singles/songs "Give It To Me Baby" and "Super Freak" resulted in Rick James becoming a star and paved the way for the future direction of explicitness in funk.

a) True

Quiz 3-60) What is William Earl Collin's nickname?

a) Bootsy
b) Scratch
c) King Tubby
d) Prince

Quiz 3-61) What is Bootsy's real name?

a) William Earl Collins
b) James Earl Jones
c) Earl Grey Williams
d) James Brown
e) Rick James
f) James Earl Brown

Quiz 3-62) Bootsy's real name is James Earl Jones.

a) False

Quiz 3-63) Bootsy's real name is William Earl Collins.

a) True

Quiz 3-64) William Earl Collins' nickname is "King Tubby."

a) False

Quiz 3-65) William Earl Collins' nickname is "Bootsy."

a) True

Quiz 3-66) James Brown's frenzied vocals, frequently punctuated with screams and grunts, channeled the "ecstatic ambiance of the "Black Church" in a secular context.

a) True

Quiz 3-67) Rick James's frenzied vocals, frequently punctuated with screams and grunts, channeled the "ecstatic ambiance of the "Black Church" in a secular context.

a) False

Quiz 3-68) James Brown's frenzied vocals, frequently punctuated with screams and grunts, channeled the "ecstatic ambiance of the "Lutheran Church" in a secular context.

a) False

Quiz 3-69) James Brown's frenzied vocals, frequently punctuated with screams and grunts, channeled the "ecstatic ambiance of the "Black Church" in a secular context.

a) James Brown
b) Rick James
c) Lee Perry

d) Prince
e) Black Church
f) Baptist Church
g) Evangelical Church
h) Lutheran Church

Quiz 3-70) William Earl Collins' nickname is "Prince."

a) False

Quiz 4 Question Bank

Quiz 4-1) Hip-Hop is a cultural movement that developed in NYC in the 1970s primarily among African and Latino Americans.

a) True

Quiz 4-2) Hip-Hop is a cultural movement that developed in Philadelphia in the 1970s primarily among African and Asian Americans.

a) False

Quiz 4-3) Hip-Hop is a cultural movement that developed in (_____) in the 1970s primarily among African and (_____) Americans.

a) New York City
b) Philadelphia, Pennsylvania
c) Chicago, Illinois
d) Columbia, South Carolina
e) Latino
f) Asian
g) Native
h) Caucasian

Quiz 4-4) Hip-Hop is a cultural movement that developed in Chicago, Illinois, in the 1980s primarily among African and Caucasian Americans.

a) False

Quiz 4-5) The Griots of West Africa are a group of traveling singers and poets, whose vocal style is similar to that of rappers and who are part of an oral tradition dating back hundreds of years.

a) True

Quiz 4-6) The (_____) of West Africa are a group of traveling singers and poets, whose vocal style is similar to that of rappers and who are part of an oral tradition dating back hundreds of years.

a) Griots
b) Skalds
c) Bards
d) Azmari
e) Marabout

Quiz 4-7) The Griots of (_____) are a group of traveling singers and poets, whose vocal style is similar to that of rappers and who are part of an oral tradition dating back hundreds of years.

a) North Africa
b) South Africa
c) East Africa
d) Central Africa
e) West Africa
f) Central Asia
g) West Indies

Quiz 4-8) The Griots of Central Asia are a group of traveling singers and poets, whose vocal style is similar to that of rappers and who are part of an oral tradition dating back hundreds of years.

a) False

Quiz 4-9) Identify two essential elements of Hip-Hop:

a) Riff oriented
b) Shuffle/Triplet
c) Overt backbeat
d) Twelve bar blues
e) Rapping/MC-ing
f) DJ-ing (Sampling/Beat Making)

Quiz 4-10) Identify two essential elements of Hip-Hop:

a) Twelve bar blues
b) Riff oriented
c) Shuffle/Triplet
d) Overt backbeat
e) Breaking (B-boyin'/B-girlin')
f) Graffiti

Quiz 4-11) Identify two essential elements of Hip-Hop:

a) Twelve bar blues
b) Riff oriented
c) Shuffle/Triplet
d) Overt backbeat
e) Graffiti
f) Rapping/MC-ing

Quiz 4-12) Identify two essential elements of Hip-Hop:

a) Twelve bar blues
b) Riff oriented
c) Shuffle/Triplet
d) Overt backbeat
e) Breaking (B-boyin'/B-girlin')
f) Rapping/MC-ing

Quiz 4-13) Two "Cultural Foundations" for Hip-Hop as explained in the lecture include Poetry and Comedy.

a) True

Quiz 4-14) Two "Cultural Foundations" for Hip-Hop as explained in the lecture include Storytelling and Rhyming.

a) True

Quiz 4-15) Two "Cultural Foundations" for Hip-Hop as explained in the lecture include explicit lyrics and an overt backbeat.

a) False

Quiz 4-16) Pick two "Cultural Foundations" for Hip-Hop as explained in the lecture:

a) Explicit lyrics
b) Misogyny
c) Silver Screen
d) Storytelling
e) Poetry

Quiz 4-17) Pick two "Cultural Foundations" for Hip-Hop as explained in the lecture:

a) Explicit lyrics
b) Misogyny
c) Silver Screen
d) Poetry
e) Comedy

Quiz 4-18) Pick two "Cultural Foundations" for Hip-Hop as explained in the lecture:

a) Explicit lyrics
b) Misogyny
c) Silver Screen
d) Rhyming/Rhymes
e) Storytelling, etc.

Quiz 4-19) Pick two "Cultural Foundations" for Hip-Hop as explained in the lecture:

a) Explicit lyrics
b) Misogyny
c) Silver Screen
d) Rhyming/Rhymcs
e) Comedy

Quiz 4-20) Pick two "Cultural Foundations" for Hip-Hop as explained in the lecture.

a) Explicit lyrics
b) Misogyny
c) Silver Screen
d) Rhyming/Rhymes
e) Poetry

Quiz 4-21) List two comedians that have influenced Hip-Hop as explained in the lecture:

a) Redd Foxx
b) Richard Pryor
c) Bernie Mac
d) Chris Tucker
e) Martin Lawrence
f) Steve Harvey
g) Kevin Hart

Quiz 4-22) List two comedians that have influenced Hip-Hop as explained in the lecture:

a) Eddie Murphy
b) Dave Chappelle
c) Bernie Mac
d) Chris Tucker
e) Martin Lawrence
f) Steve Harvey
g) Kevin Hart

Quiz 4-23) List two comedians that have influenced Hip-Hop as explained in the lecture:

a) Dave Chappelle
b) ChrisRock
c) Bernie Mac
d) Chris Tucker
e) Martin Lawrence
f) Steve Harvey
g) Kevin Hart

Quiz 4-24) List two comedians that have influenced Hip-Hop as explained in the lecture:

a) Redd Foxx
b) Pigmeat Markham
c) Bernie Mac
d) Chris Tucker
e) Martin Lawrence
f) Steve Harvey
g) Kevin Hart

Quiz 4-25) What country was DJ Kool Herc born in?

a) Jamaica
b) United States
c) United Kingdom
d) Canada
e) Barbados
f) Dominican Republic

Quiz 4-26) What is the name of the Jamaican-born DJ known as the "Father of Hip-Hop"

a) Clive Campbell
b) Glenn Campbell

c)   Lawrence Parker
d)   Antonio Hardy
e)   Carlton Ridenhour   ,
f)   William Drayton

Quiz 4-27) DJ Kool Herc was born in Barbados.

a)   False

Quiz 4-28) DJ Kool Herc was born in Jamaica.

a)   True

Quiz 4-29) DJ Kool Herc is credited as being the "Father of Dub."

a)   False

Quiz 4-30) DJ Kool Herc is credited as being the "Father of Hip-Hop."

a)   True

Quiz 4-31) DJ Kool Herc is credited as being the

a)   "Father of Hip-Hop"
b)   "Father of Soul"
c)   "Father of R&B
d)   "Father of Rap"
e)   "Father of Dub"

Quiz 4-32) The Jamaican tradition of boasting, impromptu poetry, and sayings over music is known as

a)   Toasting
b)   Locking
c)   Popping
d)   Breaking
e)   Rapping

Quiz 4-33) The Jamaican tradition of boasting, impromptu poetry, and sayings over music is known as Toasting.

a)   True

Quiz 4-34) The Jamaican tradition of boasting, impromptu poetry, and sayings over music is known as Popping.

a)   False

Quiz 4-35) The isolation of one particular section of a musical composition, in order to serve as a vamp for an Emcee, or for B-Boys/B-Girls to dance to is known as

a)   The Break
b)   The Beat
c)   The Backbeat
d)   The Downbeat
e)   The Upbeat

Quiz 4-36) The isolation of one particular section of a musical composition, in order to serve as a vamp for an Emcee, or for B-Boys/B-Girls to dance to is known as The Break.

a)   True

Quiz 4-37) The isolation of one particular section of a musical composition, in order to serve as a vamp for an Emcee, or for B-Boys/B-Girls to dance to is known as The Backbeat.

a)   False

Quiz 4-38) The rhythmic spoken delivery of rhymes and wordplay, delivered over a beat or without accompaniment is known as

a)   MCing/Rapping
b)   Boasting
c)   Locking
d)   DJing
e)   Beatboxing
f)   Beboping

Quiz 4-39) The rhythmic spoken delivery of rhymes and wordplay, delivered over a beat or without accompaniment is known as MCing/Rapping.

a)   True

Quiz 4-40) The rhythmic spoken delivery of rhymes and wordplay, delivered over a beat or without accompaniment is known as Beatboxing.

a)   False

Quiz 4-41) (_____) is more metaphorically advanced and more rhythmically complex than rap.

a)   Emceeing/MCing
b)   Boasting
c)   Locking
d)   DJing
e)   Beatboxing
f)   Beboping

Quiz 4-42) Breaking is a dynamic style of dance that developed as part of the Hip-Hop culture in the East.

a)   True

Quiz 4-43) (_____) is a dynamic style of dance that developed as part of the Hip-Hop culture in the East.

a)   Breaking
b)   Beboping
c)   Locking
d)   Rocking
e)   Popping

Quiz 4-44) Select two Turntablist techniques:

a) Beatboxing
b) Breaking
c) Rapping
d) Mixing and/or Cutting
e) Scratching
f) MCing

Quiz 4-45) Select two Turntablist techniques:

a) Beatboxing
b) Breaking
c) Rapping
d) MCing
e) Spinning
f) Sampling

Quiz 4-46) Select two Turntablist techniques:

a) Beatboxing
b) Breaking
c) Rapping
d) MCing
e) Song choice/criteria
f) Spinning

Quiz 4-47) Select two Turntablist techniques:

a) Beatboxing
b) Breaking
c) Rapping
d) MCing
e) Mixing and/or Cutting
f) Song choice/criteria

Quiz 4-48) Select two Turntablist techniques:

a) Beatboxing
b) Breaking
c) Rapping
d) MCing
e) Spinning
f) Scratching

Quiz 4-49) Rapper's Delight by the Sugar Hill Gang was performed over a breakdown section from the song "Good Times" by Chic.

a) True

Quiz 4-50) The breakdown section from "Good Times" by Chic served as the basis for which song?

a) "Rapper's Delight"
b) "The Breaks"
c) "Positive Force"
d) "The Message"
e) "Planet Rock"

Quiz 4-51) Which group used the breakdown section from "Good Times" by Chic as the basis for the track "Rapper's Delight."

a) Cameo
b) The Sugar Hill Gang
c) Cyprus Hill
d) Run-DMC
e) New York City Breakers
f) Rock Steady Crew

Quiz 4-52) Rapper's Delight by the Sugar Hill Gang was performed over a breakdown section from the song "Candy" by Cameo.

a) False

Quiz 4-53) Joseph Saddler is best known as Grand Master Flash.

a) True

Quiz 4-54) Grand Master Flash's real name is

a) Clive Campbell
b) Joseph Saddler
c) Lawrence Parker
d) Antonio Hardy
e) Carlton Ridenhour
f) William Drayton

Quiz 4-55) Grand Master Flash's real name is Clive Campbell.

a) False

Quiz 4-56) Joseph Saddler is best known as Kool Herc.

a) False

Quiz 4-57) "The Breaks" was the first Rap Song to be certified gold.

a) True

Quiz 4-58) "Rapper's Delight" was the first Rap Song to be certified gold.

a) False

Quiz 4-59) The First Certified Gold Rap Song:

a)   Positive Force
b)   Rapper' s Delight
c)   The Breaks
d)   The Message
e)   Planet Rock
f)   Sucka MCs

Quiz 4-60) Who was the first rapper to sign with a major label?

a)   Run DMC
b)   Kool Herc
c)   Kurtis Blow
d)   Afrika Bambaataa
e)   Grand Master Flash

Quiz 4-61) Kool Herc was the first rapper to sign with a major label.

a)   False

Quiz 4-62) Kurtis Blow was the first rapper to sign with a major label.

a)   True

Quiz 4-63) What is Run-D.M.C.'s place of origin?

a)   The Bronx, NYC
b)   Staten Island, NYC
c)   Hollis, Queens, NYC
d)   Brooklyn, NYC
e)   Queensbridge, NYC

Quiz 4-64) Run-D.M.C. originates from Queensbridge, NYC

a)   False

Quiz 4-65) Run-D.M.C. originates from the Hollis neighbourhood of Queens, NYC.

a)   True

Quiz 4-66) Which two of the following media outlets named Run-D.M.C. as the "Greatest Hip-Hop Group of All Time"?

a)   MTV
b)   VH1
c)   BET
d)   Rolling Stone
e)   Billboard
f)   MUCH MUSIC

Quiz 4-67) Billboard and Rolling Stone named Run-D.M.C as the "Greatest Hip-Hop Group of All Time."

a) False

Quiz 4-68) MTV and VH1 named Run-D.M.C. as the "Greatest Hip-Hop Group of All Time."

a) True

Quiz 4-69) MTV and VH1 named Grandmaster Flash and the Furious Five as the "Greatest Hip-Hop Group of All Time."

a) False

Quiz 4-70) Who was the first Hip-Hop artist/group to be inducted into the Rock and Roll Hall of Fame?

a) Run-D.M.C.
b) Grand Master Flash and the Furious Five
c) Kool Herc
d) Kurtis Blow
e) The Sugar Hill Gang

Quiz 4-71) The Sugar Hill Gang was the first Hip-Hop group to be inducted into the Rock and Roll Hall of Fame.

a) False

Quiz 4-72) Grand Master Flash and the Furious Five was the first Hip-Hop group to be inducted into the Rock and Roll Hall of Fame.

a) True

Quiz 4-73) What is the name of the track by Grandmaster Flash and the Furious Five that is sometimes cited as heralding the birth of "serious" Hip-Hop?

a) "The Message"
b) "Positive Force"
c) "Rapper' s Delight"
d) "The Breaks"
e) "Planet Rock"
f) "Sucka MCs"

Quiz 4-74) "The Message" by Grandmaster Flash and the Furious Five is sometimes cited as the birth of "serious" Hip-Hop.

a) True

Quiz 4-75) "Planet Rock" by Grandmaster Flash and the Furious Five is sometimes cited as the birth of "serious" Hip-Hop.

a) False

Quiz 4-76) "Rapper's Delight" by The Sugar Hill Gang is sometimes cited as the birth of "serious" Hip-Hop.

a) False

Quiz 4-77) Identify the early "Breaking" crew from the East Coast:

a)   Rock Steady Crew
b)   Run-D.M.C.
c)   The Sugar Hill Gang
d)   Grand Master Flash and the Furious Five
e)   Cyprus Hill

Quiz 4-78) Identify the early "Breaking" crew from the East Coast:

a)   New York City Breakers
b)   Run-D.M.C.
c)   The Sugar Hill Gang
d)   Grand Master Flash and the Furious Five
e)   Cyprus Hill

Quiz 4-79) The Rock Steady Crew and the New York City Breakers were two early "Breaking" crews from the East Coast.

a)   True

Quiz 4-80) The Rock Steady Crew and the New York City Breakers were two early "Breaking" crews from the West Coast.

a)   False

Quiz 4-81) Grand Master Flash and the Furious Five and The Sugar Hill Gang were two early "Breaking" crews from the East Coast.

a)   False

Quiz 4-82) Graffiti Terms: The act of creating Graffiti art or a particular style of Graffiti in which the entire train car is covered with Graffiti is called:

a)   Bombing
b)   Fade
c)   Families
d)   Floaters
e)   Freights

Quiz 4-83) Graffiti Terms: The graduation of colors:

a)   Bombing
b)   Fade
c)   Families
d)   Floaters
e)   Freights

Quiz 4-84) Graffiti Terms: Rows of throw ups (Graffiti) of the same name:

a)   Bombing
b)   Fade

c)   Families
d)   Floaters
e)   Freights

Quiz 4-85) Graffiti Terms: Throw ups (Graffiti) done on subway car panels at window level:

a)   Bombing
b)   Fade
c)   Families
d)   Floaters
e)   Freights

Quiz 4-86) Graffiti Terms: Rows of throw ups (Graffiti) of the same name are known as "Floaters."

a)   False

Quiz 4-87) Graffiti Terms: Rows of throw ups (Graffiti) of the same name are known as "Families."

a)   True

Quiz 4-88) TAKI 183 is one of the most influential graffiti writers.

a)   True

Quiz 4-89) Match the artist and the year of the following track: "Rapper's Delight"

a)   Sugar Hill Gang
b)   Grand Master Flash and the Furious Five
c)   Afrika Bambaataa
d)   Run-D.M.C.
e)   1979
f)   1980
g)   1982
h)   1984

Quiz 4-90) Match the artist and the year of the following track: "The Message"

a)   Sugar Hill Gang
b)   Grand Master Flash and the Furious Five
c)   Kurtis Blow
d)   Run-D.M.C.
e)   1979
f)   1980
g)   1982
h)   1984

Quiz 4-91) Match the artist and the year of the following track: "The Breaks"

a)   Sugar Hill Gang
b)   Grand Master Flash and the Furious Five
c)   Kurtis Blow
d)   Run-D.M.C.

e) 1979
f) 1980
g) 1982
h) 1984

Quiz 4-92) Match the artist and the year of the following track: "Sucka MC's"

a) Sugar Hill Gang
b) Grand Master Flash and the Furious Five
c) Kurtis Blow
d) Run-D.M.C.
e) 1979
f) 1980
g) 1982
h) 1984

Quiz 5 Question Bank

Quiz 5-1) Which of the following groups recorded "Roxanne, Roxanne"?

a) U.T.F.O.
b) Roxanne Shante
c) The Juice Crew
d) KRS-One
e) Run-DMC

Quiz 5-2) The song "Roxanne, Roxanne" was recorded by The Police.

a) False

Quiz 5-3) The song "Roxanne, Roxanne" was recorded by U.T.F.O.

a) True

Quiz 5-4) Big Daddy Kane is considered to be "one of the most influential and skilled Emcees in Hip-Hop."

a) True

Quiz 5-5) Which of the following artists is considered to be "one of the most influential and skilled Emcees in Hip-Hop?"

a) Big Daddy Kane
b) KRS-One
c) Marley Marl
d) MC Shan
e) Mr. Magic
f) Masta Ace

Quiz 5-6) Masta Ace is considered "one of the most influential and skilled rappers in Hip-Hop."

a) False

Quiz 5-7) Identify two members of The Juice Crew:

a) Grand Master Flash
b) Kool Herc
c) KRS-One
d) Kurtis Blow
e) Marley Marl
f) Roxanne Shanté

Quiz 5-8) Identify two members of The Juice Crew:

a) Grand Master Flash
b) Kool Herc
c) KRS-One
d) Kurtis Blow
e) Biz Markie
f) MC Shan

Quiz 5-9) Identify two members of The Juice Crew: Grand Master Flash

a) Grand Master Flash
b) Kool Herc
c) KRS-One
d) Kurtis Blow
e) Big Daddy Kane
f) Mr. Magic

Quiz 5-10) Identify two members of The Juice Crew:

a) Grand Master Flash
b) Kool Herc
c) KRS-One
d) Kurtis Blow
e) Kool G Rap
f) DJ Polo

Quiz 5-11) Identify two members of The Juice Crew:

a) Grand Master Flash
b) Kool Herc
c) KRS-One
d) Kurtis Blow
e) Masta Ace
f) Craig G

Quiz 5-12) Select the place of origin for The Juice Crew:

a) South Bronx, The Bronx, NYC
b) Staten Island, NYC
c) Hollis, Queens, NYC
d) Bedford-Stuyvesant, Brooklyn, NYC
e) Queensbridge, Queens, NYC

Quiz 5-13) Who are the founders of The Juice Crew?

a)   Marley Marl and Mr. Magic
b)   Kool G Rap and DJ Polo
c)   Big Daddy Kane and Craig G
d)   Masta Ace and Mr. Magic
e)   Biz Markie and MC Shan
f)   Biz Markie and Marley Marl

Quiz 5-14) Biz Markie and Marley Marl founded The Juice Crew.

a)   False

Quiz 5-15) Marley Marl and Mr. Magic founded The Juice Crew.

a)   True

Quiz 5-16) What is KRS-One's city of origin?

a)   South Bronx, The Bronx, NYC
b)   Staten Island, NYC
c)   Hollis, Queens, NYC
d)   Bedford-Stuyvesant, Brooklyn, NYC
e)   Queensbridge, Queens, NYC

Quiz 5-17) What is KRS-One's birth name?

a)   Clive Campbell
b)   Glenn Campbell
c)   Lawrence Parker
d)   Antonio Hardy
e)   Carlton Ridenhour
f)   William Drayton
g)   Peter Parker

Quiz 5-18) The Bridge Wars were widely regarded as having been won by which group, through which track?

a)   KRS-One and the BDP Crew
b)   The Juice Crew
c)   Run-DMC
d)   "The Bridge"
e)   "The Bridge Is Over"
f)   "Kill That Noise"
g)   "South Bronx"

Quiz 5-19) The Bridge Wars were widely regarded as having been won by KRS-One and the BDP Crew, with the track "The Bridge Is Over."

a)   True

Quiz 5-20) The Bridge Wars were widely regarded as having been won by The Juice Crew, with the track "The Bridge."

a) False

Quiz 5-21) What is Big Daddy Kane's birth name?

a) Clive Campbell
b) Glenn Campbell
c) Lawrence Parker
d) Antonio Hardy
e) Carlton Ridenhour
f) William Drayton
g) Peter Parker

Quiz 5-22) The Acronym KRS-ONE stands for "Knowledge Reigns Supreme Over Nearly Everyone."

a) True

Quiz 5-23) As KRS-One adopted a (_____) less violent approach, he turned away from his (_____) persona and toward that of "The Teacha."

a) Humanist
b) Blastmaster
c) The Teacha
d) Professa
e) Doctah
f) Lawyer
g) Beatsmaster
h) Masterblaster

Quiz 5-24) As KRS-One adopted a "Pacifist," less violent approach, he turned away from his "MasterBlaster" persona and toward that of "The Professa/Lawyer."

a) False

Quiz 5-25) As KRS-One adopted a "humanist," less violent approach, he turned away from his "Blastmaster" persona and toward that of "The Teacha/Philosopher."

a) True

Quiz 5-26) KRS-One is credited with innovating the (_____) side of freestyle battling via battles with (_____) in Cedar Park.

a) Aggressive
b) Philosophical
c) Metaphoric
d) Conscious
e) MC Shan
f) Marley Marl
g) Mr. Magic
h) DJ Polo

Quiz 5-27) What does the acronym KRS-ONE stand for?

a) Kris Rolls Spliffs Out Near Eastchester
b) Key Resistance Security Officer, North East
c) Kremlin Republic Security Office, North East
d) Kwanzaa Rational Savings Officer, National Estuary
e) Knowledge Reigns Supreme Over Nearly Everyone
f) Kwanzaa Rational Savings Office Non-Partisan Establishment

Quiz 5-28) What is the first song associated with The Bridge Wars?

a) "Kill That Noise"
b) "South Bronx"
c) "The Bridge"
d) "The Bridge Is Over"

Quiz 5-29) What is the second song associated with The Bridge Wars?

a) "Kill That Noise"
b) "SouthBronx"
c) "The Bridge"
d) "The Bridge Is Over"

Quiz 5-30) What is the third song associated with The Bridge Wars?

a) "Kill That Noise"
b) "South Bronx"
c) "The Bridge"
d) "The Bridge Is Over"

Quiz 5-31) What is the fourth and final song associated with The Bridge Wars?

a) "Kill That Noise"
b) "South Bronx"
c) "The Bridge"
d)"The Bridge Is Over"

Quiz 5-32) What is the name of the group formed by DJ Scott La Rock and KRS-One?

a) Boogie Down Productions
b) Death Row Records
c) Ciroc Entertainment
d) Maybach Music Group
e) Def Jam Recordings

Quiz 5-33) DJ Scott La Rock and KRS-One formed the company called Boogie Down Productions.

a) True

Quiz 5-34) DJ Scott La Rock and KRS-One formed the company called Ciroc Entertainment

a) False

Quiz 5-35) DJ Polo and Big Daddy Kane formed the company called Boogie Down Productions.

a)   False

Quiz 5-36) Marley Marl and Mr. Magic formed the company called Boogie Down Productions.

a)   False

Quiz 5-37) What is Big Daddy Kane's place of origin:

a)   South Bronx, The Bronx, NYC
b)   Staten Island, NYC
c)   Hollis, Queens, NYC
d)   Bedford-Stuyvesant, Brooklyn, NYC
e)   Queensbridge, Queens, NYC

Quiz 5-38) Name the FIRST "professional street dance" to gain prominence on the West Coast as well as one subcategory of this dance.

a)   Locking
b)   Toasting
c)   Popping
d)   Breaking
e)   Rapping

Quiz 5-39) Name the FIRST "professional street dance" to gain prominence on the West Coast as well as one subcategory of this dance.

a)   Locking
b)   Toasting
c)   Strutting
d)   Breaking
e)   Rapping

Quiz 5-40) Name the FIRST "professional street dance" to gain prominence on the West Coast as well as one subcategory of this dance.

a)   Locking
b)   Toasting
c)   Hittin'
d)   Breaking
e)   Rapping

Quiz 5-41) Name the FIRST "professional street dance" to gain prominence on the West Coast as well as one subcategory of this dance.

a)   Locking
b)   Toasting
c)   Boogaloo
d)   Breaking
e)   Rapping

Quiz 5-42) Name the FIRST "professional street dance" to gain prominence on the West Coast as well as one subcategory of this dance.

a) Locking
b) Toasting
c) Ticking
d) Breaking
e) Rapping

Quiz 5-43) Afrika Bambaataa created what is now known as (Electro-Funk), a style of "funk" driven by synthesizers and the electronic rhythm of the (_____) drum machine.

a) P-Funk
b) Electro-Funk
c) Hyper Funk
d) Punk-Funk
e) Chicago Funk

Quiz 5-44) Afrika Bambaataa created what is now known as Electro-Funk, a style of "funk" driven by synthesizers and the electronic rhythm of the (TR-808) drum machine.

a) TR-808
b) DR-55
c) HR-16B
d) SP-12
e) CR-78
f) TR-909

Quiz 5-45) (_____) created what is now known as Electro-Funk, a style of "funk" driven by synthesizers and the electronic rhythm of the (_____) drum machine.

a) Afrika Bambaataa
b) KRS-One
c) Kool Herc
d) Big Daddy Kane
e) MC Shan
f) DJ Polo

Quiz 5-46) Vocabulary: What many MC's call the music they perform to

a) Beats
b) Freestyle/Rap
c) Flow
d) MC/Emcee
e) Old School
f) Underground
g) Whack

Quiz 5-47) Vocabulary: To vocally improvize in a lyrical fashion across a range of subject matter:

a) Beats
b) Freestyle/Rap

c) Flow
d) MC/Emcee
e) Old School
f) Underground
g) Whack
h) Bite

Quiz 5-48) Vocabulary: A lyricist's/rapper's "cadence":

a) Beats
b) Freestyle/Rap
c) Flow
d) MC/Emcee
e) Old School
f) Underground
g) Whack
h) Bite

Quiz 5-49) Vocabulary: Master of ceremonies; the same in the realm of the Hip-Hop culture:

a) Beats
b) Freestyle/Rap
c) Flow
d) MC/Emcee
e) Old School
f) Underground
g) Whack
h) Bite

Quiz 5-50) Vocabulary: Reminiscent of past processes, virtues or actions:

a) Beats
b) Freestyle/Rap
c) Flow
d) MC/Emcee
e) Old School
f) Underground
g) Whack
h) Bite

Quiz 5-51) Vocabulary: Music that is not mainstream or formatted for radio:

a) Beats
b) Freestyle/Rap
c) Flow
d) MC/Emcee
e) Old School
f) Underground
g) Whack
h) Bite

Quiz 5-52) Vocabulary: This word is used to describe work of poor quality, to say that something or someone is terrible, or that their actions reflect a poor decision:

a) Beats
b) Freestyle/Rap
c) Flow
d) MC/Emcee
e) Old School
f) Underground
g) Whack
h) Bite

Quiz 5-53) Vocabulary: Plagiarism; to steal styles, concepts or lyrics from someone else:

a) Beats
b) Freestyle/Rap
c) Flow
d) MC/Emcee
e) Old School
f) Underground
g) Whack
h) Bite

Quiz 5-54) Vocabulary: "Old School" is "Reminiscent of past processes, virtues or actions."

a) True

Quiz 5-55) Vocabulary: "Old School" is "Music that is not mainstream or formatted for radio."

a) False

Quiz 5-56) Vocabulary: "Whack" means "Plagiarism; to steal styles, concepts or lyrics from someone else."

a) False

Quiz 5-57) Vocabulary: "Whack" is used "used to describe work of poor quality; to say that something or someone is terrible, or that their actions reflect a poor decision."

a) True

Quiz 5-58) Which song was recorded by U.T.F.O.?

a) "Roxanne, Roxanne"
b) "Roxanne"
c) "Kill That Noise"
d) "South Bronx"
e) "The Bridge"
f) "The Bridge Is Over"

Quiz 6 Question Bank

Quiz 6-1) Terms like "slow flow" and "mesmeric" are used to describe this MC:

a) MC G.U.R.U.
b) Rakim
c) KRS-One
d) MC Shan
e) Mr. Magic
f) Masta Ace

Quiz 6-2) Terms like "slow flow" and "mesmeric" are used to describe Rakim.

a) True

Quiz 6-3) Terms like "slow flow" and "mesmeric" are used to describe MC G.U.R.U.

a) False

Quiz 6-4) Which two terms are used to describe Rakim?

a) Slow Flow
b) Mesmeric
c) Aggressive
d) Humanist
e) Philosophical
f) Metaphoric
g) Conscious

Quiz 6-5) Terms like "humanist" and "conscious" are used to describe Rakim

a) False

Quiz 6-6) What year was *Paid In Full* by Eric B. and Rakim released?

a) 1985
b) 1986
c) 1987
d) 1988
e) 1989
f) 1990

Quiz 6-7) What is the title of American Hip-Hop duo Eric B. and Rakim's debut studio album?

a) *Paid in Full*
b) *Follow The Leader*
c) *Let The Rhythm Hit 'Em*
d) *Don' t Sweat the Technique*
e) *Bigger and Deffer*
f) *Rock the House*

Quiz 6-8) Identify the artist/group that recorded the album *Paid In Full*.

a) Eric B. and Rakim
b) Public Enemy
c) LL Cool J
d) DJ Jazzy Jeff and The Fresh Prince Gangstarr
e) Salt-n-Pepa

Quiz 6-9) *Paid In Full* is the debut studio album of American Hip-Hop duo Eric B. and Rakim released in 1987.

a) True

Quiz 6-10) *Paid In Full* is the debut studio album of American Hip-Hop duo DJ Jazzy Jeff and The Fresh Prince released in 1987.

a) False

Quiz 6-11) *Paid In Full* was one of the first Hip-Hop records to fully embrace (_____)

a) *70s Funk Samples*
b) *Funky Drummers*
c) *Drum Machines*
d) *Sampled Drum Beats*
e) *Explicit Lyrics*
f) *Break Beats*

Quiz 6-12) Which of the following albums was the first Hip-Hop record to fully embrace 70s Funk Samples?

a) *Paid in Full*
b) *Follow the Leader*
c) *Let the Rhythm Hit 'Em*
d) *Don't Sweat the Technique*
e) *Bigger and Deffer*
f) *Rock the House*

Quiz 6-13) *Paid in Full* was one of the first Hip-Hop records to fully embrace explicit lyrics

a) False

Quiz 6-14) *Paid in Full* was one of the first Hip-Hop records to fully embrace 70s Funk Samples

a) True

Quiz 6-15) *Let the Rhythm Hit 'Em* was one of the first Hip-Hop records to fully embrace 70s Funk Samples.

a) False

Quiz 6-16) *Paid in Full*'s heavy use of sampling by Eric B, such as from Bobby Byrd's "I Know You Got Soul," became influential in Hip-Hop production.

a) True

Quiz 6-17) *Paid in Full*'s heavy use of sampling by Eric B, such as from Bobby Byrd's "I Know You Got Soul," became influential in Hip-Hop production.

a)   Sampling
b)   Explicit Lyrics
c)   Funky Drumming
d)   Break Beats
e)   "I Know You Got Soul"
f)   "Get Up (I Feel Like Being A) Sex Machine"
g)   "Mother Popcorn"
h)   "Cold Sweat"

Quiz 6-18) With the emergence of a new generation of samplers such as the AKAI S900 producers were at last free of the need for tape.

a)   True

Quiz 6-19) With the emergence of a new generation of (_____) such as the (_____) producers were at last free of the need for (_____).

a)   Samplers
b)   Drum Machines
c)   Synthesisers
d)   Turntables
e)   AKAI S900
f)   TR-808
g)   DR-55
h)   TR-909
i)   Tape Loops
j)   Vinyl
k)   CDs

Quiz 6-20) Public Enemy is an American Hip-Hop group formed on Long Island, NY, in the year 1982.

a)   True

Quiz 6-21) Erik B. and Rakim are an American Hip-Hop group formed on Long Island, NY, in the year 1982.

a)   False

Quiz 6-22) What is Public Enemy's place of origin?

a)   The Bronx, NYC
b)   Staten Island, NYC
c)   Hollis, Queens, NYC
d)   Brooklyn, NYC
e)   Queensbridge, NYC
f)   Long Island, NY

Quiz 6-23) In what year was Public Enemy formed?

a)   1980
b)   1981

c)   1982
d)   1983
e)   1984
f)   1985

Quiz 6-24) Public Enemy is known for its politically charged lyrics and its criticism of the American Media.

a)   True

Quiz 6-25) Public Enemy is known for its (_____) and its criticism of the (_____).

a)   Politically Charged Lyrics
b)   Explicit Lyrics
c)   Metaphorical Lyrics
d)   American Media
e)   American Government
f)   Parents Music Resource Center

Quiz 6-26) Public Enemy is known for its explicit lyrics and its criticism of the Parents Music Resource Center.

a)   False

Quiz 6-27) Identify two member of Public Enemy by their birth name:

a)   Clive Campbell
b)   Glenn Campbell
c)   Lawrence Parker
d)   Antonio Hardy
e)   Carlton Ridenhour
f)   William Drayton
g)   Peter Parker

Quiz 6-28) Clive Campbell and Lawrence Parker are the birth names of two members of Public Enemy.

a)   False

Quiz 6-29) Carlton Ridenhour and William Drayton are the birth names of two members of Public Enemy.

a)   True

Quiz 6-30) LL Cool J stands for:

a)   Ladies Love Cool James
b)   Love Lost Cool James
c)   Long Live Cool James
d)   Lyric Loopin' Cool Jimmy

Quiz 6-31) LL Cool J stands for "Ladies Love Cool James."

a)   True

Quiz 6-32) LL Cool J stands for "Long Live Cool James."

a)   False

Quiz 6-33) Which of the following tracks is a romantic ballad by LL Cool James?

a)   "I Need Love"
b)   "Positive Force"
c)   "The Message"
d)   "Candy"
e)   "Give it to Me Baby"
f)   "I Loved and I Lost"

Quiz 6-33) Which of the following tracks is a romantic ballad by LL Cool James?

a)   "Around the Way Girl"
b)   "Positive Force"
c)   "The Message"
d)   "Candy"
e)   "Give it to Me Baby"
f)   "I Loved and I Lost"

Quiz 6-33) Which of the following tracks is a romantic ballad by LL Cool James?

a)   "Hey Lover"
b)   "Positive Force"
c)   "The Message"
d)   "Candy"
e)   "Give It To Me Baby"
f)   "I Loved and I Lost"

Quiz 6-34) What is LL Cool J's place of origin?

a)   Queens, NYC
b)   The Bronx, NYC
c)   Staten Island, NYC
d)   Hollis, Queens, NYC
e)   Brooklyn, NYC
f)   Queensbridge, NYC

Quiz 6-35) LL Cool J originates from Queensbridge, NYC.

a)   False

Quiz 6-36) LL Cool J originates from Queens, NYC

a)   True

Quiz 6-37) Pick two techniques involved in using a sample in a new song:

a)   Electronic drum machines began to replace funky drummers
b)   Lyrics became more graphic and sexually explicit

c)   Mixing and/or Cutting
d)   Diminution/Augmentation of original sample
e)   Increase/decrease tempo (BPM)

Quiz 6-38) Pick two techniques involved in using a sample in a new song:

a)   Electronic drum machines began to replace funky drummers
b)   Lyrics became more graphic and sexually explicit
c)   Mixing and/or Cutting
d)   Addition of beats, instrumentation, solos, and/or vocals
e)   Metaphorical Manipulation

Quiz 6-39) Pick two techniques involved in using a sample in a new song:

a)   Electronic drum machines replace funky drummers
b)   Lyrics became more graphic and sexually explicit
c)   Mixing and/or Cutting
d)   Substitution or alteration of the original (philosophical) the me
e)   Increase/decrease tempo (BPM)

Quiz 6-40) Identify two characteristics of earlier styles versus later styles:

a)   Break Beats vs. No Break Beats
b)   Drum Machines vs. Sampled Drum Line
c)   "Funky" Drummers vs. Drum Machines
d)   Live musicians vs. Synthesizers
e)   Synthesizers vs. Live Musicians
f)   Metaphorical Lyrics vs. Explicit Lyrics

Quiz 6-41) Identify two characteristics of earlier styles versus later styles:

a)   Tape Loops vs. Sampler
b)   Drum Machines vs. Sampled Drum Line
c)   "Funky" Drummers vs. Drum Machines
d)   Live musicians vs. Synthesizers
e)   Synthesizers vs. Live Musicians
f)   Metaphorical Lyrics vs. Explicit Lyrics

Quiz 6-42) Identify two characteristics of earlier styles versus later styles:

a)   Tape Loops vs. Sampler
b)   Break Beats vs. No Break Beats
c)   "Funky" Drummers vs. Drum Machines
d)   Live musicians vs. Synthesizers
e)   Synthesizers vs. Live Musicians
f)   Metaphorical Lyrics vs. Explicit Lyrics

Quiz 6-43) The Fresh Prince, AKA Will Smith along with DJ Jazzy Jeff, AKA Jeffrey Townes formed the group DJ Jazzy Jeff and the Fresh Prince.

a)   True

Quiz 6-44) The Fresh Prince, AKA (_____) along with DJ Jazzy Jeff, AKA (_____) formed the group DJ Jazzy Jeff and the Fresh Prince.

a) Will Smith
b) Will Drayton
c) James A very
d) Jeffrey Townes
e) Geoffrey Butler
f) Carlton Banks
g) Carlton Ridenhour
h) Joseph Marcell

Quiz 6-45) The Fresh Prince, AKA Will Drayton along with DJ Jazzy Jeff, AKA Geoffrey Butler formed the group DJ Jazzy Jeff and the Fresh Prince.

a) False

Quiz 6-46) Which track won the first Grammy award for Best Rap Performance?

a) "Parents Just Don't Understand"
b) "Kill That Noise"
c) "Rapper' s Delight"
d) "The Breaks"
e) "Positive Force"
f) "The Message"
g) "Planet Rock"

Quiz 6-47) What year was the first Grammy award for Best Rap Performance handed out?

a) 1985
b) 1986
c) 1987
d) 1988
e) 1989
f) 1990

Quiz 6-48) The first Grammy Award for Best Rap Performance was first handed out in 1988.

a) False

Quiz 6-49) The track "The Message" won the first Grammy Award for Best Rap performance in 1989.

a) False

Quiz 6-50) Salt-N-Pepa are a best selling female rap group comprised of Cheryl Wray, Sandra Denton and Dee Dee Roper.

a) True

Quiz 6-51) What is Salt's real name?

a) Cheryl Wray
b) Sandra Denton

c) Dee Dee Roper
d) JoAnn Berry
e) Dana Owens

Quiz 6-52) What is Pepa's real name?

a) Cheryl Wray
b) Sandra Denton
c) Dee Dee Roper
d) JoAnn Berry
e) Dana Owens

Quiz 6-53) What is DJ Spinderella's real name?

a) Cheryl Wray
b) Sandra Denton
c) Dee Dee Roper
d) JoAnn Berry
e) Dana Owens

Quiz 6-54) DJ Spinderella's real name is Sandra Denton.

a) False

Quiz 6-55) Pepa's real name is Cheryl Wray.

a) False

Quiz 6-56) Salt-N-Pepa are a best selling female rap duo/group, featuring Dana Owens, JoAnn Berry and Dee Dee Roper.

a) False

Quiz 6-57) Name the title and year of the video by Gangstarr shown in class:

a) "Jazz Thing"
b) "Positive Force"
c) "Planet Rock"
d) "The Message"
e) 1989
f) 1990
g) 1991
h) 1992

Quiz 6-58) Gangstarr's style combined elements of Jazz and Rap

a) True

Quiz 6-59) Gangstarr's style combined elements of (_____) and (_____)

a) Jazz
b) Rap

c)   Funk
d)   Blues
e)   Gospel
f)   Soul
g)   R&B

Quiz 6-60) Gangstar's style combined elements of Gospel and Blues

a)   False

Quiz 6-61) Which group's style combined elements of Jazz and Rap?

a)   Gangstarr
b)   The Juice Crew
c)   Eric B. and Rakim
d)   DJ Jazzy Jeff and The Fresh Prince
e)   Public Enemy
f)   Salt-n-Pepa

Quiz 6-62) What is Gangstarr's city of origin?

a)   New York City, NY
b)   Philadelphia, PA
c)   Boston, Mass
d)   Chicago, Illinois
e)   Austin, Texas
f)   Brooklyn, NY

Quiz 6-63) Pick the artist and year associated with the following track: "Paid in Full."

a)   Eric B. and Rakim
b)   Salt-N-Pepa
c)   DJ Jazzy Jeff and the Fresh Prince
d)   Public Enemy
e)   1987
f)   1988
g)   1990
h)   1991

Quiz 6-64) Pick the artist and year associated with the following track: "Push It."

a)   Eric B. and Rakim
b)   Salt-N-Pepa
c)   DJ Jazzy Jeff and the Fresh Prince
d)   Public Enemy
e)   1987
f)   1988
g)   1990
h)   1991

Quiz 6-65) Pick the artist and year associated with the following track: "Summertime."

a) Eric B. and Rakim
b) Salt-N-Pepa
c) DJ Jazzy Jeff and the Fresh Prince
d) Public Enemy
e) 1987
f) 1988
g) 1990
h) 1991

Quiz 6-66) Pick the artist and year associated with the following track: "Paid in Full."

a) Eric B. and Rakim
b) Salt-N-Pepa
c) DJ Jazzy Jeff and the Fresh Prince
d) Public Enemy
e) 1987
f) 1988
g) 1990
h) 1991

Quiz 7 Question Bank

Quiz 7-1) Which artist recorded the track "P.S.K. (What Does It Mean?)"?

a) Schoolly D
b) Eazy-E
c) Kool G Rap
d) Gang Starr
e) KRS-One
f) Ice-T

Quiz 7-2) What year was "P.S.K. (What Does It Mean?)" released?

a) 1983
b) 1984
c) 1985
d) 1986
e) 1987
f) 1988

Quiz 7-3) What is Schoolly D's city of origin?

a) Philadelphia, Pennsylvania
b) Newark, New Jersey
c) Crenshaw, Los Angeles, California
d) Compton, California
e) Queens, New York City
f) Boston, Massachusetts
g) Chicago, Illinois
h) Austin, Texas

Quiz 7-4) Which track did Schoolly D record in 1985?

a) "P.S.K. (What Does It Mean?)"
b) "6 'n the Mornin'"
c) "Two to the Head"
d) "Boyz -n- the-Hood"
e) "Mixed Up"
f) "I Ain't New Ta This"

Quiz 7-5) Ice-T recorded the track "P.S.K. (What Does It Mean?)" in 1985.

a) False

Quiz 7-6) Schoolly D recorded the track "P.S.K. (What Does It Mean?)" in 1985.

a) True

Quiz 7-7) Which artist recorded "6 'n the Mornin'"?

a) Schoolly D
b) Ice-T
c) Eazy-E
d) Kool G Rap
e) Gang Starr
f) KRS-One
g) Public Enemy

Quiz 7-8) What year was the single "6 'n the Mornin'" released?

a) 1983
b) 1984
c) 1985
d) 1986
e) 1987
f) 1988

Quiz 7-9) Which track did Ice-T record in 1986?

a) "P.S.K. (What Does It Mean?)"
b) "6 'n the Mornin'"
c) "Two to the Head"
d) "Boyz -n- the-Hood"
e) "Mixed Up"
f) "I Ain't New Ta This"

Quiz 7-10) What city was Ice-T born in?

a) Philadelphia, Pennsylvania
b) Newark, New Jersey
c) Los Angeles, California
d) Compton, California
e) Queens, New York City

f)   Boston, Massachusetts
g)   Chicago, Illinois
h)   Austin, Texas

Quiz 7-11) What city did Ice-T establish his career in?

a)   Philadelphia, Pennsylvania
b)   Newark, New Jersey
c)   Crenshaw, Los Angeles, California
d)   Compton, California
e)   Queens, New York City
f)   Boston, Massachusetts
g)   Chicago, Illinois
h)   Austin, Texas

Quiz 7-12) Ice-T recorded the track "6 'n the Mornin'" in 1986.

a)   True

Quiz 7-13) Eazy-E recorded the track "6 'n the Mornin'" in 1986.

a)   False

Quiz 7-14) What is Ice-T's birth name?

a)   Tracy Marrow
b)   Nathaniel T. Wilson
c)   Eric Lynn Wright
d)   Carlton Ridenhour
e)   William Drayton
f)   Antonio Hardy

Quiz 7-15) Ice-T established his career in Newark, New Jersey.

a)   False

Quiz 7-16) Ice-T was born in Crenshaw, Los Angeles, California.

a)   False

Quiz 7-17) Which artist recorded *Eazy-Duz-It*?

a)   Schoolly D
b)   Ice-T
c)   Eazy-E
d)   Kool G Rap
e)   Gang Starr
f)   KRS-One
g)   Public Enemy

Quiz 7-18) Schoolly D recorded *Eazy-Duz-It*.

a)   False

Quiz 7-19) Eazy-E recorded *Eazy-Duz-It*.

a)   True

Quiz 7-20) What is Eazy-E's real name?

a)   Tracy Marrow
b)   Nathaniel T. Wilson
c)   Eric Lynn Wright
d)   Carlton Ridenhour
e)   William Drayton
f)   Antonio Hardy

Quiz 7-21) What is Eazy-E's city of origin?

a)   Philadelphia, Pennsylvania
b)   Newark, New Jersey
c)   Crenshaw, Los Angeles, California
d)   Compton, California
e)   Queens, New York City
f)   Boston, Massachusetts
g)   Chicago, Illinois
h)   Austin, Texas

Quiz 7-22) Eazy-E is from Crenshaw, Los Angeles, California.

a)   False

Quiz 7-23) Eazy-E is from Compton, California.

a)   True

Quiz 7-24) Eazy-E's real name is Eric Lynn Wright.

a)   True

Quiz 7-25) Eazy-E's real name is Nathaniel T. Wilson.

a)   False

Quiz 7-26) Which album was recorded by Eazy-E?

a)   We Can't Be Stopped
b)   Rhyme Pays
c)   Eazy-Duz-It
d)   Home Invasion
e)   Justiceville
f)   Power
g)   O.G. Original Gangster

Quiz 7-27) Identify two records from Ice-T's discography:

a)   We Can't Be Stopped
b)   5150: Home 4 tha Sick
c)   It's On (Dr. Dre) 187um Killa
d)   Str8 off tha Streetz of Muthaphukkin Compton
e)   Impact of a Legend
f)   Rhyme Pays
g)   Justiceville

Quiz 7-28) Identify two records from Ice-T's discography:

a)   Wanted: Dead or Alive
b)   5150: Home 4 tha Sick
c)   Road to the Riches
d)   Str8 off tha Streetz of Muthaphukkin Compton
e)   Live and Let Die
f)   The Iceberg/Freedom of Speech… Just Watch What You Say
g)   O.G. Original Gangster

Quiz 7-29) Identify two records from Ice-T's discography:

a)   Wanted: Dead or Alive
b)   5150: Home 4 tha Sick
c)   It's On (Dr. Dre) 187 um Killa
d)   Live and Let Die
e)   Impact of a Legend
f)   Power
g)   Home Invasion

Quiz 7-30) Gangster Rap emphasized skills on the street if not more than skills on the mic; lyrics vary from accurate reflections to fictional accounts.

a)   True

Quiz 7-31) Gangster Rap emphasized skills _____ if not more than skills _____; lyrics vary from accurate reflections to fictional accounts.

a)   On the Street
b)   On the Mic
c)   On the Beat
d)   On the Stage
e)   On the Turntable
f)   On the Drum Machine

Quiz 7-32) What is Kool G Rap's birth name?

a)   Tracy Marrow
b)   Nathaniel T. Wilson
c)   Eric Lynn Wright
d)   Carlton Ridenhour
e)   William Drayton
f)   Antonio Hardy

Quiz 7-33) Nathaniel T. Wilson is better known as

a) Schoolly D
b) Ice-T
c) Eazy-E
d) Kool G Rap
e) Gang Starr
f) KRS-One

Quiz 7-34) Tracy Marrow is better known as

a) Schoolly D
b) Ice-T
c) Eazy-E
d) Kool G Rap
e) Gang Starr
f) KRS-One

Quiz 7-35) Eric Lynn Wright is better known as

a) Schoolly D
b) Ice-T
c) Eazy-E
d) Kool G Rap
e) Gang Starr
f) KRS-One

Quiz 7-36) What is Kool G Rap's city of origin?

a) Philadelphia, Pennsylvania
b) Newark, New Jersey
c) Los Angeles, California
d) Compton, California
e) Corona, Queens, New York City
f) Boston, Massachusetts
g) Chicago, Illinois
h) Austin, Texas

Quiz 7-37) Kool G Rap is from Newark, New Jersey:

a) False

Quiz 7-38) Identify two albums from Kool G Rap's discography with DJ Polo:

a) *Road to the Riches*
b) *Wanted: Dead or Alive*
c) *Power*
d) *Rhyme Pays*
e) *O.G. Original Gangster*
f) *Justiceville*

Quiz 7-39) Identify two albums from Kool G Rap's discography with DJ Polo:

a) *Live and Let Die*
b) *Wanted: Dead or Alive*
c) *Rhyme Pays*
d) *Power*
e) *Justiceville*
f) *O.G. Original Gangster*

Quiz 7-40) Identify two records from Eazy-E's discography:

a) 5150: Home 4 tha Sick
b) It's On (Dr. Dre) 187um Killa
c) Live and Let Die
d) Wanted: Dead or Alive
e) Justiceville
f) We Can't Be Stopped

Quiz 7-41) Identify two records from Eazy-E's discography:

a) Str8 off tha Streetz of Muthaphukkin Compton
b) Impact of a Legend
c) "6 'n the Mornin'"
d) Power
e) Rhyme Pays
f) Wanted: Dead or Alive

Quiz 7-42) What is another slang term for the Gangsta Rap subgenre?

a) West Coast Hip-Hop
b) P-Funk
c) Hyper Funk
d) Electro-Funk
e) Punk Funk
f) Chicago Funk

Quiz 7-43) What is another slang term for the Gangsta Rap subgenre?

a) G-Funk
b) P-Funk
c) Hyper Funk
d) Electro-Funk
e) Punk Funk
f) Chicago Funk

Quiz 7-44) Identify two factors that led to the evolution of Gangsta Rap on the West Coast:

a) Crack Cocaine
b) Reagonomics (inflation, etc.)
c) Rural America—later 1970s, early 1980s
d) Tax hikes
e) Tax cuts

f)   War in Vietnam
g)   War in Iraq

Quiz 7-45) Identify two factors that led to the evolution of Gangsta Rap on the West Coast:

a)   Urban America—later 1980s, early 1990s
b)   Community rage expressed through music
c)   Rural America—later 1970s, early 1980s
d)   Tax hikes
e)   Tax cuts
f)   War in Vietnam
g)   War in Iraq

Quiz 7-46) Identify two factors that led to the evolution of Gangsta Rap on the West Coast:

a)   Crack Cocaine
b)   Community rage expressed through music
c)   Rural America—later 1970s, early 1980s
d)   Tax hikes
e)   Tax cuts
f)   War in Vietnam
g)   War in Iraq

Quiz 7-47) Identify two factors that led to the evolution of Gangsta Rap on the West Coast:

a)   Reagonomics (inflation, etc.)
b)   Community rage expressed through music
c)   Rural America—later 1970s, early 1980s
d)   Tax hikes
e)   Tax cuts
f)   War in Vietnam
g)   War in Iraq

Quiz 7-48) Identify one of the Foundations of Violence in Gangsta Rap:

a)   Media/The Silver Screen: Cowboys vs. Indians, Mobsters, Hustlers, Dealers, Gangs
b)   Tax Cuts
c)   Being drafted to fight in conflicts overseas
d)   Racial profiling, beatings and shootings by the police
e)   Poverty and being forced to live in ghettos and "projects"
f)   Few job opportunities and easy money made through criminal activities

Quiz 7-49) Identify one of the Foundations of Violence in Gangsta Rap:

a)   Virtual Reality vs. Real Conflict: Definition and comparison to video games
b)   Tax Cuts
c)   Being drafted to fight in conflicts overseas
d)   Racial profiling, beatings and shootings by the police
e)   Poverty and being forced to live in ghettos and "projects"
f)   Few job opportunities and easy money made through criminal activities

Quiz 7-50) Identify one of the Foundations of Violence in Gangsta Rap:

a) Perceptions and Interpretation Vs. Intentions: Real/False Beefs
b) Tax Cuts
c) Being drafted to fight in conflicts overseas
d) Racial profiling, beatings and shootings by the police
e) Poverty and being forced to live in ghettos and "projects"
f) Few job opportunities; easy money made through criminal activities

Quiz 7-51) Identify one of the Foundations of Violence in Gangsta Rap:

a) Desensitization: Enactment
b) Tax Cuts
c) Being drafted to fight in conflicts overseas
d) Racial profiling, beatings and shootings by the police
e) Poverty and being forced to live in ghettos and "projects"
f) Few job opportunities; easy money made through criminal activities

Quiz 7-52) Identify two Foundations of Violence in Gangsta Rap:

a) Contextual "false" Misogyny
b) Fiction
c) Comedy
d) Break Beats
e) Rhyming/Rhymes and Early Connotations, etc.
f) Drum machines replaced by sampled beats

Quiz 7-53) Identify two Foundations of Violence in Gangsta Rap:

a) Fiction
b) Extensive use of metaphors
c) Explicit lyrics
d) Break Beats
e) Rhyming/Rhymes and Early Connotations, etc.
f) Drum machines replaced by sampled beats

Quiz 7-54) Identify two Foundations of Violence in Gangsta Rap:

a) Extensive use of metaphors
b) Metaphors used as modules for sociopolitical observation
c) Comedy
d) Break Beats
e) Rhyming/Rhymes and Early Connotations, etc.
f) Drum machines replaced by sampled beats

Quiz 7-55) Identify two Foundations of Violence in Gangsta Rap:

a) Metaphors used as modules for sociopolitical observation
b) Contextual "false" Misogyny
c) Explicit lyrics
d) Comedy
e) Rhyming/Rhymes and Early Connotations, etc.
f) Drum machines replaced by sampled beats

Quiz 7-56) Identify two Foundations in Violence of Gangsta Rap:

a)   Contextual "false" Misogyny
b)   Extensive use of metaphors
c)   Explicit lyrics
d)   Break Beats
e)   Rhyming/Rhymes and Early Connotations, etc.
f)   Comedy

Quiz 7-57) What is the name of the record label founded in 1993 by producer, rapper and entrepreneur Sean "Diddy" Combs.

a)   Bad Boy Records
b)   Boogie Down Productions
c)   Death Row Records
d)   Ciroc Entertainment
e)   Maybach Music Group
f)   Def Jam Recordings

Quiz 7-58) What is the name of the artist who founded Bad Boy Records in 1993?

a)   Sean "Diddy" Combs
b)   Schoolly D
c)   Ice-T
d)   Eazy-E
e)   Kool G Rap
f)   Gang Starr

Quiz 7-59) Bad Boy Records is a record label founded in 1993 by producer, rapper and entrepreneur Sean "Diddy" Combs.

a)   True

Quiz 7-60) Death Row Records is a record label founded in 1993 by producer, rapper and entrepreneur Sean "Diddy" Combs.

a)   False

Quiz 7-61) Bad Boy Records is a record label founded in 1993 by rapper Ice-T.

a)   False

Quiz 7-62) The need to "Keep It Real" blurred the line between business and the streets.

a)   True

Quiz 7-63) The need to "Keep It Real" blurred the line between (_____) and (_____).

a)   Business
b)   Artistry
c)   The Streets
d)   The Studio
e)   The Crib
f)   The Trap

Quiz 7-64) The need to "Keep it Fresh" blurred the line between the studio and the streets.

a)   False

Quiz 7-65) The need to (_____) blurred the line between business and the streets.

a)   Keep It Real
b)   Keep It Fresh
c)   Keep It Chill
d)   Max It Out
e)   Stay Cool
f)   Stay Authentic

Quiz 7-66) Match the artist and year to the following track: "I Ain't New Ta This."

a)   Ice-T
b)   Kool G Rap & DJ Polo ft. The Geto Boys and Ice Cube
c)   Scarface and the Geto Boys
d)   Eazy-E
e)   1991
f)   1992
g)   1993
h)   1994

Quiz 7-67) Match the artist and year to the following track: "Two to the Head."

a)   Ice-T
b)   Kool G Rap & DJ Polo ft. The Geto Boys and Ice Cube
c)   Scarface and the Geto Boys
d)   Eazy-E
e)   1991
f)   1992
g)   1993
h)   1994

Quiz 7-68) Match the artist and year to the following track: "Mixed Up."

a)   Ice-T
b)   Kool G Rap & DJ Polo ft. The Geto Boys and Ice Cube
c)   Scarface and the Geto Boys
d)   Eazy-E
e)   1991
f)   1992
g)   1993
h)   1994

Quiz 7-69) Match the artist and year to the following track: "Mind Playin' Tricks On Me."

a)   Ice-T
b)   Kool G Rap & DJ Polo ft. The Geto Boys and Ice Cube
c)   Scarface and the Geto Boys
d)   Eazy-E

e) 1991
f) 1992
g) 1993
h) 1994

Quiz 7-70) Which album does "Two to the Head" by Kool G Rap & DJ Polo appear on?

a) *Live and Let Die*
b) *Power*
c) *We Can't Be Stopped*
d) *O.G. Original Gangster*
e) *Justiceville*
f) *Rhyme Pays*

Quiz 7-71) Which album does "I Aint New Ta This" by Ice-T appear on?

a) *Home Invasion*
b) *Power*
c) *We Can't Be Stopped*
d) *O.G. Original Gangster*
e) *Justiceville*
f) *Rhyme Pays*

Quiz 8 Question Bank

Quiz 8-1) Vocabulary: A guide for behaviour and problem solving that is developed and stored in memory, and is characterized by aggression.

a) Aggressive Script
b) Ethnocentrism
c) Actor-observer effect
d) Anticonformity
e) Frustration-aggression hypothesis

Quiz 8-2) Vocabulary: A pattern of increased hostility toward out-groups accompanied by increased loyalty to one's in-group.

a) Aggressive Script
b) Ethnocentrism
c) Actor-observer effect
d) Anticonformity
e) Frustration-aggression hypothesis

Quiz 8-3) Vocabulary: The tendency for people to attribute their own behavior to external causes but that of others to internal factors.

a) Aggressive Script
b) Ethnocentrism
c) Actor-observer effect
d) Anticonformity
e) Frustration-aggression hypothesis

Quiz 8-4) Vocabulary: Opposition to social influence on all occasions, often caused by psychological reactance.

a) Aggressive Script
b) Ethnocentrism
c) Actor-observer effect
d) Anticonformity
e) Frustration-aggression hypothesis

Quiz 8-5) Vocabulary: The theory that frustration causes aggression.

a) Aggressive Script
b) Ethnocentrism
c) Actor-observer effect
d) Anticonformity
e) Frustration-aggression hypothesis

Quiz 8-6) Vocabulary: Pick the definition for "Aggressive Script."

a) A guide for behaviour and problem solving that is developed and stored in memory, and is characterized by aggression.
b) A pattern of increased hostility toward out-groups accompanied by increased loyalty to one's in-group.
c) The tendency for people to attribute their own behaviour to external causes but that of others to internal factors.
d) Opposition to social influence on all occasions, often caused by psychological reactance.
e) The theory that frustration causes aggression.

Quiz 8-7) Vocabulary: Pick the definition for "Ethnocentrism."

a) A guide for behaviour and problem solving that is developed and stored in memory, and is characterized by aggression.
b) A pattern of increased hostility toward out-groups accompanied by increased loyalty to one's in-group.
c) The tendency for people to attribute their own behaviour to external causes but that of others to internal factors.
d) Opposition to social influence on all occasions, often caused by psychological reactance.
e) The theory that frustration causes aggression.

Quiz 8-8) Vocabulary: Pick the definition for "Actor-observer effect."

a) A guide for behaviour and problem solving that is developed and stored in memory, and is characterized by aggression.
b) A pattern of increased hostility toward out-groups accompanied by increased loyalty to one's in-group.
c) The tendency for people to attribute their own behaviour to external causes but that of others to internal factors.
d) Opposition to social influence on all occasions, often caused by psychological reactance.
e) The theory that frustration causes aggression.

Quiz 8-9) Vocabulary: Pick the definition for "Anticonformity."

a) A guide for behaviour and problem solving that is developed and stored in memory, and is characterized by aggression.
b) A pattern of increased hostility toward out-groups accompanied by increased loyalty to one's in-group.
c) The tendency for people to attribute their own behaviour to external causes but that of others to internal factors.
d) Opposition to social influence on all occasions, often caused by psychological reactance.
e) The theory that frustration causes aggression.

Quiz 8-10) Vocabulary: Pick the definition for "Frustration-aggression hypothesis."

a)   A guide for behavior and problem-solving that is developed and stored in memory and is characterized by aggression.
b)   A pattern of increased hostility toward out-groups accompanied by increased loyalty to one's in-group.
c)   The tendency for people to attribute their own behavior to external causes but that of others to internal factors.
d)   Opposition to social influence on all occasions, often caused by psychological reactance.
e)   The theory that frustration causes aggression.

Quiz 8-11) Vocabulary: "Aggressive Script" refers to "A guide for behavior and problem-solving that is developed and stored in memory, and is characterized by aggression."

a)   True

Quiz 8-12) Vocabulary: "Aggressive Script" refers to "The theory that frustration causes aggression."

a)   False

Quiz 8-13) Vocabulary: "Ethnocentrism" refers to "A pattern of increased hostility toward out-groups accompanied by increased loyalty to one's in-group."

a)   True

Quiz 8-14) Vocabulary: "Ethnocentrism" refers to "Opposition to social influence on all occasions, often caused by psychological reactance."

a)   False

Quiz 8-15) Vocabulary: "Actor-observer effect" refers to "The tendency for people to attribute their own behavior to external causes but that of others to internal factors."

a)   True

Quiz 8-16) Vocabulary: "Actor-observer effect" refers to "A pattern of increased hostility toward out-groups accompanied by increased loyalty to one's in-group."

a)   False

Quiz 8-17) Vocabulary: "Anticonformity" refers to "Opposition to social influence on all occasions, often caused by psychological reactance."

a)   True

Quiz 8-18) Vocabulary: "Anticonformity" refers to "A pattern of increased hostility toward out-groups accompanied by increased loyalty to one's in-group."

a)   False

Quiz 8-19) Vocabulary: "Frustration-aggression hypothesis" refers to "The theory that frustration causes aggression."

a)   True

Quiz 8-20) Vocabulary: "Frustration-aggression hypothesis" refers to "A guide for behavior and problem-solving that is developed and stored in memory, and is characterized by aggression."

a)   False

Quiz 8-21) (_____) is a subgenre of Hip-Hop music that evolved from hardcore Hip-Hop and purports to reflect urban crime and the violent lifestyles of inner-city youths.

a)   Gangsta Rap
b)   G-Rap
c)   Hyper Rap
d)   P-Funk
e)   G-Hop
f)   Gangsta Funk

Quiz 8-22) Gangsta Rap is a subgenre of Hip-Hop music that evolved from (_____) and purports to reflect urban crime and the violent lifestyles of inner-city youths.

a)   Hardcore Hip-Hop
b)   G-Rap
c)   Hyper Rap
d)   P-Funk
e)   G-Hop
f)   Gangsta Funk

Quiz 8-23) Gangsta Rap is a subgenre of Hip-Hop music that evolved from hardcore Hip-Hop and purports to reflect urban crime and the violent lifestyles of (_____).

a)   Inner-city youths
b)   High School Students
c)   Mafia Members
d)   College and University Students
e)   Rural Youth
f)   Suburban Youth

Quiz 8-24) Gangsta Rap is a subgenre of Hip-Hop music that evolved from hardcore Hip-Hop and purports to reflect urban crime and the violent lifestyles of College and University Students.

a)   False

Quiz 8-25) Gangsta Rap is a subgenre of Hip-Hop music that evolved from hardcore Hip-Hop and purports to reflect urban crime and the violent lifestyles of inner-city youths.

a)   True

Quiz 8-26) Name the founders of Compton's Most Wanted:

a)   MC Eiht
b)   MC Eight
c)   MC A.T.E.
d)   Tha Chill

e)   MC Cool
f)   MC Kool

Quiz 8-26) Name the founders of Compton's Most Wanted:

a)   MC Eiht
b)   Tha Chill
c)   MC Ren
d)   Dr. Dre
e)   DJ Yella
f)   Eazy-E

Quiz 8-27) MC A.T.E. and MC Kool are the founders of Compton's Most Wanted.

a)   False

Quiz 8-28) MC Eiht and Tha Chill are the founders of Compton's Most Wanted.

a)   True

Quiz 8-29) What is Compton's Most Wanted's city of origin?

a)   Philadelphia, PA
b)   Newark, New Jersey
c)   Crenshaw, Los Angeles, CA
d)   Compton, CA
e)   Queens, NYC
f)   Boston, Mass.
g)   Long Beach, CA
h)   Austin, Texas

Quiz 8-30) Compton's Most Wanted was founded in Crenshaw, Los Angeles, California.

a)   False

Quiz 8-31) Compton's Most Wanted was founded in Compton, California.

a)   True

Quiz 8-32) What is Ice Cube's real name?

a)   O'Shea Jackson
b)   Calvin Cordozar Broadus
c)   Andre Romelle Young
d)   Tracy Morrow
e)   Nathaniel T. Wilson
f)   William Drayton

Quiz 8-33) What is O'Shea Jackson's nickname?

a)   Ice Cube
b)   Ice T
c)   Snoop Dogg

d) Dr. Dre
e) Eazy E
f) Kool G Rap

Quiz 8-34) O'Shea Jackson's nickname is Ice T.

a) False

Quiz 8-35) O'Shea Jackson's nickname is Ice Cube.

a) True

Quiz 8-36) What is Snoop Dogg's real name?

a) O'Shea Jackson
b) Calvin Cordozar Broadus
c) Andre Romelle Young
d) Tracy Morrow
e) Nathaniel T. Wilson
f) William Drayton

Quiz 8-37) What is Calvin Cordozar Broadus' nickname:

a) Ice Cube
b) Ice T
c) Snoop Dogg
d) Dr. Dre
e) Eazy E
f) Kool G Rap

Quiz 8-38) What is Snoop Dogg's city of origin?

a) Philadelphia, P A
b) Newark, New Jersey
c) Crenshaw, Los Angeles, CA
d) Compton, CA
e) Queens, NYC
f) Boston, Mass.
g) Long Beach, CA
h) Austin, Texas

Quiz 8-39) Calvin Cordozar Broadus' nickname is Snoop Dogg.

a) True

Quiz 8-40) Calvin Cordozar Broadus' nickname is Ice Cube.

a) False

Quiz 8-41) What is Dr. Dre's real name?

a) O'Shea Jackson
b) Calvin Cordozar Broadus

c) Andre Romelle Young
d) Tracy Morrow
e) Nathaniel T. Wilson
f) William Drayton

Quiz 8-42) What is Andre Romelle Young's nickname?

a) Ice Cube
b) Ice T
c) Snoop Dogg
d) Dr. Dre
e) Eazy E
f) Kool G Rap

Quiz 8-43) What is N.W.A's city of origin?

a) Philadelphia, P A
b) Newark, New Jersey
c) Crenshaw, Los Angeles, CA
d) Compton, CA
e) Queens, NYC
f) Boston, Mass.
g) Long Beach, CA
h) Austin, Texas

Quiz 8-44) Identify two members of N.W.A.:

a) MC Chill
b) MC Eiht
c) Snoop Dogg
d) Kool G Rap
e) Arabian Prince
f) DJ Yella

Quiz 8-45) Identify two members of N.W.A.:

a) MC Chill
b) MC Eiht
c) Snoop Dogg
d) Kool G Rap
e) Dr. Dre
f) Eazy-E

Quiz 8-46) Identify two members of N.W.A.:

g) MC Chill
h) MC Eiht
i) Snoop Dogg
j) Kool G Rap
k) Ice Cube
l) MC Ren

Quiz 8-47) Identify two members of N.W.A.:

a) MC Chill
b) MC Eiht
c) Snoop Dogg
d) Kool G Rap
e) DJ Yella
f) MC Ren

Quiz 8-48) Identify two members of N.W.A.:

a) MC Chill
b) MC Eiht
c) Snoop Dogg
d) Kool G Rap
e) Arabian Prince
f) MC Ren

Quiz 8-49) Identify two members of N.W.A.:

a) MC Chill
b) MC Eiht
c) Snoop Dogg
d) Kool G Rap
e) DJ Yella
f) MC Ren

Quiz 8-50) Identify two members of N.W.A.:

a) MC Chill
b) MC Eiht
c) Snoop Dogg
d) Kool G Rap
e) DJ Yella
f) Ice Cube

Quiz 8-51) Pick two albums from N.W.A.'s discography:

a) *Straight Outta Compton*
b) *Niggaz4life*
c) *AmeriKKKa's Most Wanted*
d) *Death Certificate*
e) *The Chronic*
f) *2001*

Quiz 8-52) Pick two albums from Ice Cube's discography:

a) *Straight Outta Compton*
b) *Niggaz4life*
c) *AmeriKKKa's Most Wanted*
d) *Death Certificate*
e) *The Chronic*
f) *2001*

Quiz 8-53) Pick two albums from Ice Cube's discography:

a)   *Straight Outta Compton*
b)   *Niggaz4life*
c)   *The Predator*
d)   *Lethal Injection*
e)   *The Chronic*
f)   *2001*

Quiz 8-54) Pick two albums from Dr. Dre's discography:

a)   *Straight Outta Compton*
b)   *Niggaz4life*
c)   *The Predator*
d)   *Lethal Injection*
e)   *The Chronic*
f)   *2001*

Quiz 8-55) Pick two albums from Dr. Dre's discography:

a)   *Straight Outta Compton*
b)   *Niggaz4life*
c)   *The Predator*
d)   *Lethal Injection*
e)   *The Chronic*
f)   *Detox*

Quiz 8-56) List two albums from Snoop Dogg's discography:

a)   *Straight Outta Compton*
b)   *Niggaz4life*
c)   *The Predator*
d)   *Lethal Injection*
e)   *The Chronic*
f)   *Detox*
g)   *Doggystyle*
h)   *Tha Doggfather*

Quiz 8-57) List two albums from Snoop Dogg's discography:

a)   *Straight Outta Compton*
b)   *Niggaz4life*
c)   *The Predator*
d)   *Lethal Injection*
e)   *The Chronic*
f)   *Detox*
g)   *No Limit Top Dogg*
h)   *Malicen Wonderland*

Quiz 8-58) List two albums from Snoop Dogg's discography:

a) *Straight Outta Compton*
b) *Niggaz4life*
c) *The Predator*
d) *Lethal Injection*
e) *The Chronic*
f) *Detox*
g) *Doggumentary*
h) *R&G(Rhythm&Gangst*a)*: TheMasterpiece*

Quiz 8-59) Ruthless Records was founded by Eazy E and Jerry Heller in 1987.

a) True

Quiz 8-60) Bad Boy Records was founded by Eazy E and Jerry Heller in 1986.

a) False

Quiz 8-61) Name the founders of Ruthless Records:

a) Eazy E
b) Jerry Heller
c) DJ Yella
d) Ice Cube
e) Ice T
f) MC Eiht

Quiz 8-62) Ruthless records was founded by Ice Cube and Jerry Heller in 1988.

a) False

Quiz 8-63) What year was Ruthless Records founded?

a) 1985
b) 1986
c) 1987
d) 1988
e) 1989
f) 1990

Quiz 8-64) Pick the artist and year associated with the following track: "Straight Outta Compton."

a) N.W.A.
b) Dr. Dre
c) Compton' s Most W anted
d) Snoop Dogg
e) 1988
f) 1991
g) 1992
h) 1993

Quiz 8-65) Pick the artist and year associated with the following track: "Nuthin' But A G Thang."

a) N.W.A.
b) Dr. Dre
c) Compton's Most W anted
d) Snoop Dogg
e) 1988
f) 1991
g) 1992
h) 1993

Quiz 8-66) Pick the artist and year associated with the following track: "The Dayz of Way Back"

a) N.W.A.
b) Dr. Dre
c) Compton's Most W anted
d) Snoop Dogg
e) 1988
f) 1991
g) 1992
h) 1993

Quiz 8-67) Pick the artist and year associated with the following track: "Hood Took Me Under."

a) N.W.A.
b) Dr. Dre
c) Compton's Most Wanted
d) Snoop Dogg
e) 1988
f) 1991
g) 1992
h) 1993

Quiz 8-68) Ruthless Records' first successful single was Eazy E's "Boyz-n-the-Hood" followed by N.W.A.'s (_____) and (_____)

a) "Dopeman"
b) "8-Ball"
c) "Hood Took Me Under"
d) "Warning"
e) "The Dayz of Way Back"
f) "Nuthin' But A G Thang"

Quiz 8-69) Ruthless Records' first successful single was Eazy E's "Boyz-n-the-Hood" followed by N.W.A.'s "Dopeman" and "8-Ball."

a) True

Quiz 8-70) Ruthless Records' first successful single was Eazy E's "Hood Took Me Under" followed by N.W.A.'s "Warning" and "The Dayz of Way Back."

a) False

Quiz 8-71) Name the title and artist behind Ruthless Records' first successful single

a) Eazy E
b) N.W.A.
c) Compton' s Most W anted
d) Ice Cube
e) "Boyz -n- the-Hood"
f) "Nuthin' But A 'G' Thang"
g) "The Dayz of Way Back"
h) "Hood Took Me Under"

Quiz 8-72) Compton's Most Wanted's track "Hood Took Me Under" is the sample for Notorious B.I.G.'s "Warning" from the album *Ready to Die.*

a) True

Quiz 8-73) Which track by which artist did Notorious B.I.G. sample for his track "Warning" on the album *Ready to Die?*

a) Eazy E
b) N.W.A.
c) Compton's Most Wanted
d) Ice Cube
e) "Boyz -n- the-Hood"
f) "Nuthin' But A 'G' Thang"
g) "The Dayz of Way Back"
h) "Hood Took Me Under"

Quiz 8-74) What was the title of the first full-length album released by Ruthless Records and what certification did it receive?

a) *Straight Outta Compton*
b) *Niggaz4life*
c) *The Predator*
d) *Lethal Injection*
e) *Gold*
f) *Platinum*
g) *Multi-Platinum*
h) *Diamond*

Quiz 8-75) Ruthless Records' first full-length release was N.W.A.'s *Straight Outta Compton* which was eventually certified multi-platinum.

a) True

Quiz 8-75) Ruthless Records' first full-length release was N.W.A.'s *Niggaz4life* which was eventually certified gold.

a) False

Quiz 8-76) Eazy E did not want to split the royalties from N.W.A's first album on Ruthless Records.

a) True

Quiz 8-77) (Eazy E) did not want to split the royalties from N.W.A's first album on Ruthless Records.

a)   Arabian Prince
b)   DJ Y ella
c)   Dr. Dre
d)   Eazy E
e)   Ice Cube
f)   MC Ren
g)   Jerry Heller

Quiz 8-78) Ice Cube did not want to split the royalties from N.W.A's first album on Ruthless Records.

a)   False

Quiz 8-79) Who is credited with the rise AND fall of N.W.A.?

a)   Arabian Prince
b)   DJ Yella
c)   Dr. Dre
d)   Eazy E
e)   Ice Cube
f)   MC Ren
g)   Jerry Heller

Quiz 8-80) NWA's manager, Jerry Heller is credited with the Rise and Fall of NWA.

a)   True

Quiz 8-81) NWA's manager, Berry Gordy is credited w/ the Rise and Fall of NWA.

a)   False

Quiz 8-82) What was the initial amount offered to the members of N.W.A.?

a) $5,000
b) $10,000
c) $50,000
d) $75,000
e) $100,000
f) $1,000,000

Quiz 8-83) $75,000 was the initial amount offered to the members of N.W.A.

a)   True

Quiz 8-84) $1,000,000 was the initial amount offered to the members of N.W.A.

a)   False

Quiz 8-85) Upon his departure from NWA Dr. Dre formed a record company named Death Row Records with an ex-bodyguard named Suge Knight.

a)   True

Quiz 8-86) Upon his departure from NWA Dr. Dre formed a record company named (_____) with an ex-bodyguard named (Suge Knight).

a)   Bad Boy Records
b)   Death Row Records
c)   Boogie Down Productions
d)   Def Jam Recordings
e)   Suge Knight
f)   Jay-Z
g)   Tupac Shakur
h)   Notorious B.I.G

Quiz 8-87) Upon his departure from NW A Ice Cube formed a record company named Bad Boy Records with an ex-bodyguard named Jerry Heller.

a)   False

Quiz 8-88) Upon it's release in 1990, Ice Cube's first solo album (_____) was certified Gold in just two weeks.

a)   True

Quiz 8-89) Upon it's release in 1990, Ice Cube's first solo album (_____) was certified (Gold) in just two weeks.

a)   *AmeriKKKa's Most Wanted*
b)   *Death Certificate*
c)   *The Predator*
d)   *Lethal Injection*
e)   Gold
f)   Platinum
g)   Multi-Platinum
h)   Diamond

Quiz 8-90) Upon it's release in (1990), (Ice Cube)'s first solo album *AmeriKKKa's Most Wanted* was certified Gold in just two weeks.

a)   1987
b)   1988
c). 1990
d)   1991
e)   Ice Cube
f)   Dr. Dre
g)   Eazy E
h)   MC Ren

Quiz 8-91) Upon it's release in 1990, Ice Cube's first solo album *Death Certificate* was certified Platinum in just two weeks.

a)   False

Quiz 8-92) N.W.A.-Ice Cube Feud, Round 1: N.W.A. attacked Ice Cube's debut album with the track ("100 Miles and Runnin'") and Ice Cube responded with the single (_____)

a)   "100 Miles and Runnin'"
b)   "Jackin' for Beats"
c)   "No Vaseline"
d)   "Real Niggaz"

Quiz 8-93) N.W.A.-Ice Cube Feud, Round 1: N.W.A. attacked Ice Cube's debut album with the track "100 Miles and Runnin'" and Ice Cube responded with the single "Jackin' for Beats."

a)   True

Quiz 8-94) N.W.A.-Ice Cube Feud, Round 1: N.W.A. attacked Ice Cube's debut album with the track "No Vaseline" and Ice Cube responded with the single "Real Niggaz."

a)   False

Quiz 8-95) N.W.A.-Ice Cube Feud, Round 2: N.W.A. then attacked with (_____) and the feud was finally shut down with Ice Cube's (_____) from the album (*Death Certificate.*)

a)   "100 Miles and Runnin'"
b)   "Jackin' for Beats"
c)   "No Vaseline"
d)   "Real Niggaz"
e)   *Death Certificate*
f)   *AmeriKKKa's Most Wanted*

Quiz 8-96) N.W.A.-Ice Cube Feud, Round 2: N.W.A. then attacked with "Real Niggaz," and the feud was finally shut down with Ice Cube's "No Vaseline" from the album *Death Certificate*.

a)   True

Quiz 8-97) N.W.A.-Ice Cube Feud, Round 2: N.W.A. then attacked with "No Vaseline," and the feud was finally shut down with Ice Cube's "*100 Miles and Runnin'*" from the album *AmeriKKKa's Most Wanted*.

a)   False

Quiz 8-98) Isaac Hayes' track "Walk On Bye" was sampled for both Notorious B.I.G.'s "Warning" and Compton's Most Wanted's "Hood Took Me Under."

a)   True

Quiz 8-99) James Brown's track "Cold Sweat" was sampled for both Notorious B.I.G.'s "Warning" and Compton's Most Wanted's "Hood Took Me Under."

a)   False

Quiz 8-100) Name the original artist and track that was sampled in both Notorious B.I.G.'s "Warning" and Compton's Most Wanted's "Hood Took Me Under":

a) Isaac Hayes
b) William Smokey Robinson
c) James Brown
d) Marvin Gaye
e) "Walk On Bye"
f) "I Loved and I Lost"
g) "In Between The Sheets"
h) "For The Easy Listeners"

Week 9 Question Bank

Quiz 9-1) Bi-coastal feuds went from battling as Emcees/Rappers to the fact of, "which crew would prevail in physical combat."

a) True

Quiz 9-2) Bi-coastal feuds went from battling as Emcees/Rappers to the fact of, "which crew would prevail in artistic integrity."

a) False

Quiz 9-3) Bi-coastal feuds went from battling as Emcees/Rappers to the fact of, "which crew would prevail in":

a) Record sales
b) Physical combat
c) Commercial endorsements
d) Artistic integrity
e) YouTube views
f) Facebook page likes
g) Profits from narcotic sales

Quiz 9-4) Bi-coastal feuds went from battling as Emcees/Rappers to the fact of, "which crew would prevail in YouTube views.

a) False

Quiz 9-5) Bi-coastal feuds went from battling as Emcees/Rappers to the fact of, "which crew would prevail in Facebook page likes.

a) False

Quiz 9-6) Tupac's diss-video "Hit 'Em Up" from 1996 is the defining moment in the East coast West Coast beef.

a) True

Quiz 9-7) Tupac's diss-video "Hit 'Em Up" from 1996 is the defining moment in the reconciliation of the East coast West Coast beef.

a) False

Quiz 9-8) Tupac's diss-video (_____) from (_____) is the defining moment in the East coast West Coast beef.

a) "Hit 'Em Up"
b) "I Used to Love H.E.R."
c) "Ether"
d) "Supa Ugly"
e) 1995
f) 1996
g) 1997
h) 1998

Quiz 9-9) Jay-Z's dis-video "Takeover" from 2001 is the defining moment in the East coast West Coast beef.

a) False

Quiz 9-10) Tupac's diss-video "Hit 'Em Up" from 1996 is the (_____) East coast West Coast beef.

a) Defining moment in the
b) Beginning of
c) Reconciling of
d) Ending of
e) Truce that ended the

Quiz 9-11) Tupac Shakur died tragically on September 11, 2001.

a) False

Quiz 9-12) Tupac Shakur died tragically on September 13, 1996.

a) True

Quiz 9-13) Jay-Z died tragically on September 13, 1996.

a) False

Quiz 9-14) Tupac Shakur died tragically on (_____) in the year (_____).

a) September 11
b) September 12
c) September 13
d) September 22
e) 1995
f) 1996
g) 2000
h) 2001

Quiz 9-15) (_____) died tragically on September 13, 1996.

a) Tupac Shakur
b) Jay-Z
c) Nas
d) 50 Cent
e) Ja Rule

Quiz 9-16) Identify two notable beefs mentioned in the last lecture

a) Cyprus Hill vs. LL Cool J
b) Jay-Z vs. Westside connection
c) DMX vs. Nas
d) Jermain Dupree vs. Eminem
e) LL Cool J vs. Jay-Z
f) Cypress Hill vs. Westside Connection
g) Jermaine Dupree vs. Dr. Dre

Quiz 9-17) Identify two notable beefs mentioned in the last lecture

a) Cyprus Hill vs. LL Cool J
b) Jay-Z vs. Westside connection
c) DMX vs. Nas
d) Jermain Dupree vs. Eminem
e) LL Cool J vs. Jay-Z
f) Foxy Brown vs. Lil Kim
g) Jermaine Dupree vs. Dr. Dre

Quiz 9-18) Identify two notable beefs mentioned in the last lecture

a) Cyprus Hill vs. LL Cool J
b) Jay-Z vs. Westside connection
c) DMX vs. Nas
d) Jermain Dupree vs. Eminem
e) LL Cool J vs. Jay-Z
f) Canibus vs. LL Cool J
g) Cypress Hill vs. Westside Connection

Quiz 9-19) Identify two notable beefs mentioned in the last lecture

a) Cyprus Hill vs. LL Cool J
b) Jay-Z vs. Westside connection
c) DMX vs. Nas
d) Jermain Dupree vs. Eminem
e) LL Cool J vs. Jay-Z
f) DMX vs. Ja Rule
g) Canibus vs. LL Cool J

Quiz 9-20) Identify two notable beefs mentioned in the last lecture

a) Cyprus Hill vs. LL Cool J
b) Jay-Z vs. Westside connection
c) DMX vs. Nas
d) Jermain Dupree vs. Eminem
e) LL Cool J vs. Jay-Z
f) Benzino vs. Eminem
g) Jay-Z vs. Nas

Quiz 9-21) Identify two notable beefs mentioned in the last lecture

a) Cyprus Hill vs. LL Cool J
b) Jay-Z vs. Westside connection
c) DMX vs. Nas
d) Jermain Dupree vs. Eminem
e) LL Cool J vs. Jay-Z
f) Jay Z vs. Mobb Deep
g) Benzino vs. Eminem

Quiz 9-22) Identify two notable beefs mentioned in the last lecture

1. Cyprus Hill vs. LL Cool J
2. Jay-Z vs. Westside connection
3. DMX vs. Nas
4. Jermain Dupree vs. Eminem
5. LL Cool J vs. Jay-Z
6. Benzino vs. Eminem
7. Foxy Brown vs. Lil Kim

Quiz 9-23) Identify two notable beefs mentioned in the last lecture

a) Cyprus Hill vs. LL Cool J
b) Jay-Z vs. Westside connection
c) DMX vs. Nas
d) Jermain Dupree vs. Eminem
e) LL Cool J vs. Jay-Z
f) Canibus vs. LL Cool J
g) Benzino vs. Eminem

Quiz 9-24) Identify two notable beefs mentioned in the last lecture

a) Cyprus Hill vs. LL Cool J
b) Jay-Z vs. Westside connection
c) DMX vs. Nas
d) Jermain Dupree vs. Eminem
e) LL Cool J vs. Jay-Z
f) Jay Z vs. Nas
g) Foxy Brown vs. Lil Kim

Quiz 9-25) Identify two notable beefs mentioned in the last lecture

a) Cyprus Hill vs. LL Cool J
b) Jay-Z vs. Westside connection
c) DMX vs. Nas
d) Jermain Dupree vs. Eminem
e) LL Cool J vs. Jay-Z
f) Jermaine Dupree vs. Dr. Dre
g) Benzino vs. Eminem

Quiz 9-26) Two of the notable beefs mentioned in the last lecture include Cypress Hill vs. Westside Connection and DMX vs. Ja Rule.

a) True

Quiz 9-27) Two of the notable beefs mentioned in the last lecture include Cypress Hill vs. Ja Rule and DMX vs. Westside Connection.

a)   False

Quiz 9-28) Two of the notable beefs mentioned in the last lecture include Foxy Brown vs. Lil Kim and Jay Z vs. Nas.

a)   True

Quiz 9-29) Two of the notable beefs mentioned in the last lecture include Foxy Brown vs. Foxxy Cleopatra and DMX vs. Run-DMC.

a)   False

Quiz 9-30) Two of the notable beefs mentioned in the last lecture include Canibus vs. LL Cool J and Jay Z vs. Nas.

a)   True

Quiz 9-31) Jay-Z/Nas Beef, Round 1: In 2001 Jay-Z came out with the track (_____) dissing Nas. Nas responded with ("H to the OMO") dissing Jay-Z. This track also sampled the beats from (_____)

a)   "Take Over"
b)   "H to the OMO"
c)   Erik B and Rakim's "Paid In Full"
d)   "Ether"
e)   "Supa Ugly"
f)   "Westside Slaughterhouse."
g)   "The 'B****' In Yoo"
h)   James Brown's "I Know You Got Soul"
i)   LL Cool J's "Hey Lover"

Quiz 9-32) Jay-Z/Nas Beef, Round 1: Jay-Z started the beef with the track "Take Over" in 2001.

a)   True

Quiz 9-33) Jay-Z/Nas Beef, Round 1: Jay-Z started the beef with the track "Supa Ugly" in 2001.

a)   False

Quiz 9-34) Jay-Z/Nas Beef, Round 1: Nas responded to Jay-Z with the track "H to the OMO."

a)   True

Quiz 9-35) Jay-Z/Nas Beef, Round 1: Nas responded to Jay-Z with the track "Supa Ugly."

a)   False

Quiz 9-36) Nas sampled the beats from Erik B and Rakim's track "Paid In Full" for "H to the OMO."

a)   True

Quiz 9-37) Nas sampled the beats from LL Cool J's track "Hey Lover" for "H to the OMO."

a)   False

Quiz 9-38) Jay-Z/Nas Beef, Round 2: In 2002 for the second round of disses, Nas dissed Jay-Z with (_____) and Jay-Z dissed Nas with (_____)

a)   "Takeover"
b)   "H to the OMO"
c)   "Ether"
d)   "Supa Ugly"
e)   "Westside Slaughterhouse"
f)   "The 'B****' In Yoo"
g)   "Hit 'Em Up"
h)   "I Used to Love H.E.R."

Quiz 9-39) Jay-Z/Nas Beef, Round 2: Nas dissed Jay-Z with "Ether."

a)   True

Quiz 9-40) Jay-Z/Nas Beef, Round 2: Jay-Z dissed Nas with "Supa Ugly."

a)   True

Quiz 9-41) Jay-Z/Nas Beef, Round 2: Jay-Z dissed Nas with "Ether."

a)   False

Quiz 9-42) Jay-Z/Nas Beef, Round 2: Nas dissed Jay-Z with "Supa Ugly."

a)   False

Quiz 9-43) Jay-Z/Nas Beef, Round 2: Nas dissed Jay-Z with "H to the OMO."

a)   False

Quiz 9-44) Jay-Z/Nas Beef, Round 2: Jay-Z dissed Nas with "Takeover."

a)   False

Quiz 9-45) Rapper 50 Cent's first major diss-track was targeted at whom?

a)   Jay-Z
b)   Nas
c)   Ja Rule
d)   LL Cool J
e)   Westside Connection

Quiz 9-46) Rapper 50 Cent's first major diss-track was targeted at Jay-Z.

a)   True

Quiz 9-47) Rapper 50 Cent's first major diss-track was targeted at Ja Rule

a)   False

Quiz 9-48) Which crew did rapper 50 Cent have his biggest beef with?

a)   Murder Inc.
b)   Westside Connection
c)   DMX
d)   Cyprus Hill
e)   Mobb Depp
f)   Canibus

Quiz 9-49) Rapper 50 Cent's biggest beef was with Murder Inc.

a)   True

Quiz 9-50) Rapper 50 Cent's biggest beef was with the Westside Connection.

a)   False

Quiz 9-51) Who is the leader of Murder Inc.?

a)   Ja Rule
b)   Jay-Z
c)   50 Cent
d)   Nas
e)   Common
f)   Ice Cube

Quiz 9-52) Ja Rule is the leader of Murder Inc.

a)   True

Quiz 9-53) Jay-Z is the leader of Murder Inc.

a)   False

Quiz 9-54) At the 1996 (_____) Death Row Records and Bad Boy staff "square off."

a)   Soul T rain Music A wards
b)   Grammy A wards
c)   BET A wards
d)   MTV Awards
e)   VH1 Video Awards
f)   Juno A wards
g)   iHeartRadio MMV A Award

Quiz 9-55) At the 1996 Soul Train Music Awards (_____) and (_____) staff "square off."

a)   Death Row Records
b)   Bad Boy Records

c) Def Jam Recordings
d) Ruthless Records
e) Boogie Down Productions
f) Maybach Music Group

Quiz 9-56) At the 1996 Soul Train Music Awards Death Row Records and Bad Boy Records staff "square off."

a) True

Quiz 9-57) At the 2001 iHeartRadio MMVA awards Ruthless Records and Boogie Down Productions staff "square off."

a) False

Quiz 9-58) At the 1996 Soul Train Music Awards Death Row Records and Bad Boy Records staff peacefully resolve their long-standing feud, leading to a golden age of collaboration between the two companies.

a) False

Quiz 9-59) Common's 1994 track (_____) describes the tale of a girlfriend in the form of a (Metaphor) to describe Hip-Hop's fate on the West Coast.

a) Metaphor
b) Allegory
c) Story
d) Parable
e) "I Used to Love H.E.R."
f) "Westside Slaughterhouse"
g) "The 'B****' in Yoo"
h) "Hit 'Em Up"

Quiz 9-60) Ice Cube and (_____) response to Common's 1994 commentary on the fate of Hip-Hop on the West Coast was the 1995 video "Westside Slaughterhouse."

a) "I Used to Love H.E.R."
b) "Westside Slaughterhouse"
c) "The 'B****' in Yoo"
d) "Hit 'Em Up"
e) Murder Inc.
f) The Westside Connection
g) DMX
h) Cyprus Hill

Quiz 9-61) Common's 1994 track "I Used to Love H.E.R." describes the tale of a girlfriend in the form of a Metaphor to describe Hip-Hop's fate on the West Coast.

a) True

Quiz 9-62) Common's 1994 track "I Used to Love H.E.R." describes the fate of his Bentley while on a tour of the West Coast.

a) False

Quiz 9-63) Ice Cube's 1995 video "Westside Slaughterhouse" was a response to Common's 1994 track "I Used to Love H.E.R."

a)   True

Quiz 9-64) Ice Cube's 1995 video "Westside Slaughterhouse" is a commentary on the fate of Hip-Hop on the West Coast.

a)   False

Quiz 9-65) In 1996 Common responded to Ice Cube and the West Side Connection with (_____)

a)   "B**** What?"
b)   "The B**** in Yoo"
c)   "You my B****"
d)   "Hit 'Em Up"
e)   "I Used to Love H.E.R."
f)   "Westside Slaughterhouse"

Quiz 9-66) In 1996 Common responded to Ice Cube and the West Side Connection with "The B**** in Yoo."

a)   True

Quiz 9-67) In 1996 Ice Cube and the West Side Connection responded to Common with "The B**** in Yoo."

a)   False

Quiz 9-68) In 1996 Common responded to Ice Cube and the West Side Connection with "I Used to Love H.E.R."

a)   False

Quiz 9-69) Common's response to the Westside Connection transcended his normally (_____) style of MC-ing.

a)   Conscious
b)   Lyrical
c)   Political
d)   Metaphorical
e)   Humourous
f)   Cynical

Quiz 9-70) Common's response to the Westside Connection transcended his normally conscious style of MC-ing.

a)   True

Quiz 9-71) Common's response to the Westside Connection transcended his normally political style of MC-ing.

a)   False

Quiz 9-72) List two ways in which the media propagandizes Hip-Hop culture:

a)   Instigation
b)   Publicity
c)   Humiliation

d) Celebration
e) Exaggeration
f) Fabrication
g) Gossip

Quiz 9-73) Two ways that the media propagandizes Hip-Hop culture is through instigation and publicity.

a) True

Quiz 9-74) Two ways that the media propagandizes Hip-Hop culture is through humiliation and exaggeration.

a) False

Quiz 9-75) Two of the notable beefs mentioned in the last lecture include Beyonce vs. Foxxy Cleopatra and LL Cool J vs. Jay-Z

a) False

Quiz 10 Question Bank

Quiz 10-1) The term "Turntablism" was first coined by DJ Babu in the year 1995.

a) True

Quiz 10-2) The term "Turntablism" was first coined by Lee "Scratch" in the year 1985.

a) False

Quiz 10-3) The term "Turntablism" was first coined by (_____) in the year (1995).

a) DJ Babu
b) Christopher Oroc
c) Lee "Scratch" Perry
d) King Tubby
e) 1980
f) 1985
g) 1990
h) 1995

Quiz 10-4) Which term was first coined by DJ Babu?

a) Turntablism
b) Slip-cueing
c) Illbient
d) Baby Scratch
e) Transformer Scratch

Quiz 10-5) The term "Illbient" was first coined by DJ Babu in the year 1995.

a) False

Quiz 10-6) (_____) music from the (_____) is a precursor to DJ-ing and turntablism.

a) Jamaican Dub
b) P-Funk
c) Psychedelic Rock
d) Disco
e) 1970s
f) 1980s
g) 1990s
h) 2000s

Quiz 10-7) Jamaican Dub music from the 1970s is a precursor to DJ-ing and turntablism.

a) True

Quiz 10-8) Psychedelic Rock music from the 1970s is a precursor to DJ-ing and turntablism.

a) False

Quiz 10-9) List two pioneers of Jamaican Dub music

a) DJ Babu
b) Christopher Oroc
c) Lee "Scratch" Perry
d) King Tubby
e) Francis Grasso
f) Grand Wizard Theodore
g) GrandMixer DXT

Quiz 10-10) Lee "Scratch" Perry and King Tubby are two pioneers of Jamaican Dub music.

a) True

Quiz 10-11) DJ Babu and Christopher Oroc are two pioneers of Jamaican Dub music.

a) False

Quiz 10-12) Lee "Scratch" Perry and King Tubby are two pioneers of (_____) music.

a) Jamaican Dub
b) Gangsta Rap
c) P-Funk
d) G-Funk
e) Funk
f) Disco
g) Turntablism

Quiz 10-13) The first disco DJ from New York City to blend records in the 1970s was Francis Grasso. This technique is called slip-cueing.

a) Francis Grasso
b) DJ Babu
c) Christopher Oroc

d) Lee "Scratch" Perry
e) Slip-cueing
f) Baby-Scratching
g) Flare-Scratching
h) Crab-Scratching

Quiz 10-14) The first disco DJ from New York City to blend records in the 1970s was Francis Grasso. This technique is called slip-cueing.

a) True

Quiz 10-15) The first disco DJ from New York City to blend records in the 1970s was DJ Babu. This technique is called Baby-Scratching.

a) False

Quiz 10-16) The first DJ to scratch was Grand Wizard Theodore. His technique is known as the baby scratch.

a) True

Quiz 10-17) The first DJ to scratch was Lee "Scratch" Perry. His technique is known as slip-cueing.

a) False

Quiz 10-18) The first DJ to scratch was (_____). His technique is known as the (baby scratch).

a) Grand Wizard Theodore
b) Grand Mixer DXT
c) Christopher Oroc
d) Baby Scratch
e) Flare Scratch
f) Transformer Scratch
g) Crab Scratch
h) DJ Babu

Quiz 10-19) Grand Wizard Theodore was the first DJ to:

a) Scratch
b) Rap
c) Slip-cue
d) Flare Scratch
e) Battle
f) Break Dance

Quiz 10-20) Identify two other types of scratching techniques

a) Flare Scratch
b) Transformer Scratch
c) Slip-cueing
d) Digging
e) Battling
f) Rapping

Quiz 10-21) Identify two other types of scratching techniques

a) Flare Scratch
b) Crab Scratch
c) Slip-cueing
d) Digging
e) Battling
f) Rapping

Quiz 10-22) Identify two other types of scratching techniques

a) Transformer Scratch
b) Crab Scratch
c) Slip-cueing
d) Digging
e) Battling
f) Rapping

Quiz 10-23) Slip-cueing and Digging are two other types of scratching techniques

a) False

Quiz 10-24) The Transformer Scratch and the Crab Scratch are two other types of scratching techniques.

a) True

Quiz 10-25) The Crab Scratch and Flare Scratch are two other types of scratching techniques.

a) True

Quiz 10-26) Who was the first DJ to popularize the turntable as an instrument?

a) Grand Mixer DXT
b) DJ Babu
c) Grand Wizard Theodore
d) Christopher Oroc
e) Lee "Scratch" Perry
f) King Tubby

Quiz 10-27) Grand Mixer DXT was the first DJ to popularize the turntable as an instrument.

a) True

Quiz 10-28) Grand Wizard Theodore was the first DJ to popularize the turntable as an instrument.

a) False

Quiz 10-29) Grand Mixer DXT was the first DJ to

a) Popularize the turntable as an instrument
b) Scratch records

c) Use the technique of slip-cueing
d) Use the technique of Baby Scratching
e) Use the term "turntablist"
f) Dig for rare records

Quiz 10-30) Which DJ was showcased on the track "Rockit"?

a) Grand Mixer DXT
b) DJ Babu
c) Grand Wizard Theodore
d) Christopher Oroc
e) Lee "Scratch" Perry
f) King Tubby

Quiz 10-31) Grand Mixer DXT was showcased on which track by which artist?

a) "Rockit"
b) "So What"
c) "Koko"
d) "Crepuscule With Nellie"
e) Miles Davis
f) Charlie Parker
g) Herbie Hancock
h) Thelonious Monk

Quiz 10-32) Which awards show was the performance of Herbie Hancock's "Rockit" broadcast on?

a) Grammy Awards
b) BET Awards
c) MTV Awards
d) Soul Train Music Awards
e) VH1 Video Awards
f) Juno Awards
g) iHeart Radio Award

Quiz 10-33) What year was "Rockit" by Herbie Hancock broadcast during an awards ceremony?

a) 1982
b) 1983
c) 1984
d) 1985
e) 1986
f) 1987

Quiz 10-34) Grand Mixer DXT was featured on the track "So What" by Miles Davis at the Grammy Awards in 1984.

a) False

Quiz 10-35) Grand Mixer DXT was featured on the track "Rockit" by Herbie Hancock at the Soul Train Music Awards in 1985.

a) False

Quiz 10-36) Grand Wizard Theodore was featured on the track "Rockit" by Herbie Hancock at the 1986 Grammy Awards.

a)   False

Quiz 10-37) Grand Mixer DXT was featured on the track "Rockit" by Herbie Hancock at the Grammy Awards in 1984.

a)   True

Quiz 10-38) What is the title and year of the first all-turntablism album?

a)   Return of the DJ
b)   Return of the Jedi
c)   DJ's at the Door
d)   Revenge of the DJ
e)   Army Group DJ
f)   First National Bank o' DJ
g)   1995
h)   1996
i)   1997
j)   1998

Quiz 10-39) The first all-turntablist album was *Revenge of the DJ*, released in 1990.

a)   False

Quiz 10-40) The first all-turntablist album was *Return of the DJ*, released in 1995

a)   True

Quiz 10-41) The 1995 album *Return of the DJ*:

a)   Was the first all-turntablist album
b)   Was the second all-turntablist album
c)   Was the first all-turntablist album to win a Grammy Award
d)   Was the first all-turntablist album to receive the R.I.A.A.'s Gold designation
e)   Was the first all-turntablist album to receive the R.I.A.A.'s Platinum designation
f)   Had a popular video single on MTV

Quiz 10-42) The 1995 album *Return of the DJ* is significant for being the first all-turntablist record to receive the R.I.A.A.'s Gold designation.

a)   False

Quiz 10-43) Identify two artists/crews that appeared on the album *Return of the DJ*:

a)   DJ Babu
b)   The Beat Junkies
c)   Christopher Oroc
d)   Lee "Scratch" Perry
e)   Grand Mixer DXT
f)   Grand Wizard Theodore

Quiz 10-44) Identify two artists/crews that appeared on the album *Return of the DJ*:

a) Invisibl Skratch Piklz
b) CutChemist
c) Christopher Oroc
d) Lee "Scratch" Perry
e) Grand Mixer DXT
f) Grand Wizard Theodore

Quiz 10-45) Identify two artists/crews that appeared on the album *Return of the DJ*:

a) DJ Babu
b) The Beat Junkies
c) Christopher Oroc
d) Lee "Scratch" Perry
e) Grand Mixer DXT
f) Grand Wizard Theodore

Quiz 10-46) Identify two artists/crews that appeared on the album *Return of the DJ*:

a) DJ Babu
b) DJ Z-Trip
c) Christopher Oroc
d) Lee "Scratch" Perry
e) Grand Mixer DXT
f) Grand Wizard Theodore

Quiz 10-47) Identify two artists/crews that appeared on the album *Return of the DJ*:

a) The Beat Junkies
b) Invisibl Skratch Piklz
c) Christopher Oroc
d) Lee "Scratch" Perry
e) Grand Mixer DXT
f) Grand Wizard Theodore

Quiz 10-48) The combination of mixing/cutting, scratching and sampling is called beat juggling.

a) True

Quiz 10-49) The combination of mixing/cutting, scratching and sampling is called slip-cuing.

a) False

Quiz 10-50) The combination of mixing/cutting, scratching and sampling is called

a) Beat Juggling
b) Slip-cuing
c) Digging
f) Baby Scratching
d) Transformer Scratching

Quiz 10-51) The term "Beat Juggling" refers to

a) A combination of mixing/cutting, scratching and sampling
b) Blending records
c) A variation of the Baby-Scratch technique
d) A variation of the Crab-Scratch Technique
e) The metrical manipulation of the beat of a preexisting track
f) The simultaneous use of a three-turntable setup

Quiz 10-52) A turntablist's basic setup includes

a) Two Turntables
b) Mixer
c) One Turntable
d) Three Turntables
e) Laser Lighting Rig
f) Pyrotechnic Displays
g) Mirror Ball

Quiz 10-53) A turntablist's basic setup includes

a) Headphones
b) Sound System
c) Quadraphonic Sound System
d) One Table
e) Mirror Ball
f) Laser Lighting Rig
g) Smoke Machines

Quiz 10-54) Part of a turntablist's basic kit includes Headphones and a Mixer.

a) True

Quiz 10-55) Part of a turntablist's basic kit includes Two Turntables and a Sound System.

a) True

Quiz 10-56) Part of a turntablist's basic kit includes a Single Turntable and a Quadraphonic Sound System.

a) False

Quiz 10-57) The substitution or alteration of the sample's an original (historical) meaning in a new, referential context is called Metaphorical Manipulation.

a) True

Quiz 10-58) The substitution or alteration of the sample's an original (historical) meaning in a new, referential context is called slip-cueing.

a) False

Quiz 10-59) The substitution or alteration of the sample's ~~an~~ or original (historical) meaning in a new, referential context is called

a) Metaphorical Manipulation
b) Metrical Manipulation
c) Slip-cueing
d) Digging
e) Transformer-Scratching

Quiz 10-60) "Metaphorical Manipulation" involves:

a) The substitution or alteration of the sample's an original (historical) meaning in a new, referential context
b) A combination of mixing/cutting, scratching and sampling
c) The metrical manipulation of the beat of a pre-existing track
d) The simultaneous use of a three-turntable setup
e) Alternating between the Baby Scratch and Crab Scratch techniques
f) Alternating between the Crab Scratch and Transformer Scratch Techniques

Quiz 10-61) The art of searching for and acquiring albums, including the search for breaks and samples according to the artist's aesthetic choices is called "digging."

a) True

Quiz 10-62) The art of searching for and acquiring albums, including the search for breaks and samples according to the artist's aesthetic choices is called "tracking."

a) False

Quiz 10-63) The term "digging" refers to

a) The art of searching for and acquiring albums, including the search for breaks and samples according to the artist's aesthetic choices
b) The substitution or alteration of the sample's an original (historical) meaning in a new, referential context
c) A combination of mixing/cutting, scratching and sampling
d) Alternating between the Baby Scratch and Crab Scratch techniques
e) An aesthetic appreciation of an album, film, etc.

Quiz 10-64) The art of searching for and acquiring albums, including the search for breaks and samples according to the artist's aesthetic choices is known as

a) Digging
b) Slip-cuing
c) Tracking
d) Turntablism
e) Disc-Juggling

Quiz 10-65) DJ Shadow is well known for his skill at digging.

a) True

Quiz 10-66) DJ Spooky is well known for his skill at digging.

a) False

Quiz 10-67) Which DJ is well known for his skill at digging?

a) DJ Spooky
b) DJ Shadow
c) DJ Babu
d) Grand Wizard Theodore
e) GrandMixer DXT

Quiz 10-68) DJ Shadow is well known for

a) His skill at "digging"
b) Coining the term "illbient"
c) Developing the Transformer Scratch technique
d) His skill at slip-cueing
e) Refining the Crab-Scratch technique

Quiz 10-69) What is the name of the largest organized DJ battle?

a) Disco Mix Club
b) Mix Master Association
c) Disc Jockeys of America Club
d) International Disc Jockey Club
e) The DJ's Death Battle Ring
f) East Coast Competitive DJ Group
g) The DJ and MC Club of America

Quiz 10-70) The Disc Jockeys of America hosts the largest annual DJ battle.

a) False

Quiz 10-71) The Disco Mix Club hosts the largest annual DJ battle.

a) True

Quiz 10-72) The Disco Mix Club is

a) One of the groups featured on *Return of the DJ*
b) The largest organized DJ Battle in America
c) The group that pioneered the slip-cueing technique
d) The group founded by GrandMixer DXT
e) The first all-female group of turntablists

Quiz 10-73) The Disco Mix Club is one of the groups featured on *Revenge of the DJ*.

a) False

Quiz 10-74) The Disco Mix Club was formed in 1987.

a) True

Quiz 10-75) The Disco Mix Club was formed in 1984.

a) False

Quiz 10-76) What year was the Disco Mix Club founded in?

a) 1984
b) 1985
c) 1986
d) 1987
e) 1988

Quiz 10-77) In formal competitive DJ battles, how long does each DJ have to present their composition?

a) 3 Minutes
b) 5 Minutes
c) 6 Minutes
d) 10 Minutes
e) 12 Minutes
f) 25 Minutes

Quiz 10-78) In formal competitive DJ battles, each DJ has 6 minutes to present their composition.

a) True

Quiz 10-79) In formal competitive DJ battles, each DJ has 3 minutes to present their composition.

a) False

Quiz 10-80) Which DJ artist/crew is known for orchestrating their compositions?

a) Invisibl Skratch Piklz
b) The Beat Junkies
c) Lee "Scratch" Perry
d) Christopher Oroc
e) GrandMixer DXT
f) Grand Wizard Theodore

Quiz 10-81) What is the group Invisibl Skratch Piklz known for?

a) Orchestrating their compositions
b) Being the first all-turntablist group to win a Grammy award
c) Being the first all-turntablist group to win have an album certified Gold
d) Their collective skill at digging for records
e) Hosting competitive DJ battles at the Disco Mix Club
f) Being the first all-female DJ collective

Quiz 10-82) What year was the DJ crew Invisibl Skratch Piklz formed?

a) 1984
b) 1985
c) 1986
d) 1987
e) 1988
f) 1989

Quiz 10-83) The DJ crew Invisibl Skratch Piklz was formed in 1989.

a)   True

Quiz 10-84) The DJ crew Invisibl Skratch Piklz was formed in 1984.

a)   False

Quiz 10-85) Identify two members of the DJ crew Invisibl Skratch Piklz.

a)   DJ Babu
b)   DJ Z-Trip
c)   Grand Wizard Theodore
d)   Grand Mixer DXT
e)   DJ Qbert
f)   Mix Master Mike

Quiz 10-86) Identify two members of the DJ crew Invisibl Skratch Piklz.

a)   DJ Babu
b)   DJ Z-Trip
c)   Grand Wizard Theodore
d)   Grand Mixer DXT
e)   DJ Qbert
f)   DJ Apollo

Quiz 10-87) Identify two members of the DJ crew Invisibl Skratch Piklz.

a)   DJ Babu
b)   DJ Z-Trip
c)   Grand Wizard Theodore
d)   Grand Mixer DXT
e)   Mix Master Mike
f)   DJ Apollo

Quiz 10-88) DJ Babu and DJ Z-Trip are members of the DJ crew Invisibl Skratch Piklz.

a)   False

Quiz 10-89) DJ Apollo and DJ Qbert are members of the DJ crew Invisibl Skratch Piklz.

a)   True

Quiz 10-90) DJ Apollo and Mix Master Mike are members of the DJ crew Invisibl Skratch Piklz.

a)   True

Quiz 10-91) Which artist got their start as a DJ in Montreal, Quebec?

a)   Kid Koala
b)   DJ Apollo
c)   Mix Master Mike
d)   DJ Babu

e) DJ Z-Trip
f) Grand Mixer DXT
g) Grand Wizard Theodore

Quiz 10-92) What is Kid Koala's city of origin?

a) Toronto, Ontario
b) Hamilton, Ontario
c) Quebec City, Quebec
d) Halifax, Nova Scotia
e) Saint-Jean-sur-Richelieu, Quebec
f) Montreal, Quebec

Quiz 10-93) Kid Koala's city of origin is Montreal, Quebec.

a) True

Quiz 10-94) Kid Koala's city of origin is Gatineau, Quebec.

a) False

Quiz 10-95) What is DJ Spooky (that Subliminal Kid)'s real name?

a) Paul D. Miller
b) Christopher Oroc
c) Lee Perry
d) Francis Grasso
e) Nathaniel T. Wilson
f) William Drayton
g) Frank Miller

Quiz 10-96) What is Paul D. Miller's stage name?

a) DJ Spooky
b) DJ Babu
c) DJ Apollo
d) DJ Z-Trip
e) Mix Master Mike
f) Grand Mixer DXT

Quiz 10-97) Paul D. Miller is better known as DJ Spooky.

a) True

Quiz 10-98) DJ Spook's real name is Christopher Oroc

a) False

Quiz 10-99) DJ Spooky (that Subliminal Kid) is credited for creating and developing:

a) A style known as "illbient"
b) His skill at digging for records
c) The slip-cuing Technique

d)   The Crab Scratch Technique
e)   The Transformer Scratch technique
f)   The art of Turntablism

Quiz 10-100) Which artist is credited for creating and developing a style known as "illbient"?

a)   DJ Spooky
b)   DJ Babu
c)   DJ Apollo
d)   DJ Z-Trip
e)   Mix Master Mike
f)   Grand Mixer DXT

Quiz 11 Question Bank

Quiz 11-1) By way of example, Michael Eric Dyson points to the early years of America, the expansion of the (_____), and the manner in which (_____) were equated with manhood and the ability to protect and care for one's (_____).

a)   Frontier
b)   Inner city
c)   Industrial Heartland
d)   Suburbs
e)   Rural areas
f)   Guns
g)   Horses
h)   Knives
i)   Jobs
j)   Family
k)   Home
l)   Business
m) Ranch

Quiz 11-2) By way of example, Michael Eric Dyson points to the early years of America, the expansion of rural areas, and the manner in which horses were equated with manhood and the ability to protect and care for one's ranch.

a)   True

Quiz 11-3) By way of example, Michael Eric Dyson points to the early years of America, the expansion of the inner city, and the manner in which jobs were equated with manhood and the ability to protect and care for one's home.

a)   False

Quiz 11-4) The ability to use (_____) skillfully and aggressively is central to being masculine in the Hip-Hop world, as is the ability to survive the (_____) that is so much a part of young, poor, and working-class men's lives.

a)   Words
b)   Rhymes
c)   Guns
d)   Knives
e)   Rhythms
f)   Violence

g) Racism
h) Depression
i) Police Brutality

Quiz 11-5) The ability to use words skillfully and aggressively is central to being masculine in the Hip-Hop world, as is the ability to survive the violence that is so much a part of young, poor, and working-class men's lives.

a) True

Quiz 11-6) The ability to use rhythms skillfully and aggressively is central to being masculine in the Hip-Hop world, as is the ability to survive the depression that is so much a part of young, poor, and working-class men's lives.

a) False

Quiz 11-7) Rap also grew out of a long tradition of (_____) in African-American culture, a tradition of boys and men (_____) for respect by projecting and proclaiming their own power and ability while simultaneously (_____) other men.

a) Male Boasting
b) Rhyming
c) Dissing
d) Drumming
e) Fighting
f) Competing
g) Playing
h) Denigrating
i) Complimenting
j) Celebrating
k) Praising

Quiz 11-8) Rap also grew out of a long tradition of male boasting in African-American culture, a tradition of boys and men fighting for respect by projecting and proclaiming their own power and ability while simultaneously denigrating other men.

a) True

Quiz 11-9) Rap also grew out of a long tradition of rhyming in African-American culture, a tradition of boys and men Competing for respect by projecting and proclaiming their own power and ability while simultaneously praising other men.

a) False

Quiz 11-10) Jackson Katz argues that males who feel (_____), (particularly men of color and working-class white men) turn to their own (_____) as a source of power. Men who have other forms of power (economic, social, political) do not have the same need to adopt this kind of (_____) physical posture.

a) Powerless
b) Powerful
c) Empowered
d) Insecure
e) Bodies
f) Cars

g) Guns
h) Women
i) Hyper-aggressive
j) Passive
k) Masculine
l) Antagonistic

Quiz 11-11) Jackson Katz argues that males who feel powerless (particularly men of color and working-class white men) turn to their own bodies as a source of power. Men who have other forms of power (economic, social, political) do not have the same need to adopt this kind of hyper-aggressive physical posture.

a) True

Quiz 11-12) Jackson Katz argues that males who feel insecure, (particularly men of color and working-class white men) turn to their own women as a source of power. Men who have other forms of power (economic, social, political) do not have the same need to adopt this kind of antagonistic physical posture.

a) False

Quiz 11-13) (_____) is so much a part of American culture that we have become (_____) to it. It is found not only in rap music, but across the culture in movies, sports, video games, and the real-world politics of (militarism and war).

a) Violence
b) Racism
c) Misogyny
d) Homophobia
e) Desensitized
f) Hyper-sensitive
g) Sensitized
h) Oblivious
i) Militarism and War
j) Women's Rights
k) Race Relations
l) Gender Studies
m) Gay and Trans Rights

Quiz 11-14) Violence is so much a part of American culture that we have become desensitized to it. It is found not only in rap music, but across the culture in movies, sports, video games and the real-world politics of militarism and war.

a) True

Quiz 11-15) Racism is so much a part of American culture that we have become oblivious to it. It is found not only in rap music, but across the culture in movies, sports, video games and the real-world politics of race relations.

a) False

Quiz 11-16) Chuck D. argues that instead of challenging the notion that (_____) violence is natural, the industries that produce popular culture actually exploit stories and images of (_____) for profit.

a) Black Male
b) Homophobic
c) Misogynistic

d) Racial
e) Black Death
f) Spousal Abuse
g) Sexual Violence
h) Gang Violence

Quiz 11-17) Chuck D. argues that instead of challenging the notion that misogynistic violence is natural, the industries that produce popular culture actually exploit stories and images of sexual violence for profit.

a) False

Quiz 11-18) Chuck D. argues that instead of challenging the notion that black male violence is natural, the industries that produce popular culture actually exploit stories and images of black death for profit.

a) True

Quiz 11-19) These sorts of (_____) are not unique to Hip-Hop. (_____) bodies are everywhere. They appear throughout American culture, in films, advertisements, television programs etc. However, across the landscape of music video, this is virtually the only vision of (_____) available.

a) Images
b) Attitudes
c) Lyrics
d) Behaviors
e) Objectified female
f) Muscled male
g) Mutilated
h) Women
i) The Black Male
j) Street Life
k) Adulthood

Quiz 11-20) These sorts of attitudes are not unique to Hip-Hop. Muscled male bodies are everywhere. They appear throughout American culture, in films, advertisements, television programs etc. However, across the landscape of music video, this is virtually the only vision of the black male available.

a) False

Quiz 11-21) These sorts of images are not unique to Hip-Hop. Objectified female bodies are everywhere. They appear throughout American culture, in films, advertisements, television programs etc. However, across the landscape of music video, this is virtually the only vision of women available.

a) True

Quiz 11-22) Beverly Guy-Shetfall argues that black people don't believe (_____) is as urgent a social issue as (_____).

a) Sexism
b) Homophobia
c) Racism
d) Islamophobia
e) Transphobia
f) Poverty

g)   Domestic Violence
h)   Gender Identity and Expression

Quiz 11-23) Beverly Guy-Shetfall argues that black people don't believe sexism is as urgent a social issue as racism.

a)   True

Quiz 11-24) Beverly Guy-Shetfall argues that black people don't believe homophobia is as urgent a social issue as poverty.

a)   False

Quiz 11-25) But Michael Eric Dyson points out that both (_____) men and black women are victimized by (_____) and (_____).

a)   Sexism
b)   Homophobia
c)   Racism
d)   Islamophobia
e)   Transphobia
f)   Poverty
g)   Domestic Violence
h)   Gender Identity and Expression
i)   Black
j)   Gay
k)   Transgendered
l)   Racialized
m)   Muslim

Quiz 11-26) But Michael Eric Dyson points out that both black men and black women are victimized by sexism and racism.

a)   True

Quiz 11-27) But Michael Eric Dyson points out that both gay men and black women are victimized by homophobia and domestic violence.

a)   False

Quiz 11-28) (_____) black women (_____) after the age of 18.

a)   Are raped
b)   Get pregnant
c)   Complete high school
d)   Are accepted into University
e)   Find employment
f)   1 in 4
g)   1 in 5
h)   1 in 50
i)   1 in 100

Quiz 11-29) 1 in 4 black women are raped after the age of 18.

a)   True

Quiz 11-30) 1 in 25 black women are accepted into university after the age of 17.

a)   False

Quiz 11-31) Black women are 35% (_____) to (_____) than white women.

a)   More likely
b)   Less likely
c)   Finish high school
d)   Get into university
e)   Be assaulted
f)   Find a job
g)   Experience teenage pregnancy

Quiz 11-32) Black women are 35% less likely to finish high school than white women.

a)   False

Quiz 11-33) Black women are 35% more likely to be assaulted than white women.

a)   True

Quiz 11-34) More than (_____) women are assaulted in the U.S. every year. This equates to one woman assaulted every (_____) seconds. 61% of the victims are under 18.

a)   50,000
b)   70,000
c)   100,000
d)   500,000
e)   700,000
f)   1,000,000
g)   45
h)   60
i)   90
j)   120

Quiz 11-35) More than 50,000 women are assaulted in the U.S. every year. This equates to one woman being assaulted every 120 seconds. 61% of the victims are over 18.

a)   False

Quiz 11-36) More than 700,000 women are assaulted in the U.S. every year. This equates to one woman being assaulted every 45 seconds. 61% of the victims are under 18.

a)   True

Quiz 11-37) (_____) suggests that the women who appear in rap videos are themselves (_____) the degradation and commodification of women.

a) Beverly Guy-Shetfall
b) Jadakiss
c) Chuck D.
d) Michael Eric Dyson
e) Jackson Katz
f) Participating in
g) Protesting against
h) Empowering
i) Desensitizing

Quiz 11-38) Michael Eric Dyson suggests that the women who appear in rap videos are themselves empowering the degradation and commodification of women.

a) False

Quiz 11-39) Beverly Guy-Shetfall suggests that the women who appear in rap videos are themselves participating in the degradation and commodification of women.

a) True

Quiz 11-40) (_____) said rap should not be taken seriously because "it's just entertainment." He also argued that (_____) are some of the biggest fans of rap music that includes lyrics about "bitches and ho's" and that they in fact like hearing these words.

a) The Rapper Jadakiss
b) Beverly Guy-Shetfall
c) The Rapper Chuck D.
d) Michael Eric Dyson
e) Jackson Katz
f) Women
g) Gay men
h) White women
i) Latin women

Quiz 11-41) The rapper Jadakiss said rap should not be taken seriously because "it's just entertainment." He also argued that women are some of the biggest fans of rap music that includes lyrics about "bitches and ho's" and that they in fact like hearing these words.

a) True

Quiz 11-42) Beverly Guy-Shetfall said rap should not be taken seriously because "it's just entertainment." She also argued that white women are some of the biggest fans of rap music that includes lyrics about "bitches and ho's" and that they in fact like hearing these words.

a) False

Quiz 11-43) Hurt argues that we have become desensitized to the (_____), (_____), and (_____) of rap and that this has blinded us to how demeaning and harmful it really is.

a) Sexism
b) Misogyny

c) Sexual objectification
d) Racism
e) Homophobia
f) Islamophobia

Quiz 11-44) Hurt argues that we have become desensitized to the racism, homophobia and islamophobia of rap and that this has blinded us to how demeaning and harmful it really is.

a) False

Quiz 11-45) Hurt argues that we have become desensitized to the sexism, misogyny and sexual objectification of rap and that this has blinded us to how demeaning and harmful it really is.

a) True

Quiz 11-46) In a lot of rap music men refer to other men by demeaning, feminized terms like "bitch." Calling a man a feminine name is the greatest insult that can be inflicted. (_____) believes that this reflects the deep insecurity that many men have about their (_____).

a) Hurt
b) Jadakiss
c) Chuck D.
d) Jackson Katz
e) Masculinity
f) Race
g) Sexuality
h) Sexual orientation

Quiz 11-47) In a lot of rap music men refer to other men by demeaning, feminized terms like "bitch." Calling a man a feminine name is the greatest insult that can be inflicted. Hurt believes that this reflects the deep insecurity that many men have about their masculinity.

a) True

Quiz 11-48) In a lot of rap music men refer to other men by demeaning, feminized terms like "bitch." Calling a man a feminine name is the greatest insult that can be inflicted. Jadakiss believes that this reflects the deep insecurity that many men have about their sexuality.

a) False

Quiz 11-49) Michael Eric Dyson points out that this is also a double assault. It is an attack on (_____), through the demeaning language, and also an attack on any type of masculinity that does not fit the stereotypical, hyper-masculine image.

a) Women
b) Men
c) Sexuality
d) Religion
e) Masculinity
f) Sexual-Orientation
g) Gender Identity

Quiz 11-50) Michael Eric Dyson points out that this is also a double assault. It is an attack on men, through the demeaning language, and also an attack on any type of gender identity that does not fit the stereotypical, hyper-masculine image.

a)   False

Quiz 11-51) Michael Eric Dyson points out that this is also a double assault. It is an attack on women, through the demeaning language, and also an attack on any type of masculinity that does not fit the stereotypical, hyper-masculine image.

a)   True

Quiz 11-52) This (_____) of men for purposes of insult does not happen just in hip- hop culture but throughout (_____) culture itself, in media, interpersonal interactions and even the world of politics.

a)   Feminizing
b)   Demeaning
c)   Insulting
d)   Bullying
e)   American
f)   Black
g)   African
h)   African-American

Quiz 11-53) This bullying of men for purposes of insult does not happen just in Hip-Hop culture but throughout African-American culture itself, in media, interpersonal interactions and even the world of politics.

a)   False

Quiz 11-54) This feminizing of men for purposes of insult does not happen just in hip- hop culture but throughout American culture itself, in media, interpersonal interactions and even the world of politics.

a)   True

Quiz 11-55) The (_____) industry makes huge profits by selling (_____) of violent, materialistic, sexist, black-masculinity, and by turning the misery of black poverty into a commodity that benefits white-owned corporations.

a)   Recording
b)   News Media
c)   Publishing
d)   Journalism
e)   Images
f)   Stories
g)   Albums
h)   Accounts

Quiz 11-56) The news media industry makes huge profits by selling stories of violent, materialistic, sexist, black-masculinity and by turning the misery of black poverty into a commodity that benefits white-owned corporations.

a)   False

Quiz 11-57) The recording industry makes huge profits by selling images of violent, materialistic, sexist, black-masculinity and by turning the misery of black poverty into a commodity that benefits white-owned corporations.

a)   True

Quiz 11-58) In previous decades, when there were still many small, independent record labels, it was (_____) for more diverse and (_____) artists to obtain recording contracts and get their music out in front of the public.

a)   Easier
b)   Difficult
c)   Impossible
d)   Unheard of
e)   Positive
f)   Controversial
g)   Underground
h)   Progressive
i)   Conscious

Quiz 11-59) In previous decades, when there were still many small, independent record labels, it was impossible for more diverse and conscious artists to obtain recording contracts and get their music out in front of the public.

a)   False

Quiz 11-60) In previous decades, when there were still many small, independent record labels, it was easier for more diverse and positive artists to obtain recording contracts and get their music out in front of the public.

a)   True

Quiz 11-61) The former president of (_____) told Hurt that the rise of so-called "gangsta" rap as the dominant subgenre coincided with the takeover of independent labels by (major corporations).

a)   Def Jam Records
b)   Death Row Records
c)   Bad Boy Records
d)   Ruthless Records
e)   Major Corporations
f)   Organized Crime
g)   Pension Funds
h)   Investors

Quiz 11-62) The former president of Def Jam Records told Hurt that the rise of so-called "gangsta" rap as the dominant subgenre coincided with the takeover of independent labels by major corporations.

a)   True

Quiz 11-63) The former president of Death Row Records told Hurt that the rise of so-called "gangsta" rap as the dominant subgenre coincided with the takeover of independent labels by organized crime syndicates.

a)   False

Quiz 11-64) (_____) fans of Hip-Hop interviewed by Hurt admitted that they know little about African-American culture beyond what they hear and see in recordings and videos. They also admitted that the music they listen to tends to (_____) negative stereotypes of blacks as violent, sexually predatory and obsessed with material goods.

a) White
b) Female
c) Asian
d) Latino
e) Reinforce
f) Dispel
g) Conform to
h) Create

Quiz 11-65) Asian fans of Hip-Hop interviewed by Hurt admitted that they know little about African-American culture beyond what they hear and see in recordings and videos. They also admitted that the music they listen to tends to dispel negative stereotypes of blacks as violent, sexually predatory and obsessed with material goods.

a) False

Quiz 11-66) White fans of Hip-Hop interviewed by Hurt admitted that they know little about African-American culture beyond what they hear and see in recordings and videos. They also admitted that the music they listen to tends to reinforce negative stereotypes of blacks as violent, sexually predatory and obsessed with material goods.

a) True

Quiz 11-67) Chuck D., of the political rap group Public Enemy, called BET "the (_____) of black manhood in the world" because of their (_____) rigid stereotypes of greedy, violent, and sexist black men.

a) Cancer
b) Savior
c) Center
d) Definition
e) Promotion of
f) Challenge to the
g) Contradiction of
h) Subversion of

Quiz 11-68) Chuck D., of the political rap group Public Enemy, called BET "the saviour of black manhood in the world" because of their subversion of rigid stereotypes of greedy, violent, and sexist black men.

a) False

Quiz 11-69) Chuck D., of the political rap group Public Enemy, called BET "the cancer of black manhood in the world" because of their promotion of rigid stereotypes of greedy, violent, and sexist black men.

a) True

Quiz 11-70) Chuck D., however, points out that (_____) cannot be blamed for what is really a state of affairs brought on by (_____) itself. Artists create what they know the industry will support. The industry supports music that glamorizes sexism and violence, not music that is political or includes positive or anti- corporate messages.

a) Individual Rappers
b) The Recording Industry
c) Parents

d) White listeners
e) Female listeners
f) White corporate owners
g) The Mainstream Media

Quiz 11-71) Chuck D., however, points out that individual rappers cannot be blamed for what is really a state of affairs brought on by the recording industry itself. Artists create what they know the industry will support. The industry supports music that glamorizes sexism and violence, not music that is political or includes positive or anti-corporate messages.

a) True

Quiz 11-72) Chuck D., however, points out that the recording industry cannot be blamed for what is really a state of affairs brought on by the individual rappers themselves. Artists create what they think the industry will support. They think the industry supports music that glamorizes sexism and violence, not music that is political or includes positive or anti-corporate messages.

a) False

Quiz 11-73) The music industry is controlled by (_____) corporations, and it is therefore (_____) businessmen who make the decisions about what rap music gets released and promoted.

a) White-owned
b) Mafia-owned
c) Black-owned
d) Foreign-owned
e) White
f) Black
g) Mafioso
h) Foreign

Quiz 11-74) The music industry is controlled by white-owned corporations; and it is therefore white businessmen who make the decisions about what rap music gets released and promoted.

a) True

Quiz 11-75) The music industry is controlled by foreign-owned corporations; and it is therefore foreign businessmen who make the decisions about what rap music gets released and promoted.

a) False

Quiz 12 Question Bank

Quiz 12-1) Pick two other musical genres related to the development of the Neo Soul genre:

a) R&B
b) Soul
c) Punk
d) Rock n' Roll
e) Country & Western
f) Progressive Rock
g) Rockabilly

Quiz 12-2) Pick two other musical genres related to the development of the Neo Soul genre:

a) Funk
b) Jazz
c) Punk
d) Rock n' Roll
e) Country & Western
f) Progressive Rock
g) Psychobilly

Quiz 12-3) Pick two other musical genres related to the development of the Neo Soul genre:

a) Hip hop
b) R&B
c) Punk
d) Barbershop
e) Country & Western
f) Progressive Rock
g) Psychobilly

Quiz 12-4) Barbershop and Country & Western are two musical genres related to the development of Neo Soul.

a) False

Quiz 12-5) Soul and R&B are two musical genres related to the development of Neo Soul.

a) True

Quiz 12-6) Select two albums from Erykah Badu's discography:

a) *Baduizm*
b) *Mama's Gun*
c) *Brown Sugar*
d) *The Art of Love & War*
e) *Black Diamond*
f) *Voodoo*

Quiz 12-7) Select two albums from Erykah Badu's discography:

a) *Worldwide Underground*
b) *Mama's Gun*
c) *Legendary Status*
d) *Mahogany Soul*
e) *Brown Sugar*
f) *Urban Hang Suite*

Quiz 12-8) Select two albums from Erykah Badu's discography:

a) *New Amerykah Part Two (Return of the Ankh)*
b) *Worldwide Underground*
c) *Brown Sugar*
d) *The Art of Love & War*
e) *Legendary Status*
f) *Unexpected*

Quiz 12-9) Select two albums from Erykah Badu's discography:

a) *New Amerykah Part One (4th World War)*
b) *Worldwide Underground*
c) *Stone Love*
d) *Mahogany Soul*
e) *Black Diamond*
f) *The Art of Love & War*

Quiz 12-10) Select two albums from Erykah Badu's discography:

a) *Mama's Gun*
b) *New Amerykah Part Two (Return of the Ankh)*
c) *Legendary Status*
d) *Stone Love*
e) *Urban Hang Suite*
f) *Unexpected*

Quiz 12-11) Name the song by Erykah Badu played in the lecture:

a) "Apple Tree"
b) "Gettin' In The Way"
c) "Crusin'"
d) "No Games"
e) "The Exclusive"
f) "Take Notice"

Quiz 12-12) What is Erykah Badu's city of origin?

a) Dallas, Texas
b) Philadelphia, Pennsylvania
c) Richmond, Virginia
d) Brooklyn, NYC
e) Columbia, South Carolina
f) The Bronx, NYC
g) Detroit, Michigan

Quiz 12-13) Erykah Badu is from The Bronx, NYC.

a) False

Quiz 12-14) Erykah Badu is from Dallas, Texas

a) True

Quiz 12-15) What is Erykah Badu's real name?

a) Erica Abi Wright
b) Angela Laverne Brown
c) Cheryl Wray
d) Sandra Denton
e) Dee Dee Roper

f) JoAnn Berry
g) Dana Owens

Quiz 12-16) What is Erica Abi Wright's nickname?

a) Erykah Badu
b) Angie Stone
c) Pepa
d) Salt
e) Queen Latifah
f) DJ Spinderella

Quiz 12-17) Erica Abi Wright's nickname is Angie Stone.

a) False

Quiz 12-18) Erica Abi Wright's nickname is Erykah Badu.

a) True

Quiz 12-19) Erykah Badu's real name is Sandra Denton.

a) False

Quiz 12-20) Erykah Badu's real name is Erica Abi Wright.

a) True

Quiz 12-21) What is Jill Scott's city of origin?

1. Dallas, Texas
2. Philadelphia, Pennsylvania
3. Richmond, Virginia
4. Brooklyn, NYC
5. Columbia, South Carolina

f) The Bronx, NYC

Quiz 12-22) Jill Scott is from Columbia, South Carolina.

a) False

Quiz 12-23) Jill Scott is from Philadelphia, Pennsylvania.

a) True

Quiz 12-24) Name the song by Jill Scott played in the lecture:

a) "Apple Tree"
b) "Gettin' in the Way"
c) "Crusin'"
d) "No Games"

e) "The Exclusive"
f) "Take Notice"

Quiz 12-25) Select two albums from D'Angelo's discography

a) *New Amerykah Part Two (Return of the Ankh)*
b) *Worldwide Underground*
c) *Brown Sugar*
d) *The Art of Love & War*
e) *D' Angelo' s Urban Hang Suite*
f) *Voodoo*

Quiz 12-26) What is D'Angelo's city of origin?

a) Dallas, Texas
b) Philadelphia, Pennsylvania
c) Richmond, Virginia
d) Brooklyn, NYC
e) Columbia, South Carolina
f) The Bronx, NYC

Quiz 12-27) D'Angelo's city of origin is Dallas, Texas.

a) False

Quiz 12-28) D'Angelo's city of origin is Richmond, Virginia.

a) True

Quiz 12-29) What is D'Angelo's real name?

a) Michael Eugene Archer
b) Gerald Maxwell Rivera
c) John Percy Simon
d) Christopher Oroc
e) Lee Perry
f) Paul D. Miller
g) Nathaniel T. Wilson

Quiz 12-30) What is Michael Eugene Archer's nickname?

a) D'Angelo
b) Maxwell
c) Percee P.
d) J Dilla
e) Common
f) Questlove

Quiz 12-31) Michael Eugene Archer's nickname is Questlove.

a) False

Quiz 12-32) Michael Eugene Archer's nickname is D'Angelo.

a)   True

Quiz 12-33) D'Angelo's real name is Nathaniel T. Wilson.

a)   False

Quiz 12-34) D'Angelo's real name is Michael Eugene Archer.

a)   True

Quiz 12-35) Name the song by D'Angelo (but originally sung by Smokey Robinson) played in the lecture:

a)   "Apple Tree"
b)   "Gettin' In The Way"
c)   "Crusin'"
d)   "No Games"
e)   "The Exclusive"
f)   "Take Notice"

Quiz 12-36) List one album from Maxwell's discography (year and title):

a)   *Maxwell's Urban Hang Suite*
b)   *Maxwell's New Amerykah Part Two (Return of the Ankh)*
c)   *Maxwell's Brown Sugar*
d)   *Maxwell's Original Instant Coffee*
e)   *Maxwell's Art of Love & War*
f)   *Maxwell's Legendary Status*

Quiz 12-37) What is Maxwell's real name?

a)   Michael Eugene Archer
b)   Gerald Maxwell Rivera
c)   John Percy Simon
d)   Christopher Oroc
e)   Maxwell Power
f)   Paul D. Miller
g)   Nathaniel T. Wilson

Quiz 12-38) What is Gerald Maxwell Rivera's nickname?

a)   Geraldo Rivera
b)   Maxwell
c)   D'Angelo
d)   Maxwell
e)   Percee P .
f)   J Dilla
g)   Common
h)   Questlove

Quiz 12-39) Gerald Maxwell Rivera's nickname is Geraldo Rivera

a)   False

Quiz 12-40) Gerald Maxwell Rivera's nickname is Maxwell

a)   True

Quiz 12-41) What is Maxwell's city of origin?

a)   Dallas, Texas
b)   Philadelphia, Pennsylvania
c)   Richmond, Virginia
d)   Brooklyn, NYC
e)   Columbia, South Carolina
f)   The Bronx, NYC
g)   Detroit, Michigan

Quiz 12-42) Maxell's city of origin is The Bronx, NYC.

a)   False

Quiz 12-43) Maxell's city of origin is Brooklyn, NYC.

a)   True

Quiz 12-44) Select two albums from Angie Stone's discography:

a)   *Baduizm*
b)   *Mama's Gun*
c)   *Brown Sugar*
d)   *The Art of Love & War*
e)   *Black Diamond*
f)   *Voodoo*

Quiz 12-45) Select two albums from Angie Stone's discography:

a)   *Worldwide Underground*
b)   *Stone Love*
c)   *Legendary Status*
d)   *Mahogany Soul*
e)   *Brown Sugar*
f)   *Angie's Urban Hang Suite*

Quiz 12-46) Select two albums from Angie Stone's discography:

a)   *New Amerykah Part Two (Return of the Ankh)*
b)   *Worldwide Underground*
c)   *Brown Sugar*
d)   *The Art of Love & War*
e)   *Legendary Status*
f)   *Unexpected*

Quiz 12-47) Select two albums from Angie Stone's discography:

a) *New Amerykah Part One (4th World War)*
b) *Worldwide Underground*
c) *Stone Love*
d) *Mahogany Soul*
e) *Black Diamond*
f) *New Amerykah Part Two (Return of the Ankh)*

Quiz 12-48) Select two albums from Angie Stone's discography:

a) *Mama's Gun*
b) *New Amerykah Part Two (Return of the Ankh)*
c) *Legendary Status*
d) *Stone Love*
e) *Erykah's Urban Hang Suite*
f) *Unexpected*

Quiz 12-49) What is Angie Stone's city of origin?

a) Dallas, Texas
b) Philadelphia, Pennsylvania
c) Richmond, Virginia
d) Brooklyn, NYC
e) Columbia, South Carolina
f) The Bronx, NYC
g) Detroit, Michigan

Quiz 12-50) Angie Stone is from Columbia, South Carolina.

a) True

Quiz 12-51) Angie Stone is from Charleston, South Carolina.

a) False

Quiz 12-52) What is Angie Stone's real name?

a) Erica Abi Wright
b) Angela Laverne Brown
c) Cheryl Wray
d) Sandra Denton
e) Dee Dee Roper
f) JoAnn Berry
g) Dana Owens

Quiz 12-53) Angie Stone's real name is Angela Laverne Brown.

a) True

Quiz 12-54) Angie Stone's real name is Angela Laverne Shirley.

a) False

Quiz 12-55) What is Angela Laverne Brown's nickname?

a) Shirley Laverne
b) Angie Stone
c) DJ Spinderella
d) Erykah Badu
e) Pepa
f) Salt

Quiz 12-56) Angela Laverne Brown's nickname is Angie Stone.

a) True

Quiz 12-57) Angela Laverne Brown's nickname is Shirley Laverne

a) False

Quiz 12-58) Identify two members of the group The Soulquarians:

a) Angie Stone
b) Maxwell
c) Jill Scott
d) DJ Spinderella
e) Christopher Oroc
f) Common
g) Erykah Badu

Quiz 12-59) Identify two members of the group The Soulquarians:

a) Angie Stone
b) Maxwell
c) Jill Scott
d) DJ Spinderella
e) Christopher Oroc
f) Questlove
g) Bilal

Quiz 12-60) Identify two members of the group The Soulquarians:

a) Angie Stone
b) Maxwell
c) Jill Scott
d) DJ Spinderella
e) Christopher Oroc
f) D'Angelo
g) James Poyser

Quiz 12-61) Identify two members of the group The Soulquarians:

a) Angie Stone
b) Maxwell
c) Jill Scott
d) DJ Spinderella

e)   Christopher Oroc
f)   Mos Def
g)   Q-Tip

Quiz 12-62) Identify two members of the group The Soulquarians:

a)   Angie Stone
b)   Maxwell
c)   Jill Scott
d)   DJ Spinderella
e)   Christopher Oroc
f)   Talib Kweli
g)   Pino Palladino

Quiz 12-63) Identify two members of the group The Soulquarians:

a)   Angie Stone
b)   Maxwell
c)   Jill Scott
d)   DJ Spinderella
e)   Christopher Oroc
f)   J Dilla
g)   Mos Def
h)   Mos Eisely

Quiz 12-64) What is J Dilla's city of origin?

a)   Dallas, Texas
b)   Philadelphia, Pennsylvania
c)   Richmond, Virginia
d)   Brooklyn, NYC
e)   Columbia, South Carolina
f)   The Bronx, NYC
g)   Detroit, Michigan

Quiz 12-65) J Dilla is from The Bronx, NYC.

a)   False

Quiz 12-66) J Dilla is from Detroit, Michigan.

a)   True

Quiz 12-67) What is one of J Dilla's alternate nicknames?

a)   Jay Dee
b)   Jay Zee
c)   J.C.
d)   Jay Cee
e)   Dee Jay
f)   Zee Jay
g)   Jay Dawg

Quiz 12-68) What is one of J Dilla's alternate nicknames?

a) Dilla Dawg
b) Dilla Pilla
c) Pilla Dilla
d) Killa Dawg
e) Snoop Dawg
f) Hogg Dawg
g) Killa Dilla
h) Dilla Killa

Quiz 12-69) One of J Dilla's nicknames is Jay Cee.

a) False

Quiz 12-70) One of J Dilla's nicknames is Jay Dee.

a) True

Quiz 12-71) One of J Dilla's nicknames is Dilla Dawg.

a) True

Quiz 12-72) One of J Dilla's nicknames is Dilla Killa.

a) False

Quiz 12-73) Which subgenre of Hip-Hop does J Dilla Represent?

a) G-Funk
b) Jazz Rap
c) Underground
d) Gangsta Rap
e) Illbient
f) Turntablist

Quiz 12-74) J Dilla represents the "Illbient" subgenre of Hip-Hop.

a) False

Quiz 12-75) J Dilla represents the "Underground" subgenre of Hip-Hop.

a) True

Quiz 12-76) What is Percee P's real name?

a) Michael Eugene Archer
b) Gerald Maxwell Rivera
c) John Percy Simon
d) Christopher Oroc
e) Maxwell Power
f) Paul D. Miller
g) Nathaniel T. Wilson

Quiz 12-77) What is John Percy Simon's nickname?

a)   D'Angelo
b)   Maxwell
c)   Percee P.
d)   J Dilla
e)   Common
f)   Questlove

Quiz 12-78) Percee P's real name is Nathaniel T. Wilson

a)   False

Quiz 12-79) Percee P's real name is John Percy Simon

a)   True

Quiz 12-80) John Percy Simon's nickname is Q-Tip

a)   False

Quiz 12-81) John Percy Simon's nickname is Percee P.

a)   True

Quiz 12-82) What is Percee P's city of origin?

a)   Dallas, Texas
b)   Philadelphia, Pennsylvania
c)   Richmond, Virginia
d)   Brooklyn, NYC
e)   Columbia, South Carolina
f)   The Bronx, NYC
g)   Detroit, Michigan

Quiz 12-83) Percee P is from Brooklyn, NYC.

a)   False

Quiz 12-84) Percee P is from The Bronx, NYC.

a)   True

Quiz 12-85) Pick two albums from Percee P's Discography:

a)   Oh No vs. Percee P
b)   Legendary Status
c)   Brown Sugar
d)   Voodoo
e)   Black Diamond
f)   Mahogany Soul
g)   Stone Love

h) Unexpected

Quiz 12-86) Pick two albums from Percee P's Discography:

a) Perseverance
b) Legendary Status
c) Brown Sugar
d) Voodoo
e) Black Diamond
f) Mahogany Soul
g) Stone Love
h) Unexpected

Quiz 12-87) Pick two albums from Percee P's Discography:

a) Perseverance
b) Oh No vs. Percee P
c) Brown Sugar
d) Voodoo
e) Black Diamond
f) Mahogany Soul
g) Stone Love
h) Unexpected

Quiz 12-88) MP3: Identify the Artist, Song Title, Album Title and Year of the following track:

a) J Dilla
b) Percee P
c) Jaylib
d) "Take Notice"
e) "The Exclusive"
f) "Don't Sleep"
g) "No Games"
h) *RuffDraft*
i) *Promo*
j) *Champion Sound*
k) 2003
l) 2004
m) 2005

Quiz 12-89) MP3: Identify the Artist, Song Title and Album title of the following track:

a) J Dilla
b) PerceeP
c) Jaylib
d) "Take Notice"
e) "The Exclusive"
f) "Don't Sleep"
g) "No Games"
h) *Ruff Draft*
9. *Promo*
j) *Champion Sound*

k) 2003
l) 2004
m) 2005

Quiz 12-90) MP3: Identify the Artist, Song Title and Album title of the following track:

a) J Dilla
b) Percee P
c) Jaylib
d) "Take Notice"
e) "The Exclusive"
f) "Don't Sleep"
g) "No Games"
h) *Ruff Draft*
i) *Promo*
j) *Champion Sound*
k) 2003
l) 2004
m) 2005

Quiz 12-91) MP3: Identify the Artist, Song Title and Album title of the following track:

a) J Dilla
b) Percee P
c) Jaylib
d) "Take Notice"
e) "The Exclusive"
f) "Don't Sleep"
g) "No Games"
h) *Ruff Draft*
i) *Promo*
j) *Champion Sound*
k) 2003
l) 2004
m) 2005

Quiz 13 Question Bank

Quiz 13-1) What sport is credited with being responsible for "sneaker culture"?

a) Basketball
b) Football
c) Tennis
d) Cricket
e) Soccer
f) Baseball
g) Track and Field

Quiz 13-2) Tennis is the sport credited with responsibility for "sneaker culture."

a) False

Quiz 13-3) Basketball is the sport credited with responsibility for "sneaker culture."

a)   True

Quiz 13-4) Which of the following is credited to the sport of basketball?

a)   "Sneaker Culture"
b)   The term "felon sneakers"
c)   Origin of Kangol Hats
d)   Origin of Levi's Jeans
e)   Laccless sneakers
f)   Leather jackets

Quiz 13-5) The element of "style" in sneaker culture is credited to what genre of music?

a)   Hip-Hop/Rap
b)   Soul
c)   Bebop
d)   Funk
e)   Disco
f)   Hyper Funk

Quiz 13-6) The element of "style" in sneaker culture is credited to the Hip Hop/Rap genre of music.

a)   True

Quiz 13-7) The element of "style" in sneaker culture is credited to the Hyper Funk genre of music.

a)   False

Quiz 13-8) What initially determined sneakers selection by B-Boys and B-Girls?

a)   Comfort
b)   Brand
c)   Gang affiliation
d)   Hood of origin
e)   Sole material
f)   Traction/Slipperiness

Quiz 13-9) Initially the Brand of a pair of sneakers was instrumental in determining selection by B-Boys and B-Girls.

a)   False

Quiz 13-10) Initially the comfort of a pair of sneakers was instrumental in determining selection by B-Boys and B-Girls.

a)   True

Quiz 13-11) Identify two supporting fashions to "sneaker culture" of the 1980s:

a)   Le Tigre Shirt
b)   Lee Rider Jeans
c)   Adidas Hat

d)   Track pants
e)   Ray Ban Sunglasses
f)   Leather Jackets

Quiz 13-12) Identify two supporting fashions to "sneaker culture" of the 1980s:

a)   Levi's Jeans
b)   Kangol Hat
c)   Adidas Hat
d)   Track pants
e)   Ray Ban Sunglasses
f)   Leather Jackets

Quiz 13-13) Identify two supporting fashions to "sneaker culture" of the 1980s:

a)   Shoe Laces/Fat Laces and/or accessories
b)   Kangol Hat
c)   Adidas Hat
d)   Track pants
e)   Ray Ban Sunglasses
f)   Leather Jackets

Quiz 13-14) Adidas hats and Ray Ban sunglasses were two supporting fashions to "sneaker culture" of the 1980s.

a)   False

Quiz 13-15) Kangol Hats and Levi's Jeans were two supporting fashions to "sneaker culture" of the 1980s.

a)   True

Quiz 13-16) Which of the following groups dominated the sneaker "look" of the 1980s?

a)   B-Boys/B-Girls
b)   MCs
c)   DJs
d)   Gangstas
e)   Rappers
f)   Turntablists
g)   Pimps

Quiz 13-17) MCs and DJs dominated the sneaker "look" of the 1980s.

a)   False

Quiz 13-18) B-Boys/B-Girls dominated the sneaker "look" of the 1980s.

a)   True

Quiz 13-19) The mindset of "cleaning" your sneakers came from which of the following?

a)   Necessity
b)   Peer pressure

c) Collectability of shoes
d) Scarcity of shoes
e) Cultural Traditions
f) Pride

Quiz 13-20) The mindset of "cleaning" your sneakers was a result of necessity.

a) True

Quiz 13-21) The mindset of "cleaning" your sneakers was a result of the collectible nature of sneakers which were often bought, sold and traded by sneaker enthusiasts.

a) False

Quiz 13-22) Back then, shoe laces matched which of the following items?

a) Hat (with Brand Name) and/or Kangol Hat
b) Track Pants
c) Sunglasses
d) Jacket
e) Sneakers
f) Le Tigre Shirt

Quiz 13-23) Back then, shoe laces matched the Le Tigre Shirt you were wearing.

a) False

Quiz 13-24) Back then, shoe laces matched either your hat (with brand name) or Kangol hat.

a) True

Quiz 13-25) Without this your sneakers "meant nothing."

a) Accessories
b) Coordinated laces
c) Matching socks
d) Matching hat
e) Matching track pants
f) Matching Le Tigre Shirt

Quiz 13-26) Without accessories your sneakers "meant nothing."

a) True

Quiz 13-27) Without a matching Le Tigre Shirt, your sneakers "meant nothing."

a) False

Quiz 13-28) In order to "stretch" shoelaces in the "80s, which of the following household items were used"?

a) Iron
b) Hair Curler

c) Screwdriver
d) Hammer
e) Stovetop
f) Wringer apparatus on a Washing Machine
g) Cast Iron Frying Pan

Quiz 13-29) The wringer apparatus on old-fashioned washing machines was used to "stretch" shoelaces in the 1980s.

a) False

Quiz 13-30) An iron was used to "stretch" shoelaces in the 1980s.

a) True

Quiz 13-31) The concept of laceless sneakers comes from which culture?

a) Prison
b) Army
c) Navy
d) National Guard
e) Prep School
f) Private College

Quiz 13-32) The concept of laceless sneakers comes from Prep School culture.

a) False

Quiz 13-33) The concept of laceless sneakers comes from prison culture.

a) True

Quiz 13-34) 80s Fashion essentially revolved around representing which of the following?

a) The "Sneaker" Industry
b) Basketball
c) The Individual
d) Tennis
e) Corporations
f) Fashion designers
g) Pop musicians

Quiz 13-35) 80s Fashion essentially revolved around representing the Sneaker Industry.

a) False

Quiz 13-36) 80s Fashion essentially revolved around representing the individual.

a) True

Quiz 13-37) The Adidas brand is synonymous with which Rap Group?

a) Run-DMC
b) The Juice Crew

c)   The Soulquarians
d)   The Westside Connection
e)   N.W.A.
f)   Public Enemy

Quiz 13-38) The Adidas brand is synonymous with the group The Juice Crew.

a)   False

Quiz 13-39) The Adidas brand is synonymous with the group Run-DMC.

a)   True

Quiz 13-40) The classic Run-DMC "look" is known in NYC as which of the following?

a)   "Stick-Up Kid"
b)   "B-Boy"
c)   "Gangsta"
d)   "Hitman"
e)   "Pimp King"
f)   "MixMaster"
g)   "Supafly"

Quiz 13-41) The classic Run-DMC "look" is known in NYC as the "MixMaster" look.

a)   False

Quiz 13-42) The classic Run-DMC "look" is known in NYC as the "Stick-Up Kid" look.

a)   True

Quiz 13-43) Which rap group was the "Stick-Up Kid" look associated with?

a)   Run-DMC
b)   The Juice Crew
c)   The Soulquarians
d)   The Westside Connection
e)   N.W.A.
f)   Public Enemy

Quiz 13-44) What was the amount of money offered to the "famed rap group" from the film in the contract offered by Adidas

a) $10,000
b) $75,000
c) $100,000
d) $250,000
e) $1,000,000
f) $1,500,000

Quiz 13-45) Which company made offered a million-dollar endorsement contract to a famed rap group?

a)   Adidas
b)   Ray Ban

c) Adidas
d) Converse
e) Nike
f) My Fila
g) Kangol
h) Le Tigre

Quiz 13-46) Nike offered a million-dollar contract to the "famed rap group" shown in the video.

a) False

Quiz 13-47) Adidas offered a million-dollar contract to the "famed rap group" shown in the video.

a) True

Quiz 13-48) The term "Felon Sneakers" was coined by:

a) Gerald W. Deas
b) Tipper Gore
c) The Parent Music Resource Council
d) Chuck D
e) Run-DMC
f) Common
g) Ice T

Quiz 13-49) What was Gerald W. Deas' contribution to "sneaker culture"?

a) Coined the term "Felon Sneakers"
b) Convinced Adidas to offer Run-DMC an endorsement contract
c) Started a shoe store popular with B-Boys/B-Girls
d) Improved sneakers to meet the needs of B-Boys and B-Girls
e) Was the forward-thinking president and CEO of Nike
f) Was a condescending politician who disparaged "sneaker culture"

Quiz 13-50) Gerald W. Deas was famous for running a shoe store that imported all manner or rare and customer sneakers for his B-Boy/B-Girl clientele.

a) False

Quiz 13-51) Gerald W. Deas was famous for coining the term "Felon Sneakers."

a) True

Quiz 13-52) Who came up with the slogan "My Adidas"?

a) Russell Simmons
b) Gerald Deas
c) Fresh Gordon
d) LL Cool J
e) Beastie Boys
f) Busy B
g) Heavy D

Quiz 13-53) Russel Simmons coined the term "Felon Sneakers."

a)   False

Quiz 13-54) Gerald W. Deas coined the slogan "My Adidas."

a)   False

Quiz 13-55) Russel Simmons coined the slogan "My Adidas."

a)   True

Quiz 13-56) Which of the following is attributed to Russell Simmons:

a)   The slogan "My Adidas"
b)   The term "Felon Sneakers"
c)   A famous sneaker shop
d)   Offering Run-DMC an endorsement contract
e)   Wrote articles praising "sneaker culture"
f)   Wrote articles disparaging "sneaker culture"

Quiz 13-57) Michael Jordan specifically introduced which of these sneakers?

a)   Air Jordan I
b)   Air Jordan Mk 2
c)   Air Jordan Custom
d)   New Air Jordan
e)   Air Jordan Converse
f)   Air Jordan .38 Special

Quiz 13-58) Michael Jordan specifically introduced the "New Air Jordan" sneaker.

a)   False

Quiz 13-59) Michael Jordan specifically introduced the (_____) sneaker.a) True
   Quiz 13-60) What is Michael Jordan's contribution to "sneaker culture"?

a)   Introduced the "Air Jordan 1"
b)   Introduced the "New Air Jordan"
c)   Coined the term "Felon Sneakers"
d)   Coined the slogan "My Adidas"
e)   Helped Run-DMC get an endorsement deal
f)   Wrote articles praising "sneaker culture"

Quiz 13-61) Match the following artist with the sneaker: Fresh Gordon

a)   My Fila
b)   Nike
c)   Converse
d)   Air Jordan
e)   Suede Adidas
f)   Troop

Quiz 13-62) Match the following artist with the sneaker: Heavy D.

a) My Fila
b) Nike
c) Converse
d) Air Jordan
e) Suede Adidas
f) Troop

Quiz 13-63) Match the following artist with the sneaker: Busy B.

a) My Fila
b) Nike
c) Converse
d) Air Jordan
e) Suede Adidas
f) Troop

Quiz 13-64) Match the following artist with the sneaker: Beastie Boys.

a) My Fila
b) Nike
c) Converse
d) Air Jordan
e) Suede Adidas
f) Troop

Quiz 13-65) Match the following artist with the sneaker: LL Cool J.

a) My Fila
b) Nike
c) Converse
d) Air Jordan
e) Suede Adidas

f) Troop

Quiz 13-66) Match the following sneaker with the artist: My Fila.

a) Fresh Gordon
b) Heavy D
c) Busy B
d) Beastie Boys
e) LL Cool J
f) Run-DMC
g) The Juice Crew

Quiz 13-67) Match the following sneaker with the artist: Nike.

a) Fresh Gordon
b) Heavy D
c) Busy B

d) Beastie Boys
e) LL Cool J
f) Run-DMC
g) The Juice Crew

Quiz 13-68) Match the following sneaker with the artist: Converse.

a) Fresh Gordon
b) Heavy D
c) Busy B
d) Beastie Boys
e) LL Cool J
f) Run-DMC
g) The Juice Crew

Quiz 13-69) Match the following sneaker with the artist: Suede Adidas.

a) Fresh Gordon
b) Heavy D
c) Busy B
d) BeastieBoys
e) LL Cool J
f) Run-DMC
g) The Juice Crew

Quiz 13-70) Match the following sneaker with the artist: Troop.

a) Fresh Gordon
b) Heavy D
c) Busy B
d) Beastie Boys
e) LL Cool J
f) Run-DMC
g) The Juice Crew

Quiz 14 Question Bank

Quiz 14-1) What is Talib Kweli's full given name?

a) Talib Kweli Greene
b) Talib Kweli Smith
c) Talib Kweli Ibn Abdul Syeed Davis
d) Talib Kweli Jones
e) Talib Kweli Davis
f) Talib Kweli Jackson

Quiz 14-2) Talib Kweli's full given name is Talib Kweli Ibn Abdul Syeed Davis.

a) False

Quiz 14-3) Talib Kweli's full-given name is Talib Kweli Greene.

a) True

Quiz 14-4) What language is Talib Kweli's first name from and what does it mean?

a) Arabic
b) Swahili
c) Pashto
d) Urdu
e) Student/Seeker
f) Teacher/Master
g) Philosopher/Thinker
h) Truth/Honesty

Quiz 14-5) Talib Kweli's first name means "student" or "seeker" in Arabic.

a) True

Quiz 14-6) Talib Kweli's first name means "Teacher" or "Master" in Pashto.

a) False

Quiz 14-7) Which artist's first name means "student" or "seeker" in Arabic.

a) Talib Kweli
b) Mos Def
c) Nas
d) MF Doom
e) Madlib
f) Bilal

Quiz 14-8) What language is Talib Kweli's middle name from and what does it mean?

a) Arabic
b) Swahili
c) Pashto
d) Urdu
e) Student
f) Teacher
g) Philosopher
h) Truth

Quiz 14-9) Which artist's middle name means "truth" in Swahili?

a) Talib Kweli
b) Mos Def
c) Nas
d) MF Doom
e) Madlib
f) Bilal

Quiz 14-10) Talib Kweli's middle name means "truth" in Swahili.

a) True

Quiz 14-11) Talib Kweli's middle name means "philosopher" in Pashto.

a)   False

Quiz 14-12) What is Talib Kweli's city of Origin?

a)   Brooklyn, NYC
b)   Bedford-Stuyvesant, Brooklyn, NYC
c)   Queens, NYC
d)   Long Island, NY
e)   Oxnard, CA
f)   Philadelphia, P A

Quiz 14-13) Talib Kweli is from Long Island, New York.

a)   False

Quiz 14-14) Talib Kweli is from Brooklyn, New York City.

a)   True

Quiz 14-15) Identify two albums from Talib Kweli's discography:

a)   *Quality*
b)   *The Beautiful Struggle*
c)   *Black On Both Sides*
d)   *Manifest Destiny*
e)   *Illmatic*
f)   *It Was Written*

Quiz 14-16) Identify two albums from Talib Kweli's discography:

a)   *Right About Now*
b)   *Eardrum*
c)   *True Magic*
d)   *The New Danger*
e)   *Hip Hop Is Dead*

f)   *Untitled*

Quiz 14-17) Identify two albums from Talib Kweli's discography:

a)   *Quality*
b)   *Eardrum*
c)   *The New Danger*
d)   *Hip Hop Is Dead*
e)   *God's Son*
f)   *Stillmatic*

Quiz 14-18) Identify two albums from Talib Kweli's discography:

a)   *The Beautiful Struggle*
b)   *Right About Now*

c) *Street's Disciple*
d) *Distant Relatives*
e) *Born Like This*
f) *Unexpected Guests*

Quiz 14-19) Name the artist and track name of the sample used in the Talib Kweli track played in the last lecture:

a) "Planet Rock"
b) Afrika Bambaataa
c) Eric B. and Rakim
d) "Paid In Full"
e) Smokey Robinson
f) "Crusin'"
g) Compton's Most Wanted
h) "Hood Took Me Under"

Quiz 14-20) The Talib Kweli track played in the last lecture sampled "Planet Rock" by Afrika Bambaataa.

a) True

Quiz 14-21) The Talib Kweli track played in the last lecture sampled "Paid in Full" by Eric B. and Rakim.

a) False

Quiz 14-22) What is Mos Def's real name?

a) Dante Terrell Smith-Bey
b) Nasir bin Olu Dara Brown
c) Talib Kweli Green
d) Daniel Dumile
e) Otis Jackson Jr.
f) Russell Simmons

Quiz 14-23) What is Dante Terrell Smith-Bey's nickname?

a) Mos Def
b) Nas
c) Talib Kweli
d) MF Doom
e) Run
f) Madlib

Quiz 14-24) Dante Terrell Smith-Bey's nickname is Mos Def.

a) True

Quiz 14-25) Dante Terrell Smith-Bey's nickname is Nas.

a) False

Quiz 14-26) What is Mos Def's city of origin?

a) Brooklyn, NYC
b) Bedford-Stuyvesant, Brooklyn, NYC

c) Queens, NYC
d) Long Island, NY
e) Oxnard, CA
f) Philadelphia, P A

Quiz 14-27) Which of the following artists is from the Bedford-Stuyvesant neighborhood of Brooklyn, New York City?

a) Mos Def
b) Madlib
c) Nas
d) Talib Kweli
e) MF Doom
f) Run

Quiz 14-28) Mos Def is from Queens, NYC.

a) False

Quiz 14-29) Mos Def is from the Bedford-Stuyvesant neighborhood of Brooklyn, New York City.

a) True

Quiz 14-30) Identify two albums from Mos Def's discography:

a) *Black on Both Sides*
b) *Manifest Destiny*
c) *Quality*
d) *Operation Doomsday*
e) *Untitled*
f) *Distant Relatives*

Quiz 14-31) Identify two albums from Mos Def's discography:

a) *The New Danger*
b) *True Magic*
c) *The Beautiful Struggle*
d) *MM..Food*
e) *Street's Disciple*
f) *Hip Hop Is Dead*

Quiz 14-32) Identify two albums from Mos Def's discography:

a) *Mos Definite*
b) *The Ecstatic*
c) *Right About Now*
d) *Live from Planet X*
e) *Stillmatic*
f) *God's Son*

Quiz 14-33) Identify two albums from Mos Def's discography:

a) *The Ecstatic*
b) *True Magic*

c)   *Eardrum*
d)   *Born Like This*
e)   *I Am...*
f)   *Nastradamus*

Quiz 14-34) Identify two albums from Mos Def's discography:

a)   *The New Danger*
b)   *Manifest Destiny*
c)   *The Beautiful Struggle*
d)   *Unexpected Guests*
e)   *Illmatic*
f)   *It Was Written*

Quiz 14-35) What is Nas' City of Origin?

a)   Brooklyn, NYC
b)   Philadelphia, P A
c)   Bedford-Stuyvesant, Brooklyn, NYC
d)   Queens, NYC
e)   Long Island, NY
f)   Oxnard, CA

Quiz 14-36) Nas is from the Bedford-Stuyvesant neighborhood in Brooklyn, New York City.

a)   False

Quiz 14-37) Nas is from Queens, New York City.

a)   True

Quiz 14-38) What is Nas' complete given name?

a)   Nasir bin Olu Dara Brown
b)   Nasir bin Olu Dara Davis
c)   Nasir bin Olu Dara Jones
d)   Nasir bin Olu Dara Jackson
e)   Nasir bin Olu Dara Greene
f)   Nasir bin Olu Dara Ibn Abdul Syeed Davis

Quiz 14-39) Nas' complete given name is Nasir bin Olu Dara Jones.

a)   True

Quiz 14-40) Nas' complete name is Nasirideen Ibn Abdul Syeed Davis.

a)   False

Quiz 14-41) What is Nasir bin Olu Dara Jones' nickname?

a)   Mos Def
b)   Nas
c)   Talib Kweli

d) MF Doom
e) Run
f) Madlib

Quiz 14-42) What is the title of the track played by Nas in the last lecture and the title of the track that Nas sampled?

a) "It Ain't Hard To Tell"
b) "Human Nature"
c) "Planet Rock"
d) "Paid in Full"
e) "Hood Took Me Under"
f) "Crusin'"

Quiz 14-43) Identify two albums from Nas' Discography:

a) *Untitled*
b) *Distant Relatives*
c) *The Ecstatic*
d) *True Magic*
e) *Eardrum*
f) *Born Like This*

Quiz 14-44) Identify two albums from Nas' Discography:

a) *Street's Disciple*
b) *Hip Hop Is Dead*
c) *Mos Definite*
d) *The Ecstatic*
e) *Right About Now*
f) *Live from Planet X*

Quiz 14-45) Identify two albums from Nas' Discography:

a) *Stillmatic*
b) *God's Son*
c) *The Beautiful Struggle*
d) *MM..Food*
e) *The New Danger*
f) *Manifest Destiny*

Quiz 14-46) Identify two albums from Nas' Discography:

a) *I Am...*
b) *Nastradamus*
c) *The New Danger*
d) *True Magic*
e) *Manifest Destiny*
f) *Quality*

Quiz 14-47) Identify two albums from Nas' Discography:

a) *Illmatic*
b) *It Was Written*

c) *Black on Both Sides*
d) *Manifest Destiny*
e) *Quality*
f) *Operation Doomsday*

Quiz 14-48) Which two MC's form the duo Blackstar?

a) Mos Def
b) Talib Kweli
c) Nas
d) MF Doom
e) Madlib
f) Run

Quiz 14-49) What is the name of the duo formed by Mos Def and Talib Kweli?

a) Blackstar
b) Madvillian
c) Underground Kingz
d) Jonzun Crew
e) Geto Boys
f) Run-DMC

Quiz 14-50) Mos Def and Talib Kweli formed the duo Madvillan.

a) False

Quiz 14-51) Mos Def and Talib Kweli formed the duo Blackstar.

a) True

Quiz 14-52) Blackstar is a duo formed by MF Doom and Madlib.

a) False

Quiz 14-53) The duo Blackstar was formed by Mos Def and Talib Kweli.

a) True

Quiz 14-54) Which country was MF Doom born in?

a) Britain
b) Barbados
c) Nigeria
d) Congo Republic
e) Trinidad
f) Brazil

Quiz 14-55) Which of the following artists were born in Britain?

a) Mos Def
b) Talib Kweli

c) Nas
d) MF Doom
e) Madlib
f) Run

Quiz 14-56) MF Doom was born in Barbados.

a) False

Quiz 14-57) MF Doom was born in Britain.

a) True

Quiz 14-58) What is MF Doom's real name?

a) Daniel Dumile
b) Nasir bin Olu Dara Jones
c) Talib Kweli Greene
d) Dante Terrell Smith-Bey
e) Otis Jackson Jr.
f) Russell Simmons

Quiz 14-59) What is Daniel Dumile's nickname?

a) Mos Def
b) Talib Kweli
c) Nas
d) MFDoom
e) Madlib
f) Run

Quiz 14-60) MF Doom's real name is Otis Jackson Jr.

a) False

Quiz 14-61) MF Doom's real name is Daniel Dumile.

a) True

Quiz 14-62) What are the three possible meanings given for the "MF" in MF Doom?

a) Metal Face, Metal Fingers or Mad Flow
b) Metal Face, Mad Fingers or Metal Flow
c) Mad Face, Metal Fingers, or Mad Flow

Quiz 14-63) The three possible meanings given for the "MF" in MF Doom are "Metal Face," "Metal Fingers" or "Mad Flow."

a) True

Quiz 14-64) The three possible meanings given for the "MF" in MF Doom are "Metal Face," "Mad Fingers" or "Metal Flow."

a) False

Quiz 14-65) What is MF Doom's city of origin?

a) Brooklyn, NYC
b) Bedford-Stuyvesant, Brooklyn, NYC
c) Queens, NYC
d) Long Island, NY
e) Oxnard, CA
f) Philadelphia, PA

Quiz 14-66) MF Doom originated from Oxnard, California.

a) False

Quiz 14-67) MF Doom originated from Long Island, NY.

a) True

Quiz 14-68) Select two albums from MF Doom's Discography:

a) *Operation Doomsday*
b) *MM.Food*
c) *The Beautiful Struggle*
d) *Illmatic*
e) *It Was Written*
f) *Black on Both Sides*

Quiz 14-69) Select two albums from MF Doom's Discography:

a) *MM..Food*
b) *Live from Planet X*
c) *Eardrum*
d) *I Am...*
e) *Nastradamus*
f) *The New Danger*

Quiz 14-70) Select two albums from MF Doom's Discography:

a) *Live from Planet X*
b) *Born Like This*
c) *Right About Now*
d) *Stillmatic*
e) *God's Son*
f) *The Beautiful Struggle*

Quiz 14-71) Select two albums from MF Doom's Discography:

a) *Born Like This*
b) *Unexpected Guests*
c) *The Beautiful Struggle*
d) *Street's Disciple*
e) *Hip Hop Is Dead*
f) *Mos Definite*

Quiz 14-72) Select two albums from MF Doom's Discography:

a) *Unexpected Guests*
b) *Operation Doomsday*
c) *Quality*
d) *Untitled*
e) *Distant Relatives*
f) *The Ecstatic*

Quiz 14-73) What is Madlib's real name?

a) Daniel Dumile
b) Nasir bin Olu Dara Jones
c) Talib Kweli Greene
d) Dante Terrell Smith-Bey
e) Otis Jackson Jr .
f) Russell Simmons

Quiz 14-74) What is Otis Jackson Jr.'s nickname?

a) Mos Def
b) Talib Kweli
c) Nas
d) MF Doom
e) Madlib
f) Run

Quiz 14-75) Madlib's real name is Otis Jackson Jr.

a) True

Quiz 14-76) Madlib's real name is Dante Terrell Smith-Bey.

a) False

Quiz 14-77) Otis Jackson Jr's nickname is Mos Def.

a) False

Quiz 14-78) Otis Jackson Jr's nickname is Madlib.

a) True

Quiz 14-79) What is Madlib's city of origin?

a) Brooklyn, NYC
b) Bedford-Stuyvesant, Brooklyn, NYC
c) Queens, NYC
d) Long Island, NY
e) Oxnard, CA
f) Philadelphia, P A

Quiz 14-80) Madlib is from Long Island, NY.

a)   False

Quiz 14-81) Madlib is from Oxnard, California.

a)   True

Quiz 14-82) What does the acronym MADLIB stand for?

a)   Mind Altering Demented Lessons In Beats
b)   Mad Attacks Demanding Loyalty In Blood
c)   Miserable Atrophy Degrading Life In Brooklyn
d)   My Aunt's Dog Likes It's Bone
e)   Mental Alterations Done Live In Bedford

Quiz 14-83) The acronym MADLIB stands for "Mind Altering Demented Lessons In Beats."

a)   True

Quiz 14-84) The acronym MADLIB stands for "Miserable Atrophy Degrading Life In Brooklyn."

a)   False

Quiz 14-85) Which two MC's form the duo Madvillian?

a)   Mos Def
b)   Talib Kweli
c)   Nas
d)   MFDoom
e)   Madlib
f)   Run

Quiz 14-86) What is the name of the duo formed by MF Doom and Madlib?

a)   Blackstar
b)   Madvillian
c)   Underground Kingz
d)   Jonzun Crew
e)   Geto Boys
f)   Run-DMC

Quiz 14-87) MF Doom and Madlib formed the duo Blackstar.

a)   False

Quiz 14-88) MF Doom and Madlib formed the duo Madvillian.

a)   True

Quiz 14-89) Madvillian is a duo formed by MF Doom and Mos Def.

a)   False

Quiz 14-90) Madvillian is a duo formed by Madlib and MF Doom.

a)   True

Quiz 14-91) MP3: Identity the artist, track title and album title of the following excerpt.

a)   Madlib
b)   MF Doom
c)   Madvillian
d)   Talib Kweli
e)   Mos Def
f)   Nas
g)   "Set Me At Ease"
h)   "Camphor"
i)   "Curls"
j)   "We Got the Beat"
k)   "Mathematics"
l)   "Every Ghetto"
m)   *Shades of Blue*
n)   *Special Herbs Vol. 7&8*
o)   *Madvillainy*
p)   *The Beautiful Struggle*
q)   *Black On Both Sides*
r)   *StIllmatic*

Quiz 14-92) MP3: Identity the artist, track title and album title of the following excerpt.

a)   Madlib
b)   MFDoom
c)   Madvillian
d)   Talib Kweli
e)   Mos Def
f)   Nas
g)   "Set Me At Ease"
h)   "Camphor"
i)   "Curls"
j)   "We Got the Beat"
k)   "Mathematics"
l)   "Every Ghetto"
m)   *Shades of Blue*
n)   *SpecialHerbsVol.7&8*
o)   *Madvillainy*
p)   *The Beautiful Struggle*
q)   *Black On Both Sides*
r)   *StIllmatic*

Quiz 14-93) MP3: Identity the artist, track title and album title of the following excerpt.

a)   Madlib
b)   MF Doom
c)   Madvillian
d)   Talib Kweli

e)   Mos Def
f)   Nas
g)   "Set Me At Ease"
h)   "Camphor"
i)   "Curls"
j)   "We Got The Beat"
k)   "Mathematics"
l)   "Every Ghetto"
m)   *Shades of Blue*
n)   *Special Herbs Vol. 7&8*
o)   *Madvillainy*
p)   *The Beautiful Struggle*
q)   *Black On Both Sides*
r)   *StIllmatic*

Quiz 14-94) MP3: Identity the artist, track title and album title of the following excerpt.

a)   Madlib
b)   MF Doom
c)   Madvillian
d)   Talib Kweli
e)   Mos Def
f)   Nas
g)   "Set Me at Ease"
h)   "Camphor"
i)   "Curls"
j)   "We Got the Beat"
k)   "Mathematics"
l)   "Every Ghetto"
m)   *Shades of Blue*
n)   *Special Herbs Vol. 7&8*
o)   *Madvillainy*
p)   *The Beautiful Struggle*
q)   *Black On Both Sides*
r)   *StIllmatic*

Quiz 14-95) MP3: Identity the artist, track title and album title of the following excerpt.

a)   Madlib
b)   MF Doom
c)   Madvillian
d)   Talib Kweli
e)   Mos Def
f)   Nas
g)   "Set Me At Ease"
h)   "Camphor"
i)   "Curls"
j)   "We Got The Beat"
k)   "Mathematics"
l)   "Every Ghetto"
m)   *Shades of Blue*
n)   *Special Herbs Vol. 7&8*

o)   *Madvillainny*
p)   *The Beautiful Struggle*
q)   *Black On Both Sides*
r)   *StIllmatic*

Quiz 14-96) MP3: Identity the artist, track title and album title of the following excerpt.

a)   Madlib
b)   MF Doom
c)   Madvillian
d)   Talib Kweli
e)   Mos Def
f)   Nas
g)   "Set Me At Ease"
h)   "Camphor"
i)   "Curls"
j)   "We Got The Beat"
k)   "Mathematics"
l)   "Every Ghetto"
m)   *Shades of Blue*
n)   *Special Herbs Vol. 7&8*
o)   *Madvillainny*
p)   *The Beautiful Struggle*
q)   *Black On Both Sides*
r)   *StIllmatic*

Quiz 14-97) MP3: Identity the artist, track title and album title of the following excerpt.

a)   Madlib
b)   MF Doom
c)   Madvillian
d)   Talib Kweli
e)   Mos Def
f)   Nas
g)   "Set Me At Ease"
h)   "Camphor"
i)   "Curls"
j)   "We Got The Beat"
k)   "Mathematics"
l)   "Every Ghetto"
m)   *Shades of Blue*
n)   *Special Herbs Vol. 7&8*
o)   *Madvillainny*
p)   *The Beautiful Struggle*
q)   *Black On Both Sides*
r)   *StIllmatic*

Quiz 15 Question Bank

Statement 1: Hip-Hop is ubiquitous throughout the world (its "global-ness"): In some form, or another, a local or regional Hip-Hop culture exists in almost every country.

Quiz 15-1) Hip-Hop is (_____) throughout the world: In some form, or another, a local or regional Hip-Hop culture (_____) in almost every country.

a) Ubiquitous
b) Reviled
c) Revered
d) Scarce
e) Exists
f) Is repressed
g) Is celebrated
h) Is suppressed

Quiz 15-2) Hip-Hop is reviled throughout the world (its "unglobal-ness"): In some form, or another, a local or regional Hip-Hop culture is censored in almost every country.

a) False

Quiz 15-3) Hip-Hop is ubiquitous throughout the world (its "global-ness"): In some form, or another, a local or regional Hip-Hop culture exists in almost every country.

a) True

Quiz 15-4) Hip-Hop is ubiquitous throughout (_____): In some form, or another, a local or regional Hip-Hop culture exists in almost every (_____).

a) The world (its "global-ness")
b) The United States (its "communal-ness")
c) North and South America (its "universal-ness")
d) North America (its "common-ness")
e) City
f) State
g) Province
h) Country
i) Continent

Statement 2: According to the U.S. Department of State, Hip-Hop is "now the center of a mega music and fashion industry around the world" that breaks down social barriers and cuts across racial lines.

GLOBAL Hip-Hop: Global Innovations:
Quiz 15-5) According to the (_____), Hip-Hop is "now the center of a mega music and fashion industry around the world" that breaks down (_____) barriers and cuts across (_____) lines.

a) U.S. Department of State
b) Parents Music Resource Council
c) U.S. Department of Art and Culture
d) Recording Industry Association of America
e) Social
f) Racial
g) Economic

h)   Class
i)   Gender
j)   Artistic
k)   Musical

Quiz 15-6) According to the U.S. Department of Art and Culture), Hip-Hop is "now the center of a mega music and fashion industry around the world" that breaks down economic barriers and cuts across artistic lines.

a)   False

Quiz 15-7) According to the U.S. Department of State, Hip-Hop is "now the center of a mega music and fashion industry around the world" that breaks down social barriers and cuts across racial lines.

a)   True

Quiz 15-8) According to the U.S. Department of State, Hip-Hop is "now the center of a mega (_____) and (_____) industry around the (_____)" that breaks down social barriers and cuts across racial lines.

a)   Music
b)   Fashion
c)   Entertainment
d)   Sneaker
e)   Country
f)   Continent
g)   World
h)   Film

Statement 3: "For most music-addicted earthlings, Hip-Hop culture is the predominant global youth subculture of today."

THE AUDACITY OF Hip-Hop—From Hip-Hop World by Dalton Higgins:

Quiz 15-9) "For most music-addicted earthlings, Hip-Hop culture is (_____) global youth subculture of today."

a)   The predominant
b)   Subculture
c)   Counterculture
d)   An underground
e)   Culture
f)   Fad
g)   An obscure

Quiz 15-10) "For most music-addicted earthlings, Hip-Hop culture is an obscure global youth fad of yesterday."

a)   False

Quiz 15-11) "For most music-addicted earthlings, Hip-Hop culture is the predominant global youth subculture of today."

a)   True

Quiz 15-12) "For most (_____)-addicted earthlings, Hip-Hop culture is the predominant global youth subculture of today."

a) Music
b) Drug
c) Money
d) Car
e) Youth
f) Gangster
g) Criminal
h) Delinquent

Statement 4: Hip-Hop's globally common function serves as the voice of Society's disenfranchised, oppressed, marginalized, or repressed, who challenges the status quo.

Quiz 15-13) Hip-Hop's globally common function serves as the voice of Society's (_____) who (_____) the status quo.

a) Disenfranchised, oppressed, marginalized or repressed
b) Entitled, oppressive, marginalizing or repressive
c) Yearning, tired, or poor, huddled masses
d) Privileged, elite, bourgeois or upper-class
e) Challenges
f) Maintains
g) Enforces
h) Ignores

Quiz 15-14) Hip-Hop's globally common function serves as (_____) of Society's disenfranchised, oppressed, marginalized, or repressed who challenges (_____).

a) The voice
b) The rallying cry
c) The herald
d) A banner
e) Authority
f) The status quo
g) The patriarchy
h) Capitalism

Quiz 15-15) Hip-Hop's globally common function serves as the voice of Society's disenfranchised, oppressed, marginalized, or repressed who challenges the status quo.

a) True

Quiz 15-16) Hip-Hop's globally common function serves as the voice of Society's poor, tired, or yearning huddled masses who comply with the status quo.

a) False

Statement 5: Irrespective of its projected values, the music continues to provide a sense of identity shared among its artists and audiences around the globe.

Quiz 15-17) Irrespective of its projected (_____), the music continues to provide a sense of (_____) shared among its artists and audiences around the globe.

a) Values
b) Message
c) Image
d) Morals
e) Identity
f) Belonging
g) Friendship
h) Individuality

Quiz 15-18) Irrespective of its projected values, the music continues to provide a sense of identity shared among its (_____) and (_____) around the globe.

a) Artists
b) Producers
c) Celebrities
d) Audiences
e) Management
f) Executives
g) Royalty

Quiz 15-19) Irrespective of its projected values, the music continues to provide a sense of identity shared among its artists and audiences around the globe.

a) True

Quiz 15-20) Irrespective of its projected image, the music continues to provide a sense of belonging shared among its producers and executives around the globe.

a) False

Statement 6: Its American roots (African-American primarily) is universally recognized; yet, each local culture has adapted it in ways both musically and thematically to make it their own.

Quiz 15-21) Its American roots (_____) primarily) is universally recognized; yet, each local culture has adapted it in ways both musically and thematically to make it their own.

a) American
b) Global
c) African-American
d) African
e) North American
f) Western
g) Eastern
h) North African

Quiz 15-22) Its African-American roots (African primarily) is universally recognized; yet, each local culture has adapted it in ways both musically and thematically to make it their own.

a) False

Quiz 15-23) Its American roots (African-American primarily) is universally recognized; yet, each local culture has adapted it in ways both musically and thematically to make it their own.

a) True

Quiz 15-24) Its American roots (African-American primarily) are universally (_____); yet, each local culture has (_____) in ways both musically and thematically to make it their own.

a) Adapted it
b) Rejected it
c) Assimilated it
d) Changed it
e) Recognized
f) Acknowledged
g) Unknown h) Disregarded

Statement 7) Perhaps the very fact that its musical components were relatively simple to replicate, and that its core was a lyric-based message made it an adaptable, user-friendly structure onto which far-flung performers could graft their own local subjects, narratives, and concerns. This quote makes reference to Hip-Hop's accessibility.

Quiz 15-25) Perhaps the very fact that its (_____) components were relatively simple to replicate, and that its core was a (lyric)-based message made it an adaptable, user- friendly structure onto which far-flung performers could graft their own local subjects, narratives, and concerns. This quote makes reference to Hip-Hop's (_____).

a) Musical
b) Lyrical
c) Rhythmic
d) Lyric
e) Violence
f) Misogynistic
g) Accessibility
h) Inaccessibility

Quiz 15-26) Perhaps the very fact that its musical components were relatively simple to replicate, and that its core was a lyric-based message made it an adaptable, user-friendly structure onto which far-flung performers could graft their own local subjects, narratives, and concerns. This quote makes reference to Hip-Hop's accessibility.

a) True

Quiz 15-27) Perhaps the very fact that its lyrical components were relatively simple to replicate, and that its core was a violence-based message made it an inflexible, difficult structure onto which far-flung performers could not graft their own local subjects, narratives, and concerns. This quote makes reference to Hip-Hop's inaccessibility.

a) False

Quiz 15-28) Perhaps the very fact that its musical components were relatively simple to replicate, and that its core was a lyric-based message made it an (_____), (_____) structure onto which far-flung performers (could) graft their own local subjects, narratives, and concerns. This quote makes reference to Hip-Hop's (_____).

a) Adaptable
b) Inflexible
c) User-friendly
d) Difficult

e) Could
f) Could not
g) Accessibility
h) Inaccessibility

Statement 8: Once a form of social protest in the United States, rap appears to be anything but that now. In contrast, outside of the US, rap music articulates and addresses local political and social concerns.

Quiz 15-29) Once a form of (_____) protest in the United States, rap appears to be anything but that now. In contrast, outside of the US, rap music articulates and addresses local (_____) and social concerns.

a) Political
b) Social
c) Ethnic
d) Racial
e) Economic
f) Democratic
g) Religious

Quiz 15-30) Once a form of social protest (_____), rap appears to be anything but that now. In contrast, (_____), rap music articulates and addresses local political and social concerns.

a) In the United States
b) Outside of the United States
c) Around the world
d) Global
e) Local
f) Regional
g) International

Quiz 15-31) Once a form of social protest in the United States, rap appears to be anything but that now. In contrast, outside of the US, rap music articulates and addresses local political and social concerns.

a) True

Quiz 15-32) Once a form of (_____) outside the United States, rap appears to be anything but that now. In contrast, in the US, rap music (_____) local racial and economic concerns.

a) False

Quiz 15-33) Once a form of social protest in the United States, rap appears to be anything but that now. In contrast, outside of the United States, rap music articulates and addresses local political and social concerns.

a) Individual expression
b) Social protest
c) Novel entertainment
d) Artistic expression
e) Articulates and addresses
f) Suppresses and ignores
g) Trivializes and belittles

Quiz 15-34) Once a form of novel entertainment in the United States, rap appears to be anything but that now. In contrast, outside of the United States, rap music trivializes and belittles local political and social concerns.

a) False

Statement 9: Tapping into Hip-Hop's potential as a force for social change should be easy to realize, but the question of "realistically expecting solutions to complex world problems from teens and twenty-something" is one that has been raised. This attitude though, perhaps, demonstrates a lack of awareness that any socio-political problem needs to be firstly identified and widely publicized before it will be acknowledged by the power structures of society.

Quiz 15-35) Tapping into Hip-Hop's potential as a force for (_____) should be easy to realize, but the question of "realistically expecting solutions to complex world problems from teens and twenty-something" is one that has been raised. This attitude though, perhaps demonstrates a lack of awareness that any socio-political problem needs to be firstly identified and widely publicized before it will be acknowledged by the (_____) of society.

a) Social Change
b) Good
c) Anarchy
d) A lack of
e) A thorough
f) Power Structures
g) Political Elite
h) Whole

Quiz 15-36) Tapping into Hip-Hop's potential as a force for social change should be easy to realize, but the question of "realistically expecting solutions to complex world problems from teens and twenty-something" is one that has been raised. This attitude though, perhaps demonstrates a lack of awareness that any socio-political problem needs to be firstly identified and widely publicized before it will be acknowledged by the power structures of society.

a) True

Quiz 15-37) Tapping into Hip-Hop's potential as a force for anarchy should be easy to realize, but the question of "realistically expecting solutions to complex world problems from teens and twenty-something" is one that has been raised. This attitude though, perhaps demonstrates a thorough awareness that any socio-political problem needs to be firstly identified and widely publicized before it will be acknowledged by the political elites of society.

a) False

Quiz 16 Question Bank

Quiz 16-1) What is Scarface's real name?

a) Brad Terrence Jordan
b) Jay Wayne Jenkins
c) André Benjamin
d) Antwan Patton
e) Bernard Freeman
f) Chad Butler
g) Radric Davis
h) Clifford Joseph Harris, Jr.

Quiz 16-2) What is Brad Terrence Jordan's nickname?

a) Scarface
b) Lil Boosie
c) Webbie
d) Juicy J
e) T.I.

f) Rick Ross
g) Gucci Mane
h) Ludacris

Quiz 16-3) Scarface's real name is Brad Terrence Jordan.

a) True

Quiz 16-4) Scarface's real name is Clifford Joseph Harris, Jr.

a) False

Quiz 16-5) Brad Terrence Jordan's nickname is Scarface

a) True

Quiz 16-6) Brad Terrence Jordan's nickname is Gucci Mane.

a) False

Quiz 16-7) What is Scarface's city of origin?

a) Houston, Texas
b) Port Arthur, Texas
c) Columbia, South Carolina
d) Miami, Florida
e) Atlanta, Georgia
f) Baton Rouge, Louisiana
g) Memphis, Tennessee
h) Carol City, Florida
i) Birmingham, Alabama

Quiz 16-8) Scarface is from Atlanta, Georgia

a) False

Quiz 16-9) Scarface is from Houston, Texas.

a) True

Quiz 16-10) List two albums from Scarface's discography

a) Mr. Scarface Is Back
b) The World Is Yours
c) Come Shop Wit Me
d) Seen It All: The Autobiography
e) Urban Legend
f) Stay Trippy
g) Too Hard to Swallow

Quiz 16-11) List two albums from Scarface's discography:

a) The Diary

b)   The Untouchable
c)   Battle of the Sexes
d)   The Red Light District
e)   Dirty Money
f)   Back to the Trap House
g)   Deeper Than Rap

Quiz 16-12) List two albums from Scarface's discography:

a)   The World Is Yours
b)   The Diary
c)   Hustle Till I Die
d)   La Flare
e)   Bad Azz
f)   Idlewild
g)   Port of Miami

Quiz 16-13) List two albums from Scarface's discography:

a)   Mr. Scarface Is Back
b)   The Untouchable
c)   Snow Season
d)   The Recession
e)   Thuggin' under the Influence (T.U.I.)
f)   Snow Season
g)   I'm Serious

Quiz 16-14) What is Young Jeezy's real name?

a)   Brad Terrence Jordan
b)   Jay Wayne Jenkins
c)   André Benjamin
d)   Antwan Patton
e)   Bernard Freeman
f)   Chad Butler
g)   Radric Davis
h)   Clifford Joseph Harris, Jr.

Quiz 16-15) What is Jay Wayne Jenkins' nickname?

a)   Scarface
b)   Lil Boosie
c)   Webbie
d)   Young Jeezy
e)   T.I.
f)   Rick Ross
g)   Gucci Mane
h)   Ludacris

Quiz 16-16) Young Jeezy's real name is Chad Butler.

a)   False

Quiz 16-17) Young Jeezy's real name is Jay Wayne Jenkins.

a)   True

Quiz 16-18) Jay Wayne Jenkins' nickname is Young Jeezy.

a)   True

Quiz 16-19) Jay Wayne Jenkins' nickname is Juicy J.

a)   False

Quiz 16-20) What is Young Jeezy's city of origin?

a)   Port Arthur, Texas
b)   Houston, Texas
c)   Columbia, South Carolina
d)   Miami, Florida
e)   Atlanta, Georgia
f)   Baton Rouge, Louisiana
g)   Memphis, Tennessee
h)   Carol City, Florida
i)   Birmingham, Alabama

Quiz 16-21) Young Jeezy is from Baton Rouge, Louisiana.

a)   False

Quiz 16-22) Young Jeezy is from Columbia, South Carolina.

a)   True

Quiz 16-23) List two albums from Young Jeezy's discography:

a)   Thuggin' under the Influence (T.U.I.)
b)   Come Shop wit Me
c)   The World Is Yours
d)   ATLiens
e)   Urban Legend
f)   Hustle Till I Die
g)   Savage Life

Quiz 16-24) List two albums from Young Jeezy's discography:

a)   Let's Get It: Thug Motivation 101
b)   The Inspiration
c)   Southernplayalisticadillacmuzik
d)   Too Hard to Swallow
e)   Bad Azz
f)   Idlewild
g)   Speakerboxxx/The Love Below

Quiz 16-25) List two albums from Young Jeezy's discography:

a)   The Recession
b)   TM:103HustlerzAmbition
c)   Underground King
d)   Dirty Money
e)   Too Hard to Swallow
f)   Trap House
g)   La Flare

Quiz 16-26) List two albums from Young Jeezy's discography:

a)   Seen It All: The Autobiography
b)   Churchin These Streets
c)   Dirty Money
d)   Battle of the Sexes
e)   Back for the First Time
f)   ATLiens
g)   Hustle Till I Die

Quiz 16-27) List two albums from Young Jeezy's discography:

a)   Trap or Die 3
b)   Snow Season
c)   Aquemini
d)   Stankonia
e)   Chicken-n-Beer
f)   Release Therapy
g)   Underground King

Quiz 16-28) What is Trina's real name?

a)   Katrina Laverne Taylor
b)   Angela Laverne Brown
c)   Erica Abi Wright
d)   Dana Owens
e)   Cheryl Wray
f)   Sandra Denton
g)   Dee Dee Roper
h)   JoAnn Berry

Quiz 16-29) What is Katrina Laverne Taylor's nickname?

a)   Trina
b)   Erykah Badu
c)   Angie Stone
d)   Pepa
e)   Salt
f)   Queen Latifah
g)   DJ Spinderella

Quiz 16-30) What is Trina's city of origin?

a) Port Arthur, Texas
b) Houston, Texas
c) Columbia, South Carolina
d) Miami, Florida
e) Atlanta, Georgia
f) Baton Rouge, Louisiana
g) Memphis, Tennessee
h) Carol City, Florida
i) Birmingham, Alabama

Quiz 16-31) Trina is from Miami, Florida.

a) True

Quiz 16-32) Trina is from Memphis, Tennessee.

a) False

Quiz 16-33) Trina's real name is Katrina Laverne Taylor.

a) True

Quiz 16-34) Trina's real name is Angela Laverne Brown.

a) False

Quiz 16-35) Katrina Laverne Taylor's nickname is Trina.

a) True

Quiz 16-36) Katrina Laverne Taylor's nickname is Angie Stone

a) False

Quiz 16-37) List two albums from Trina's discography:

a) Da Baddest Bitch
b) Diamond Princess
c) The World Is Yours
d) The Diary
e) The Red Light District
f) Release Therapy
g) Port of Miami

Quiz 16-38) List two albums from Trina's discography:

a) Diamond Princess
b) Glamorest Life
c) Back for the First Time
d) Battle of the Sexes
e) Theater of the Mind
f) Speakerboxxx/The Love Below

g) Aquemini

Quiz 16-39) List two albums from Trina's discography:

a) Glamorest Life
b) DaBaddestBitch
c) I'm Serious
d) La Flare
e) Super Tight
f) Church in These Streets
g) The Untouchable

Quiz 16-40) What are the real names of the members of duo OutKast?

a) Brad Terrence Jordan
b) Jay Wayne Jenkins
c) André Benjamin
d) Antwan Patton
e) Bernard Freeman
f) Chad Butler
g) Radric Davis
h) Clifford Joseph Harris, Jr.

Quiz 16- 41) André Benjamin and Antwan Patton are the members of which duo?

a) OutKast
b) Blackstar
c) Madvillian
d) Underground Kingz
e) Geto Boys
f) Jonzun Crew
g) Run-DMC

Quiz 16-42) Chad Butler and Bernard Freeman formed the duo OutKast.

a) False

Quiz 16-43) André Benjamin and Antwan Patton formed the duo OutKast.

a) True

Quiz 16-44) What is OutKast's city of origin?

a) Port Arthur, Texas
b) Houston, Texas
c) Columbia, South Carolina
d) Miami, Florida
e) Atlanta, Georgia
f) Baton Rouge, Louisiana
g) Memphis, Tennessee
h) Carol City, Florida
i) Birmingham, Alabama

Quiz 16-45) OutKast is from Miami, Florida.

a)   False

Quiz 16-46) OutKast is from Atlanta, Georgia

a)   True

Quiz 16-47) List two albums from OutKast's discography:

a)   Southernplayalisticadillacmuzik
b)   ATLiens
c)   The World Is Yours
d)   Come Shop Wit Me
e)   The Recession
f)   Chronicles of the Juice Man
g)   Ridin' Dirty

Quiz 16-48) List two albums from OutKast's discography:

a)   ATLiens
b)   Stankonia
c)   Stay Trippy
d)   Hustle Till I Die
e)   Trap Muzik
f)   King
g)   Too Hard to Swallow

Quiz 16-49) List two albums from OutKast's discography:

a)   Speakerboxxx/The Love Below
b)   Idlewild
c)   Incognegro
d)   Battle of the Sexes
e)   Theater of the Mind
f)   Ludaversal
g)   Word of Mouf

Quiz 16-50) List two albums from OutKast's discography:

a)   Idlewild
b)   Stankonia
c)   Side Hustles
d)   Deeper Than Rap
e)   La Flare
f)   Trap House
g)   Urban Legend

Quiz 16-51) List two albums from OutKast's discography:

a)   Aquemini
b)   ATLiens

c) Trilla
d) Trap Muzik
e) Stay Trippy
f) Hustle Till I Die
g) Trap or Die 3

Quiz 16-52) What is Lil Boosie's real name?

a) Brad Terrence Jordan
b) Jay Wayne Jenkins
c) André Benjamin
d) Antwan Patton
e) Bernard Freeman
f) Chad Butler
g) Torrence Hatch
h) Clifford Joseph Harris, Jr.

Quiz 16-53) What is Torrence Hatch's nickname?

a) Scarface
b) LilBoosie
c) Webbie
d) Juicy J
e) T.I.
f) Rick Ross
g) Gucci Mane
h) Ludacris

Quiz 16-54) Lil Boosie's real name is Torrence Hatch.

a) True

Quiz 16-55) Lil Boosie's real name is Chad Butler

a) False

Quiz 16-56) Torrence Hatch's nickname is Lil Boosie.

a) True

Quiz 16-57) Torrence Hatch's nickname is Gucci Mane

a) False

Quiz 16-58) What is Lil Boosie's city of origin?

a) Port Arthur, Texas
b) Houston, Texas
c) Columbia, South Carolina
d) Miami, Florida
e) Atlanta, Georgia
f) Baton Rouge, Louisiana

g)   Memphis, Tennessee
h)   Carol City, Florida
i)   Birmingham, Alabama

Quiz 16-59) Lil Boosie is from Atlanta, Georgia

a)   False

Quiz 16-60) Lil Boosie is from Baton Rouge, Louisiana.

a)   True

Quiz 16-61) List two albums from Lil Boosie's discography (year and title):

a)   Bad Azz
b)   Superbad: The Return of Boosie Bad Azz
c)   Thuggin' under the Influence (T.U.I.)
d)   Let's Get It: Thug Motivation 101
e)   Trap Muzik
f)   Trap House
g)   Back to the Trap House

Quiz 16-62) What is Webbie's real name?

a)   Brad Terrence Jordan
b)   Jay Wayne Jenkins
c)   André Benjamin
d)   Antwan Patton
e)   Bernard Freeman
f)   Chad Butler
g)   Webster Gradney, Jr.
h)   Clifford Joseph Harris, Jr.

Quiz 16-63) What is Webster Gradney Jr.'s nickname?

a)   Scarface
b)   Lil Boosie
c)   Webbie
d)   Juicy J
e)   T.I.
f)   Rick Ross
g)   Gucci Mane
h)   Ludacris

Quiz 16-64) Webbie's real name is Webster Gradney Jr.

a)   True

Quiz 16-65) Webbie's real name is Jay Wayne Jenkins.

a)   False

Quiz 16-66) Webster Gradney Jr.'s nickname is Webbie.

a)   True

Quiz 16-67) Webster Gradney Jr.'s nickname is Scarface.

a)   False

Quiz 16-68) What is Webbie's city of origin?

a)   Port Arthur, Texas
b)   Houston, Texas
c)   Columbia, South Carolina
d)   Miami, Florida
e)   Atlanta, Georgia
f)   Baton Rouge, Louisiana
g)   Memphis, Tennessee
h)   Carol City, Florida
i)   Birmingham, Alabama

Quiz 16-69) Webbie is from Baton Rouge, Louisiana.

a)   True

Quiz 16-70) Webbie is from Houston, Texas.

a)   False

Quiz 16-71) List two albums from Webbie's discography:

a)   Savage Life
b)   SavageLife2
c)   Thug Life
d)   Thug Life 2
e)   Gangsta Life
f)   Gangsta Life 2
g)   Trap Life
h)   Trap Life 2

Quiz 16-72) What is Juicy J's real name?

a)   Webster Gradney, Jr.
b)   Jordan Houston
c)   William Leonard Roberts
d)   Clifford Joseph Harris, Jr.
e)   Radric Davis
f)   Christopher Bridges
g)   Chad Butler
h)   Bernard Freeman

Quiz 16-73) What is Jordan Houston's nickname?

a)   Scarface
b)   Lil Boosie
c)   Webbie
d)   Juicy J
e)   T.I.
f)   Rick Ross
g)   Gucci Mane
h)   Ludacris

Quiz 16-74) Jordan Houston's nickname is Juicy J.

a)   True

Quiz 16-75) Jordan Houston's nickname is Gucci Mane.

a)   False

Quiz 16-76) Juciy J's real name is Jordan Houston.

a)   True

Quiz 16-77) Rick Ross's real name is Jordan Houston.

a)   False

Quiz 16-78) What is Juicy J's city of origin?

a)   Port Arthur, Texas
b)   Houston, Texas
c)   Columbia, South Carolina
d)   Miami, Florida
e)   Atlanta, Georgia
f)   Baton Rouge, Louisiana
g)   Memphis, Tennessee
h)   Carol City, Florida
i)   Birmingham, Alabama

Quiz 16-79) Juicy J is from Memphis, Tennessee.

a)   True

Quiz 16-80) Juicy J is from Houston, Texas.

a)   False

Quiz 16-81) List two albums from Juicy J's discography:

a)   Chronicles of the Juice Man
b)   Hustle Till I Die
c)   The World Is Y ours
d)   Let's Get It: Thug Motivation 101

e) TM:103 Hustlerz Ambition
f) Idlewild
g) Bad Azz

Quiz 16-82) List two albums from Juicy J's discography:

a) Hustle Till I Die
b) Stay Trippy
c) The Red Light District
d) Incognegro
e) Trap Muzik
f) Back to the Trap House
g) Ridin' Dirty

Quiz 16-83) List two albums from Juicy J's discography:

a) Stay Trippy
b) Chronicles of the Juice Man
c) Dirty Money
d) Too Hard to Swallow
e) Side Hustles
f) Battle of the Sexes
g) Release Therapy

Quiz 16-84) What is T.I.'s real name?

a) Webster Gradney, Jr.
b) Jordan Houston
c) William Leonard Roberts
d) Clifford Joseph Harris, Jr.
e) Radric Davis
f) Christopher Bridges
g) Chad Butler

Quiz 16-85) What is Clifford Joseph Harris, Jr.'s nickname?

a) Scarface
b) Lil Boosie
c) Ludacris
d) Gucci Mane
e) Webbie
f) Juicy J
g) T.I.
h) Rick Ross

Quiz 16-86) Clifford Joseph Harris, Jr.'s nickname is T.I.

a) True

Quiz 16-87) Clifford Joseph Harris, Jr.'s nickname is Juicy J.

a) False

Quiz 16-88) T.I.'s real name is Clifford Joseph Harris, Jr.

a)   True

Quiz 16-89) T.I.'s real name is William Leonard Roberts.

a)   False

Quiz 16-90) What is T.I.'s city of origin?

a)   Port Arthur, Texas
b)   Houston, Texas
c)   Columbia, South Carolina
d)   Miami, Florida
e)   Atlanta, Georgia
f)   Baton Rouge, Louisiana
g)   Memphis, Tennessee
h)   Carol City, Florida
i)   Birmingham, Alabama

Quiz 16-91) T.I. is from Atlanta, Georgia.

a)   True

Quiz 16-92) T.I. is from Birmingham, Alabama.

a)   False

Quiz 16-93) List two albums from T.I.'s discography:

a)   I'm Serious
b)   Trap Muzik
c)   The World Is Yours
d)   The Recession
e)   Stankonia
f)   Bad Azz
g)   Hustle Till I Die

Quiz 16-94) List two albums from T.I.'s discography:

a)   Trap Muzik
b)   Urban Legend
c)   Port of Miami
d)   La Flare
e)   Trap House
f)   Too Hard to Swallow
g)   Battle of the Sexes

Quiz 16-95) List two albums from T.I.'s discography:

a) Urban Legend
b) King
c) Trilla
d) Back to the Trap House
e) Super Tight
f) Word of Mouf
g) The Untouchable

Quiz 16-96) List two albums from T.I.'s discography:

a) I'm Serious
b) Urban Legend
c) Deeper Than Rap
d) Dirty Money
e) Back for the First Time
f) Snow Season
g) Southernplayalisticadillacmuzik

Quiz 16-97) List two albums from T.I.'s discography:

a) Trap Muzik
b) King
c) Side Hustles
d) Underground King
e) Incognegro
f) Come Shop Wit Me
g) Trap or Die 3

Quiz 16-98) What is Rick Ross' real name?

a) Webster Gradney, Jr.
b) Jordan Houston
c) William Leonard Roberts
d) Clifford Joseph Harris, Jr.
e) Radric Davis
f) Christopher Bridges
g) Chad Butler
h) Bernard Freeman

Quiz 16-99) What is William Leonard Roberts' nickname?

a) Scarface
b) Lil Boosie
c) Webbie
d) Juicy J
e) T.I.
f) Rick Ross
g) Gucci Mane
h) Ludacris

Quiz 16-100) William Leonard Roberts' nickname is Rick Ross.

a)   True

Quiz 16-101) William Leonard Roberts' nickname is Gucci Mane

a)   False

Quiz 16-102) Rick Ross' real name is William Leonard Roberts.

a)   True

Quiz 16-103) Rick Ross' real name is Christopher Bridges.

a)   False

Quiz 16-104) What is Rick Ross' city of origin?

a)   Port Arthur, Texas
b)   Houston, Texas
c)   Columbia, South Carolina
d)   Miami, Florida
e)   Atlanta, Georgia
f)   Baton Rouge, Louisiana
g)   Memphis, Tennessee
h)   Carol City, Florida
i)   Birmingham, Alabama

Quiz 16-105) List two albums from Rick Ross' discography:

a)   Port of Miami
b)   Trilla
c)   The World Is Yours
d)   Come Shop Wit Me
e)   Idlewild
f)   Release Therapy
g)   King

Quiz 16-106) List two albums from Rick Ross' discography:

a)   Trilla
b)   Deeper Than Rap
c)   Speakerboxxx/The Love Below
d)   Theater of the Mind
e)   Super Tight
f)   Ridin' Dirty
g)   La Flare

Quiz 16-107) List two albums from Rick Ross' discography:

a)   Deeper Than Rap
b)   Port of Miami
c)   Southernplayalisticadillacmuzik

d) Superbad: The Return of Boosie Bad Azz
e) Chronicles of the Juice Man
f) The State vs. Radric Davis
g) Ludaversal

Quiz 16-108) What is Gucci Mane's real name?

a) Webster Gradney, Jr.
b) Jordan Houston
c) William Leonard Roberts
d) Clifford Joseph Harris, Jr.
e) Radric Davis
f) Christopher Bridges
g) Chad Butler
h) Bernard Freeman

Quiz 16-109) What is Radric Davis's nickname?

a) Scarface
b) Lil Boosie
c) Webbie
d) Juicy J
e) T.I.
f) Rick Ross
g) Gucci Mane
h) Ludacris

Quiz 16-110) Radric Davis' nickname is Gucci Mane.

a) True

Quiz 16-111) Radric Davis' nickname is Ludacris.

a) False

Quiz 16-112) Gucci Mane's real name is Chad Butler.

a) False

Quiz 16-113) Gucci Mane's real name is Radric Davis.

a) True

Quiz 16- 114) What is Gucci Mane's city of origin?

a) Port Arthur, Texas
b) Houston, Texas
c) Columbia, South Carolina
d) Miami, Florida
e) Atlanta, Georgia
f) Baton Rouge, Louisiana
g) Memphis, Tennessee

h)   Carol City, Florida
i)   Birmingham, Alabama

Quiz 16-115) List two albums from Gucci Mane's discography:

a)   La Flare
b)   Trap House
c)   The World Is Yours
d)   Let's Get It: Thug Motivation 101
e)   Church in These Streets
f)   Aquemini
g)   Savage Life

Quiz 16-116) List two albums from Gucci Mane's discography:

a)   Trap House
b)   Back to the Trap House
c)   The Diary
d)   The Inspiration
e)   Trap or Die 3
f)   Stankonia
g)   Chronicles of the Juice Man

Quiz 16-117) List two albums from Gucci Mane's discography:

a)   La Flare
b)   Back to the Trap House
c)   The Untouchable
d)   The Recession
e)   Snow Season
f)   Speakerboxxx/The Love Below
g)   Hustle Till I Die

Quiz 16-118) List two albums from Gucci Mane's discography:

a)   Back to the Trap House
b)   The State vs. Radric Davis
c)   Thuggin' under the Influence (T.U.I.)
d)   TM:103 Hustlerz Ambition
e)   Southernplayalisticadillacmuzik
f)   Idlewild
g)   Stay Trippy

Quiz 16-119) List two albums from Gucci Mane's discography:

a)   The State vs. Radric Davis
b)   La Flare
c)   Come Shop Wit Me
d)   Seen It All: The Autobiography
e)   ATLiens
f)   Bad Azz
g)   Trap Muzik

Quiz 16-120) What are the real names of the members of duo Underground Kingz?

a) Webster Gradney, Jr.
b) Jordan Houston
c) William Leonard Roberts
d) Clifford Joseph Harris, Jr.
e) Radric Davis
f) Christopher Bridges
g) Chad Butler
h) Bernard Freeman

Quiz 16-121) What is the name of the duo formed by Chad Butler and Bernard Freeman?

a) OutKast
b) Blackstar
c) Madvillian
d) Underground Kingz
e) Geto Boys
f) Jonzun Crew
g) Run-DMC

Quiz 16-122) Chad Butler and Bernard Freeman formed the duo Underground Kingz.

a) True

Quiz 16-123) Chad Butler and Bernard Freeman formed the duo OutKast.

a) False

Quiz 16-124) What is the city of origin of the duo Underground Kingz?

a) Port Arthur, Texas
b) Houston, Texas
c) Columbia, South Carolina
d) Miami, Florida
e) Atlanta, Georgia
f) Baton Rouge, Louisiana
g) Memphis, Tennessee
h) Carol City, Florida
i) Birmingham, Alabama

Quiz 16-125) List two albums from Underground Kingz' discography:

a) The Southern Way
b) Banned
c) Ludaversal
d) Chicken-n-Beer
e) Back to the Trap House
f) Port of Miami
g) Stay Trippy

Quiz 16-126) List two albums from Underground Kingz' discography:

a) Too Hard to Swallow
b) Super Tight
c) Battle of the Sexes
d) Word of Mouf
e) Trap House
f) King
g) Hustle Till I Die

Quiz 16-127) List two albums from Underground Kingz' discography:

a) Ridin' Dirty
b) Dirty Money
c) Theater of the Mind
d) Back for the First Time
e) La Flare
f) Urban Legend
g) Chronicles of the Juice Man

Quiz 16-128) List two albums from Underground Kingz' discography:

a) Side Hustles
b) Underground King
c) The Red Light District
d) Incognegro
e) Deeper Than Rap
f) Trap Muzik
g) Savage Life

Quiz 16-129) List two albums from Underground Kingz' discography:

a) UGK 4Life
b) Super Tight
c) Release Therapy
d) The State vs. Radric Davis
e) Trilla
f) I'm Serious
g) Bad Azz

Quiz 16-130) What is Ludacris' real name?

a) Antwan Patton
b) Torrence Hatch
c) Webster Gradney, Jr.
d) William Leonard Roberts
e) Jordan Houston
f) Clifford Joseph Harris, Jr.
g) Radric Davis
h) Christopher Bridges

Quiz 16-131) What is Christopher Bridges' nickname?

a)   Scarface
b)   Lil Boosie
c)   Webbie
d)   Juicy J
e)   T.I.
f)   Rick Ross
g)   Gucci Mane
h)   Ludacris

Quiz 16-132) Ludacris' real name is Christopher Bridges

a)   True

Quiz 16-133) Ludacris' real name is Jeff Bridges

a)   False

Quiz 16-134) Christopher Bridges' nickname is Ludacris.

a)   True

Quiz 16-135) Christopher Bridges nickname is Lil Boosie

a)   False

Quiz 16-136) What is Ludacris' city of origin?

a)   Port Arthur, Texas
b)   Houston, Texas
c)   Columbia, South Carolina
d)   Miami, Florida
e)   Atlanta, Georgia
f)   Baton Rouge, Louisiana
g)   Memphis, Tennessee
h)   Carol City, Florida
i)   Birmingham, Alabama

Quiz 16-137) Ludacris is from Atlanta, Georgia.

a)   True

Quiz 16-138) Ludacris is from Memphis, Tennessee.

a)   False

Quiz 16-139) List two albums from Ludacris' discography:

a)   Incognegro
b)   Back for the First Time
c)   Mr. Scarface Is Back
d)   Savage Life

e) Deeper Than Rap
f) Too Hard to Swallow
g) Underground King

Quiz 16-140) List two albums from Ludacris' discography:

a) Word of Mouf
b) Chicken-n-Beer
c) The World Is Yours
d) Side Hustles
e) Trap House
f) Urban Legend
g) Hustle Till I Die

Quiz 16-141) List two albums from Ludacris' discography:

a) The Red Light District
b) Release Therapy
c) The Untouchable
d) TM:103 Hustlerz Ambition
e) Southernplayalisticadillacmuzik
f) ATLiens
g) Stankonia

Quiz 16-142) List two albums from Ludacris' discography:

a) Theater of the Mind
b) Battle of the Sexes
c) The Diary
d) Thuggin' under the Influence (T.U.I.)
e) Church in These Streets
f) Trap or Die 3
g) Idlewild

Quiz 16-143) List two albums from Ludacris' discography:

a) Ludaversal
b) Incognegro
c) Come Shop Wit Me
d) Snow Season
e) Hustle Till I Die
f) Port of Miami
g) Idlewild

Quiz 16-144) MP3: Identify the artist and the title of the following track:

a) Scarface
b) Ludacris
c) OutKast
d) T.I.
e) "The Diary"
f) "Undisputed"
g) "Southernplayalisticadillacmuzik"
h) "Do We have A Problem"

Quiz 16-145) MP3: Identify the artist and the title of the following track:

a) Underground Kingz'
b) Gucci Mane
c) Juicy J
d) Trina
e) "Pocket Full of Stones"
f) "77 Birds in the Trash Can"
g) "Flood Out The Club (Show The Strippers Love)"
h) "Killin' You Hoes"

Quiz 16-146) MP3: Identify the artist and the title of the following track:

a) Trina
b) Rick Ross
c) Juicy J
d) Outkast
e) "Killin' You Hoes"
f) "Rich Off Cocaine"
g) "Flood Out The Club (Show The Strippers Love)"
h) "Southernplayalisticadillacmuzik"

Quiz 16-147) MP3: Identify the artist and the title of the following track:

a) Gucci Mane
b) "77 Birds in the Trash Can"
c) Trina
d) "Killin' You Hoes"
e) Ludacris
f) "Undisputed"
g) T.I.
h) "Do We have A Problem"

Quiz 16-148) MP3: Identify the artist and the title of the following track:

a) Lil Boosie
b) "I'm Dat Nigga Now"
c) Trina
d) "Killin' You Hoes"
e) Underground Kingz
f) "Pocket Full of Stones"
g) Gucci Mane
h) "77 Birds in the Trash Can"

Quiz 16-149) MP3: Identify the artist and the title of the following track:

a) Rick Ross
b) "Rich Off Cocaine"
c) Ludacris
d) "Undisputed"
e) OutKast
f) "Southernplayalisticadillacmuzik"
g) T.I.
h) "Do We have A Problem"

Quiz 16-150) MP3: Identify the artist and the title of the following track:

a) T.I.
b) "Do We Have A Problem"
c) Gucci Mane
d) "77 Birds in the Trash Can"
e) Lil Boosie
f) "I'm Dat Nigga Now"
g) Trina
h) "Killin' You Hoes"

Quiz 16-151) MP3: Identify the artist and the title of the following track:

a) Juicy J
b) "Flood Out The Club (Show The Strippers Love)"
c) Ludacris
d) "Undisputed"
e) OutKast
f) "Southernplayalisticadillacmuzik"
g) Trina
h) "Killin' You Hoes"

Quiz 16-152) MP3: Identify the artist and the title of the following track:

a) OutKast
b) "Southernplayalisticadillacmuzik"
c) Juicy J
d) "Flood Out The Club (Show The Strippers Love)"
e) Scarface
f) "The Diary"
g) Rick Ross
h) "Rich Off Cocaine"

Quiz 16-153) MP3: Identify the artist and the title of the following track:

a) Ludacris
b) "Undisputed"
c) Trina
d) "Killin' You Hoes"
e) Scarface
f) "The Diary"
g) Lil Boosie
h) "I'm Dat Nigga Now"

Quiz 17 Question Bank

Quiz 17-1) What is Lamont Coleman's stage name?

a) Big L
b) Pimp C
c) Easy E
d) Juicy J

e)   Chuck D
f)   Percee P
g)   BigC

Quiz 17-2) Lamont Coleman's stage name is Big L.

a)   True

Quiz 17-3) Lamont Coleman's stage name is Pimp C.

a)   False

Quiz 17-4) Lamont Coleman was a/an:

a)   American
b)   British
c)   Australian
d)   Canadian
e)   Rapper
f)   DJ
g)   MC
h)   Turntablist

Quiz 17-5) Lamont Coleman was a Canadian MC.

a)   False

Quiz 17-6) Lamont Coleman was an American Rapper.

a)   True

Quiz 17-7) Lamont Coleman made contributions to the music scene of which city?

a)   New York City, NY
b)   Philadelphia, PA
c)   Houston Texas, TX
d)   Boston, MA
e)   Atlanta, Georgia
f)   Miami, Florida

Quiz 17-8) Lamont Coleman made contributions to the New York City music scene.

a)   True

Quiz 17-9) Lamont Coleman made contributions to the Atlanta, Georgia, music scene.

a)   False

Quiz 17-10) What decade was Lamont Coleman active?

a)   1980s
b)   1990s
c)   2000s
d)   2010s

Quiz 17-11) Lamont Coleman was active in the 1990s.

a) True

Quiz 17-12) Lamont Coleman was active in the 1980s.

a) False

Quiz 17-13) Lamont Coleman was a member of which of the following Hip-Hop collectives?

a) D.I.T.C.
b) Run-DMC
c) OutKast
d) N.W.A.
e) Compton's Most Wanted
f) The Juice Crew

Quiz 17-14) Lamont Coleman was a member of the Hip-Hop collective D.I.T.C.

a) True

Quiz 17-15) Lamont Coleman was a member of the Hip-Hop collective The Juice Crew.

a) False

Quiz 17-16) Lamont Coleman was shot and killed in:

a) January
b) February
c) March
d) April
e) 1989
f) 1991
g) 1999
h) 2009

Quiz 17-17) Lamont Coleman was shot and killed in February 1999.

a) True

Quiz 17-18) Lamont Coleman died from a combination of sleep apnea and consumption of "Purple Drank" in December 2007.

a) False

Quiz 17-19) Sneakers are

a) Kicks
b) Flicks
c) Bones
d) Whips
e) Gats
f) Hats

Quiz 17-20) Kicks are:

a) Kicks
b) Sneakers
c) Movies
d) Cigarettes
e) Guns and Pistols
f) Cars

Quiz 17-21) Condoms are *cars*.

a) False

Quiz 17-22) Kicks are sneakers.

a) True

Quiz 17-23) Cars are kicks.

b) False

Quiz 17-24) Sneakers are kicks.

b) True

Quiz 17-25) Movies are:

a) Kicks
b) Flicks
c) Bones
d) Whips
e) Gats
f) Hats

Quiz 17-26) Flicks are:

a) Sneakers
b) Movies
c) Cigarettes
d) Guns and Pistols
e) Cars
f) Condoms

Quiz 17-27) Movies are flicks.

a) True

Quiz 17-28) Flicks are movies.

a) True

Quiz 17-29) Flicks are pistols and guns.

a)   False

Quiz 17-30) Guns and pistols are flicks.

a)   False

Quiz 17-31) Cigarettes are:

a)   Kicks
b)   Flicks
c)   Bones
d)   Whips
e)   Gats
f)   Hats

Quiz 17-32) Bones are:

a)   Sneakers
b)   Movies
c)   Cigarettes
d)   Guns and Pistols
e)   Cars
f)   Condoms

Quiz 17-33) Cigarettes are bones.

a)   True

Quiz 17-34) Bones are cigarettes.

a)   True

Quiz 17-35) Bones are condoms.

a)   False

Quiz 17-36) Condoms are bones.

a)   False

Quiz 17-37) Heated is:

a)   Mad
b)   Glad
c)   Sad
d)   Dead
e)   Missing
f)   Arrested

Quiz 17-38) Mad is:

a)   Heated

b) Bucked
c) Snuffed
d) Deleted
e) Love
f) Bad Breath

Quiz 17-39) Mad is heated.

a) True

Quiz 17-40) Heated is mad.

a) True

Quiz 17-41) Mad is deleted.

a) False

Quiz 17-42) Bucked is mad.

a) False

Quiz 17-43) The studio is:

a) The Lab
b) Your pad
c) A grill
d) Your Poke
e) A sweat box
f) Your crib

Quiz 17-44) The Lab is:

a) The studio
b) Your home
c) Your apartment
d) A long had stare
e) Your bankroll
f) A small club

Quiz 17-45) A studio is a lab.

a) True

Quiz 17-46) A lab is a studio.

a) True

Quiz 17-47) A studio is your pad.

a) False

Quiz 17-48) Your pad is the studio.

a) False

Quiz 17-49) Cars are:

a) Kicks
b) Flicks
c) Bones
d) Whips
e) Gats
f) Hats

Quiz 17-50) Whips are:

a) Sneakers
b) Movies
c) Cigarettes
d) Guns and Pistols
e) Cars
f) Condoms

Quiz 17-51) Cars are whips.

a) True

Quiz 17-52) Whips are cars.

a) True

Quiz 17-53) Cars are kicks.

a) False

Quiz 17-54) Kicks are cars.

a) False

Quiz 17-55) Guns and pistols are:
a) Kicks
b) Flicks
c) Bones
d) Whips
e) Gats
f) Hats

Quiz 17-56) Gats are:

a) Sneakers
b) Movies
c) Cigarettes
d) Guns and Pistols
e) Cars
f) Condoms

Quiz 17-57) Gats are guns and pistols.

a) True

Quiz 17-58) Guns and pistols are gats.

a) True

Quiz 17-59) Guns and pistols are flicks.

a) False

Quiz 17-60) Flicks are guns and pistols.

a) True

Quiz 17-61) A very long, hard stare is a

a) kick
b) grill
c) flick
d) bone
e) rat
f) flick

Quiz 17-62) A grill is

a) A movie
b) A gun or pistol
c) A cigarette
d) A car
e) A long, hard stare
f) A sneaker

Quiz 17-63) A very long, hard stare is a grill.

a) True

Quiz 17-64) A grill is a very long, hard stare.

a) True

Quiz 17-65) A very long, hard stare is a bone.

a) False

Quiz 17-66) A bone is a very long, hard stare.

a) False

Quiz 17-67) To get shot is to

a) Get bucked
b) Get snuffed

c)   Get Heated
d)   Max
e)   Get deleted
f)   Get stuck

Quiz 17-68) To get bucked is to

a)   Get shot
b)   Relax
c)   Get stabbed
d)   Get punched
e)   Get kicked
f)   Get mad

Quiz 17-69) To get bucked is to get shot.

a)   True

Quiz 17-70) To get shot is to get bucked.

a)   True

Quiz 17-71) To get bucked is to get punched.

a)   False

Quiz 17-72) To get punched is to get bucked.

a)   False

Quiz 17-73) Your bankroll is

a)   Your poke
b)   Your kick
c)   Your pad
d)   Your crib
e)   Your gat
f)   Your whip

Quiz 17-74) Your poke is

a)   Your bankroll
b)   Your sneaker
c)   Your house
d)   Your apartment
e)   Your gun or pistol
f)   Your car

Quiz 17-75) Your bankroll is your poke.

a)   True

Quiz 17-76) Your poke is your bankroll.

a)   True

Quiz 17-77) Your bankroll is your crib.

a)   False

Quiz 17-78) Your crib is your bankroll.

a)   False

Quiz 17-79) To be snuffed is to:

a)   Get punched
b)   Get kicked
c)   Get shot
d)   Get robbed
e)   Get murdered
f)   Get stabbed

Quiz 17-80) To be punched is to

a)   Get snuffed
b)   Get bucked
c)   Get heated
d)   Get deleted
e)   Get stuck
f)   Get whacked

Quiz 17-81) To be snuffed is to get punched.

a)   True

Quiz 17-82) To get punched is to be snuffed.

a)   True

Quiz 17-83) To be snuffed is to get murdered.

a)   False

Quiz 17-84) To get murdered is to be snuffed.

a)   False

Quiz 17-85) The dragon is:

a)   Bad breath
b)   A pistol or gun
c)   A car
d)   An STD
e)   AIDS
f)   A cigarette

Quiz 17-86) Bad breath is:

a)   The dragon

b)   The germ
c)   Heated
d)   The grill
e)   The whip
f)   The poke

Quiz 17-87) The Dragon is bad breath.

a)   True

Quiz 17-88) Bad Breath is the dragon.

a)   True

Quiz 17-89) The dragon is a gun or pistol.

a)   False

Quiz 17-90) A gun or pistol is the dragon.

a)   False

Quiz 17-91) To max is to:

a)   Relax
b)   Commit a robbery
c)   Shoot someone
d)   Kick someone
e)   Get punched
f)   Get stabbed

Quiz 17-92) To relax is to:

a)   Max
b)   Poke
c)   Buck
d)   Guerilla
e)   Kick
f)   Flick

Quiz 17-93) To max is to relax.

a)   True

Quiz 17-94) To relax is max.

a)   True

Quiz 17-95) To max is to rob someone.

a)   False

Quiz 17-96) To relax is to buck.

a)   False

Quiz 17-97) To be blind is:

a) To be in love
b) To get shot
c) To get stabbed
d) To get robbed
e) To relax
f) To get kicked

Quiz 17-98) To be in love is to:

a) Be blind
b) Max
c) Get bucked
d) Get stuck
e) Get snuffed
f) Get whacked

Quiz 17-99) To be in love is to be blind.

a) True

Quiz 17-100) To be blind is to be in love.

a) True

Quiz 17-101) To be in love is to get stuck.

a) False

Quiz 17-102) To get stabbed is to be blind.

a) False

Quiz 17-103) Guerrilla means:

a) To kick
b) To use physical force
c) To punch
d) To shoot
e) To kill
f) To stab

Quiz 17-104) To use physical force is to:

a) Guerrilla
b) Buck
c) Snuff
d) Whack
e) Poke
f) Max

Quiz 17-105) To Guerrilla is to use physical force.

a)   True

Quiz 17-106) To use physical force is to guerrilla.

a)   True

Quiz 17-107) To guerrilla is to punch.

a)   False

Quiz 17-108) To use physical force is to max.

a)   False

APPENDIX: QUIZZES

Q1.

Music born in The Americas and Europe can be referred to as _____ music

Music is differentiated from the music of other cultures based on it's _____.

The _____ is the perceptible tune of a piece of music.

A minimum of three notes, sounding simultaneously, produces a _____.

Specific [musical] patterns of long or short durations are called_____.

BPM is an acronym for _____

and refers to the _____ (speed) of a piece of music.

Melodies are derived from _____, or ordered sets of pitches from low to high or high to low.

Harmony is established by a minimum of _____ notes.

The sound "Color" or characteristic of the sound can be described as which of the following?

a. Texture/Timbre
b. Mood
c. Style

The organization of all sections of a piece of music can be referred to as the _____.

ABA structure in music is referred to as which of the following:

a. Binary
b. Ternary
c. Tertian

List/name two 'Early Jazz' legends::

a.
b.

List/name two 'Blues' legends:

a.
b.

List/name two 'Swing Era' (Big Band) legends:

a.
b.

The rhythmical accenting of beats two and four is referred to as the what?

a.

The Rhythm exists within the _____ which exists within the _____.

The melody can be based on any number of notes from the _____.

The Major scale has _____ notes.

The Chromatic scale has _____ notes

Though _____ connections may predominate, _____ within Native American and European cultures is also part of the development of African-American music.

Q2.

An angular (square) rhythmic cycle with four distinct designations of the beat is best represented by which genre of music?

a.

A circular and continuous rhythmic cycle that is less defined is best represented by which genre of music?

a.

List two *characteristics* of Rhythm and Blues:

a.
b.

List two Rhythm and Blues artists:

a.
b.

Little Milton Campbell and Curtis Mayfield represent what subgenres?

a.

Name the song played in the lecture by Curtis Mayfield and the Impressions.

a.

Name/list two Motown Artists:

a.
b.

Memphis soul is a shimmering, sultry style of soul music produced in the 1960s and 1970s at _____ Records and _____ Records in Memphis, Tennessee, as heard on recordings by the vocalist _____.
_____, also known as [nick name],_____ is the lead singer for **The Isley Brothers.**

What was the name of the Isley's selection used for Notorious B.I.G.'s Big Poppa?

a.   It's Your Thing
b.   In Between the Sheets

Name the track and artist, mentioned in the lecture, which **preceded** Notorious B.I.G.'s "Big Poppa."

a.

Name the Queen of Soul and the name of her record label.

a.
b.

Q3.

[The artist formerly known as] _____ *represents the epitome of 80s production.*

List four "funk jazz" bands of the 1970s:

a.
b.
c.
d.

Parliament Funkadelic was heavily influenced by _____ and psychedelic rock.

"Horn sections were replaced by synth keyboards." "Electronic drum machines began to replace the 'funky drummers' of the past, and the lyrics of funk songs became more graphic and sexually explicit."

Which genre do these statements most apply to?

Parliament Funkadelic, also known as_____, was founded
by_____.

In the 1980s, largely as a reaction against what was seen as the overrated popularity of
_____ many of the core elements began to be usurped by electronic machines and
synthesizers.

What are the titles and years the **three** James Brown hits mentioned the previous lecture:

a.
b.
c.

What is the title of the MP3 by "Cameo" played in the previous lecture.

a.

List **two** "Dub" legends as mentioned in the lecture:

a.
b.

The singles/songs _____and _____ resulted in Rick James becoming
a star and paved the way for the future direction of explicitness in funk.

What is Bootsy's "real" name?

a.

(Artist's name) _____ frenzied vocals, frequently punctuated with screams and grunts, channeled the "ecstatic ambiance of the _____" in a secular context.

Q4.

Hip-Hop is a cultural movement that developed in (city)_____ in the 1970s primarily among African and _____ Americans.

The _____ of West Africa are a group of traveling singers and poets, whose vocal style is similar to that of rappers and who are part of an oral tradition dating back hundreds of years.

List four **essential elements** of Hip-Hop:

a.
b.
c.
d.

[per the lecture] List four "**cultural foundations**" for Hip-Hop:

a.
b.
c.
d.

[per the lecture] List two [of four] comedians that have influenced Hip-Hop:

a.
b.

Jamaican born DJ _____(birth name) is credited as being the "Father of Hip-Hop."

The Jamaican tradition boasting impromptu poetry and sayings over music:

a.

The isolation of one particular section of a musical composition, in order to serve as a vamp for an Emcee or for B-Boys/B-Girls to dance to

a.

The rhythmic spoken delivery of rhymes and wordplay, delivered over a beat or without accompaniment:

a.

_____ is more metaphorically advanced and more rhythmically complex than rap.
_____ is a dynamic style of dance which developed as part of the Hip-Hop culture in the East.

List four Turntablist techniques:

a.
b.
c.
d.

Rapper's Delight by the Sugar Hill Gang was performed over a breakdown section
from the song _____ by _____.

Joseph Saddler (birthname) is best known as _____.

The First Certified Gold Rap Song:

a. Positive Force
b. Rapper's Delight
c. The Breaks

First Rapper to sign with a major record label:

a. Run DMC
b. Kool Herc
c. Kurtis Blow

The group RUN-DMC originates from which of the following:

a. Bronx, NYC
b. Staten Island, NYC
c. [Hollis] Queens, NYC

RUN-DMC was named "Greatest Hip Hop Group of All Time" by which of the following?

a. MTV
b. VH1
c. BET

The FIRST Hip-Hop artist/group inducted into the Rock and Roll Hall of Fame:

a. RUN-DMC
b. Grand Master Flash….
c. Kool Herc

(song title) _____ by Grandmaster Flash and the Furious Five is sometimes
cited as the birth of "serious" Hip-Hop.

Name two early (East Coast) "Breaking" crew:

a.
b.

Graffiti Terms (complete the definition w/ the appropriate term after the colon)

The act of creating Graffiti art; or a particular style of Graffiti in which the entire train car is covered with Graf:

The graduation of colors:

Rows of throw ups (Graffiti) of the same name:

Throw ups (Graffiti) done on subway car panels at <u>window level</u>:

(Graf. Name) _____ is one of the most influential graffiti writers.

Sound Bytes: Artist/Title/Year

1.
2.
3.
4.

Q5.

The song Roxanne Roxanne is by which of the following groups?

a.   Roxanne Shante
b.   UTFO
c.   The Juice Crew

"He is considered to be one of the most influential and skilled Emcees in Hip-Hop."

a.

List four members of The Juice Crew:

a.
b.
c.
d.

Select the origin for The Juice Crew:

a.   Bronx, NY
b.   Brooklyn, NY
c.   Queensbridge, NY

By whom was "The Juice Crew" founded?

a.

The Cedar Park battle was widely regarded as having been won however by
KRS-One and the BDP Crew, with the track _____.

What is KRS's origin?

a.

What is KRS-ONE's birth name?

a.   _____

List Big Daddy Kane's given name:

a.

What is the acronym for the name KRS-One?

a.   _____

As KRS-One adopted this "humanist," less violent approach, he turned
from his "_____," persona and toward that of
"_____"

KRS-One is credited with innovating the _____ side of freestyle battling via battles w/MC
_____ in Cedar Park.

List the songs that are associated with the "Cedar Park" battle, in order of sequence:

a.

b.

c.

d.

DJ Scott La Rock and KRS-One formed the company called _____.

List Big Daddy Kane's NYC borough of origin:

a.

Name the FIRST "professional street dance" prominent on the West Coast along with **three sub categories for this dance:**

(1)

a.

b.

c.

Afrika Bambaataa created what is now known as _____;
a style of "funk" driven by synthesizers and the electronic rhythm of the [brand name] _____ drum machine.

Vocabulary: (complete the definition w/ the appropriate term after the colon)

Many MC's call the music they perform to:

To vocally improvize in a lyrical fashion across a range of subject matter:

A lyricist's/rapper's "cadence":

Master of ceremonies; the same in the realm of the Hip-Hop culture:

Reminiscent of past processes, virtues or actions:

Music that is not mainstream or formatted for radio:

This word is used to describe work of poor quality; to say that something or someone is terrible or that their actions reflect a poor decision:

Plagiarism: to steal styles, concepts, or lyrics from someone else:

Q6.

The album's heavy use of _____ by Eric B, like James

Brown's (song title)_____ became influential in Hip Hop

production.

With the emergence of a new generation of _____ such as the

_____, producers were at last free of the need for _____.

PE is an American Hip Hop group formed on _____, NY

in the year _____.

PE is known for its _____ charged lyrics and it's criticism of

the _____.

List two members of PE by birth name:

a.

b.

LL Cool J stands for:

a.   _____

LL Cool J is known for romantic ballads such as

(song title) _____, and_____

LL Cool J's origin is which of the following cities and states?

a.   Queens, NY
b.   Bronx, NY
c.   Brooklyn, NY

Breakdown of song to Sample: list qualities

a.

b.

c.

d.

Earlier styles vs Later Style: list qualities

a.

b.

c.

The Fresh Prince, AKA _____, along with (birth name)

_____ formed the group DJ Jazzy Jeff and the Fresh Prince.

The title song that won the first Grammy for rap was

_____, from the year_____.

_____ is a best selling female rap duo/group.

Cheryl Wray AKA _____

Sandra Denton AKA _____

DJ named _____

Name the title track and year of the "Gangstarr" Video shown in class:

a.

b.

"Gangstarr's" style combined elements of _____ and _____.

"Gangstarr" emanates from what city and state:

a.   New York, NY
b.   Philadelphia, PA
c.   Boston, Mass

Terms like "slow flow" and "mesmeric" are used to describe this MC:

a. MC G.U.R.U.
b. RAKIM
c. KRS-ONE

_____ is the debut studio album of American hip
hop duo _____, released in 1987.
(con't)
This album was one of the first Hip-Hop records to fully embrace
_____.

Sound Bytes: Artist /Title/ Year

a.
b.
c.
d.

Q7.

(artist)_____ (City)_____ Park Side Killers-1985
(artist) _____, Six In the Morning (year)_____
(title)_____, Easy E- (year)1987/88

Ice T (birth name):
Born :
Industry Origin:

Discography: two

a.
b.

Gangster Rap emphasized _____, if not more than skills on the
mic; lyrics vary from accurate reflections to _____accounts;

Other slang terms for this subgenre include: name two

a.
b.

List FOUR factors leading to the evolution of Gangster Rap on the West Coast

a.
b.
c.
d.

Eazy E (birthname):
Origin:

Discography:

a.
b.

List four "cultural foundations" of violence:

1.
2.
3.
4.

List four "key-elements" of Gangster Rap:

a.
b.
c.
d.

Kool G Rap (birth name)-

Origin:

Played the Kool G Rap track _____ from the 1992 album

_____, in the lecture.

Discography (with DJ Polo): list two

a.
b.

_____ is a record label founded in 1993 by producer/rapper/

entrepreneur _____.

The need to "_____" blurred the line between business and the streets.

Sound Bytes: Artist /Title/ Year

a.
b.
c.
d.

Q8.

CMW-Members

a.
b.

Origin:

CMW's track, _____, is the sample for Notorious B.I.G.'s track

_____from the B.I.G. album Ready to Die.

Ruthless Records

    Founders:
    Where:
    Year of Formation:

Ruthless' first successful single was Eazy's "_____," followed by N.W.A.'s "Dopeman" and "8-Ball."

Label's first **full-length release** was N.W.A.'s _____ which was eventually certified multi-platinum.

NWA Origin:
Members:

a.

b.

c.

d.

Discography: two (album/year)

a.

b.

Ice Cube- Birth Name:

Discography: two

a.

b.

Dr. Dre- Birth Name:

Discography: Two (album/ year)

a.

b.

Original Sample and Artist for B.I.G.'s "Warning" and CMW's "Hood Took Me Under":

a.

b.

Snoop Dogg- Birth Name:

Origin:

Discography:

a.

b.

-

_____ did not want to split the royalties from the first album on Ruthless Records

NWA's manager, _____, is credited w/ the Rise AND Fall of NWA.

$_____ was the initial amount offered to the members of NWA.

Upon his departure from NWA, Dr. Dre formed a record company named_____ with an ex-bodyguard named _____.

Upon its release in 1990, Ice Cubes first solo album_____ achieved

_____ [status] in just two weeks.

NWA attacked Ice Cubes debut with the track_____.

Ice Cube responded w/ the Single _____.

NWA , then, attacked w/ the Single_____.

Ice Cube shut the feud down w/ the track _____ from the Album

_____.

Sound Bytes: Artist /Title/ Year

a.

b.

c.

d.

Q9.

Rapper 50 cent's first major diss-track was issued against whom?

a.

50 cent's biggest beef was held with what crew?

a.

Who is the leader of this [nemesis] crew?

a.

Feuds went from battling as MC's to which crew would prevail in _____.
In 1996 @ the (event, _____, _____ and Bad Boy Records
"Squared Off."
[MC] Common's "I use to love her," from 1994, describes the tale of a girlfriend in the form of a
_____ to describe Hip Hop's fate on the West Coast.
Ice Cube and the _____ responded in 1995 w/ the video
"_____."

[MC] Common responded with which single from 1996?

a.

Common's response transcended his normally _____ style of Emceeing:

List two ways in which the media propagandizes Hip Hop culture: any combination

a.

b.

Tupac's Diss-video, _____, from the year, _____, is the defining moment in the East coast
West coast beef.
Tupac Shakur died tragically on this day and year: _____

Notable Beefs: any three mentioned

a.

b.

c.

In the first round of disses in 2001 Jay-Z came out with the track "_____" (dissing Nas).

In response, Nas came out with "_____" (dissing Jay-Z), which used

Eric B and Rakim's "_____" beat.

In the second round of disses, Nas responded with "_____" (dissed Jay-Z) and

Jay-Z's response was "_____" (dissing Nas).

Q10.

1) "Turntablism" was first coined by _____ in the year _____.

2) Jamaican _____ music from the _____ (decade) is a precursor to DJ-ing and turntablism.

3) List two pioneers of the type of music you identified in question 2:
   a. _____
   b. _____

4) The first disco DJ from New York City to blend records in the 1970s was _____.
   a. This technique is called _____ (synchronizing the switch and fade between records).

5) The first DJ to scratch was _____. His technique is known as the _____.

6) List two other types of scratching techniques:
   a. _____
   b. _____

7) The first DJ to popularize the turntable as an instrument was _____.
   a. He was showcased as a soloist on _____ (song name).
   b. This was performed with Herbie Hancock on what television broadcast? _____.
   c. The year of this broadcast was _____.

8) Give the **name** and **year** of the first all-turntablism album:
   a. Name: _____.
   b. Year: _____.

9) List 3 artists or crews (from class) that appeared on the album in question 8:
   a. _____.
   b. _____.
   c. _____.

10) The combination of mixing/cutting, scratching and sampling is called _____.

11) A turntablist's basic setup includes:
    a. _____.
    b. _____.
    c. _____.
    d. _____.

12) The substitution or alteration of the sample's an original (historical) meaning in a new, referential context is called _____.

13) The art of searching for and acquiring albums, including the search for breaks and samples according to the artist's aesthetic choices is called _____.

14) Name the DJ from class that is well known for your answer in question 13: _____.

15) The largest organized DJ battle is called:
   a.   _____ (full name).
   b.   It was founded in the year _____.
   c.   How long does each DJ have to present their composition? _____.

16) The DJ crew who is known for orchestrating their compositions is:
   a.   _____.
   b.   They were formed in the year _____.

17) List the three original core members of the crew from question 16:
   a.   _____.
   b.   _____.
   c.   _____.

18) Kid Koala got his start as a DJ in which city/region? _____.

19) The birth name of DJ Spooky (that Subliminal Kid) is _____.

20) DJ Spooky (that Subliminal Kid) is credited for creating and developing a style known as _____.

Q11.

By way of example, _____ points to the early years of America, the expansion of the frontier, and the manner in which guns were equated with _____ and the ability to protect and care for one's family.

The ability to use words skillfully and aggressively is central to being _____ in the hip hop world, as is the ability to survive the _____that is so much a part of young, poor, and working-class men's lives.

Rap also grew out of a long tradition of _____ in African American culture, a tradition of boys and men fighting for respect by projecting and proclaiming their own power and ability while simultaneously _____ other men.

_____ argues that males who feel powerless (particularly men of color and working-class white men) turn to their own bodies as a source of power. Men who have other forms of power (economic, social, political) do not have the same need to adopt this kind of _____ physical posture.

Violence is so much a part of American culture that we have become _____ to it. It is found not only in rap music, but across the culture in movies, sports, video games and the real-world politics of _____ and war.

But _____ argues that instead of challenging the notion that black male violence is

natural, the industries that produce popular culture actually _____stories and images of black death for profit.

These sorts of images are not unique to Hip-Hop. _____ female bodies are everywhere. They appear throughout American culture, in films, advertisements, television programs, etc. However, across the landscape of music video, this is virtually the only _____ of women available.

_____ argues that black people don't believe sexism is as urgent a social issue as racism.

But Michael Eric Dyson points out that both black men and black women are _____ by sexism and racism

1 in 4 black women are raped _____.

Black women are 35% more likely to be _____ than white women.

More than _____ women are assaulted in the U.S. every year. This equates to one woman being assaulted every 45 seconds. 61% of the victims are under 18.

_____ suggests that the women who appear in rap videos are themselves participating in the degradation and _____ of women.

The rapper _____ said rap should not be taken seriously because "_____." He also argued that women are some of the biggest fans of rap music that includes lyrics about "bitches and ho's" and that they in fact like hearing these words.

Hurt argues that we have become _____to the sexism, misogyny and sexual _____of rap and that this has blinded us to how demeaning and harmful it really is.

In a lot of rap music men refer to other men by _____, feminized terms like "bitch." Calling a man a feminine name is the greatest insult that can be inflicted. Hurt believes that this reflects the deep insecurity that many men have about their _____.

Michael Eric Dyson points out that this is also a (two words) _____. It is an attack on women, through the demeaning language, and also an attack on any type of masculinity that does not fit the stereotypical, _____ image.

This _____of men for purposes of insult does not happen just in Hip-Hop culture but throughout American culture itself, in media, interpersonal interactions and even the world of _____.

The recording industry makes huge profits by selling images of violent, materialistic, sexist, black-masculinity, and by turning the misery of _____ into a commodity that benefits white-owned corporations.

In previous decades, when there were still many small, _____ record labels, it was easier for more _____ and positive artists to obtain recording contracts and get their music out in front of the public.

The former president of Def Jam Records told Hurt that the rise of so-called "gangsta" rap as the dominant subgenre coincided with the takeover of _____ by major corporations.

White fans of Hip-Hop interviewed by Hurt admitted that they know little about _____ culture beyond what they hear and see in recordings and videos.

They also admitted that the music they listen to tends to _____ negative stereotypes of blacks as violent, sexually predatory and obsessed with material goods.

Chuck D., of the political rap group _____, called BET "the _____of black manhood in the world" because of their promotion of rigid stereotypes of greedy, violent, and sexist black men.

Chuck D., however, points out that individual rappers cannot be blamed for what is really a state of affairs brought on by the _____ industry itself. Artists create what they know the industry will support. The industry supports music that glamorizes sexism and violence, not music that is political or includes positive or _____ messages.

The _____ is controlled by white-owned corporations; and it is therefore white businessmen who make the decisions about what rap music gets released and promoted.

Q12.

List two other musical genres related to the development of Neo Soul music:

a.

List two albums by Erykah Badu (year and title):

a.
b.

Name the song played in the lecture by Erykah Badu:

a.

Erykah Badu—Origin:

a.

List Erykah Badu's given name:

a.

5. Name Jill Scott's originating city:

a.

Name the song played in the lecture by Jill Scott:

a.

List two albums by D' Angelo (year and title):

a.
b.

List D' Angelo's given name:

a.

Name D' Angelo's originating city:

a.

Name the song played in the lecture by D' Angelo and the song originally sung by Smokey Robinson:

a.
b.

List ONE album by Maxwell (year and title):

a.

List Maxwell's given name:

a.

Name Maxwell's originating city:

a.

List ONE album by Angie Stone (year and title):

a.

Name Angie Stone's originating city:

a.

List Angie Stone's given name:

a.

List four members of the group The Soulquarians:

a.
b.
c.
d.

Name J Dilla's originating city:

a.

Name two alternate "nick-names" for J Dilla:

a.
b.

Percee P-originating city:

a.

List Percee P's given name:

a.

Percee P Discography: list one (year and title)

a.

Sound Bytes: Artist /Title/ Year

a.
b.
c.
d.

Q13–14.

List Talib Kweli's full given name:

a.

Talib's first name in _____ means
"_____" or "_____."

List 2 Talib Kweli Studio Albums by Title and Year:

a.
b.

Which American city and state is Talib Kweli from?

a.

Name the Sample to the Talib Kweli track played in the lecture:

a.

Talib's middle name in _____(spelling) means "_____."

List Mos Def's given name:

a.

Which American city and state is Mos Def from?

a.

List two Mos Def Studio Albums by year and title:

a.
b.

Name the Nas track w/ Sample played in the last lecture:

a.

Which American city and state is Nas from?

a.

What two MC's are known together as *Blackstar?*

a.
b.

MF Doom was born in which countries?

a.

What American city is MF Doom from?

a.

MF Doom Discography: year/title

a.
b.

List MF Doom's given name:

a.

What American city is Madlib from?

a.

Madlib Discography: year/title

a.
b.

List Madlib's given name:

a.

What does the name Madlib stand for?

a.

What two MC/ Producers are represented by the term "Madvillain"?

a.
b.

Sound Bytes: Artist /Title/ Year

a.
b.
c.
d.
e.

Q15.

1. Hip-Hop is _____throughout the world (its "global-ness"): In some form or another, a local or regional Hip-Hop culture exists in almost every country.
2. According to the U.S. Department of State, Hip-Hop is "now the center of a mega music and fashion industry around the world" that _____ social _____ and cuts across _____lines.
3. "For most music-addicted earthlings, Hip-Hop culture is the _____ global youth _____of today."
4. Hip-Hop's globally common function serves as the voice of society's _____, or _____ _____that challenges the _____.
5. "Irrespective of its projected values, the music continues to provide a sense of _____shared among its artists and audiences around the globe."
6. Its American _____(and afro-American primarily) is universally recognized, yet each local culture has _____it in ways both _____and _____to make it their own.
7. "Perhaps the very fact that its musical components were, technically, relatively simple to replicate and that its_____ was a lyric-based message made it an adaptable, user-friendly structure onto which far-flung performers could graft their own _____subjects, narratives, and concerns."
8. The quote in question #7 is making reference to Hip-Hop's_____.
9. "Once a form of social protest in the United States, rap appears to be anything but that now. In contrast, outside of the US, rap music articulates and addresses local _____and _____concerns."
10. Tapping into Hip-Hop's potential as a force for social change should be easy to realize, but the question of "realistically _____solutions to complex world problems from teens and twenty-something" is one that has been raised. This attitude though, perhaps, demonstrates a lack of awareness that any socio-political problem needs to be first identified and widely publicized before it will be acknowledged by the _____ of society.

Q16.

Scarface
Origin:
Birth Name:

a.

Discography:

a.
b.

Young Jeezy
Origin:
Birth Name:

a.

Discography:

a.
b.

Trina
Origin:
Birth Name:

a.

Discography:

a.
b.

OutKast
Origin:
Birth Names:

a.
b.

Discography:

a.
b.

Lil Boo$ie
Origin:
Birth Name:

a.

Discography:

a.
b.

Webbie
Origin:
Birth Name:

a.

Discography:

a.
b.

Juicy J
Origin:
Birth Name:

a.

Discography:

a.
b.

T.I.
Origin:
Birth Name:

a.

Discography:

a.
b.

Rick Ross
Origin:
Birth Name:

a.

Discography:

a.
b.

Gucci Mane
Origin:
Birth Name:

a.

Discography:

a.
b.

UGK
Origin:
Birth Names:

a.
b.

Discography:

a.
b.

Ludacris
Origin:
Birth Name:

a.

Discography:

a.
b.

Sound Bytes: Artist /Title/ Year

a.

b.

c.

d.

e.

f.

Q17.

Fill In:

_____, also known by his stage name _____,

was an _____ who made significant contributions to the

_____ music scene in the 1990s as a member of the Hip-Hop

collective _____.

He was shot and killed in _____ (month/year) before releasing his second album.

Slang Test:

Whips are_____

Kicks are_____

Movies are _____

Cigarettes are _____.

If you get "bucked," you got _____.

Your "bankroll" is your_____.

If you get _____ that mean you got punched.

If you got bad breath, you got the _____.

To relax is the same as [to] _____.

The "lab" is the _____.

If you're "mad," you are _____.

If you're in love, you are _____.

A very hard, long stare is a _____.

To "guerrilla" means to use _____.

Intro: https://youtu.be/NQ_eU-SFdHU
Ep. 1 https://youtu.be/bFQyRRBy99o
Ep. 2 https://youtu.be/lOd7DcU-74E
Ep. 3 https://youtu.be/D2Zc2HEVJ7k
Ep. 4 https://youtu.be/WCgzkEqLIzk
Ep. 5 https://youtu.be/fPhCMP31tkY

I created the term Jazz-Hop in 2009—as a composer's musical-metaphor of the equal dominion, or Magisteria, of jazz and Hip-Hop. The corresponding web-links serve as a candid look at "the author" in action, in interview and on stage as a musician, providing conceptual evidence of some of the many concepts that have emerged since Westray's Jazz-Hop.

www.ingramcontent.com/pod-product-compliance
Lightning Source LLC
Chambersburg PA
CBHW050352110426
42812CB00008B/2442